This Book

is one of

Eighteen Volumes

of

THE CANADIAN CENTENARY SERIES

being presented in its entirety

to selected Canadian Libraries

by the

RICHARDSON CENTURY FUND

which was established in 1957

to commemorate the

Hundredth Anniversary

of

JAMES RICHARDSON & SONS, LIMITED

THIRTIETH FLOOR, RICHARDSON BUILDING, ONE LOMBARD PLACE

WINNIPEG, CANADA R3B 0Y1

CANADA
1957-1967

J.L. GRANATSTEIN

CANADA
1957-1967

The Years of Uncertainty and Innovation

The Canadian Centenary Series

McClelland and Stewart

Canadian Cataloguing in Publication Data
Granatstein, J.L., 1939-
Canada 1957-1967

(The Canadian centenary series ; 19)
Includes bibliographical references and index.
ISBN 0-7710-3515-2

1. Canada – History – 1945- 2. Canada – Politics and government – 1957-1963. 3. Canada – Politics and government – 1963-1968. I. Title. II. Series

FC620.G72 1986 971.064'2 C85-099058-0
F1034.2.G72 1986

McClelland and Stewart Limited
The Canadian Publishers
25 Hollinger Road
Toronto, Ontario
M4B 3G2

Printed and bound in Canada by John Deyell Co.

For
Michael,
1963-1985

A History of Canada

Ramsay Cook, EXECUTIVE EDITOR

*1. *Tryggvi J. Oleson* Early Voyages and Northern Approaches, 1000-1632

*2. *Marcel Trudel* The Beginnings of New France, 1524-1663

*†3. *W.J. Eccles* Canada Under Louis XIV, 1669-1701

4. *Dale Miquelon* Canada from 1701 to 1744

*5. *G.F.G. Stanley* New France, 1744-1760

*†6. *Hilda Neatby* Quebec, 1760-1791

*†7. *Gerald M. Craig* Upper Canada, 1784-1841

*†8. *Fernand Ouellet* Lower Canada, 1792-1840

*†9. *W.S. MacNutt* The Atlantic Provinces, 1712-1857

*†10. *J.M.S. Careless* The Union of the Canadas, 1841-1857

*†11. *E.E. Rich* The Fur Trade and the Northwest to 1857

*†12. *W.L. Morton* The Critical Years, 1857-1873

*†13. *P.B. Waite* Canada, 1874-1896

*†14. *R. Craig Brown and G.R. Cook* Canada, 1896-1921

*†15. *John Herd Thompson with Allen Seager* Canada, 1922-1939

*†16. *Morris Zaslow* The Opening of the Canadian North, 1870-1914

17. *Morris Zaslow* The North, 1914-1967

*18. *D.G. Creighton* Canada, 1939-1957

*19. *J.L. Granatstein* Canada, 1957-1967

VOLUMES STARRED ARE PUBLISHED

†ALSO AVAILABLE IN PAPERBACK

Volumes I, III, VII, and XII of The Canadian Centenary Series were published with the help of grants from the Humanities Research Council of Canada.

CONTENTS

Canada 1957–1967

For material in the illustration section of this book, acknowledgement is made to the following sources:

The Public Archives of Canada for John Diefenbaker at 1956 Progressive Conservative Leadership Convention; Donald Fleming and James Coyne; [D. Cameron] Howard Green with J.G. Diefenbaker and Governor General Vincent Massey; Réal Caouette; L.B. Pearson and Jean Lesage at Quebec Liberal Convention; the Stratford Shakespearean Festival; L.B. Pearson with new flag; Gerda Munsinger; Rassemblement pour l'indépendance nationale demonstration; Expo 67; [Duncan Cameron] Admiral Landymore at parliamentary hearing; Pierre-Elliott Trudeau with Daniel Johnson.

For Duncan Macpherson cartoons, John Diefenbaker as the Tory "team"; "Let Them Eat Cake"; "Blast Off"; "The Old Smoothie"; "A simple 'Yes' or 'No' will suffice", reprinted with permission – The Toronto Star.

The National Liberal Federation for *The Election Colouring Book.*

The J.F. Kennedy Library for L.B. Pearson with John F. Kennedy.

York University, Toronto *Telegram* collection, for Unemployment Insurance demonstration; T.C. Douglas at NDP leadership convention; Bomarc missile; Meeting of the Royal Commission on Bilingualism and Biculturalism at London, Ont.; NDP rally, Maple Leaf Gardens; Vietnam War protest, Toronto; Progressive Conservative Leadership Convention, 1967; Pierre-Elliott Trudeau with Joey Smallwood.

Saskatchewan Archives/Toronto *Telegram* for "Keep Our Doctors" rally, Regina.

The Canadian Centenary Series

Half a century has elapsed since *Canada and Its Provinces*, the first large-scale co-operative history of Canada, was published. During that time, new historical materials have been made available in archives and libraries; new research has been carried out, and its results published; new interpretations have been advanced and tested. In these same years Canada itself has greatly grown and changed. These facts, together with the centenary of Confederation, justify the publication of a new co-operative history of Canada.

The form chosen for this enterprise was that of a series of volumes. The series was planned by the editors, but each volume will be designed and executed by a single author. The general theme of the work is the development of those regional communities which have for the past century made up the Canadian nation; and the series will be composed of a number of volumes sufficiently large to permit adequate treatment of all the phases of the theme in the light of modern knowledge.

The Centenary History, then, was planned as a series to have a certain common character and to follow a common method but to be written by individual authors, specialists in their fields. As a whole, it will be a work of specialized knowledge, the great advantage of scholarly co-operation, and at the same time each volume will have the unity and distinctive character of individual authorship. It was agreed that a general narrative treatment was necessary and that each author should deal in a balanced way with economic, political, and social history. The result, it is hoped, will be an interpretative, varied, and comprehensive account, at once useful to the student and interesting to the general reader.

The difficulties of organizing and executing such a series are apparent: the overlapping of separate narratives, the risk of omissions, the imposition of divisions which are relevant to some themes but not to others. Not so apparent, but quite as troublesome, are the problems of scale, perspective, and scope, problems which perplex the writer of a one-volume history and are magnified in a series. It is by deliberate choice that certain parts of the history are told twice, in different volumes from different points of view, in the belief that the benefits gained outweigh the unavoidable disadvantages.

W.L. MORTON,
Executive Editor.
D.G. CREIGHTON,
Advisory Editor.

Executive Editor's Preface

W.L. Morton and D.G. Creighton, two of Canada's most distinguished historians, together conceived the Canadian Centenary Series, divided the work, recruited the authors, and presided over the publication of fifteen volumes. Regrettably, neither lived to see the final four books through the press. That responsibility has fallen to me. I intend to carry it through according to the letter and the spirit of the introductory statement written by the first editors, which will continue to appear in each volume. The series remains theirs, an appropriate reminder of the seminal contributions that they made to the understanding of Canada's past. Having served my apprenticeship as a historian with each of them, in different ways, it is a signal privilege for me to be able to oversee the completion of this fine series of Canadian historical volumes.

In this volume Professor J.L. Granatstein brings his demonstrated talents as a historian of twentieth-century Canadian public life to bear on the tumultuous, seemingly confused years of the Diefenbaker and Pearson governments. Basing his study on an impressive range of unpublished manuscript material, most used here for the first time, he demonstrates that political instability and federal-provincial friction did not prevent the development of innovative new policies in social, cultural, and defence matters. So, too, he carefully details the initiatives that were taken by provincial governments in fields where the federal government had assumed dominance. The well-chosen themes of this book make understandable a period of contemporary history that once seemed chaotic. That is a substantial achievement.

RAMSAY COOK

PREFACE

The Years of Uncertainty and Innovation

This book, chronologically the last volume in the Centenary Series, is an examination of the years from 1957 to 1967, the "tenth decade" of post-Confederation Canada. It is a study of a nation changing rapidly from an entity that had seemed to understand the verities of life to one that was uneasily adrift on a sea of conflicting choices and too rapid change. It is also about a period so recent that to historians it verges on being current events. In an earlier volume in this series, Craig Brown and Ramsay Cook justly noted that their book on the 1896-1921 era was "a progress report on Canadian scholarship," one that relied heavily on the "exciting work that has been accomplished, though often not yet published, by a new generation of Canadian historians." This volume has little such work on which to rely, very few scholars having yet worked through the materials of the 1957-1967 era. In a sense, then, this book, which rests heavily on manuscript sources, is a first scholarly attempt to sketch in the outlines of a critical period of uncertainty in Canadian politics and policy. Its "case study" approach has been shaped by the lack of monographic literature. Very simply, it seemed fruitless to attempt to write the history of the entire decade when so much basic research remained undone.

This work could not have been undertaken without the assistance of many people and organizations. I am deeply indebted to the Killam Programme of the Canada Council and to the Social Science and Humanities Research Council for generous assistance that made possible the research and writing. After some initial hesitation, York University co-operated splendidly. Chapter VI was first printed in a somewhat different form in the *Canadian Historical Review* published by the University of Toronto Press. Like everyone working on the recent Canadian past, I have benefited greatly from *Canada Since 1945*, the work of my friends Robert Bothwell, Ian Drummond, and John English. Their influence herein has been pervasive – if not always completely persuasive.

I am especially grateful to those individuals and institutions who so kindly let me make use of their papers and read their mail and to the archivists who gamely carried record boxes that were astonishing in their number. Equally so were the number and the variety of archival collections that proved to be available, either freely to everyone or with special permission. This book is among the first to make use of a fairly complete range of sources for the 1957-1967 period, and the selected bibliography of primary sources and the detailed reference notes are intended as a guide to what is now available. And it is only proper to add that the many sources to which I could get access (as well as the very few to which I could not) tended to shape the resulting book. The Canada Council, for example, is examined in one of the case studies as a way of looking at the arts because of its importance to culture and the growth of higher education during the decade, but also because the council's officers generously gave me almost unlimited access to its records. Similarly, Saskatchewan medicare is examined as the example for the beginnings of the shift in initiative from Ottawa to the provinces both because of its own importance and because the key Saskatchewan public figures, unlike most of their provincial counterparts elsewhere in the country, have made their records available virtually without conditions. In no case did access restrictions to the private papers or government records used in this book prove onerous; in no case did the owners of material ask for any deletions of substance – and that, I am especially pleased to add, includes the Privy Council Office and the Departments of External Affairs, National Defence, and Finance, all of which co-operated fully.

Among the legion of archivists who were most helpful yet again were Ian Wilson of the fine Saskatchewan Archives, Ann McDermaid of the Queen's University Archives, and Carman Carroll, Ian McClymont, Jerry O'Brien, and their staffs at the Public Archives of Canada. Several major actors in the events described here read chapter drafts or sections concerning their lives and times and saved me from many errors: Hon. J.W. Pickersgill, Hon. Allan Blakeney, H.B. Robinson, James Coyne, J.R. Beattie, Louis Rasminsky, David Bartlett, Dr. A.W. Trueman, and Hon. Paul Hellyer. I am very happy to state the simple truth that I know some will not believe: none of these participants tried to impose either a point of view or an *apologia pro vita sua* on me. Colleagues and friends assisted: Pat Kyba, Rod Byers, J.T. Jockel, Des Morton, Malcolm Taylor, and Mel MacLeod read and commented upon drafts of specific sections or chapters; Norman Hillmer facilitated my research at National Defence Headquarters; Bill Young provided Chinese food and Occidental shelter; Jim Pitsula looked after me very well in Regina; Peter Neary suggested material; and John English allowed me to read drafts of his own work. Scholarship is, as always, a co-operative venture, and if, on every occasion, I did not take the advice that was suggested, it probably would have been better if I had.

I always did follow – almost always – the inspired editorial advice of Ramsay Derry and Janet Craig and the suggestions/orders of the Executive Editor of the Centenary Series, my colleague Ramsay Cook. Again, the book would have been better if I had done everything they wanted. They, like the others who tried to warn me, are blameless.

Finally, my wife, Elaine, and my children, Carole and Michael, as always assisted in the most important ways. Michael did not live to see the book appear, but it is his nonetheless.

J.L.G.
Toronto, Fall, 1985

CHAPTER 1

Canada at the Coming of the Prophet

Astonishment. That was the only word that could describe the nation's feeling when Canadians awoke on the morning of June 11, 1957. The Liberals had been beaten in the general election the day before, and for the first time since 1935 the country faced a change in government. Under Mackenzie King and Louis St. Laurent, the Liberal party had held power through the last part of the Great Depression, the Second World War, and the post-war reconstruction and subsequent boom; a whole generation had reached maturity with the near certainty that the good, grey, competent Grits would always be there. The "Government Party" had seemed absolutely unbeatable. But the Liberals had been toppled by John Diefenbaker and his Progressive Conservative party. The new prime minister-designate, the leader chosen at a great national party convention in December 1956, was sixty-one years old, a Saskatchewan lawyer who had been an Opposition Member of Parliament since 1940.

The country seemed excited at the prospect of change. The headlines the day after the election of June 10 were almost ecstatic as the editors, as much as the voters, scratched their heads and pondered just how they had done the deed. The opinion polls and the pundits had agreed that Diefenbaker had no chance, but there he was, poised to take over the reins. The Chief's perfervid and almost evangelical speeches had obviously struck a responsive chord in the voters, sick of Liberal arrogance. The governing Liberals, Diefenbaker had repeated endlessly during the campaign, had been in office so long that they assumed Canada was theirs to rule by divine right. There was truth in that – the Liberals had grown smug and complacent in power – and the self-proclaimed champion of the little man had readily found sufficient examples to prove his claims to his own satisfaction and to that of enough voters in Ontario, the Maritimes, and the West to elect a Conservative minority government. The next March Diefenbaker would repeat the same arguments to excoriate the Grits again and lead his party to the most sweeping victory in Canadian history up to that time. Canada was now John Diefenbaker's to command and lead, and the adulation that showered upon him was unceasing and apparently heartfelt.

The country that Diefenbaker and his party had won was vastly different from what it had been when the new prime minister had first entered Parliament seventeen years before. The war and post-war economic expansion erased memories of the depressed 1930s; the boom proceeded almost without interruption, and Canada was now a prosperous country. There were huge oil and gas reserves in the West just beginning to be exploited; the nation's mineral resources were enormous; and there were great deposits of uranium, the essential element of the atomic age. The farms were productive, and the factories of the heartland produced manufactured goods with relative efficiency. Canadians lived in God's country, and most of them realized it.

There were 16.1 million of them in 1956, up almost four million since the beginning of the decade. By 1967, the country's population would be 20.3 million, a steady and impressive growth to be sure but still far from confirming that the twentieth century would ever belong to Canada. Ontario remained the most heavily populated province at 5.4 million inhabitants in the mid-decade census of 1956, with Quebec following at 4.6 million; British Columbia at 1.4 million and Alberta at 1.1 million were next, while Prince Edward Island with just under 100,000 people was still below its population of seventy-five years earlier. In the still largely unsettled North there were only 12,190 persons in the Yukon and 19,313 in the Northwest Territories (counting Caucasians, Eskimos, and Indians – the terms Inuit and Dene were not yet in use), both figures well below the totals recorded in the 1901 census.[1]

The distribution of the people was still changing. The 1956 population was divided into approximately 9.3 million urban dwellers and 6.8 million rural; the urban population would increase massively to 12.6 million ten years later. Of the rural population in 1956 only 2.6 million lived on farms, and by 1966 farmers had dropped to 1.9 million while the total rural population had risen by only a half-million people.[2] The farm population, in other words, was decreasing steadily as the historic drift of the sons and daughters of rural Canada to the towns and cities continued apace. As the countryside emptied, the organizations, schools, clubs, and baseball teams that had once flourished there gradually ceased to exist, thus increasing rural isolation and leaving only the church – with each minister having four or five congregations in his care – and the television set as links to the outside world. Mechanization had reduced the number of workers necessary (male farm labour declining by one third between 1957 and 1967),[3] but the hard work and daily drudgery remained as did the poor monetary return and the vagaries of weather; many of the best and brightest left for what they believed was an easier life in the cities. It was still too soon to argue that the family farm was finished even though farm holdings fell by 145,000 from 1956 to 1966,[4] but by the mid-1960s the cornerstone of Canadian agriculture was under siege and agribusiness was just around the corner.

If agricultural Canada was entering a period of decline, the cities were beginning to boom. The growth was remarkable. Montreal increased from a metropolitan population of 1.83 million in 1956 to one of 2.57 million ten years later; over the same period Toronto rose from 1.57 million to 2.29 million while Vancouver increased from 694,000 to 933,000 people. Calgary went from 201,000 to 330,000 and Edmonton from 275,000 to 425,000.[5] The same pattern of growth was evident all across the land as immigrants from overseas and Canadians from the rural areas flocked to the opportunities of the cities. The pressures on land and housing were intense – every average family of 3.9 persons in 1961 apparently felt itself entitled to a house and garden, to a large American-designed automobile (passenger vehicles increased from 3.4 million in 1957 to 5.9 million ten years later)[6] with good roads and expressways to drive upon, and to a public transit system as well. And the city governments, watching their budgets escalate and their debts rise as they tried to keep up with the demands for services, sewers, and roads, raised their taxes higher and increased their demands on the provinces and Ottawa; some, like Toronto, consolidated their smaller urban councils into more manageable units and created a regional government with enough power to service a huge population. The increase in numbers in the cities also allowed and encouraged the growth of amenities. New theatres developed and symphonies began to flourish. Good restaurants sprang up and offered a variety of cuisine in place of the overcooked roast beef, Yorkshire pudding, and boiled vegetables that had been the standard offering of even the best eating places (outside Quebec City and Montreal). Cooks in restaurants and at home experimented with new foods and spices; garlic became a staple no longer confined to Italian groceries. And shops and boutiques sold broader ranges of goods to a more demanding clientele.

For all their new sophistication, the Canadian people were still overwhelmingly of British and French stock in 1957. The 1951 census had found 5.7 million of British origin and 4.3 million of French; ten years later, the figures were 8 million and 5.54 million respectively, but as the government's immigration policy changed so too did the composition of the country's inhabitants.

Canadian immigration regulations had been applied with rigour during the Depression and the Second World War to keep out "undesirable elements," a group that was interpreted broadly to include many Jews and others fleeing the Nazi persecutions. After the war, the government in 1947 had proclaimed a policy that sought "to ensure the careful selection and permanent settlement of such numbers of immigrants as can advantageously be absorbed in our national economy. . . ." And as Prime Minister Mackenzie King added, there was "general agreement with the view that the people of Canada do not wish, as a result of mass immigration, to make a fundamental alteration in the character of our population."[7] In effect that policy prevailed until 1957, with a "most-preferred" status being given to immigrants from Britain and the United States and, after 1948, to French immigrants. Nationals from Belgium, Luxembourg, Norway, Denmark, Sweden, and Switzerland with skills needed in Canada were accepted next on the priority list; prospective immigrants from other parts of the world were restricted severely, their access to Canada being defined by the presence of sponsors or close relatives already in residence or by a need for their skills. The policy, in other words, was fundamentally based on race.

But in 1956 and 1957, the St. Laurent government had moved with substantial speed to admit thousands of Hungarians who had fled their country after Soviet tanks had put down a popular revolt in October and November 1956. The Minister of Citizenship and Immigration, J.W. Pickersgill, had created a special programme to process the refugees, and no selectivity was practised in granting entry visas. There was much imagination shown – the entire Faculty of Forestry of the University of Sopran consisting of 300 professors, students, and their families, was admitted *en bloc* to Canada and attached to the University of British Columbia – and in all more than 32,000 Hungarians, large numbers of whom were well educated and young, came to Canada in 1957.[8]

Not until the Diefenbaker government was in power, however, did the fundamental bases of Canadian immigration policy substantially alter. Initially, the Conservatives turned off the tap as unemployment began to increase in 1957 and 1958, but in 1962, Ellen Fairclough, the Minister of Immigration and Citizenship, announced a policy that substituted new criteria for the old one of race. Henceforth, immigrants were to be "personally suitable and . . . have the required background and training to become worthwhile citizens." That standard was to be applied "consistently to all who seek admission to this country. . . ."[9] That was a major change, an end to the old racialism, and a step into a new era of openness. And the government of Lester Pearson continued and built on that change, suggesting a planned immigration policy in a White Paper in 1966 aimed at replacing the "tap on – tap off" system of the past that had seen immigration fluctuate with the Canadian economy's ups and downs with "a steady policy of recruitment based on long-term considerations of economic growth."[10]

The result of the immigration policies could only be measured in the numbers who came to Canada. In 1957, thanks to the Hungarian refugees and to an extraordinarily large exodus from post-Suez Britain, there were 282,164 new arrivals; the next year there were only 124,851 and in 1959 only 106,928. The low point during the Diefenbaker years was 1961, with 71,689 arrivals, the smallest number since 1947. Under the Liberals totals climbed again to 194,743 in 1966 and 222,876 in 1967, the highest post-war total except for the extraordinary year of 1957. The sources of immigrants were also changing, with British migrants arriving in large and steady waves each year and with substantial increases from southern European countries. British arrivals between 1957 and 1967 were never fewer than 11,870 (1961) and in 1957 numbered 108,989; Italian immigrants averaged more than twenty thousand a year over the same period, an influx that effectively altered cities like Toronto, where huge numbers settled. There were, in addition, over five thousand a year from Greece and Portugal, most of whom settled in Toronto and Montreal. But Asian immigration through the period remained tiny, and migrants from western Europe continued to arrive in significant and steady numbers – an average of about ten thousand a year from West Germany, three thousand a year from France, two thousand a year from the Netherlands. American arrivals averaged about fifteen thousand each year as well.[11]

The government offered some assistance to the new arrivals, but never enough to ease the psychological shock of coming to a strange country. Norman Levine, the expatriate Canadian author who returned to Canada on an "emigrant ship" for an extended visit in 1956, coldly described the Canadian welcome that greeted immigrants in Halifax:

> I entered a large drill hall. I was marched with the others inside a tall wire cage that was open at the top and told to sit down on a wooden bench. Around the walls of the drill hall hung the shields of the various provinces. Four Union Jacks hung down from the walls. They were all faded, two had moth holes. The drill hall was divided by toilets into two squares. A sign

> between the toilets said WELCOME TO CANADA in seven languages. . . .
> Our first sign of welcome came after we left this room . . . a pale, narrow-shouldered man in a shabby brown suit . . . held out his hand. . . . He gave each of us a sample box of corn flakes. . . . He also gave each of us pamphlets that said a Bank welcomed us to Canada, a telephone company, and if we wanted to develop a Canadian habit we should buy certain patent medicines.[12]

In its own way, that scene was symptomatic. Canada wanted immigrants and needed them, but it was not quite willing to greet them. The "ethnics" (a word that was just beginning to come into use as a replacement for the slur "D.P.s" – displaced persons) were told again and again that Canada was a mosaic, not a melting pot, that they could maintain a separate identity in Canada. The statement was to some extent true, but the immigrants – even those who had been in Canada for a generation or two – somehow remained virtually out of sight and out of mind. The political parties, seeking the votes of new Canadian citizens, published literature in a variety of languages; they sometimes appointed loyal supporters to patronage posts and occasionally even to a Senate seat; Diefenbaker made a Ukrainian, Michael Starr from Oshawa, Ontario, a Cabinet minister, but that was hardly a share of power. The ultimate comment on the invisibility of the non-charter-group Canadians was the appointment of the Royal Commission on Bilingualism and Biculturalism in 1963 by the Pearson government. As an afterthought, two representatives of ethnic communities were included among the commissioners, and the terms of reference were revised to include an examination of the other Canadians' place in the mosaic that was dominated by "b&b." The inclusion of ethnics smacked of nothing so much as tokenism, and that slight and a hundred thousand others delivered daily to a hundred thousand new Canadians created the first stirrings of protest. By the late 1960s these were strong enough to encourage a government policy of "multiculturalism" as a device to entrench and enshrine the political mosaic alongside the bicultural reality of Canada.

If immigrants and new Canadians at 25.2 per cent of the 1961 population were absent from the centres of power, so too were those who constituted 49.25 per cent of the population: women. No woman was named to a federal cabinet until John Diefenbaker made Ellen Fairclough a member of his 1957 government; women were almost totally absent from senior positions in the federal and provincial bureaucracies. Moreover there were almost no women executive officers in business according to John Porter's *The Vertical Mosaic* (1965), a detailed study of the country's élites during the 1950s; indeed, there is not even an entry for women in Porter's index.

But women were present in society and in the labour force. In 1959, for example, 26.7 per cent of all women over fourteen years of age and 17.9 per cent of married women were in the labour force;[13] by 1967 the figures were 33.8 and 28.3 per cent respectively and were continuing to rise. Typically, women's jobs were the lowest paid and most transitory. In 1961, for example, females made up only 2.2 per cent of the total number of architects, 6.8 per cent of doctors, and 2.6 per cent of lawyers; they did, however, constitute 96.8 per cent of all secretaries.[14]

The birth-rate remained very high in 1957, a limiting factor on the number of married women in the labour force. The post-war peak in the birth-rate had occurred in 1947 with 28.9 births per thousand women, and the rate in 1957 was 28.2; over the following decade, however, there was a steady and very rapid decline to 18.2 births per thousand in 1967, the lowest rate recorded to that point. That decline demonstrated the effectiveness of the contraceptive pill, which liberated women from the tyranny of unwanted pregnancies and allowed more to work longer after marriage. On the other hand, and despite the introduction of effective contraception, the number of illegitimate births increased substantially from 1957 to 1967, rising from 4 per cent of live births to 8.3 per cent, again a record.[15] Undoubtedly the increase was a reflection of changing sexual attitudes among the young – and to ineffective sex education.

Women's liberation was an undiscovered idea in 1957, and it remained so – for a very large number of women – through the rest of the decade. Probably the most important influence in making women think about their place in society was *The Feminine Mystique* (1963), a book by American writer Betty Friedan that had a major and dramatic part in convincing North American women that, for all the comforts and modern appliances at their disposal, they were still unfulfilled and unhappy. But change was slow to come, and even among the radical young, in revolt throughout the mid-1960s against almost all the conventions of society, women played a subordinate role. "Women, brought into new left organizations as the lovers of male members," one Canadian participant remembered, "were the 'camp followers' of the new left. . . . If a woman had any status, it was the reflected one of being the property of an important man, and in this role she was expected to be 'loyal' and support his views. The 'sexual revolution' . . . simply served to increase the access men had to women."[16] But change did come and, while there were protests from many men and some women, by 1967 the federal government had appointed the Royal Commission on the Status of Women, one key recognition of the fact that government had a role to play in winning women the equality that was their right. Ten years before, such a move would have been virtually inconceivable. In addition, in 1968 Canadian divorce laws were loosened, producing further dramatic change. The divorce rate per hundred thousand population had been 40.3 in 1957 and 54.8 in 1967; by 1974, under the new legislation, it was 200.6.[17]

If women were raising their consciousness and using American models to do so, so too were Indians in Canada. The Red Power movement was beginning in the United States, itself patterned after the rise of American Blacks who, with their white supporters, were struggling to win their civil rights in the South and elsewhere. Minorities everywhere were becoming conscious of their identities and seeking to improve their lot. And in Canada it was the native peoples who suffered from the highest unemployment and infant mortality, a very high rate of alcoholism, and substandard housing on their squalid reserves and in towns and cities. The federal government's paternalistic role, sanctioned and ordained by the Indian Act, had failed disastrously, but there was no consensus either in society as a whole (which largely chose to ignore the problem) or among native groups on how to remedy matters. In 1969, for example, when Ottawa suggested doing away with the act and integrating natives into Canadian life, the idea was quickly rejected. The natives wanted to find and maintain their own identities.

So too did young people. According to census figures, in 1956 46.8 per cent of the population had been under twenty-four; in 1961, 48.3 per cent; and in 1966, 49.4 per cent. The young were consumers, spending billions each year on movies, records, clothes, pop and bubble gum; they were, once they reached the age of twenty-one, voters in civic, provincial, and federal elections; and they were flooding into the universities in record numbers as their parents urged them on to higher education. The young mattered.

And the young were increasingly unhappy as the years after 1957 went on. On the streets of Yorkville in Toronto and Kitsilano in Vancouver they were unhappy about Canada's close ties to the United States through the North American Air Defence Command and NATO, links that the war in Vietnam brought home to them. They were unhappy at the prospect of dying in a nuclear holocaust, a possibility that few could dismiss after the Soviet-American confrontation over Cuba in 1962. They were unhappy with the low percentage of Canadian professors and textbooks and courses in their universities. They were unhappy about the way the Diefenbaker government had been brought down by what many saw as American intervention, and after the philosopher George Grant produced his book *Lament for a Nation: The Defeat of Canadian Nationalism* in 1965, they had a text that blamed Canadian Liberalism for destroying the possibility of building an alternative to the American republic on the northern half of the continent. The Liberals, Grant argued, "were in office during the years when the possible basis for nationalism disappeared. It was under a Liberal regime that Canada became a branch-plant society; it was under Liberal leadership that our independence in defence and foreign affairs was finally broken. . . . The Liberals," he went on, "failed to recognize that the real danger to nationalism lay in the incipient continentalism of English-speaking society, rather than in any Quebec separatism. Their economic policies homogenized the culture of Ontario with that of Michigan and New York." It was Diefenbaker, the conservative philosopher maintained, who had tried to resist Americanization, but the continentalist pulls were stronger than the tattered lures of Tory nationalism.[18]

This powerful message found ready believers, and Grant, while his book mourned the death of Canadian nationalism, was as responsible as any man for the nationalist cast that Canadian protest in the mid-1960s took. In the United States, the young protested the Vietnam War (gruesomely visible to all on television each evening) and capitalism's excesses; in Canada (in the new McLuhanesque global village, the same television footage was available everywhere), the protest was against *American* imperialism and the war and in favour of a more nationalist foreign and economic policy from the government. The difference was clear – young Canadians seemed to want to free their nation from the Americans' grasp; in Quebec, in increasing numbers, the young wanted to create their own nation. It was not just the university students who believed in an independent Canada. Their professors, organized in such groups as the University League for Social Reform, and businessmen and politicians such as Walter Gordon shared the same vision.

Most businessmen had only contempt for the new nationalism and those who espoused it. American business was the most advanced and most powerful in the world, and Canada's capitalists, increasingly centred in Toronto as the 1960s continued, wanted the share of the action to which they believed themselves entitled. The links between Bay Street and Wall Street, the two countries' financial centres, were strong, and American investment in Canadian oil, mines, and factories had propelled the great post-war boom. By 1957, American money controlled 70 per cent of the oil industry, 56 per cent of the manufacturing industries, and 52 per cent of the mining sector.[19] All those percentages would increase over the decade, as would the amount of Canadian investment abroad (a large part of it in the United States), which rose from $2.16 billion in 1957 to $4.47 billion in 1967, suggesting that higher profits could be made elsewhere.[20] Again in 1957, exports to the United States were four times those to Britain, and

Canadian imports from the United States were almost eight times as large as those from the old Mother Country.[21] Those disparities would also continue to increase. Canadian business, in other words, was too tightly tied to the United States, its major and increasingly its only market and source of capital, to look with favour on nationalist policies.

Industry did not look with much more favour on regional development policies – unless there were tax write-offs and incentives offered by federal, provincial, or civic governments, desperate to fight persistently high unemployment rates and to keep population in the area. Manufacturers wanted to be near their markets, and those were in Ontario and Quebec; there was a real reluctance to go to the Prairies or the Maritimes. One study of Nova Scotia's experience, for example, noted that only 3 of 350 firms that established themselves in Quebec and Ontario between 1959 and 1962 had even considered Nova Scotia as a possible location. One reason was that there was at least a 5-percent comparative cost advantage in being set up in Ontario and Quebec, most of it because of cheaper costs of transportation. Nor was the Atlantic province any more successful in generating its own growth, being laggard in the movement away from family business and partnerships to incorporated companies.[22] The provincial government in Halifax, however, was active in encouraging firms to locate there, its concessions to business being substantial. The record of success of these enticements in Nova Scotia, as in Prince Edward Island, Newfoundland, Manitoba, Saskatchewan, eastern Ontario, and eastern Quebec, regions that lagged behind their provincial economies, was not very good, many companies taking the money and running when the going became difficult.[23]

But resource industries were developing outside the Montreal-Toronto axis. The St. Lawrence Seaway, a giant project that had cost a billion dollars, displaced 6,500 people from their homes, destroyed some towns and led to the creation of others, and taken years to complete, opened with great ceremony on June 26, 1959, and put the agricultural and industrial products of the heartland within easy reach of Europe. By the time the first shipping season ended on December 3, 6,595 ships had used the route, and the traffic was up by two thirds over the previous year. At Toronto, ships from thirty-nine lines around the world had come into port with more than 700,000 tons of cargo in the first season, a satisfying increase of 150 per cent over 1958. That new access to world markets – to say nothing of the cheap hydroelectric power generated by the Seaway's works – spurred the development of manufacturing in Ontario especially. But just as important, the Seaway allowed huge bulk freighters to carry the iron ore of the Quebec-Labrador region cheaply to the foundries of Ohio and Pennsylvania. The opportunity created jobs at Sept-Îles, Quebec, and at the Iron Ore Company's mines in Labrador where none had existed before; but it did little to create any manufacturing, and Canadians, while they provided the raw materials, still had to import many finished products from the United States.

Oil and natural gas could easily be refined for market in Canada, however, and petroleum and its products altered the face of Alberta. Home to only a third of the Prairies' population in 1941, the foothills province could claim 40 per cent in 1961 mainly as a result of the prosperity that oil brought. In 1935, as the historian of the region, Gerald Friesen, noted, over half of the province's income came from agriculture and 10 per cent only from resource production, including oil extraction and mining; but by 1971, agriculture accounted for just 15 per cent, and the oil and mining sector now produced 40 per cent of the much expanded gross provincial product.[24] What this meant was clear: employment in the oil industry almost doubled between 1957 and 1967 as the value of production was increasing from $465 million to $1.23 billion in the same period.[25] This was all the more impressive because with oil in world oversupply through most of the 1950s and 1960s, Alberta's relatively high-cost reserves were being exploited at only 50 per cent of capacity.

In the circumstances, what Alberta's Social Credit government could offer the oil companies was stability. "We told them," Premier Ernest Manning recalled, "that Alberta was a stable, sound place for long-range investment. The government would not get involved in the oil industry, but we would create a good business climate" with royalties fixed for ten-year periods.[26] The policy worked well for the province as the foreign firms poured in the money and created jobs; they also took away the lion's share of the profits.

If Canadian industry was booming, labour unions were in stasis. Over the ten years from 1957 to 1967 the percentage of workers belonging to unions stayed almost steady at just over 32 per cent, although the total number of union members rose from 1.39 million to 1.92 million. Over that same period the number of strikes increased and the percentage of working time lost also rose substantially. The creation of the Canadian Labour Congress in 1956 had at last reunited a divided movement and brought most of organized labour under one roof; even so, 71 per cent of unionized workers in 1957 belonged to international – or American-controlled – unions.[27] What was perhaps most unusual in the labour picture during the years 1957 to 1967 was the rise of government employees' unions. The province of Saskatchewan had led the way by giving its employees the right to strike in

1944; Quebec followed suit in 1966, and in 1967, honouring a Liberal party promise made in the 1963 election, the federal government did the same. New Brunswick and British Columbia were not far behind. Over the same period, close to 100 per cent of the country's public employees were unionized, making the Canadian Union of Public Employees the largest union in the nation by 1965.[28] Eventually those civil service unions would negotiate salaries in government jobs to a point where they exceeded those in the private sector, but that was not yet the case in the years from 1957 to 1967.

In 1960, 78 per cent of the labour force was salaried, and earnings, as always, varied quite substantially. According to the 1961 census, a bus driver earned $5,831 a year on the average (a sum that would be less if he drove his bus on Barrington Street in Halifax and more if he drove on Yonge Street in Toronto) and a fisherman took home only $1,902. Among professionals, doctors and surgeons earned $15,365, dentists $11,339, and teachers and professors only $3,474.[29] The disparities between rich and poor persisted.

Moreover, there were signs of trouble in the economy by 1957. Unemployment, just 3.4 per cent in 1956 (3.9 per cent for men and 1.9 per cent for women workers), was beginning to climb, and in 1958 it reached 7 per cent. That was worrisome, as was the fact that joblessness in the forestry, fishing, and trapping industries climbed to 29.2 per cent and in construction to 19.2 per cent.[30] The shock of unemployment fortunately was eased substantially by the safety net of social welfare measures that had been put in place since the Depression. The Unemployment Insurance Commission kept watch on the labour situation and provided benefits to those without work; family allowances went to every mother with young children; and the Central Mortgage and Housing Corporation helped subsidize mortgage rates. But there was still only a rudimentary system of old age pensions, no national contributory pension plan, and as yet no national system of hospital or medical care insurance. The welfare state had arrived, but it was far from complete.

The provincial governments generally seemed unaware of and unconcerned by the gathering clouds. In Quebec Maurice Duplessis's Union Nationale seemed virtually unbeatable as it kept a tight rein on the province's unions and the seriously underfunded universities. The Roman Catholic Church lived up to Duplessis's boast that the bishops ate out of his hand, but it was nonetheless a powerful force. The Quiet Revolution might have been aborning, but as Gérard Pelletier remembered, "Quebec seemed frozen for all time in the glaciers of conservatism."[31] In Ontario, the Conservatives were equally entrenched under "Old Man Ontario" Leslie Frost, who ran a brilliantly effective government and party machine. In British Columbia, the government of W.A.C. Bennett and his Social Credit party, in power since 1952, had transformed the populist rhetoric developed by William Aberhart in Alberta in the 1930s into a small-p progressive, small-c conservative regime that relied on its close relationship with the resource industries as its basic prop. In Saskatchewan, the Co-operative Commonwealth Federation government of T.C. Douglas was as different as could be. That provincial government was almost alone in taking an activist position and in trying to build a small but efficient public service able to proffer advice on most questions. Across the country in 1957, there were three Liberal and three Conservative governments, two Social Credit, one CCF, and one Union Nationale. The Liberals might continue their hegemony nationally, but on the provincial level there was wide diversity.

The Liberal government that had seemed all-powerful before the 1957 election had in fact been showing its age for some time. Prime Minister St. Laurent was seventy-five in 1957 and very tired; Bruce Hutchison, the British Columbia newspaper editor who was very close to the Liberals and to many senior mandarins, wrote to a friend to say that "the boys in Ottawa may not realize it but St. Laurent has just quietly faded out of the picture in the last six months. . . ."[32]

If the Prime Minister had slipped, so too had his control over the government. It was harder to get agreement in Cabinet on difficult questions, and C.D. Howe, the "Minister of Everything," was also aging and increasingly fatigued. Walter Harris, the Minister of Finance and one of the ablest men left in the ministry, was reported by a journalist to have said that "Howe had become an impossible colleague . . . more determined to bull things through. Walter said that if you really thought about it you would realize that everything Howe touches now goes sour."[33] Certainly that had been true in the Trans-Canada Pipe Lines affair when, in mid-1956, the government had rammed its bill to finance the pipeline through the House of Commons with the repeated use of closure. In the process, the Speaker's integrity was judged by many to have been compromised,[34] the opposition parties pulled together for the first time, thanks to the tactical genius of Stanley Knowles, the CCF member for Winnipeg North, and the government was painted across the land as dictatorial and arrogant. Some years later, St. Laurent, who had sat through much of the debate slumped in depression behind his desk in the House, admitted that his government had made errors. "People do make mistakes, you know."[35]

What was striking about the pipeline affair was that it not only reinforced existing fears but also fed them. Liberal arrogance seen in action was the spur to the Conservative party's burning conviction that Canada's freedom was in danger. It was a "black day in Canada's history," Gordon Churchill, a Winnipeg Tory M.P., had written to his family after the pipeline debate, "the sordid spectacle of parliament in decay and the emergence of naked tyranny. . . ."[36] Donald Fleming, Davie Fulton, and George Drew had led the Conservatives through the draining struggle, and Opposition Leader Drew's health had cracked under the strain. Ironically, it was John Diefenbaker, the Prince Albert M.P. and one of the few front-bench Tories who had said almost nothing during the heated sessions, who was to become the main beneficiary of the new mood in the country.

CHAPTER 2

The Chief in Power

The Chief was the son of a Prairie homesteader. John Diefenbaker's father, William, had come west from Ontario in 1903 with his wife and two sons and taken up a homestead at Borden in the Northwest Territories while supporting the family by teaching school. In 1905 the first ten acres were broken, in July 1906 a shack was built, and from October of that year the family lived on their land in what, after 1905, was the province of Saskatchewan. Until 1909, the Diefenbakers never farmed more than thirty acres or owned more than three cows and a single horse, and the value of the entire operation, including the $250 spent for the lumber needed to build the house, was only some $400.[1] Like so many others in those years, William Diefenbaker could not make a success of Prairie farming.

The family moved to Saskatoon when John was almost fifteen, and while his father worked as a civil servant he attended high school and entered the University of Saskatchewan in 1912. During the Great War he enlisted, like almost all the young men of his generation, and went overseas as a lieutenant, but Diefenbaker suffered a training injury and was invalided home. That fortunate mischance probably saved his life – infantry subalterns had an infinitesmal life span in the trenches – and allowed young Diefenbaker to complete his education with a degree in law. In 1919 he began to practise in Wakaw, Saskatchewan, and three years later he moved to Prince Albert, his home for most of the rest of his life. There, his law career developed well, he built an enviable reputation as an able and fiery defence counsel, and he became known as a defender of the little man, a champion of civil rights.

His political career, however, was completely unsuccessful, one disaster following another. His first try for office was in 1925 when he contested the Prince Albert seat for the federal Conservatives and lost. The next year he ran against Mackenzie King in the same riding and lost again, in 1929 he lost a campaign for the Saskatchewan legislature and in 1933 he was defeated when he ran for mayor of his town. In 1936, despite this abysmal record, he was elected leader of the moribund Saskatchewan Conservative party, but when he made another attempt for a seat in the legislature in 1938 he lost again. Until the age of forty-three, Diefenbaker had lost every election he had contested, but, undaunted, he tried yet again in the 1940 federal contest in the riding of Lake Centre and, despite a national Liberal sweep, he squeaked into Parliament. He was to hold that constituency until, he always claimed, it was gerrymandered out from under him before the 1953 election when he won the Prince Albert constituency, which he held until his death.

The new M.P. had his ambitions, and they led him to try for the party leadership in 1942. He did not succeed then, losing to John Bracken, nor did he fare better in 1948, when Lieutenant-Colonel George Drew, the Premier of Ontario, won the crown. But if he was unsuccessful in winning the top post, he did earn a reputation as a good Commons performer, one who participated in debates, did his homework, and took care of his constituents' needs. He was, however, a difficult subordinate in caucus for, in a Tory party that seemed to see itself (and was often seen by the public) as the voice of Orange Ontario and Bay Street, Diefenbaker was a lonely Westerner and an advocate of increased social welfare. In 1944, for example, he was virtually alone in the caucus in supporting the idea of family allowances. As a result, his relations with the party leaders from 1942 to 1956 were often cool. But there was no overt break, and Diefenbaker, who went out of his way to befriend bright young members of the party caucus (and some of the not-so-bright, too), developed a coterie of devoted admirers. That paid off in the 1956 convention.

His first wife, Edna Brower, had been his greatest supporter during the lean years. Bright and vivacious, Edna had always seemed more lively than her dour and disappointed husband, and the marriage had its difficulties. Edna died in 1951, and two years later Diefenbaker married Olive Palmer, a childhood friend now widowed. Gracious and calm but as harsh on her husband's critics as Diefenbaker himself, and very protective of her husband's health, Olive was the Chief's greatest asset, a rock of stability amid the political turmoil.[2]

The man's character was not easy to fathom. He was very conscious of the snubs he had suffered because of his German-sounding surname, and the discrimination he had borne led him to feel strongly about the need for a "Canadian citizenship that knew no hyphenated consideration." There should be no German-Canadians, no Jewish- or French-Canadians, only Canadians pure and simple. "I never deviated from this purpose," Diefenbaker said. "It's the reason I went into public life."[3] That was an admirable and egalitarian aim, even if it did neglect some of the basic Canadian and Quebec realities. Even so, the abuse he had suffered because of his origins probably helped make Diefenbaker a man who trusted few men and never forgave those who crossed him. He remembered slights and attacks for years, and he could not readily accept the Conservatives who had run against him for leader in 1942, 1948, or 1956, who had disagreed with him on issues or tactics, or even those who had loyally supported the party leaders. It was not easy to explain matters to him. "He won't read papers," General George Pearkes, a caucus colleague remembered, "he won't attend Committee meetings – and when you go in to talk to him he was getting more deaf. . . ." In addition, the British Columbia M.P. said, he "would much rather talk than listen; and when you went in to see him you would start to explain things and then he'd start telling you. . . ."[4] He was also averse to fine points, particularly on complex questions of foreign policy, and he preferred to stay on "fairly broad terms" and was almost always impatient with detailed agendas.

Nor did Diefenbaker have the habit of working out problems on paper. He was not a reflective man; rather, like many lawyers, he operated best on his feet when he had those intuitive flashes that made him a leading member of the bar and one of the great parliamentary orators of Canadian history. He was freshest in the morning, "the time we usually try to get decisions from him," an aide said, noting that "this becomes less easy as the day wears on."[5] He had little idea of administration or teamwork, and (a not unusual trait) he preferred to have people around who agreed with him, not those who might question. Already in his sixties and set in his ways, John Diefenbaker after seventeen years in opposition was now to be prime minister.

I

John Diefenbaker had begun his campaign for the leadership of the Progressive Conservative party within days of George Drew's decision to resign as leader at the beginning of October 1956. As soon as Drew's announcement had come, Gordon Churchill was on the telephone to Diefenbaker to urge him to run. And within a day Churchill was meeting with his colleagues in the caucus, solidifying support for the Saskatchewan lawyer. The aim, as Churchill said as early as October 11, was to get "John elected on the first ballot. That means being sure of 800 delegates out of the 1,400 who will be present. My hope is that 300 delegates from the Western provinces will offset any block of votes in the East and with 90% of the Maritime vote plus very substantial support from Ontario we should manage it."[6] By the end of October, 80 per cent of the Conservative M.P.s were committed to Diefenbaker, a striking tribute to his perceived electability at the convention, to the belief that he could be sold to the nation in a general election, and to the resentment at the Old Guard that festered within the party's ranks. The Old Guard was said to include the men around Drew, the party bigwigs in Toronto, and the ineffectual party machine in Quebec. These were the men who had failed to crack Liberalism's stranglehold on the country; more immediately, they were believed to be the ones who had denied preferment within the party to members who did not measure up to their conception of Conservatism.

Significantly, Diefenbaker had little support in the party establishment – although Churchill, for one, had been thought to be part of the "in" group.[7] Indeed, the day the convention was called, a group that included Donald Fleming, the party's financial critic, J.M. Macdonnell, another Toronto M.P. with strong business connections, Grattan O'Leary of the Ottawa *Journal*, Léon Balcer, one of the party's few Quebec M.P.s and president of the Progressive Conservative Association, George Nowlan, a Nova Scotia M.P., and R.A. Bell, long a key figure in the party's national organization, met to discuss ways of stopping Diefenbaker. As Bell remembered, the consensus was that Fleming was not strong enough to do the job; instead, Sidney Smith, the president of the University of Toronto and a man who had almost run for the leadership in 1942, was to be sounded out. But Smith declined, and the "Stop John" campaign was derailed before it began.[8] Instead, Fleming decided to run, and Balcer and Bell were named convention co-chairmen. Ottawa was always a gossipy small town, and the suspicious Diefenbaker must have been convinced that his opponents would go to any length to deny him the prize that he had first sought fourteen years earlier.[9]

One major convention problem for Diefenbaker was Quebec. Diefenbaker had been a strong conscriptionist during the war, and some of his phrases of condemnation still rankled in Quebec. He was also a fervent advocate of civil rights, and as such he had denounced the "Padlock Law" that Maurice Duplessis's government had put on the statute books to control communism – and used to harass Jehovah's Witnesses and other groups.[10] That made Diefenbaker unpopular with Union Nationale supporters, the natural Conservative backers in Quebec, and was therefore a concern. Churchill put the best possible face on matters, stating that "we are assured of considerable support from that province, we have several influential people there working for us, and every effort will be made to establish good relations with our friends in Quebec." But Churchill conceded, "Our major efforts, however, will naturally be made in the West, the Maritimes and in Ontario. . . ."[11] Diefenbaker did have some supporters in Quebec, most notably Pierre Sévigny, a war hero who was a link to the largely hostile Duplessis government, Wilfrid Dufresne, M.P., and a number of old party warhorses, yet all in all, as Churchill had to admit, "Diefenbaker will get some support in Quebec but it is a very difficult province and has so many factions operating that no one can determine in advance just what they will do." True enough; no one in Diefenbaker's camp expected much from French Canada, and Quebec was expected to vote *en bloc* for Donald Fleming.[12]

Diefenbaker also had to face half-truths and rumours. He was too old, in ill health, and difficult to get along with, some said. In Quebec, the rumour was also spread that he was Jewish.[13] Diefenbaker was sixty-two, he had been an M.P. since 1940, and he was twenty-two years older than Davie Fulton (the British Columbia M.P. who was in the race) and ten years Fleming's senior. As for the complaints that Diefenbaker was a moody loner, a turbulent force in caucus, and a man who had not always lent his full support to the party leader, Churchill explained to a Winnipeg friend, Duff Roblin, that "much of his difficulty in the past has arisen from the fact that he has not had sufficient assistance for him to keep up with his work and his correspondence. I am finding him very reasonable and very frank and easy to deal with."[14]

All the rumours, however, were as nothing against the widespread belief that Diefenbaker was going to win. Churchill was certain that "unless something unexpected happens there is no doubt as to the outcome,"[15] and even some of those who were nominally supporting other candidates wanted Diefenbaker to win.

It was all over, bar the shouting. There were ruckuses at the Ottawa convention, tales of plots and conspiracies, but the only disturbance to John Diefenbaker's triumphal procession came when he refused to have a French Canadian speak to his nomination. His choices were Premier Hugh John Flemming of New Brunswick and General George Pearkes of British Columbia. The General was prepared to stand aside, but Diefenbaker would have none of it. As he said later, "This is one country. I didn't neglect Quebec in any way. In 1948 I had a seconder from Quebec. This time, without any intention whatsoever in the slightest to do anything detrimental . . . I decided to follow the example of Mr. Bennett in 1927" and have representatives of East and West. In fact, Diefenbaker said, he had used French in his convention speech for the first time in the campaign, although he was no linguist, and he had done that deliberately to "show my attitude."[16]

Perhaps it was as Diefenbaker said. But there could be little doubt that his adamant refusal to allow Pearkes to withdraw split the convention into French and English blocs, polarizing most Quebec delegates behind Fleming and probably sending some English-speaking Fleming delegates into Diefenbaker's camp.[17] It was an unhappy augury for the future, and even Pierre Sévigny, loyally working for Diefenbaker, wrote to warn of the serious consequences if the impression that Diefenbaker was against French Canadians were not corrected.[18]

The Quebec delegates may not have wanted the Prince Albert lawyer, but the country seemed to. A poll released by the Canadian Institute of Public Opinion on November 26, just days before the convention began, showed that Diefenbaker had the support of 55 per cent of Conservative voters compared to 14 per cent for Fleming and 2 per cent for Fulton; in addition, he was preferred to his rivals by more Liberal voters and supporters of other parties. The Diefenbaker campaign, gloating just a bit, argued that this proved "beyond the shadow of a doubt that we have a man who commands not only overwhelming support in our own Party but tremendous spontaneous endorsation by the Floating Vote which went to other parties in the last election."[19] That was the clincher, for Diefenbaker swept the delegates, taking 774 votes to 393 for Fleming and 117 for Fulton on the first and only ballot. It was the Diefenbaker party now.[20]

Once the euphoria of the convention had dissipated, the Conservatives remembered that they were still far from power at the beginning of 1957. In the election of 1953 the party had managed to elect only fifty-one Members of Parliament on 31 per cent of the popular vote, and Conservatism was strong only in Ontario (thirty-two M.P.s) and desperately weak elsewhere – most particularly in Quebec (four M.P.s). Few observers could see any sign of a resurgence. In the West, for example, Premier Tommy Douglas of Saskatchewan was convinced that the "battle is going to be between the CCF and Social Credit."[21] The polls did not quite agree, one on December 1, 1956, showing Social Credit with 26 per cent of the support on the Prairies and in British Columbia, the Conservatives at 17, Liberals at 37, and the CCF at 19 per cent. Nationally, the Liberals stood at 50 per cent, the Conservatives at 31, CCF at 10, and Social Credit at 9. That was a comfortable Liberal lead, and the government was ahead in every region. The only worrisome sign was that in Ontario the Liberals led the Conservatives by only one percentage point, but even that was an improvement over the August poll that had shown the government trailing a point.[22]

Those numbers did not frighten the Conservatives. Few thought the party could win, but almost all expected that the Liberal government's substantial majority could be reduced and, with the new leader, the P.C.s prepared to take power at the election after next. One man with a theory was Gordon Churchill. The Manitoban considered himself a student of elections, and in his view the Conservative party had long misapplied its resources. His analysis of voting since 1935 had demonstrated to his own satisfaction that the party had little chance in Quebec, which the results seemed to have confirmed. Was the answer to sink more scarce resources into a vain attempt to resuscitate Conservatism in French Canada? Not to Churchill, who was angry that in 1953, by his reckoning, 45 per cent of the party's election funds had been spent in Quebec to produce four seats while in his own province the party's candidates had been starved for cash. As he put it in a memorandum that he had first drafted in 1954, "The Conservatives now hold 50 seats. 87 more are required. If 20 more seats are gained in Quebec where we now have 4, there still remain 67 seats which have to be obtained elsewhere in Canada" for a majority. The logic was clear: ". . . the major effort of the Conservative Party must be made in Ontario and to an almost equal degree in the Maritimes and the West. In these areas the Party has formerly had considerable strength whereas in Quebec it has had very little strength since 1891 and practically none at all since 1935."[23] As the M.P. closest to the new leader, Churchill was in a position to press that position on Diefenbaker, and it soon became policy. In practical terms what it meant was that each constituency received $3,000 from the party treasury for the election, a marked change from 1953 when some had received nothing and others, mainly in Quebec, had received up to $10,000.[24]

Diefenbaker also reorganized party headquarters in Ottawa. The national director, W.L. Rowe (whose father, Earl Rowe, had endorsed Fleming's candidacy at the convention), was replaced. Then Diefenbaker made Allister Grosart national director. Under Grosart was Dalton Camp as the director of advertising and general supervisor of the headquarters. Both men were to work closely with Churchill, and the triumvirate effectively decentralized the party's election machinery, giving far more power to provincial campaign committees than in the past.[25] In addition, the advertising budget, tentatively set at $800,000, was put mainly in the hands of the McKim and Locke-Johnson agencies with Churchill, Camp, and Grosart to decide on the division and with Churchill to arbitrate any disputes between the two advertising men who had come from the competing agencies. The same trio was to decide on publicity and to have the opportunity to discuss any political decision intended to be made public.[26]

The creative thrust came from Camp. The New Brunswick-born adman had a genius for picking out campaign themes. In mid-

February, for example, he sent a long memorandum to Churchill that detailed the pros and cons of different media strategies and his assessment of probable issues. Camp went over the list – the rights of Parliament, the restoration of the two-party system, the economic problems of the have-not provinces, the United Nations, the Commonwealth and the United States, fiscal policy and inflation, and "the personal appeal of Diefenbaker, both to latent Conservatives and independent voters." As Camp said, "The important consideration with regard to all these issues is, to me, the fact that only one of them can honestly be said to be truly national in scope, and that is the personal appeal of the leader himself. . . . In all candour, it has not always been possible for a political party to consider its leader as its first asset and best issue." He went on, "Flattery is useless here. . . . But in actual fact there is every evidence that what we describe as the average voter appears to have an intuitive confidence and liking for this party's leader. Translated into publicity it means that our newspaper and magazine advertising, if it is to have the greatest effect on the greatest number of people, will give the highest priority to Mr. Diefenbaker."[27]

The focus was to be on the Chief, as he was already being called, and this approach was ratified by the members of the National Campaign Committee in Ottawa on April 7.[28] Within the next two weeks, the leader's national tour had been planned and staff assigned. George Hogan, a wealthy Toronto auto dealer, became executive assistant, Derek Bedson the private secretary, and, most important, Merril Menzies, a young Ph.D. in economics, the research assistant. It was Menzies, with his able memoranda on any and every subject, who was to provide the intellectual coherence to the campaign.[29]

But it was Diefenbaker who set the heather afire as the campaign began in the spring of 1957. With his fierce eyes and marcelled grey-white hair, the Chief would have been a striking individual in appearance alone, but when he began to speak the effect was electric. The words flowed forth, mixing Biblical rhetoric and parables with down-home humour; the arms waved, the fingers pointed, the gaze mesmerized. "I have come here tonight, my fellow Canadians," Diefenbaker said in one typical address in the Maritimes, "to discuss with you the future of Canada – not just of this section or of that section – but of the nation as a whole. My theme is One Country – One Policy: our policy embraces the whole of Canada. . . . I have come here with a vision of our nation's destiny, with a positive message of hope and progress." That was Diefenbaker on the high road, pledging that no section would receive special treatment, a message that implicitly suggested that Quebec would be treated no better than any other region. In the Maritimes and on the Prairies, parts of the country that believed themselves short-changed by the Liberals, that was important; it was also important that Diefenbaker was not a Central Canadian come to visit the country bumpkins. He seemed to understand regional needs as in Truro, Nova Scotia, where he said that "any project which is truly beneficial and essential to the welfare and prosperity of a region or province is by definition – at least by Conservative definition – in the national interest. Can I be more specific than that?"[30] There was a forthrightness there that won support.

But occasionally Diefenbaker showed a complete unwillingness to be open with the press. For example, in a televised press conference early in his leadership he was asked what he would do to resolve the railway strike then disrupting the country. "Well, now, of course I'm not going to indulge in hypothesis and answer speculations," he said; ". . . I'm not going to be placed in the position of saying what I would do." Wasn't it time to speak up fearlessly as he had said he would? one reporter asked. The reply was that "any speaking up fearlessly is to be done in the House of Commons."[31]

Most politicians, of course, do that, yet somehow Diefenbaker sounded fresher and franker than his competitors. He could also be very funny on occasion, as when he recalled the situation he faced as leader in 1957: ". . . the Gallup polls and the punsters and the pollsters and the paragons of all the political perfections who in their punditry are able to predict and forget the prediction after the election, they all said there wasn't any hope. . . ."[32]

No one thought there was, and certainly not the Liberals. Brooke Claxton, a long-time Liberal minister and in 1957 chairman of the Canada Council, wrote to a friend that the pipeline and other "boobs" had lowered government prestige, and the organization and candidates were all four years older than in 1953. There might also be a small turnout, and that could hurt. But the worst he foresaw was the loss of twenty or so seats, even if, as he anticipated, the Conservatives were to conduct "an anti-Catholic, anti-French, anti-American, anti-Jewish, anti-Canadian, anti-Pearson campaign which may be effective in some parts of Ontario and the Maritimes."[33] Certainly there was truth in the comments on the age of the government. It was old; its ministers stayed in Ottawa, only rarely returning to their constituencies. One of C.D. Howe's aides lamented that his minister "just never comes home. We finally had to dig up an anniversary so we could put on a special dinner. Then he had to come."[34]

Still the polls continued to look good for the government, although there was a concern that 70-per-cent support in Quebec masked slippage in the East and West.[35] The press remained solid, even if there was a slightly grudging tone. The Ottawa *Citizen*, for example, said that ordinarily it might be a good thing to change governments after a generation. "But in this case there is simply no alternative in sight . . . ."[36] Nonetheless worries kept appearing. A Manitoba Liberal wrote to party headquarters early in May to say that "somehow or other this election is not going right. Ministers appearing in the Province are getting a fair reception but seem unable to get close to the electors, either in their person or in their mental attitudes." The government, he said, "had lost touch with the grass roots."[37] Even Prime Minister St. Laurent seemed to sense that when he told a Windsor, Ontario, audience that "this is a curious election. Every time we turn around we are confronted with the argument that, well, yes, things are going fairly well – but if the Tories had only been in power everything would be absolutely perfect."[38]

In his own way Diefenbaker had zeroed in on the same point. He hammered at the arrogance of the government, telling a Winnipeg audience that Howe had said on one occasion, "If we wanted to get away with it, who would stop us?" and had added on another, "If we have overstepped our powers, I make no apology for having done so."

> That's strength. Those are strong powerful words.
> "Who would stop us?"
> Perhaps, that is the real issue in this election.
> "Who would stop them?"
> My fellow Canadians, I hope *you* for nobody else can!

Later, in a television address, Diefenbaker cited what he saw as a "ground-swell of protest – against things done and things left undone by the St. Laurent government. It is a protest against want in the midst of plenty . . . against arrogance where there should be understanding." There was "righteous indignation – against a government which is just beginning to wake up to the fact that no matter how powerful any group of men may be they cannot fool all the people all the time." And, most powerfully of all, in a national address on CBC-TV on June 5, Diefenbaker referred to the pipeline debate, which demonstrated that the Cabinet had reached the "point where it believes itself to be infallible." He said, ". . . I give you this pledge, sometimes I may be wrong in the future, as in the past, but I'll never be on the side of wrong, and this party, so long as I am its leader, will not be on the side of wrong."[39]

That was the Tory leader on the attack. In a more positive vein, Diefenbaker was promising much: a new deal for the provinces in federal-provincial fiscal relations, an offer that was to win him the wholehearted support of Premier Leslie Frost of Ontario. In "his quiet but enormously effective method,'' Gordon Churchill remembered, Frost ''swung his people in behind the Federal Conservatives.''[40] That galvanized the party's troops in Ontario, which had not happened when Drew was leader. There were promises of aid to all the regions. There was a vision of a new Canada and a new policy of national development. Alvin Hamilton, the (highly unsuccessful) leader of the Saskatchewan Progressive Conservative party since 1949 and in the 1957 election a federal candidate, bombarded Diefenbaker with memoranda on the need for such a policy, on a ''Roads to Resources'' programme, and on the necessity for the South Saskatchewan River Dam. Merril Menzies reinforced Hamilton's importunings with his own memoranda and shrewd advice on wheat policy.[41] The campaign began catching fire, and there were huge crowds out to see Diefenbaker, the people cheering him to the echo.

The Liberals were getting a different response. Senator T.A. Crerar wrote to a friend about one meeting held by C.D. Howe in Morris, Manitoba:

> The farmers of the district . . . are as steady in their thinking as would be found anywhere; but they are frustrated and incensed over wheat marketing. Clarence has never been more inept than at this meeting. The storm signals had been flying, and the grandfatherly talk that if they just continued to be good boys everything would be alright, when the Suez problem and a few other matters were cleared up, simply infuriated the audience . . . there can be little doubt there is mounting resentment across the Prairies. Farmers have only been able to market a few bushels per acre of their last year's crop. Many have unmarketed grain grown as far back as 3 or 4 years ago. . . . The fact is the Govt . . . when everything was going well took all the credit. . . . Now when matters are going badly Clarence and Jimmy [Gardiner, the Minister of Agriculture] cannot satisfy the farmers with bedtime stories. . . .[42]

The ineptitude played into the Conservatives' hands. Their basic advertisement downplayed the party name by focusing on the slogan ''It's Time for a Diefenbaker Government!'' above a large photograph of the leader and the words ''A New National *Policy*. . . . Unity requires it . . . Freedom Demands it . . . Vision will ensure it. . . .''[43] But the Tories were flexible enough to improvise. In British Columbia a candidate in Vancouver-Burrard, John Taylor, had his slogan ''Follow John'' used on posters and simply showing two footprints. Somehow that caught on in that province and became almost universally employed there for the Diefenbaker campaign, despite the fears of the party's local advertising agency that it could become an object of ridicule. As Diefenbaker's executive assistant wrote to headquarters, ''All over B.C. today you see on the back of cars, on sidewalks, on fences and walls, these two footprints and the words 'Follow John'. Mr. Diefenbaker's name has attracted such magic, and there appears to be such a halo around John's head . . . that there is no danger in this election of the slogan becoming ridiculous. On the contrary, it is having a bandwagon effect, and all sorts of people are turning up wearing Follow John badges just as a sort of fad."[44] The craze soon spread across the land.

But still almost no one expected the Conservatives to win. Chubby Power, Liberal senator and old campaigner, guessed 142 Liberals to 78 Conservatives on June 4, six days before the election.[45] George Hogan, travelling with Diefenbaker, did a province-by-province breakdown on election morning and estimated that Diefenbaker would take not less than 75 seats nor more than 111; his best guess was 82, with the Liberals winning 150.[46] Only Grant Dexter, the Liberal-leaning journalist with the Winnipeg *Free Press*, foresaw large Liberal losses in the East, noting resentment in Ontario and general fuming at the measly six-dollar increase in the Old Age Pension that the Liberals had grudgingly given before the election. "We may be in the process of going over the dam," he wrote.[47]

Over the government went. On the evening of June 10, Canadians discovered that they had elected 112 Conservatives, 105 Liberals, 25 CCFers, 19 Social Crediters, and 4 independents. The Diefenbaker party had increased its popular vote from 31 per cent in 1953 to 38.9, and although that left them trailing the Liberals who had garnered 40.9 per cent, that figure was skewed by massive Grit support (57.6 per cent) in Quebec. Indeed, only in Quebec and Newfoundland, a Liberal fiefdom since Confederation in 1949, did the Liberals hold a lead in seats (sixty-two to nine and seven to six, respectively) and popular vote. But it was Ontario that elected Diefenbaker, returning sixty-one Tories on 48 per cent of the popular vote to only twenty Liberals, far more than the mere twenty-one Conservatives elected in Western Canada. It was a Diefenbaker triumph, a wholly unexpected victory that was a tribute to the leader's personality and drive – and to the shrewd campaign his party had mounted. The earth had moved, the pipeline affair had been avenged, and as historian Frank Underhill noted, "Mackenzie King was at last dead."[48]

But what would the St. Laurent government do? In a narrow minority situation, it could reasonably stay in power and attempt to secure CCF or Social Credit support to continue governing. But that was not St. Laurent's way. The gentlemanly prime minister took his defeat "like a man worthy of the great office he held," Power, who was with him as the result became certain, wrote. "There was no drama, no noble sentiments; he might have been discussing a law case he had lost." St. Laurent said that "he should not attempt to carry on his administration with certain defeat in eight of ten provinces and nine of his best [cabinet] colleagues defeated," a list that included Howe, Harris, Robert Winters, and Stuart Garson.[49]

That decision came as a great relief to the Governor General. Massey had feared he might find himself in a "Governor-General's nightmare" and he kept seeing "the ghost of 1926" stalking through Rideau Hall. But when he met St. Laurent on June 12, he was relieved to learn that the Prime Minister had already talked to Diefenbaker to suggest "that he should be sworn of the Privy Council and that he should represent Canada as Prime Minister-designate" at the Commonwealth Prime Ministers' Conference scheduled to begin in the next ten days or so. That he should resign office, St. Laurent said, was his own idea,[50] but at a Cabinet on June 13 there were at least two ministers who disagreed.[51] Nonetheless, St. Laurent was determined, even though he agreed to await the delayed military voting results. The plan to name Diefenbaker Prime Minister-designate had to be scrapped – at the Commonwealth meetings, Diefenbaker had to be able to speak for Canada.

On June 15, St. Laurent attended a Rideau Hall garden party, telling Massey that it was "a good thing for foreign diplomats to see how we behave on an occasion of crisis like the one at present."[52] And on June 17, he resigned. The new prime minister was in "a bit of a daze, which he quite humbly and sincerely refers to," Massey noted. "He says he can hardly believe this had happened."[53] And the next day the Cabinet was sworn in. The Clerk of the Privy Council, having presided at the ceremony, announced that a Cabinet meeting would follow in the East Block. George Nowlan, a new minister, one who, Massey noted, "has a pleasant sense of humour, said, 'Can anyone show us where it is?' "[54] The miracle had come to pass, and even the chief mover and his aides could not believe what they had accomplished.

II

John Diefenbaker had few close political friends, and this posed problems when he had to form his Cabinet. He didn't limit himself to supporters, he remembered years later, and by then considered it an error. He took George Nowlan in – "he opposed me to the limit always" – and J.M. Macdonnell and Balcer who "did everything [they could] to prevent me from becoming leader." But none of them got important posts, Balcer, the senior Quebecker in the party, becoming Solicitor General, Macdonnell Minister without Portfolio, and Nowlan getting National Revenue. The Chief offered Davie Fulton the Speakership, and only when Fulton protested did he offer him the Justice portfolio. He had promised to have a woman in the Cabinet and thus had to offer a post to Ellen Fairclough of Hamilton, even though, as she had not supported him at the 1956 convention, he distrusted her. "I have to form a Cabinet," he told her, "and it begins to look as though I shall have to form it largely of my enemies." Fairclough became Secretary of State. Donald Fleming, a man who had sat silent in Parliament for six weeks after the 1956 convention so as not to detract from the new leader, received Finance, although he had wanted External Affairs. Gordon Churchill was offered Transport and accepted, only to be told at the last moment that he had to take Trade and Commerce, some businessmen apparently objecting to seeing George Hees in that post. Howard Green of Vancouver had been Transport critic in the last parliament, and he unwisely told journalists that he thought he might be given that portfolio. Characteristically, Diefenbaker told him he could have anything except Transport, which went to Hees instead. Green became Minister of Public Works. Angus MacLean of Prince Edward Island and William Hamilton from Montreal did not learn that Fisheries and the Postmaster-Generalship were theirs until the swearing-in. Other posts went to Douglas Harkness of Calgary (Northern Affairs and National Resources), George Pearkes of Victoria (National Defence), A.J. Brooks of New Brunswick (Veterans Affairs), Michael Starr (Labour), and W.J. Browne of Newfoundland (Minister without Portfolio). The Prime Minister himself, disregarding some naïve suggestions that he keep Lester Pearson as Secretary of State for External Affairs, took that post for himself.[55]

What was so striking about that initial Cabinet was not that it contained a Ukrainian in Starr or a woman in Fairclough; what everyone noticed was that Balcer was the sole French Canadian and that his was a junior post. There was no Quebec lieutenant – as one scholar has observed, "Diefenbaker believed as fervently in one leader as in one Canada."[56] The Prime Minister tried to deal with this in a television address the day after the swearing-in when he promised Quebec "that I shall, as soon as possible, increase the representation of your Province in the Cabinet and particularly of the French-speaking constituencies." To be fair, the choice was extremely limited. Perhaps that was why Diefenbaker had deleted a paragraph from his remarks. He was to have said that the Quebec M.P.s "are so good, in fact, that it is only with the greatest difficulty that I am able to choose between them. The quality of your choice is excellent. Perhaps I may be pardoned therefore if I express the hope that on another occasion you will do just as well in the matter of quantity."[57]

Diefenbaker soon expanded the ministry. Sidney Smith of the University of Toronto became Secretary of State for External Affairs, a move that initially was hailed as giving Diefenbaker a Pearson of his very own; it did not prove to be so. Alvin Hamilton became Minister of Northern Affairs and Harkness moved to Agriculture. Paul Comtois took the portfolio of Mines and Waldo Monteith of Stratford, Ontario, became Minister of National Health and Welfare.[58] But that was all – Quebec still had only two French-speaking ministers, and although two Francophones became parliamentary secretaries, that did not ease the hurt. Still, as Vincent Massey said, and the Prime Minister agreed, "The French-speaking members of your Cabinet are not the best element you have in your group!"[59]

Inevitably, the Cabinet was inexperienced. None had ever served in a federal ministry before, but some of the ministers were extremely able. Fulton was an intellectually gifted man of honesty and ability. Fleming worked harder than any man could or should – and gloried in it. Green was a man who followed his own moral sense. But by comparison with the Cabinet of heavyweights that had preceded it – the war ministry of Mackenzie King or the first Cabinet of Louis St. Laurent – the Diefenbaker government was lamentably weak.

One of the new government's greatest assets was the Clerk of the Privy Council, Robert B. Bryce. Bryce had been a member of the public service since 1938 when he had joined the Finance department after a first-rate education at the University of Toronto in Engineering, at Cambridge under Keynes, and at Harvard. His rise had been rapid in Finance, where he worked closely with Clifford Clark, the deputy minister, in Treasury Board, and from 1954 as Clerk of the Privy Council and Secretary to the Cabinet, the senior post in the bureaucracy. But because Bryce had worked closely with the St. Laurent government, the new prime minister initially looked on him (as on all those who had served the *ancien régime*) with suspicion. That did not last, however. Bryce knew everything – he even had to prepare a paper for Diefenbaker on how Cabinet functioned[60] – and he wisely adopted the policy of being completely straightforward with the new prime minister, offering frank advice, backing it up with the complete details on paper, and doing the many and varied jobs of his office on time and with precision. It did not take long before Diefenbaker realized that he had inherited a gem, a man who could be trusted and one whose advice was worth taking.[61]

But the suspicion of the public service persisted nonetheless. During the years of the old government, Bryce had had a regular Saturday lunch date with James Coyne and J.R. Beattie, the Governor and Deputy Governor of the Bank of Canada, and with J.W. Pickersgill, the

Liberal Minister of Citizenship and Immigration; after the election, in the atmosphere of mistrust that quickly spread through Ottawa, the lunches ceased, and Pickersgill, much of whose social life centred around the friends he had made when he was a civil servant, felt almost isolated.[62] Sometimes the suspicion affected policy. For example, when Secretary of State John Foster Dulles came to Ottawa on July 31, 1957, Diefenbaker refused to allow any officials to sit in on the visit, and the Canadian record had to be pieced together from officials' conversations with the Prime Minister – and an account provided by the American ambassador. "The new administration as you know is not very familiar with the usual habits of diplomacy," John Holmes, the acting under-secretary of state for External Affairs, wrote, although Diefenbaker "could hardly have been more friendly" and was proving to be "very willing to accept advice provided the advice is clearly and succinctly stated."[63]

There was also conflict in some departments. The Minister of Trade and Commerce, Gordon Churchill, and his deputy, Mitchell Sharp, did not get on. C.D. Howe's old department was difficult at the best of times, but Churchill and his personal aides were suspicious of Sharp, fearful that the files had been vetted or destroyed, and unwilling to put any trust in the deputy minister's impartiality.[64] Sharp resigned early in the new year, and soon, for the first time in his life, became involved in politics. George Pearkes, the Minister of National Defence, recalled that he was sure External Affairs was riddled with Grits. "Not only were many of them personal friends of Pearson and [Paul] Martin, but Pearson's son was in the department in Ottawa." There was no problem in Defence, however. "I was served loyally by the Chiefs of Staff and Department officials. However Diefenbaker felt that [the Chairman of the Chiefs of Staff Committee, General Charles] Foulkes was not [loyal]. Foulkes was a friend of Pearson but I still maintain he was loyal. . . . I doubt if he disclosed plans or policy to Pearson. . . ."[65]

On the other hand, Howard Green, often thought of as a partisan Tory, wrote to his Liberal predecessor at Public Works to say that "the department was in fine shape and one could not ask for a better deputy than Hugh Young. He has been wonderful and I have had the best of cooperation from all the officials. . . ."[66] And Alvin Hamilton in Northern Affairs got on very well with his deputy, Gordon Robertson, although their relationship was undoubtedly helped by the fact that the two men had attended the University of Saskatchewan together.[67] Yet the relationship between the new government and the officials who served it was delicate and difficult, and Diefenbaker never developed the trust that was essential to a good working relationship. The crucial figure, the liaison between a suspicious prime minister and a fearful bureaucracy, was Bryce, and if the machine of government functioned it was largely because of his efforts of interpretation.

The new government was also quick to set up its patronage network. Although there were complaints in the fall of 1957 that M.P.s' "advice concerning matters vital to their constituents," as Allister Grosart delicately phrased it in a letter to ministers, was being ignored,[68] in fact the changeover from the old Liberal lists was made quickly. In Kingston, for example, the leading local Conservative, T.A. Kidd, was sending Ottawa lists of lawyers who should get work within a month of the election. Kidd also took care to recommend men for work on the Rideau Canal locks, passed on notices of calls for tenders to his friends, and sent long lists of local firms, doctors, and dentists for the "preferred list" kept by government departments. In addition, Kidd sent the names of firms to "be no longer considered as suppliers to Government agencies" and those of individuals who might be hired as Christmas help at the post office. In Kingston, at any rate, patronage covered everything from apples to undertakers.[69]

In the meantime the government was hard at work. While the ministers tried to master their departments, the Cabinet seemed to be constantly in session. Between January 22 and February 4, 1958, for example, there were 11 meetings. In all 1956 there had been 89 meetings, R.B. Bryce was advised; in 1957 there were 111, and in 1958, 131. A later and revised count put the 1958 total at 164, a figure that Bryce considered "Unbelievable!"[70] At the same time, the amount of paper multiplied, as Cabinet documents distributed to ministers rose from 259 in 1956 to 379 in 1958.[71] So heavy was the agenda, so frequent the meetings that many ministers could barely keep abreast of their own portfolios. And some fumed as the Cabinet devoted from two to six hours on each capital punishment case, which, under the prevailing law, had to be reviewed by ministers. "The evidence would be read over again," Pearkes recollected, "and here was everybody sitting around."[72] Diefenbaker, as a lawyer, took that responsibility very seriously.

He also took seriously the Royal Visit in October 1957, when the Queen came to open Parliament. Endless hours were spent arranging ceremonial details for the opening of Parliament, but curiously the Queen was uncomfortable about the Speech from the Throne she had to read. "It was quite clear," the Governor General privately noted, "that the Queen had felt unhappy about most of the text . . . as being not the kind of thing she wished to say, nor representing the way in which she wished to say it." Nor was the Queen entirely pleased with the wine she was served at Government House. At the request of Niagara wine growers, Massey had proffered a domestic (and pre-varietal) white wine: "She said it reminded her of medicine which used to be given to her when she was a girl." The anglophilic Massey for his part had tried to persuade Diefenbaker to wear the formal court dress of Windsor uniform during the visit. "I said that people would generally approve," but fortunately good sense prevailed.[73]

The new session launched, Diefenbaker set out to put his mark on the country. Old age pensions were increased to fifty-five dollars a month, a winter works programme was begun, and the Roads to Resources scheme got under way with Ottawa putting up half the money and the provinces the rest. Taxes were cut, freeing 100,000 Canadians from income tax. The provinces received three additional tax points, and the old government's hospital insurance legislation – which had held up a federal contribution until six provinces representing a majority of the population had agreed – was amended. No longer could Ontario and Quebec stop Saskatchewan and British Columbia from implementing hospital insurance, a great addition to the social security programme. Premier Tommy Douglas said later, "I am convinced that if Mr. Diefenbaker hadn't taken that clause out, it isn't likely that we would have had hospital insurance for many years, if ever."[74] There were improvements to veterans' benefits, new Atlantic Provinces grants made without strings, large new wheat sales and cash advances for farmers, and above all there seemed to be a wholly new spirit in Ottawa. The country was on the move and John Diefenbaker was leading the way. By November 1957, as Bruce Hutchison reported from British Columbia, "Dief is stronger today, out here, than on June 10 . . . in the ordinary mind, out here, he has adopted a pretty good stance."[75]

III

While the Conservatives rejoiced in the unfamiliar exercise of power, the Liberals were struggling to regroup. Louis St. Laurent's physical and mental condition had worsened after the election defeat, and the Liberal leader was deeply depressed and blaming himself for the party's loss of office. But St. Laurent did not want to resign precipitately, leaving his party in the lurch during the new session of Parliament, and he was torn. At the beginning of September, his family called in Lester Pearson and Lionel Chevrier, and after a long conversation, St. Laurent decided he should step down; Pearson drafted the statement, a delicate task for a man who had intentions of running for the leadership and who, in fact, had promised St. Laurent that he would. St. Laurent was to remain as Leader of the Opposition during the session. And a Liberal leadership convention was soon set for January 14 to 16, 1958, in Ottawa.[76]

There were several credible candidates. Walter Harris, the former minister of Finance, was widely admired and respected, but he had lost his seat in the election and had to take the blame for the six-dollar increase in old age pensions that Diefenbaker had made into the symbol of an uncaring government. In the end, Harris decided not to run. Paul Martin, however, was determined to test the waters. An Ontario Francophone and a Roman Catholic, Martin had been a highly successful minister of National Health and Welfare and he had also played a substantial role in foreign policy, serving the country well at the United Nations in New York. He was also an accomplished politician, a hand-shaker with a phenomenal memory for names and faces and a tag-line – "Anyone here from Windsor?" – that had been heard all around the world. Martin had few illusions about his prospects if Pearson ran, however, and he knew that he would be flying in the face of the Liberals' "tradition" of alternating French and English leaders.[77]

Pearson was the favourite of the party establishment. The former diplomat had come into the Cabinet in 1948 and over the years built himself a glowing reputation in Canada and abroad. Pearson never seemed to be a politician, scrapping in the trenches in the House or on the hustings; instead, he seemed above the party battles, the embodiment of reason and intelligence in Canadian public life. That was why some Conservatives could seriously suggest keeping him on as Secretary of State for External Affairs in June 1957. And after Pearson was given the Nobel Peace Prize for his role during the Suez Crisis, his selection as leader seemed certain to turn into a coronation.

But there were weaknesses, and these were set out frankly by Walter Gordon, long a friend of Pearson's and now one of the key organizers of his hastily put together campaign. Against his easy personality and standing in foreign policy, Gordon said, there was Pearson's reputation for neither knowing nor caring much about domestic policy. There was also the battered condition of the party and the fact that "he has no first class associates left except Paul Martin." And, finally, he was inevitably associated with the errors of the previous administration. How could he take a new tack without repudiating his colleagues?[78] Those were all problems, and there were also elements in the party trying to push Pearson in certain directions. Gordon himself, for example, was seen by some as the proponent of "size, of combinations and monopolies." But John Deutsch, a former senior civil servant and now an economist of great repute at the University of British Columbia, lectured Pearson on the virtues of free trade, and on the need to identify with the common man: "The chief function of the state is to preserve as much as possible the freedoms that make for flexibility and economic opportunity."[79]

Obviously the January convention, like all leadership conventions, was not going to be decided on issues or policies. The Liberal delegates wanted a man who could lead them to victory again, and the popular wisdom held that an English-speaking Protestant from Ontario was necessary to restore the party's fortunes, the assumption being that Liberalism was safe in Quebec in perpetuity.[80] Everyone agreed that Martin made the best speeches, but his campaign was hurt by tactical blunders – the candidate's newspaper quoted J.W. Pickersgill in a way that suggested he supported Martin, an insinuation that was not so and that led an angry Pickersgill to make a public statement to the contrary; in addition, Martin's propaganda said that as prime minister he would have Canada's best foreign minister at his side, a reference to Pearson, of course, but one that some sensitive souls interpreted as a slight to St. Laurent, who had been Secretary of State for External Affairs from 1946 to 1948. Those errors offended delegates, and Martin took only 305 votes to Pearson's 1,084 on the first and only ballot. In his acceptance speech, a vigorous one, Pearson pledged to do all he could to defeat the Diefenbaker government at the first opportunity.[81]

That was probably a tactical error, and Pearson compounded it on January 20, 1958, when he attacked the government in his first Commons speech as Opposition Leader and then moved an amendment that cited the government's failings in trade, economic, and fiscal policies over its seven months in office. Pearson concluded by saying that "in view of the desirability, at this time, of having a government pledged to implement Liberal policies, His Excellency's advisers, should, in the opinion of this House submit their resignation forthwith"– and turn over the government to the Liberals.[82] That speech, reeking of Liberal arrogance, met with jeers in the House and in the country. It had been drafted by Pickersgill, whose intent had been to have his new leader put forward a non-confidence motion that the CCF and Social Credit would not support and therefore could not bring down the government and force a quick election. "I think as time goes on the wisdom of the course [Pearson] took in giving the Liberals the opportunity to stand up by themselves as the one Party in Opposition in the House . . . will serve us in good stead," Pickersgill wrote to a friend. "Of course, Diefenbaker scored a triumph in the Press, but his whole speech was defensive."[83]

It didn't sound that way. In his speech, the Prime Minister "tore me to shreds," Pearson admitted. "He had a better opportunity that day than ever subsequently. His was the speech of an Opposition leader, not a Prime Minister."[84] But Diefenbaker went too far. To counter

Pearson's charges about the weakening of the economy since June 1957, Diefenbaker produced a secret government report, "The Canadian Economic Outlook for 1957," that had been prepared in the Department of Trade and Commerce in March 1957, and he charged that the Liberal government had known then that an economic recession was on the way. Why had they done nothing to prevent it? The economy's decline, the rise in unemployment, the Prime Minister claimed, were the fault of the Liberals. That was probably fair comment, but to brandish a classified report in Parliament was a violation of the relationship between ministers and civil servants and of the confidentiality of the advice of the public service. The already shaky relationship between the government and its bureaucracy was further weakened, and as Paul Martin later noted, Diefenbaker's use of the report "cannot be justified . . . he knew that was a secret report. . . . But there's no doubt that, using it, together with our *gaucherie* in the amendment that we put forward, gave him an opportunity of making one of the greatest devastating speeches. . . ."[85]

There was more to come. On February 1, Diefenbaker saw the Governor General and secured his consent to dissolution. He had been talking to Massey since early November 1957 about the need for a quick election, telling him that "the longer this election is postponed, the economy, situation involving unemployment, etc., would be adverse to [the] Government's fortunes."[86] Pearson's gaffe had given Diefenbaker the opportunity to go to the people, and the quick election call denied Pearson any chance to make a mark of his own. Diefenbaker was cocky and confident, his followers loud in his praise. The chorus was not yet unanimous, however. CCF leader M.J. Coldwell wrote that "Dief will be found out in time, but that time is not yet."[87]

"I have so far found no one who wants the Liberals back," George Ferguson, the editor of the *Montreal Star*, wrote to a friend on February 8, 1958, at the opening of the election campaign. "The Govt. has done a deal of floundering and it has not found its feet, but it has done various very popular things and there is no chance of hanging unemployment on it." A very experienced journalist with good Liberal and Tory connections, Ferguson added, "The Lib. criticism is weak and gravely hampered by the fact that every time they say something shd. be done, it's pat to reply 'why didn't you do it yourself?' "[88] That was the 1958 election in a nutshell.

It seemed that Diefenbaker could do not wrong. The secret report furore died down quickly, many Canadians apparently considering that the Prime Minister had done nothing untoward. And Diefenbaker attacked the Liberals unmercifully. "They said they had no confidence in us,'' he said in his speech opening the campaign at Winnipeg on February 12. "The [January 20] amendment showed they had no confidence in the people either. I want to be fair. Such an amendment in the diplomatic world might have got by. But as a parliamentary manoeuvre it couldn't.'' The Liberals were questioning the necessity of an election, the Prime Minister said. "We called the election because it was called for. . . . They say that I called an election because of fear, fear to face responsibilities. I don't believe that to trust the people is ever evidence of fear.''

The Chief then roused the audience – and the country – with his programme for the future, "one that is calculated to give young Canadians, motivated by a desire to serve, a lift in the heart, and Faith in Canada's Future, Faith in her Destiny.'' This was Diefenbaker's Vision, and the components of it were the Pine Point Railway to Great Slave Lake, the pressing forward of hydro development on the Columbia River, a national conference on conservation, farm rehabilitation, a second Trans-Canada highway, progress on Arctic research to develop routes and resources in the North, improvement of the Hudson Bay route, and increased self-government in the Yukon and Northwest Territories. "This is the message I give to you my Fellow Canadians – not one of defeatism – Jobs! Jobs for hundreds of thousands of Canadian people. A new vision! A new hope! A new soul for Canada.'' The cheers almost tore the roof off.[89]

The Vision, as everyone soon called it, had had its first try-out in the 1957 election. It was refined for the 1958 campaign by Menzies, Alvin Hamilton, and Roy Faibish, Hamilton's private secretary and the draftsman of the text Diefenbaker employed at Winnipeg.[90] But the phraseology and the passion were the Prime Minister's, and the Vision swept the land, never more so than when Pearson unwisely quipped that it would provide roads from igloo to igloo. Canadians did not understand their North or go to it, but it was theirs, and when Diefenbaker promised to develop it, he struck a responsive chord.

The Liberals had nothing to counter the Conservative pitch. The party promised a $400-million tax cut, but as Bruce Hutchison privately noted, "The public thinks it is phony, a death-bed repentance, an obvious piece of bait.'' Pearson's campaign, he added, "has never got off the ground out here [in B.C.].'' The voters wanted to give Diefenbaker a chance and they had "forgotten'' Pearson's Nobel Prize and his fine record of service.[91]

Few Liberals, however, saw the size of the approaching disaster. There was some initial nervousness in Quebec, Chubby Power reported, "largely on account of the great show of number[s] at the Diefenbaker meetings and the conventions and to a large extent because [Liberals] began to realize that a champagne appetite carefully nurtured in the past would have to be satisfied with a beer diet," but the fears had abated. The Tory crowds had been bought and paid for, Diefenbaker's Quebec tour had not been a success, and the Tories had failed to appoint any French-speaking ministers with standing. "Moreover, as the Diefenbaker candidates appear, they are largely of very inferior capacity and calibre."[92] That sounded hopeful enough, even though it neglected the efforts of Premier Duplessis's organizers for the Conservatives and the expenditure of $750,000 in Union Nationale funds in fifty selected ridings.[93] Still, Senator J.J. Connolly, running the Liberal campaign, could write as late as three weeks before the March 31 election that the party would not lose any seats it had held in 1957, and he was even forecasting gains in British Columbia and on the Prairies.[94] Tommy Douglas in Saskatchewan was also optimistic, telling Coldwell that the CCF campaign in the province was better than at any time since 1945. "The one thing that troubles me," the Premier added, "is that in the main the Liberal candidates are extraordinarily weak and no one knows where the Liberal vote will go."[95]

Meanwhile Diefenbaker continued to stump the country, buoyed up by the extraordinary response his very presence inspired. In a national TV address on March 13, he spoke of the economy:

> It is with deep personal satisfaction, my fellow Canadians, that I am able to come before you tonight and say to you – much sooner than even I and my colleagues had hoped for – that there are good reasons for believing that the clouds are beginning to disappear, that we are on the verge of a turn in the tide of gloom and fear which was the legacy we inherited when we took office last June. I refer, of course, to unemployment, tight money, trade deficits, the housing slump, high interest rates, and the loose and harmful talk that we were heading into an economic depression. . . .

What had turned the tide? he asked, and gave his own answer: "The vigorous measures which we took and are still taking. . . ."[96]

The people believed. An opinion poll on March 15 showed the Conservatives with 56 per cent support, the Liberals with 32, and the CCF with 7. "If there were no explanation," Senator Connolly wrote to Liberals, "this would be discouraging . . . many candidates will be upset." The explanation, the Senator said, bravely whistling past the graveyard, was that the poll had been taken before Pearson's campaign hit its stride.[97] Perhaps, but the final poll, released just before election day, still showed Diefenbaker with 56 per cent; even more incredible, the Liberals were trailing in Quebec, 44 per cent to 41, and being decimated in Ontario, 63 per cent to 29.[98]

The results confirmed the polls' findings. Diefenbaker won 208 seats on 53.6 per cent of the popular vote, and he led the Liberals everywhere except in Newfoundland. In Quebec, the *bleus* won fifty seats on 49.6 per cent of the vote, the best Tory showing since the palmy days of Sir John A. In Ontario, it was sixty-seven Conservatives to fifteen Liberals, while the Grits were shut out in the West and managed only eight seats in the Maritimes. Pearson had seen his following reduced to forty-nine seats, the CCF won only eight, and Social Credit was wiped out. Some of the Conservative gains were incredible. In Quebec East, St. Laurent's old seat, a 1957 Liberal majority of more than 17,000 turned into a Conservative victory; in York-Scarborough, the Liberals had won in 1953 but lost in 1958 by over 35,000 votes. It was a tidal wave.[99] "We've lost everything," Maryon Pearson, a reluctant political wife, told her husband, "we've even won our own constituency!"[100]

Clearly Pearson was destined to be overwhelmed no matter what he had done. But as even Liberals wondered, did the defeat have to be as bad as it was? Pearson had not run an effective election, and some were asking if their leader was "cut out for this particular job."[101] Pearson himself pondered the question, for all doubts about Diefenbaker's fallibility had been swept away. The Chief was in power and obviously in charge, the leader of an impregnable party and government. The Conservative era had begun in earnest.

IV

Despite its great majority – or perhaps because of it – the government's second-term record was lacklustre. The back-bench M.P.s who arrived in vast numbers faced the standard feeling of diminution that all new members suffered. "You are a great big frog in your own pond," Ged Baldwin of Peace River said, "and suddenly you were just another faceless cipher." For some, the shock was even more profound. Erik Nielsen, the Conservative member for Yukon, said he arrived in 1958 as an idealist only to become cynical when he discovered that ministers refused to believe what they were told about areas and subjects he knew well. Instead, they listened to their bureaucrats, few of whom had seen the North.[102] It was all disillusioning. So too was the simple fact that there was very little for the untried M.P.s to do beyond attending committee meetings or sitting in the House and voting the way the party whips directed.

In the Cabinet, by contrast, the ministers were grossly overworked. There was the heavy schedule of Cabinet sessions, attendance in the House, the receiving of deputations, and trips to Canada and abroad as well as the daily administrative and policy work. The strain was severe, and Gordon Churchill remembered looking around the Cabinet table one Christmas at the white, tense faces of his colleagues and thinking that all needed a holiday.[103]

The Quebec ministers and M.P.s had it hardest. There was the shock of being translated into a wholly English-speaking world – the city of Ottawa and the government of Canada effectively operated only in English, and the Cabinet meetings were unilingual as well. Scarcely a memo in the public service was written other than in English, and a *député* either became fluent in the other language or resigned himself to giving up true participation in the affairs of state. One large step forward was the introduction of simultaneous translation in Parliament, a measure that made the Commons truly functional for all M.P.s for the first time.

But that did not satisfy French Canada. Léon Balcer, the Solicitor General until 1960 and the Minister of Transport thereafter, observed that while simultaneous translation might have been hailed in 1955, after the late 1950s and the onset of the Quiet Revolution in Quebec it was seen as tokenism. The problem, Balcer believed, was that Diefenbaker was a centralist, and that made it hard for Quebec's Conservatives. His own role in Cabinet was limited to saying "What about Quebec?" whenever plans were being made, a remark that indicates how little Quebec weighed on the minds of the Prime Minister and Cabinet.[104] Alvin Hamilton expressed the same kind of attitude when he wrote to Diefenbaker in July 1959 to say that he knew the press continually speculated that Quebec was key to the party's fortunes. "I hold another view, namely, that we must hold the West. With the Maritimes and Ontario reasonably steady and the West with us a good number of Quebec seats will always come to us. Therefore the West must remain the key."[105] Diefenbaker obviously agreed. Nevertheless he could say in a 1960 speech: "They said I didn't understand Quebec and that Quebec didn't understand me. They were wrong then, and they are wrong now. I say to you, my friends, that nowhere in Canada do I feel the things for which I stand are more completely understood than they are in the Province of Quebec."[106]

The Prime Minister was deluding himself, for by that point Quebec ministers were already warning of impending collapse. "Our chief organizers are depressed and indifferent," Pierre Sévigny, the Associate Minister of National Defence, wrote to Allister Grosart in 1960. "Some have quit altogether and do not hesitate to say so. Fewer and fewer people are calling on Ministers or Members of Parliament and we are receiving fewer invitations to speak . . . no one wishes to contribute. . . . Our press has been bad and we are being murdered over the television and radio networks."[107] Quebec was changing with extraordinary rapidity as the Quiet Revolution burst forth under the direction of the new Liberal government of Jean Lesage, and Diefenbaker could neither accept nor respond adequately to the new directions.

There were also difficulties with others of the provincial governments, most notably Newfoundland. In 1958, the Royal Commission on Newfoundland Finances reported, thus fulfilling Term 29 in the Terms of Union of Newfoundland and Canada of 1949. The Royal Commission had been directed to review the financial position of the province and "to recommend the form and scale of additional financial assistance, if any," required to bring provincial government services in Newfoundland to the level of those in the Maritime Provinces. The Liberal government of Joey Smallwood had asked for $15 million a year, but the commission recommended the additional payment of $6.6 million in 1957-58, rising to only $8 million in 1962-63, and thereafter at the same level. Although Smallwood pressed the Diefenbaker government to be generous and to pay the $15 million sought, in March 1959 Diefenbaker accepted the advice of his Minister of Finance and confounded and outraged the Newfoundlander by offering only the Royal Commission's recommended sums – and by declaring that payments were to be cut off completely in 1962.[108]

Perhaps that decision had been shaped by the other great issue of the winter of 1958-59 between St. John's and Ottawa, the question of the use of the Royal Canadian Mounted Police against striking members of the International Woodworkers of America. In February 1959, Smallwood had a bill passed in his legislature decertifying the IWA, on strike for a fifty-four-hour work week at $1.22 an hour. Violence soon erupted, and the RCMP was hard pressed to control matters. Acting under the terms of the province's contract with the Police, Smallwood asked for fifty additional constables, a request that the RCMP Commissioner agreed had to be met. But Diefenbaker disagreed, condemning Smallwood for seeking to use the Police as strikebreakers. Commissioner L.H. Nicholson of the RCMP promptly resigned, and relations between Newfoundland and Ottawa hit their nadir.[109] Diefenbaker's response was the decent one; it was also wrong. What was important about the problems between the Prime Minister and Smallwood was that they indicated that Quebec was not alone in feeling misunderstood. The high hopes of 1957 for a new deal for the provinces had gone aglimmering.

But there were real achievements, too. One was the Bill of Rights. Cynics were unimpressed with Diefenbaker's long campaign for a charter of the rights of Canadians, expecting that it would "degenerate into a Declaration. The Dief will declare himself for God and against adultery," the acerbic George Ferguson laughed, "though as a friend of mine said, he personally was in favour of both. Not the Dief: my friend."[110] There were some grounds for scepticism, for everyone recognized that the federal government's role under the constitution was limited, but there was substantial importance even in a declaration of principle. The government decided to enact the bill as a simple statute, not as a constitutional amendment. "I considered that it would be impossible to pass an amendment to the British North America Act which would be binding both on the provinces and the Dominion," Diefenbaker wrote, bemoaning the provinces' jealous protection of their constitutional rights. Of course, any subsequent administration could simply repeal the Bill of Rights, but Diefenbaker was confident – and rightly – that none would dare. Nor did he expect to see any legislation passed with a "notwithstanding the Bill of Rights" clause in it, and again he was correct.[111] The bill, declaratory as it was, forced a continuing review of wording and of arbitrary actions permissible under Canadian law. As Davie Fulton, the Minister of Justice, noted, it obliged the government to ensure that its legislation did not infringe the rights of the people.[112]

The government also continued its push on national development. The sparkplug was Alvin Hamilton, the Minister of Northern Affairs, and the able team around him. In the spring of 1958 Roy Faibish and Merril Menzies had proposed that a development planning group be set up in the Privy Council Office to do long-range planning and to coordinate the work of the many departments involved.[113] By the end of the year a small research staff had been created in the PCO and a Cabinet Committee on Planning of Resource Development set up.[114] Hamilton's efforts got his department's budget increased, and he got things done. The Roads to Resources programme, the basic policy for which had been passed by Cabinet in February 1958, was under way in eight provinces by the end of that year. That meant, for example, roads from Stewart to Cassiar in British Columbia, to Uranium City in Saskatchewan, and along the Cabot Trail in Nova Scotia, the latter road a testimony to the government's decision to consider tourism a resource.[115] There was also the South Saskatchewan River Project, technically under the Department of Agriculture but really Hamilton's. This was the largest development ever undertaken by the government of Saskatchewan, and the costs to the province alone were more than $100 million. The scheme would create a vast lake, ultimately to be called Lake Diefenbaker, containing 8 million acre-feet of water to be used for power generation, recreation, and irrigation.[116] And Hamilton pressed for the Resources for Tomorrow Conference of October 1961, "the first time since 1906," Peter Newman wrote, "that federal and provincial agencies had met in plenary session for the purpose of formulating a program for the better conservation and management of the nation's natural resources."[117] But by the time of the conference, Hamilton had moved on to the Department of Agriculture (where he became a phenomenally successful salesman for Canadian wheat and the force behind the successful Agricultural Rehabilitation and Development Act of 1961), and under his successor, Walter Dinsdale, the North's development stalled. Still, Diefenbaker's Vision, as drafted by Menzies and Faibish and implemented by Hamilton, was one of the government's great successes.

The triumphs of 1957 and 1958 had turned quickly into the problems of running an administration and a country, and whatever his qualities, effective management was not the Prime Minister's forte. Diefenbaker was willing to seek consensus in Cabinet; indeed, he was too willing, so that endless debates re-hashing old questions took place as the ministers around him vainly sought a formula that all – and the Chief – could accept. That desire for acceptable solutions led to charges that he was politically timid and vacillating. In a sense, that was unfair, for while Diefenbaker could procrastinate, he could also move with great speed in following his intuitive instincts, sometimes with success. But the Prime Minister too often felt obliged to take on jobs himself because he did not trust the judgements or abilities of his colleagues. Very often he would assign the same task to two staff members with the inevitable result that, when this was discovered, the workers had to collude to ensure that both did not send the same material to the Prime Minister.[118] The government simply was not efficient.

That hurt, but inefficiency probably could not have brought Diefenbaker down by itself. His fall took an extraordinary concatenation of events in foreign policy, in the economy, in financial policy, and in defence questions. The crisis might have been managed with a different prime minister in charge, but not with John Diefenbaker at the helm.

CHAPTER 3

The End of the Empire Tie

The Suez Crisis of 1956 was a watershed in Canadian relations with Britain. To John Diefenbaker and his party, it had seemed to be only a further example of the Liberal government's willingness to follow Washington's policy, but once the Progressive Conservatives were in office they gradually came to realize that the British tie was much weaker than it had been. Suez had demonstrated that Britain (and France, too) no longer had an independent military capacity that would permit decisive and quick action; it had also shown everyone the extent of American control over the economies of the West. What was Canada's place in such a world with approximately three quarters of Canadian trade going to the United States? What was the significance of the Commonwealth in this new world? And could someone like Diefenbaker, an emotional monarchist and a lifelong believer in Britain and the British, adjust to the realities of mid-century? Questions of trade and race would put the Conservative prime minister to the test, and in the process, while relations with Britain deteriorated, the hollowness of Canada's links with the old Mother Country would be exposed.

I

John Diefenbaker was exhilarated by his attendance at the Commonwealth Prime Ministers' Conference in the days immediately after the election of 1957. To be in London as the first Conservative prime minister of Canada since 1935 was the fulfilment of long-held dreams. And the British warmed to the Canadian too. The Agent-General for Saskatchewan, Graham Spry, reported to Regina that Diefenbaker was "making a very favourable impression here by his energy and directness. He is, of course, being welcomed here in all Conservative circles with enormous rejoicing and to read some of the cheaper newspapers one would think that Canada had not only rejoined the Commonwealth, but was almost going to amalgamate with the United Kingdom."[1] In the circumstances, it was probably inevitable that when the emotional prime minister returned to Canada on July 7 he told a press conference that it was his government's "planned intention" to divert 15 per cent of Canada's purchases from the United States to the United Kingdom. This was, Diefenbaker said later, "a direct challenge to British industry and initiative."[2]

The Ottawa bureaucracy, which had known nothing of this idea, was stunned by the Prime Minister's remarks. The pledge was simply impossible to meet. The figures were very clear, as the Cabinet was shown in a memorandum from the Department of Finance on August 8. A 15-per-cent diversion meant that the British share of total Canadian imports would have to increase from 8.5 per cent, where it stood in 1956, to 19.5 per cent or, in dollar terms, by $625 million. That was a problem, not least because Britain's share of the Canadian market had been dropping continuously – from 56.1 per cent in 1870 to 16.8 per cent in 1921-31, and to the 8.5 figure in 1956. In that last year, American imports made up almost three quarters of the Canadian total.

The historical trend was significant enough, but there were also other factors. First, the British had no chance whatsoever to enter half the Canadian import market either because they did not export the goods in question or because their products were unsuitable for Canada for reasons of styling or design or lack of industrial capacity. There were also barriers caused by international marketing arrangements, patents, and the General Agreement on Tariffs and Trade, which forbade Canada from giving advantages to any one country. There were some prospects for a shift of trade, but "a diversion of 15 percent of Canadian imports from the United States to the United Kingdom would, in effect, mean diverting roughly 35 percent of Canadian imports from the United States to the United Kingdom in those trade categories which appear to offer scope. . . ." That meant, the officials said, that British exporters would have to increase their sales in Canada between three and four times. That was highly unlikely.[3]

In other words, the Diefenbaker "diversion" was a dead duck, a policy pronouncement made without any understanding of the facts. The British could calculate just as well as the Canadian officials, and when a British minister brought a free trade proposal to Ottawa on September 9, it was immediately countered by Diefenbaker who said "that he recognized the advantages it would provide to U.K. exports, but could not see what advantage there would be in it for Canada."

The idea was rejected firmly and officially on September 10.[4] Something that threatened Canadian producers was not to be welcomed. The result was that Cabinet ministers also began to back off from the Prime Minister's diversion pledge,[5] and Donald Fleming, the Finance minister, even told a Joint United States–Canada Committee on Trade and Economic Affairs meeting that it was all the doing of the press. The newspapers, Fleming said, "had reported a statement of Mr. Diefenbaker's as involving a definite proposal to divert imports. . . . He explained that what Mr. Diefenbaker had in mind was mainly the fact that if a shift of the order of 15% were to take place among the sources of Canadian imports, without injury to Canadian producers, this would largely remove the problem of imbalance which was worrying so many Canadians. Mr. Diefenbaker," Fleming added, "was not suggesting that it would be possible or desirable to carry out a transfer of this kind overnight . . . any shift would be expected to proceed in a way which would not injure Canadian producers. . . ."[6]

The demise of the trade diversion was a minor episode. But it did demonstrate a certain rashness on the part of the Prime Minister, and it is likely that it led the British to have some doubts about the detailed planning that might underlie the new government's policy promises. The dénouement also demonstrated that Diefenbaker's fervent Britishness could be waived if the implementation of any policy might ultimately cause hardship to Canadian producers.

II

The same disposition was apparent during the long battle between London and Ottawa over Great Britain's attempt to enter the European Common Market. To London, entry into the EEC seemed a necessity if Britain was to maintain a place in the world politically and to survive economically. To Ottawa, London's approach to Europe was almost treason, a virtual betrayal of the Commonwealth and of the hundred thousand Canadians who had died to defend Britain in the two World Wars. The sense of outrage, when heightened by the potential losses in trade preferences, was pronounced indeed.

There seemed to be a good deal at stake. A Finance department paper prepared in 1958 noted that Britain was Canada's second-largest market and her principal market for wheat. The Common Market countries also took substantial amounts of Canadian goods – to the tune of $402 million in 1957 – and Britain and the Six supplied about one quarter of Canada's imports. There had been cautious enthusiasm for European unity under the Liberal government, and traces of this remained in the public service in 1958. "It is recognized that a strong and prosperous Europe can play a vital role in the expansion of world trade. However," and here the true fear was evident, "if the regional arrangements in Europe were to develop along restrictive lines they would create divisive forces with serious implications for the interests of all concerned." The Treaty of Rome, the basis of the Common Market, caused concern, in large part because the new common tariff, carefully balanced to satisfy all the Six, seemed likely to be higher than the existing tariffs in some areas.[7] There was an additional fear, too. "To the extent that new European arrangements lessen our markets overseas," one memorandum prepared for a meeting of ministers and officials on December 28, 1959, observed, "our dependence on the United States market will inevitably be increased."[8] Given John Diefenbaker's desire to increase trade with Britain, the prospect of having to expand trade with the Americans in an attempt to replace lost British markets was not a palatable thought.

But for the moment London was not part of the Six; instead it belonged to the "Seven," the European Free Trade Area and, as British officials told their Canadian counterparts at the United Kingdom/Canada Continuing Committee on Trade and Economic Affairs in June 1960, the only practical solution they could see was for some form of association between the Six and the Seven. But because of French attitudes, this did not seem a suitable time to reach a long-range agreement. "The United Kingdom's present course was to consolidate the Seven and permit a situation to develop until . . . a new approach became feasible. In the meantime they were reassessing their position and examining all their possibilities, consistent with the existence of the Six and the Seven as two separate groups and with their wider obligations toward the Commonwealth and in the G.A.T.T."[9] In other words, Britain was keeping all its options open and waiting for something to turn up.

Within a very few months, however, the British were once again looking toward the Common Market with yearning eyes. In September 1960, Diefenbaker wrote, he received notice of Britain's intention to renew negotiations with the European Economic Community.[10] A meeting in London gave the Canadians the chance to put forward "strong" arguments against this that "undoubtedly gave U.K. Ministers some food for thought," or so Norman Robertson, the Under-Secretary of State for External Affairs, wrote.[11] Prime Minister Diefenbaker had his first chance to put his concerns directly to Prime Minister Harold Macmillan when the British leader visited Ottawa on April 10, 1961. What would happen to Commonwealth preferences if Britain joined the Common Market? "We would have to negotiate,"

Macmillan said, " – that is why we have not joined." But moments later, Macmillan admitted that the preferences would probably have to be reduced. Was it not better that Britain should join Europe and become a live partner in a growing trade association than become bankrupt on its own and thereby cease to be a profitable market for anyone? To the British, the choice was between the short-run advantages of the Commonwealth preferences and the long-run advantages that came from access to a large, rich market. That did not calm Diefenbaker, nor did Macmillan's comment that he had no fear of European common institutions evolving in due course.[12] The British also made clear that the Kennedy Administration wanted them to go into Europe – London's reliability as an ally could help stabilize the situation between France and Germany.[13]

But if the government was alarmed by British approaches to the Common Market, Canadian business seemed remarkably calm. The president of INCO saw radical changes as possible but, he warned, Canadians should not assume "that Britain is obligated over the indefinite future to do buying here. . . ." The deputy manager of the Bank of Montreal took a similar line, adding that only small proportions of Canada's trade would be affected and that losses in one area would be offset by gains in others.[14] But the Ottawa view was different, and, faithfully reflecting it, the High Commissioner in London, George Drew, told British audiences that they should compare the immense potential of the Commonwealth with the sadly limited raw materials of Europe.[15]

The battle lines were being drawn even before Britain made its application for Common Market membership on July 31, 1961. Duncan Sandys, the Secretary of State for Commonwealth Relations, came to Ottawa in mid-July, and the Canadians prepared thoroughly for the meeting, marshalling their political arguments and their trade data. In the first place, the Ottawa ministers and officials claimed to fear for the future of the multiracial Commonwealth if Britain entered Europe. But Ottawa also wished to be cautious, not wanting to obstruct London in protecting the British national interest – and not wanting to take the blame if Britain was refused entry by the Six. In trade terms, studies demonstrated that 35 per cent of Canada's industrial exports to Britain would be unaffected if Britain joined, and an additional 25 per cent could probably be given free entry. On a further 7 per cent of Canadian exports, the loss of preference would not cause problems. On some other materials, amounting to 10 per cent of exports, the preference was small and officials believed that the Canadian competitive position could be preserved. All in all, 77 per cent of Canadian industrial exports to the United Kingdom, or half of all Canadian exports to Britain, would not be hurt if Britain joined the Common Market. The major damage would be to the export of semi-manufactured goods – $163 million in trade in 1960. There were also threats to agricultural sales, notably wheat and barley.

Surely the British could negotiate with the Six to protect Canada's interests? Not so, said the Canadian officials: ". . . the prospects are that the U.K. is not in a strong negotiating position. . . . Moreover, the U.K. is likely to use up a good deal of its limited negotiating strength to accommodate the more specialized problems of certain other parts of the Commonwealth which depend on a narrower range of products."[16]

Sandys made his case to the cool Canadians on July 13. There were uncertainties for British industries too – some might "go to the wall" – if Britain joined Europe; "the over-riding consideration, however, was the virtual certainty that the United Kingdom would suffer a severe economic decline if it stayed out of Europe." He hoped that Commonwealth trade could expand, but Britain recognized its limitations and realized that Commonwealth free trade was not practicable, a mild shot at the Canadian rejection of the idea a few years before. The minister had examined Canada's trade with Britain, and he admitted that one-sixth would be affected by the Common Market's agricultural policy, still to be settled. "He was hopeful though that Canadian hard wheat exports would not suffer. . . . For foodstuffs generally he thought duty-free quotas might be a solution." Sandys expected that Canadian raw materials could be safeguarded, and he was pessimistic only about terms of entry for manufactured goods "which, although they represent only 2% of Canada's total exports, were still of great importance. . . ."[17]

According to a Canadian reporter in London who saw Sandys's confidential report on his visit, the British minister had not been impressed with Canadian arguments. The Canadians had not yet read the Treaty of Rome, he said, and their objections were made in ignorance and coloured by political considerations.[18] That was unworthy as comment, but it was paralleled by Canadian editorials that were beginning to denounce Ottawa's "dog in the manger" attitudes to Britain and the Market.[19]

The dog was soon howling. At the Commonwealth Economic Consultative Council meeting in Accra, Ghana, in mid-September 1961, Donald Fleming, the Minister of Finance, and George Hees, the Minister of Trade and Commerce since October 1960, gave full vent to their outrage at Britain's attempt to desert the Empire. Fleming told the meeting that Canada – and the Commonwealth – viewed the British step with "disappointment and grave apprehension," while his colleague warned that American protectionist moves might result. Hees also doubted that the Commonwealth would survive – it was "held together by tradition, trust and trade, and any weakening of any one of those would weaken all three." As the press put it, Canada had told Britain to choose either Europe or the Commonwealth.[20]

London was agog at the Canadian vehemence and at the very critical communiqué issued by the meeting. The *Sunday Telegraph* described it "as a deliberate attempt to sabotage British entry altogether," the policy "only of the Canadians whose eloquent Finance Minister, Mr. Fleming, drafted the document. Mr. Fleming . . . is well aware of the value of appealing over the heads of the British Government to the profound fund of Commonwealth sentiment that exists in this country."[21] Curiously, the Cabinet in Ottawa was upset, the ministers seeing the noise from Ghana as "unwise policy and unwise politics" and they urged that "Canada should now accept as a fait accompli" the British decision to go into Europe.[22] Similar views seem to have been held by Prime Minister Diefenbaker, who was "boiling," R.A. Bell, Fleming's parliamentary secretary, wrote to his minister. "He called me into the lobby . . . then asked if I did not believe you and Hees were 'going a long distance in endeavouring to destroy the British Commonwealth' . . . then said 'unless they learn to behave themselves I will call them both home and immediately.' "[23]

Fleming was chastened – and called back early – but he nonetheless told the House of Commons on his return that "what was said . . . not only by Canada but by others, was that if the United Kingdom adheres to the community on the basis of the treaty of Rome, there will inevitably follow a change in political relationships. That is the inevitable consequence of the treaty of Rome. . . ."[24] Perhaps, but the *Globe and Mail* denounced Fleming's "Song of Woe," and O.J. Firestone, a former government economist close to the Tories, told Diefenbaker that Canada was being pushed into a rigid position that was being interpreted as "ganging up" on the British, and even worse using superficial statistics that exaggerated the trade losses to do so. Nor had the government put forward any alternatives, a negative position not in keeping with the status of senior dominion.[25] Leon Ladner, a leading British Columbia Conservative, also wrote to Diefenbaker to say that his province's forest industry believed Britain had already decided to enter the Common Market and, the implicit message was, further comments like those in Ghana could only harm future sales to Britain and Europe.[26]

But despite the criticism in Cabinet and out, there was no sign of any change in the government position. A delegation sent to London for conversations between September 18 and 28 reported that although the British had urged Canada to be more "constructive," it had maintained its mandate of "ascertaining, in the light of the assurances which had been given by British Ministers, what measures the United Kingdom proposed to ensure that damage to essential Canadian interests would be avoided" if Britain joined.[27]

What was the attitude of the Canadian public? The British thought they knew, and their press regularly reported that the Diefenbaker government's position had little support. Certainly the polls found that 50 per cent of informed Canadians disapproved of the government's position.[28] This worried George Drew in London who fretted that the government case was not being well made and particularly in Britain. "Nothing is said by most of the British writers about the political consequences. . . . Then there is the key question. What does protection of the position of members of the Commonwealth really mean. Surely it means what it says. Our trade in every field . . . must be protected and that doesn't mean partial protection or switches which might advance primary as against secondary sales." To Drew, always feisty and bitterly unhappy with British actions, his government's position had to be based "on the preservation and increase of Canadian jobs. . . . The Canadian Government has not sought to tell the British Government how to run its own business. But it has a duty as well as a right to tell the Canadian people what the result would be of any particular course."[29] For the former Ontario premier and national Tory leader, the main issues were trade and jobs; but if the loss in trade would be small, as Canadian officials and some businessmen had said, then other factors were at work.

Most important was the fear that if Britain went into the Common Market Canada's only alternative would be to throw in its economic lot wholly with the Americans. This was what ultimately concerned Diefenbaker, Drew, Fleming, and Hees. But that choice had in fact been made years before, and the great bulk of Canada's trade already was with the United States, only a trickle continuing to cross the sea. The Commonwealth, greatly expanded, racially mixed, and already turning into a foreign aid organization, simply was not a strong force in world policy. The ministers were out of date; the public, instinctively, had grasped the reality. And some officials in Ottawa, looking at the long view, were already beginning to think of free trade with the United States once again as the answer.[30]

Perhaps Ottawa's best hope might be France. In the late fall of 1961, however, with Britain already deep in negotiation with the Six, President de Gaulle told Donald Fleming, "We are willing to have the United Kingdom in the Common Market, but not the Commonwealth."[31] That was no comfort, for Ottawa believed that to be essentially London's view too, a feeling that was strengthened when Macmillan told the Minister of Finance a few days later that he would "try" to protect Commonwealth interests. The British prime minister did not reply to questions that asked him to define "protection." About all that the Canadians could cling to were the remarks of Edward Heath, the Lord Privy Seal, who had said at the beginning of the negotiations with the Six that "Britain could not join the EEC under conditions in which this [Commonwealth] trade connection was cut with grave loss, even ruin for some of the Commonwealth countries."[32] No one suggested that Canada faced either ruin or grave loss. Fleming, therefore, must have been mildly receptive when his friend Grattan O'Leary wrote to say that he had little confidence in British promises. "What I fear, alas, – it may only be my Fenian youth coming back on me – is that you will discover what the Irish learned through four centuries, namely: That when it comes to their own advantage the English will sell you down the river every time, assuring you that it is God's will and for your own gain."[33] The news from the Brussels talks early in December, where the British had made no headway in the negotiations to protect Commonwealth trade, was that London wanted Canada to agree to water down its position.[34] The O'Leary-like fears in Ottawa were increasing.

The officials concerned, however, professed not to be surprised. Most took the view that Britain should go into Europe in its own interest and in the interest of making Europe as strong as possible. Most appear to have considered the threat to Canadian trade to be relatively minor and, in any case, to be justified by the political gains in Europe. But for some, Canada had to bargain as toughly as possible with the British if only to save those preferences that could be preserved.[35] In any case, as Norman Robertson wrote to his minister, Howard Green, on January 2, 1962, "Nothing in the course of the negotiations so far seems to call for a reassessment of our view that Britain will find it virtually impossible to maintain satisfactory terms of access for Canadian exports to the British market."[36] No one expected much, in other words.

Nonetheless, meetings between Edward Heath and Canadian ministers early in January calmed the worried in Cabinet. Heath repeated his pledges about protecting Canadian exports, and Fleming stated that he was satisfied that London was doing everything it could in the negotiations.[37] At a March meeting, the Canadians told Heath that the British proposals on foodstuffs and industrial items "were just not good enough and that they should go back and press strongly for something a good deal better." That was tough talk. Heath could only promise that there would be a prime ministers' meeting in the fall, after which

Britain would have to decide for itself whether to join the Market or not.[38]

But the old paranoia was resurfacing. George Drew – sending telegrams marked, to the despair of External Affairs, for the Prime Minister only – said that Britain "is engaged in the unilateral planning of the fragmentation of the Commonwealth. . . ." If that was accepted, Drew said, referring to the special terms London was seeking for the trade of the African and Asian members, "all the King's horses and all the King's men may never be able to put it together again."[39] Drew's warnings emerged when Diefenbaker and Macmillan met at the end of April in Ottawa. The Canadian stressed "the importance of Commonwealth preferences to Canada as a means of staving off United States domination," and he added that "the Government was keenly concerned with the preservation of the Commonwealth and feared that its future would be endangered by the political implications of United Kingdom entry." The Commonwealth was an important part of the Canadian identity, Diefenbaker said, almost certainly believing his own words, and he "could not be unconcerned that, if the United Kingdom should join the E.E.C., the basic buttress of the Commonwealth might go."[40] Macmillan did not seem moved by the rhetoric.

Nonetheless, by August 5, the negotiations in Brussels had been adjourned until October without agreement. The Prime Ministers' Conference, set to begin September 10, would thus take place without a firm offer on the table. Still, as Macmillan told Diefenbaker, the negotiations had progressed sufficiently so that Britain could present a reasonably comprehensive outline of terms of entry.[41] Sadly battered by the June 1962 election and in the throes of an austerity programme, the Diefenbaker government was not in its best condition, but Diefenbaker was ready to fight.

His officials advised caution. Britain was going to go into Europe, they said, not least because everyone was manoeuvring to avoid being saddled with the blame for keeping it out. That should include Canada: "We think Canada should not get into the position of leading any open opposition to British entry or being blamed as a principal cause of failure of British efforts to enter." The British would not get better terms, the officials said, and this meant that all Canada's preferences in the U.K. market would be gone by 1970. And when the question was asked, as it inevitably would be, whether Britain had lived up to its promises to protect Commonwealth interests, the officials suggested phrasing an answer to suggest that the injuries to Canadian trade would not be intolerable in the light of the benefits to be obtained.[42]

If Diefenbaker was not convinced – "British entry into the E.E.C.," he told Cabinet, "would be the occasion, if not the cause, of the dissolution of the Commonwealth by about 1970" – increasingly his ministers were. On August 30 and 31 the Cabinet discussed the forthcoming prime ministers' meeting and heard Gordon Churchill, the former Trade and Commerce minister, say that only 17 per cent of Canada's trade was with the U.K. and only 10 per cent would be affected by British entry. "We were not in such a difficult position as New Zealand," Churchill said, a view he reiterated to Diefenbaker in a forceful memorandum, and "we must remember that what we say in Britain about the effects on our trade will come back to Canada." That seemed to be the general view, and the ministers urged that there be no ganging up against Britain. Simply keep the Canadian position in view, they said.[43]

The Prime Minister did not listen. When the conference opened on September 10, Diefenbaker was full of fire. Although, as one British newspaper put it, "Mr. Diefenbaker, it was confidently expected, would be speaking for the benefit of the yokels back on the prairies," that was not the way it turned out. "But as Mr. Macmillan watched and Mr. Diefenbaker adjusted the microphone on Tuesday morning [September 11], it was at once plain that something was badly wrong." The *Sunday Observer* went on to say that the Canadian "was obviously in a highly emotional state. . . . He was rejecting the whole tenor of Mr. Macmillan's speech. . . . This wasn't aimed at the yokels. This was a direct assault on the British government."[44]

That description was not far wrong. Diefenbaker began by saying that he had listened to Macmillan's address with its exposition of the political and economic reasons why Britain sought to go into Europe. He shared the concern for the future of Europe and "recognised that the prosperity of every member of the Commonwealth depended on that of Britain," a state of affairs that had not been true for Canada, at least, for over a half century. But there were still unanswered questions. Macmillan had said Britain was dependent on trade and needed the larger market of Europe to grow. But "if that argument was sound then it would seem to follow that Canada should seek a similar close relationship with the United States." Yet, despite many offers, Canada had refused to do this because it would have meant a weakening of the relationship with Britain and the Commonwealth.

Diefenbaker then gave close scrutiny to all the stated British reasons for wanting to join Europe, doubted that Britain would ever achieve great influence in Europe, and turned to a dissection of pledges by British ministers since 1959. What had changed since those promises were made? He was disappointed that the Common Market countries had failed to show more understanding of Commonwealth trade needs, and he feared that "very few of the basic exports of Canada would be unaffected. He would like to know whether it would be possible to maintain traditional sales of Canadian wheat under the levy system. Would sales of canned salmon be maintained when the prices were forced up by the tariff? . . . He would like to ask whether some Canadian manufactures could not be considered for nil duties. . . ." Diefenbaker then said that while he understood the difficulties about foodstuffs, "he would be less than frank if he did not say that the arrangements outlined did not provide a genuine assurance that Canadian trade would continue at satisfactory levels."

The Canadian said that he had tried to give a realistic assessment of the incomplete settlement that had been brought back from Brussels. He thought that a further prime ministers' meeting might be necessary after the final round of negotiations. And Diefenbaker concluded by expressing his fervent feeling for the Commonwealth. "He thought they should weigh all the considerations carefully before deciding on what would be a fundamental change of course. He was not at this stage saying that it was the wrong course: only asking whether it was the only course."[45]

Called a Cassandra by the *Observer*, Diefenbaker was not alone. All the prime ministers who spoke on September 11 objected to Britain's joining the Market on the present terms. "Macmillan had hoisted the flag of Europe," the *Sunday Observer* wrote, but Diefenbaker and his colleagues were shooting it down, and Diefenbaker drew an ovation from his peers. "One of the Ghanaians, as he told the Queen a few nights later, 'was so moved that I thought I was going to cry.' "[46]

The result was that on September 17 Macmillan defined four points on which all were agreed: the expansion of world trade; improvement of the market for primary foodstuffs; recognition by the developed countries that trade was important to the less developed; and the need for measures to regulate the disposal of agricultural surpluses to meet the requirements of those in want. Those points, he said, would be in the minds of his negotiators in Brussels. On that basis, the conferees agreed that Britain should return to the table to renew the negotiations – which in any case none of them could have prevented and all claimed to desire. As for Diefenbaker, his last word – and one that did not find its way into the communiqué – was to call for all the trading nations "to meet at the earliest practicable date to give consideration to how to deal with trading problems before us in a way which will be to the mutual advantage of all."[47]

In effect, the result of the conference was reserved judgement on the British application. If the terms were better after the next round of negotiations a reasonable assumption was that the Commonwealth could not say nay; if not . . .

But all the Commonwealth huffing and puffing turned out to be for naught. In a press conference on January 14, 1963, President de Gaulle revealed his "unbending attitude toward any significant concessions designed to facilitate British entry into the Common Market," or so an External Affairs memorandum paraphrased him.[48] The Brussels negotiations came to their end with a French veto on January 29, and Britain, much to the relief of the Diefenbaker government, blamed only the French for this.

The Common Market crisis was over for the Progressive Conservative government. Diefenbaker and his increasingly reluctant ministers and officials had fought with vigour and with substantial effect – but for what? The trade, except for that in a few sectors, was small in proportion to the total Canadian trade, and the Commonwealth as some ministers had admitted around the Cabinet table was probably doomed to disintegration and, therefore, of less importance to Canada than hitherto.[49] What the Conservatives had been fighting for was not trade but the idea of the Commonwealth as it existed in John Diefenbaker's mind, a British-led community of nations that fought the good fight and co-operated on all things. It was a figment of the imagination, but not for Diefenbaker. To admit that was to admit that Canada was doomed to slide into the American maw, and he could not do that. The thought that somehow Canada might stand on its own as an independent North American state did not seem to occur to the Prime Minister.

III

If the Common Market crisis had revealed Diefenbaker's Imperial emotionalism and showed him at his worst, the question of South Africa showed him at his best, genuinely concerned for human rights in the world. The question was whether South Africa would be permitted to continue its Commonwealth membership after it became a republic, an issue of importance because of the country's policy of apartheid or racial separation. The blacks, by far the largest part of the population, were kept separate from the white minority and, the implication was clear, were to remain in a subservient status. This was reprehensible at any time, but by the end of the 1950s the world and the Commonwealth were changing quickly. Former colonial states were securing their independence, taking seats at the United Nations, and beginning to weigh offers from the protagonists in the Cold War. The Third World was an area of contention between the West and Moscow and Peking, and in those circumstances South Africa's racial policies did damage to Western policy. Equally important to the Diefenbaker government, if the Commonwealth were to survive as a multiracial institution, the South African question would have to be resolved or, at the very least, somewhat ameliorated. If the sore continued to fester, the non-white members might depart, leaving Britain, Canada, Australia, New Zealand, and South Africa alone in a very different world. To avoid that was the Canadian aim.

On the other hand, South Africa was a sister dominion, a state that had shared in the World Wars, a nation that had built itself, much like Canada, out of the struggles of two racial-linguistic groups. For most Canadians, South Africa was a democracy (for whites), a good if rather limited trading partner, a friend and ally. Could Canada turn on South Africa and help to eject it from the Commonwealth?[50]

Those kinds of questions troubled the Prime Minister. South Africa was an independent nation, and Canada had to be careful about criticizing the internal workings of its friends. Even so, as Basil Robinson, the External Affairs officer in the Prime Minister's Office, noted in February 1959, while Diefenbaker might refrain from open criticism of South African racial policies, no one should assume that "in his mind absence of public criticism equals an effort to cultivate friendship. . . ."[51] Still, the Prime Minister was not prepared to lead any assault on the Boers. That was amply clear on January 28, 1960, when the Canadian Labour Congress urged Canada to take a lead in pushing South Africa out of the Commonwealth. Diefenbaker "blew up" and told the labour leaders that "the Commonwealth was an association of independent states each with responsibility for its own internal affairs and that he had no intention whatever of raising the question of South Africa's racial policies at the [May 1960] Prime Ministers' Meeting with a view to causing South Africa to leave the Commonwealth."[52] In fact, as Robinson privately told R.B. Bryce, the Prime Minister "shrinks from expulsion,"[53] and that feeling persisted even after the Sharpeville massacre on March 21 when South African police fired into demonstrating black crowds and killed scores.

At the 1960 Prime Ministers' Conference, the question of South African racialism was hotly argued. Diefenbaker himself saw Eric Louw, the South African foreign minister, in two private meetings and left him in no doubt of the Canadian lack of sympathy. But there was no indication of any willingness to ease restrictions on blacks, and the Prime Minister, as he wrote in his memoirs, said that the inevitable result was certain to be a bloodbath: "You can't carry on like this. Your nation's stand will turn the whole continent of Africa . . . against you. Your policies are not only wrong, but dangerous."[54] But when the South Africans asked the Commonwealth states if South Africa was still welcome in the association, there was general agreement. The foreign minister then announced that his government proposed to hold a referendum to see if the electorate favoured a republican constitution. Before making this public, his government wished to receive Commonwealth consent to continuance in the association. There was more contention among the members, fear that a statement of the type desired would help the South African government in its campaign, and the resulting communiqué noted only that if a republican South Africa desired to remain in the Commonwealth, "the Meeting suggested that the South African Government should then ask for the consent of the other Commonwealth Governments. . . ." There was, in other words, no guarantee of automaticity.[55]

There was also the question of the reaction of the non-white members if South Africa sought to stay in the Commonwealth. In July 1960, Bryce went as a Canadian representative to the Commonwealth Study Group meeting at Chequers, the British prime minister's official country estate. The study group was looking at a variety of constitutional points, but Bryce took the occasion to steer the conversation to the South African problem. His conclusion, as he reported to Ottawa, was: "There seems to be no doubt that if and when South Africa becomes a republic if she wishes to continue in the Commonwealth she must secure agreement of all the other members." Bryce noted that "British officials present did not like being reminded of this and were clearly unhappy, but there was no way around it." The Secretary to the Cabinet expressed his own doubts that unanimity could be achieved, a forecast none disputed. The Indian representative said he thought it unlikely Malaya and Ghana would agree; his own country and Pakistan might be expected to accept South Africa if there was no controversy, but if Malaya and Ghana objected, India, Pakistan, and probably Ceylon would have to oppose re-admission as well. To Bryce, the best solution in the circumstances was "to endeavour to persuade South Africa not to apply for continuation or re-admission but rather to leave the issue dormant and have those of us who are interested take such legal steps as are necessary to continue arrangements regarding preferences, citizenship, etc."[56] This was a critical meeting in shaping Canadian attitudes, not least because it put Bryce on record as opposing re-admission if it meant a black-white split of the Commonwealth.

But the Department of External Affairs did not agree. There was a distinct aversion there to being a party to forcing the South Africans out. "We would prefer to have South Africa remain in the Commonwealth in its present status," one Commonwealth Division memorandum said in August 1960, "but failing that we should like to retain some vestige of connection'' to make re-entry possible should conditions change.[57] Later position papers struggled manfully to find ways to postpone a decision at least until another prime ministers' meeting and, if possible, even after such a meeting.[58]

But if External seemed clear in its position, so too was Bryce. As he told George Glazebrook of External Affairs, he could agree with everything in the department's memorandum "except the conclusion. . . . This is going to be such an important issue on which the Prime Minister feels so deeply and is so perplexed that I think he should cogitate on this well argued case." Bryce's convictions were based on his own view of the Commonwealth as a club which "can do a little to bridge the gulf between the white and coloured – a gulf which I think will get wider and more visible in the next five or ten years. We need to preserve all the bridges we can across it." If the South African membership was reaffirmed, Bryce argued, "that action will be interpreted widely as implying some approval or at least toleration of South Africa's policies. . . ." If the decision went the other way "then people . . . will realize with a start that the Commonwealth does mean seriously what it says from time to time in woolly phrases. . . . My own view is that at the meeting [of prime ministers now scheduled for March 1961] Canada should take the lead on this matter" and "express its view contrary to re-affirmation basing it upon the effect of the nature and reputation of the Commonwealth." In the circumstances, Bryce suggested, the majority would stand with Canada, and South Africa would leave at once "and blame us for rejecting them."[59]

If the bureaucratic positions were clear, the Prime Minister still remained torn. In November 1960 he told Robinson that "he did not see how he could support South Africa's readmission if the Union Government continued to refuse to pay even lip service to the idea of racial equality." And, Diefenbaker added, he thought it a good idea to tell the South Africans this, warning them that "unless some solid sign of moderation were displayed on the racial issue they could not count on Canadian support. . . ."[60] He said as much in a telegram to Macmillan later that month.[61] But early in 1961 his position seemed to soften, probably in response to a message in reply from the British leader. Macmillan, worried about the "troublesome" and "holier than thou" Diefenbaker, argued that racialism was an internal South African question, just as much as the change from monarchy to republic was. Come to the conference uncommitted, he urged, for if South Africa were forced out, there would be no chance of liberalization there.[62] That weighed on Diefenbaker, and he told Robinson that "his present view was that the time for 'abrupt action' had not arrived . . . the best course would be to give notice again to South Africa that its status as a member of the Commonwealth was in jeopardy." All his emotional reactions were favourable to the South Africans, he added, except on racial policy, and his intent was to put the onus on them, to force them to make concessions or leave. "It was clear," Robinson noted, that "he would be most reluctant to be responsible for South Africa's expulsion from the Commonwealth at least until a further opportunity has been given for changes. . . ."[63]

And in February, less than a month before the Prime Ministers' Meeting and after a long Cabinet discussion that focused on the fear that the Canadian public might condemn the government if it took the lead in forcing South Africa out of the club, Diefenbaker told Robinson that his "first aim" was to try "once again to bring about some concession on the part of South Africa, a concession of sufficient significance to forestall extreme measures. . . ." But if Prime Minister H.F. Verwoerd would concede nothing, then Diefenbaker said "he favoured 'postponement.' " What he wanted, Robinson believed, was either some promise of concessions or "some other respectable way of taking the heat off."[64] In other words, the Canadian Prime Minister went to London uncertain in his own mind and with the intention of finding some way around the problem that could keep both South Africa and the African and Asian members in the Commonwealth.

Diefenbaker found the British still trying to argue that South Africa was entitled to automatic re-admission, a position that Duncan Sandys put to the Prime Minister when they met on March 9.[65] That was a non-starter, but what Diefenbaker wanted was a declaration of principles, a form of Commonwealth Bill of Rights. As Bryce scribbled it down in a garbled form, the Canadian statement read, "We propose that the Conference should announce forthwith, at the same time as it announced the continuation in membership of South Africa, that it has been decided at the next Conference the making of a declaration of principles to which all members of the Commonwealth will be expected to subscribe (and adhere). It should be stated as a minimum that this declaration will specify that member governments of the Commonwealth believe that all men in each nation are entitled to equal rights."[66] The Prime Minister envisaged incorporating such a declaration in a communiqué that South Africa would either have to accept and amend its race policies or reject and thereby dissociate itself from the Commonwealth. That was a tough but tactful formula.[67]

When the South African question came up on March 13 at the meeting, Diefenbaker began with his efforts to seek a delay. As South Africa was not scheduled to become a republic until May 31, "the constitutional processes . . . were by no means complete. It could not be said that South Africa had yet decided to become a republic . . . the issue had again been raised prematurely." But that, he said, did not affect the need for a statement of the Commonwealth's belief in the principle of equality of rights. The idea did not get very far, however, and discussion for the remainder of the day focused on the wording of the draft communiqué, as the inflexible Verwoerd and the Afro-Asian premiers, aided by Diefenbaker, fought over language. The Canadian, for example, insisted that the communiqué include a statement that it was the firm view of the meeting (other than the Prime Minister of South Africa) that South Africa's racial policy was inconsistent with the basic ideals of the Commonwealth and with the Charter of the United Nations.[68]

The next day, Diefenbaker again raised his "principles" idea and tried in vain to get the South Africans to take some step to indicate that they were prepared to move towards according some representation to those South Africans who were at present disfranchised. While Verwoerd was willing to accept some references to South Africa's racial policies in the draft communiqué prepared by Macmillan, he was generally unforthcoming and insisted on including his defence of his country's policies. The crisis came on March 15 with Diefenbaker, joined by Nehru of India, arguing that the revised draft gave too much prominence to Verwoerd's views. Then the Ghanaian and Indian prime ministers attacked South Africa sharply, Dr. Nkrumah indicating that he might have to reconsider his country's position in the association. After one or two more prime ministers had spoken, Macmillan adjourned the session so that all could reconsider their positions. When the meeting began again, Verwoerd announced that he was withdrawing South Africa's application.[69]

Verwoerd had made the decision himself, and while Diefenbaker as the only leader of a white nation to support the Afro-Asians had played a major part, he had not had to cast a veto on continued membership. That was something he had desperately wanted to avoid, and he had. But the South Africans blamed him in any case, Verwoerd agreeing with his foreign minister that the Canadian was "a vicious fellow" and telling Pretoria that Diefenbaker had supported the black Africans in "strong and hostile terms."[70]

Canadian opinion did not agree. Diefenbaker was hailed in the press and in Parliament, although some thought he had not tried hard enough to keep South Africa in the Commonwealth. It was a triumph for Diefenbaker. Despite his natural doubts and concerns, he had acted with vigour and intelligence in a good cause.

But where did the South African decision leave the Commonwealth in Canadian opinion? Canadians might cheer the idea of a multiracial Commonwealth and be delighted when their prime minister played an important part in a world forum, but despite those happy feelings the Commonwealth connection had slipped in importance. The simple truth was that the remnants of empire had ceased to matter very much. In 1956 when the Suez Crisis had sharply divided the country, the British connection had been a live issue of substantial political significance. But half a dozen years later, the emotive force was ebbing fast. Canada was more American now, John Diefenbaker notwithstanding, and the multiracial Commonwealth was less a part of the public consciousness than the old all-white club had been. The decline in trade with Britain was only one sign of the shift (as was Britain's cold-blooded willingness to sacrifice Canadian interests in her own), just as much as the constantly increasing imports to and exports from the United States. John Diefenbaker's deep gut feelings for the British connection and the Commonwealth had somehow begun to seem anachronistic in only an eye-blink of time. Ironically, Diefenbaker's attacks on British policy toward the EEC and his efforts to force South Africa out of the Commonwealth unless it moved toward racial equality had sped the process of change in Canada.

CHAPTER 4

The Economic Muddle: Coyne, the Recession, and the Declining Dollar

The Diefenbaker government's problems in dealing with Britain's attempt to join the Common Market were minor in comparison to the crisis in the domestic economy. The great post-war boom had sputtered to a halt in 1957, and the unemployment rolls began to grow. There was concern in business circles about large budget deficits, and nationalists had begun to worry aloud about the extent to which the economy had fallen into the hands of foreign investors. Donald Fleming, the Minister of Finance, struggled manfully to deal with these difficulties, but he and his ministerial colleagues were badly divided on policy, and there were serious differences within the bureaucracy, most notably between the Governor of the Bank of Canada, James Coyne, and officials in the Department of Finance. All the makings of a crisis were there.

I

The Bank of Canada's *Annual Report* is usually greeted with general indifference. The prose is dry, the statistics cold, the message invariably spartan in its call for Canada to tighten its belt and reduce expectations. But in March 1958, when the report for 1957 was made public, an election campaign was under way, and the governor's message sparked the interest of the press.

"During the recent period when the abnormally high demand for money far outran the moderate increase in the rate of savings and the moderate increase in the money supply," Coyne wrote shortly after the Diefenbaker government took office and the economy began to slide into recession, "the impression seems to have arisen that the money supply was actually being contracted. This was not the case. The supply of money increased and its velocity of circulation rose very substantially. The phrase 'tight money policy' may sometimes be used to refer to matters other than monetary matters. . . . To the extent that the phrase might be taken to imply a contraction in the availability of money it is not applicable. In this sense of the phrase," the Governor of the Bank of Canada insisted, "there has never been a 'tight money policy' in Canada since the establishment of the central bank twenty-three years ago. There has been what I would call a sound money policy, and I trust there always will be."[1]

What made Coyne's report news was that the Progressive Conservatives, in power for nine months and seeking the transformation of their minority status into a majority one, were denouncing the tight money policies that had been practised, they claimed, by the previous Liberal regime. In fact, the prime rate charged by the chartered banks to their best customers was 5.25 per cent in mid-February 1958, down a half point from the peak of August 1957 and equal to the level of mid-August 1956.[2] Both those rates, however, were too high for the Diefenbaker Cabinet, worried as it was by the economy's slowdown and the rise in unemployment. In November 1957, in fact, the Cabinet had instructed the Minister of Finance to talk with Coyne and to "impress on him the necessity of taking measures to relax the present tight money policy and to remove credit restrictions."[3] The government was feeling the pinch, and its supporters were complaining that high interest rates were still in place. Donald Fleming, for one, had written privately to the editor of the Winnipeg *Tribune* in February 1958 that tight money "has very materially relaxed since we came into office. While government action is not entirely responsible for the easing . . . never the less these trends have been in keeping with Government policy, and we have played our part in bringing them about."[4]

Now Coyne was denying that tight money had ever existed, and the government was furious. One minister said that the governor had demonstrated his unfitness for office; another called the report a belated attempt to "help the Liberal Party"; and a third said, "I don't know what the move will be, but one thing is sure – the Bank of Canada will be made more responsible to Parliament."[5] Fleming argued that Coyne was putting his own definition on the meaning of tight money and, he said, the people who had to pay the high interest rates did not need to be told anything about it: ". . . they know the effects of it all too well from personal experience." Did he intend to fire the governor? the press in Vancouver asked Fleming. "No." Would the differences in opinion require the governor's resignation? "I have no reason to think so."[6] The political issue blew over after the election, although unquestionably it left strong memories.[7]

The governor, James Coyne, was forty-seven years old when he first became a subject of controversy. A brilliant, quiet man with strong emotions, Coyne had been born in Winnipeg in 1910. His father, J.B. Coyne, was a strong Liberal with the best of connections in the Gateway City, a commitment to nationalism and internationalism, and a close friendship with J.W. Dafoe, the great editor of the *Free Press*. His son inherited his father's nationalism, and a Rhodes Scholarship did nothing to dilute it, nor did the practice of law in Winnipeg. But the younger Coyne was not to be a practising lawyer for long. In 1938, he joined the Bank of Canada. The bank, opened in March 1935, gave the federal government the power to control foreign exchange and issue currency, and the existence of a central bank, if it was used to the fullest, let the government influence, if not direct, the course of the economy. Coyne's initial position was in the bank's research department (the first applied research unit in the federal bureaucracy), and there he worked on the Rowell-Sirois Royal Commission, on the planning for the Central Mortgage and Housing Corporation, and, with the onset of war, on the Foreign Exchange Control Board. Then he served on the Wartime Prices and Trade Board, did a brief stint in the Royal Canadian Air Force, and in 1944 returned to the bank. When the first governor, Graham Towers, stepped down in 1954, Coyne was both the retiring governor's and the board of directors' choice for the post.

Although Coyne had little formal training in the dismal science, his capacious mind and his great capacity for work had led him to read the classics of economics as well as the works of modern economists. He had become sceptical of J.M. Keynes's belief that an economy in depression could be set right by government spending and deliberate deficit financing, and by the time of the 1958 election he had come to the unshakeable conviction that the real enemy was inflation. By later standards, the rate of increase in the consumer price index was low – from January to October 1957 the increase was 2.5 per cent[8] – but Coyne nevertheless was afraid of its corrosive effects, fearful of the tendency of governments to spend in ways that fed the fires. Part of this was simply the mystique of the central banker, the feeling, apparently shared by all governors, that only the bank stood between wasteful politicians pandering to the electorate and the long-term health of the nation. But part was also a shrewd understanding of the system and a knowledge of the dangers inflation posed to the polity. This was why Coyne, later calling himself "a premature anti-Keynesian revisionist," tried to keep the money supply under tight control.[9]

More to the point, Coyne could do this because the Bank of Canada Act gave the governor almost untrammelled authority. The bank was wholly owned by the government, but the governor was appointed for a fixed term and thus could be removed only if his behaviour was scandalously inappropriate or if Parliament passed legislation declaring the office vacant. This was deliberate. Monetary policy was seen as a particularly sensitive and critical area and one too subject to the whims of politicians and the winds of opinion to be left to anyone other than a well-paid, well-protected official to implement. The governor had to be independent, even though the government had the ultimate responsibility for his policies and any governor had to realize that he could go only so far with policies the Minister of Finance could not accept. To exceed these limits could destroy the bank and ruin a governor's career; a major clash could also have a serious impact on the economy for it had to suggest that no one was minding the store. Coyne knew all this; so too did Fleming.

Donald Fleming had been the Member of Parliament for Toronto-Eglinton since 1945. Hard working, earnest, careful and precise, as his massive memoirs demonstrate, Fleming had run for the leadership of his party in 1956 only to lose badly to John Diefenbaker. It was not in his character to rail against fate, however, and at fifty-one years of age Fleming set out to be a loyal follower of the Chief. And when the Tories won the 1957 election, Fleming got the nod for Finance.[10]

But there was one potential problem. Before the 1957 election, Fleming had assailed Walter Harris, the St. Laurent government's Minister of Finance, over interest rates. Would the government order the Bank of Canada to lower the rates? Harris's reply in June 1956 was taken by the Opposition as an evasion of governmental responsibility: according to statute, "the Bank of Canada takes the responsibility for its actions." Two months later Harris had explained away another interest rate increase by saying that "this action is the action of the governor of the bank and his responsibility alone." Fleming denounced this argument, declaring that the government "cannot shed its responsibility for full fiscal policy in the broadest sense of the word and that must include the actions of the Bank of Canada, even when, in a technical sense, those actions are taken by the Governor. . . ."

But once he had become Minister of Finance himself, the temptation to put the blame on the bank was strong. In April 1959, for example, as interest rates began to rise, Fleming did just that. "In the matter of monetary policy," he told the House, "this Parliament has placed the responsibility . . . and the power in the hands of the Bank of Canada. The government does not exercise any sway in the field of monetary policy." The minister had altered the equation significantly, saying that the responsibility and power were the bank's.[11] In the circumstances, James Coyne might have been forgiven for believing what his ministers said.

The Diefenbaker government had the bad luck to assume office just as the post-war Canadian economy began its first serious economic slowdown. The boom that had rolled on uninterruptedly was coming to a close, and Canadian productivity, growth, inflation, and unemployment rates were entering a period of uncertainty. The cycles of boom and bust were getting shorter in duration, and somehow the old economic verities and the tried and true economic remedies no longer seemed to work as well as they once had.[12]

The problems were immediately apparent to the new government. In the fall of 1957, for example, one government economist predicted that unemployment four months ahead would be at a post-war high, a result of the declining demand for the products of the resource industries, a lower level of business capital investment, a reduced consumer demand, and a decline in the housing market. The only possible benefit in all this was that the pause in expansion might halt creeping inflation.[13] This was of great importance to the government, of course, for with its minority situation in Parliament another election had to come quickly, and a weak economy would be detrimental. While a few employment-creating projects were put into effect, as R.B. Bryce wrote, the chief measure to be directed against unemployment was fiscal policy. A cash deficit of almost $1 billion was expected, compared with a modest surplus the year before, he said in February 1958. "This will be the main manner in which government policy influences employment and will be very substantial in sustaining the level of employment and income."[14]

Fleming and the government had some luck when the economy began to improve in March 1958, the month of the federal election. Unemployment dropped quickly, falling from 366,000 in May to 286,000 in July, while wages, retail sales, output, and exports all rose. And as a paper prepared in the bureaucracy noted, government expenditures were helping the economic upturn.[15] Fleming's budget in June had predicted a $1.4-billion cash deficit and was expansionist in tone.

The improved conditions seem to have given the government the confidence in the summer of 1958 to undertake a massive conversion of wartime Victory Bonds, due to mature between January 1, 1959, and September 1, 1966, and paying an average of 3 per cent, into longer-term bonds paying an average of 3.83 per cent. Organized by the Bank of Canada, the conversion loan featured patriotic hoopla; it also produced large windfall profits for brokers and advertising agencies. But the conversion was a success, as more than 90 per cent of the outstanding Victory Bonds were turned in, almost two thirds going into fourteen- and twenty-five-year maturities. The reason behind it all was, as Assistant Deputy Minister of Finance A.F.W. Plumptre later explained, that the "issuance of new government bonds could be expected to run into continual difficulties" with the heavy maturity of the Victory issues "overhanging the market." And new government issues were going to be necessary to finance the record budget deficits that Fleming was incurring.[16]

At the bank, James Coyne pumped money into the economy to support the new bonds' prices. As Coyne wrote in the 1958 *Annual Report*, the bank "stood prepared to make markets in all maturities of Government securities" during the conversion campaign "even if this should involve a substantial degree of monetary expansion."[17] It did, and it involved even more when the American bond market coincidentally weakened. Inevitably the result was that many bond purchasers saw their investments fall in value when the bank began to tighten up the money supply once more. Fleming told his Cabinet colleagues, "It is the play of forces in the market which determines the day to day price of bonds. It happens that, largely as a result of the continued erosion of the United States bond market, there have been weakening effects on market offerings for Government issues in Canada. There is no way of insulating the Canadian bond market from such influences. . . ."[18] That was probably true, but large numbers of investors were furious. And the angry complaints probably made Fleming look askance at the governor.[19]

One effect of the conversion loan may have been to drive interest rates up.[20] The prospect – and the reality – of government budget deficits aided this process as well. In November 1958, while the echoes of the conversion loan were reverberating, K.W. Taylor, the Deputy Minister of Finance, sent Fleming his tentative appraisals of the budgetary outlook for 1959-60. For someone as concerned with sound money and balanced budgets as was the minister, the memorandum could not have been pleasant reading. Revenues for 1958-59 were projected at $4,680 million and for 1959-60 at $4,975 million, while expenditures were estimated at $5,380 million and $5,875 million in those two years. The expenditure estimates were probably low, both being predicated on squeezing defence costs and keeping civil programmes under control. The deficits for 1958-59 and 1959-60 were expected to be $700 million and $900 million. "I am sure you will agree," Taylor said, "that these figures give grounds for very serious concern. . . . You will want to give a good deal of thought to your strategy and tactics in putting these problems squarely before your colleagues."[21]

That was the problem. Although no minister worked harder in his office, in Parliament, and in the country (and told everyone so), Fleming never quite managed to establish his authority with the Prime Minister or the Cabinet. Many ministers, Alvin Hamilton being one example, tended to think that they knew as much about finance, budgets, and the economy as the Minister of Finance and his officials, and Fleming had to wage constant war with his colleagues. The business community, however, frightened at the disorganization of the Diefenbaker regime, looked to Fleming as its bulwark. But given the Western populist cast of the Diefenbaker government, that was not an unalloyed benefit for Fleming.

J.M. Macdonnell, the Minister without Portfolio, was a good guide to business opinion. In March 1959 he told Fleming that the measures in the budget to deal with the deficit were the key. If business deemed the steps adequate, interest rates could be expected to drop; if the measures were weak, the rates would certainly climb – and then even high interest rates might have no effect in restoring confidence.[22] Fleming was getting similar advice from his department, and the Prime Minister was hearing the same tune from the Secretary to the Cabinet. In a memorandum on March 20, 1959, just before the first Cabinet discussion on budget policy, R.B. Bryce argued that Canada was living with the paradoxical situation of unemployment and inflation in co-existence. "The reason behind this situation lies, I think, as much in the nature of our society as in anything of a strictly economic character. We have now powerful organized groups in the community, contending with one another and using all the arts of organization, industrial power, propaganda and pressures on government to gain their ends. So far, the only way of reconciling the conflicting interests of these groups . . . is in permitting some gradual upward movement in costs and prices." To Bryce, it was necessary "to accept some cost in terms of unemployment in order to check inflation or vice versa." His budget advice was "that you should increase taxes fairly substantially in this coming year . . . something in the neighbourhood of $300 million. . . ." That would still leave a large deficit but would stimulate the economy, which could be expected to continue to improve. From a different point of view, a tax increase would decrease the government's reliance on a weak bond market and demonstrate that it had the "fiscal and economic situation under control."[23]

Fleming's budget moved in the direction suggested. And very soon afterwards interest rates began to skyrocket. R.A. Bell, the M.P. for Carleton, Ontario, and Fleming's former parliamentary assistant, wrote on August 15 to say that "the rise of 6.4% of the B. of Can. rate I find deeply disturbing. A rate .41 higher than the maximum chartered bank rate is incongruous. I'm no economist . . . but it does seem to me that there is a real chance that we are building up to a 'bust' – which will wreck the economy – and carry the Government to a Bennett-like grave." Why, Bell asked, "must the Bank of Canada be so restrictive? . . . Could it be that Coyne is making a bogey of inflation?"[24] Others were thinking that too, although the speculative interest rate spiral was broken neatly on August 20 by a shrewdly timed ministerial intervention that, Fleming wrote proudly, produced the sharpest ever drop in the Treasury Bill rate.[25] For the time being, Fleming was defending the Bank of Canada's policies and even using them as a weapon against his free-spending critics in the Cabinet. But in a volatile economic situation, allies could change.[26]

One dubious ally was the Prime Minister. According to Ken Taylor, Diefenbaker could be fully persuaded of the need for restraint until he was "buttonholed by one of the Cabinet and becomes carried away with emotional excitement, for this cause or the other cause and new commitments are made." Taylor had become convinced, he told a reporter in confidence, that the Prime Minister's interest in monetary policy had one single motive: "He wishes to put the blame for tight money or any unpopular phase of monetary policy, entirely on the Bank of Canada. But in doing so," Taylor continued, he "must meet one unanswerable criticism. Parliament created the Bank of Canada; parliament can change the statute at will. You have 208 members in a House of 265 members. If your government really thinks that the Bank of Canada is doing the wrong thing, why don't you change the act or the personnel . . .?"[27] That was Diefenbaker's dilemma, but so long as James Coyne had the support of Donald Fleming, it was unlikely that Diefenbaker could move.

But some of Fleming's colleagues were extremely unhappy with the Minister of Finance, his budgets, and his Bank of Canada. The leaders of the opposition in Cabinet were Alvin Hamilton, David Walker, and Gordon Churchill, all men considered close to the Prime Minister. As Hamilton, the Minister of Northern Affairs and National Resources, said later, he had discovered while serving on the Treasury Board that the government's expansionist direction was being reversed by the officials' desire to keep costs down. That infuriated him, and after Fleming's 1959 budget had sprung higher taxes on the country – and on the Cabinet too, Hamilton said – the angry ministers asked who was running the country, the Cabinet or the Department of Finance, the Bank of Canada, and officials afraid of inflation? As a result, Diefenbaker agreed to set up an unofficial ministerial committee – without Fleming – to look at financial policy. The committee met in the summer and fall of 1959, and the members heard many of the senior financial bureaucrats. Most, Hamilton recalled, agreed to follow the Cabinet's desired priorities, but whether Coyne met with the ministers or not, he could not be persuaded to another view and could not accept the idea that government should spend to stimulate growth. The ministers were as nationalist as Coyne, Hamilton argued, but they were not "ghetto nationalists" who believed that Canada could live behind tariff walls.[28]

There were no immediate policy results from the Cabinet revolt (Fleming produced a stand-pat budget in March 1960), nor was there much change after a series of similar meetings in late summer 1960, but in the long run an influential group of ministers came to recognize that Coyne was no friend. When Fleming finally abandoned the governor, he would be alone, and as the economy began to slide into recession in mid-1960 the relations between the governor and the minister, already delicate, became exacerbated further by Coyne's frequent and contentious public statements.

In the autumn of 1959, the Governor of the Bank of Canada began to make an extraordinary series of speeches that were, James Coyne said later, "of rather greater importance than the kind of routine speeches that central bankers do from time to time make."[29] So they were, and Coyne began his efforts to shape public opinion at the urging of the bank's directors, who wanted the central bank's position to be clear in the public mind and who wanted everyone to realize that the board, the Minister of Finance and, indeed, the government as a whole were in favour of the kind of monetary policy the bank was following. As Coyne said, his own reasons for the speeches were to foster public understanding of monetary questions, to point out how monetary policy was affected by other fields of economic policy, to point to the growing dangers to the economy from the large balance of payments deficit and the domination of economic activity by foreign corporations, and to show as forcefully as possible that unemployment could not be overcome simply by the use of monetary policy. Later Coyne was to argue that the fight against inflation was his primary concern and that he had raised these other issues to make clear that non-monetary policies were more important than monetary policy in stimulating growth and controlling the rise in the cost of living.[30]

Certainly Coyne's first major speech dealt with inflation. In his address to the Montreal Canadian Club on November 16, 1959, the governor said that "inflation is particularly insidious in that it seems to some to encourage production and employment and expansion for a time, but it continually accumulates excesses, distortions, inefficiencies and injustices which in due course produce recession, loss of confidence and contraction." Policy had to be directed at both price stability and growth: "We cannot achieve substantial and steady employment and growth without price stability and public confidence that price stability will be maintained."[31]

A few months later Coyne told the Canadian Club in Winnipeg that Canadians had to live within their means and not pursue unrealistic rates of growth, particularly when they were based "to an excessive degree on borrowed money, whether domestic or foreign." In Canada, the governor argued, "pursuit of an excessive and unsustainable rate of capital expenditure . . . has not only contributed to the unstable cycle of short-lived boom followed by recession but has also been responsible for a growing deficit in our international balance of payments, a large excess of imports . . . over our exports, increasing reliance on foreign resources to finance (directly and indirectly) both capital projects and consumption, and a great increase in our foreign debt. . . ." Coyne quoted Fleming in his support: ". . . we must all avoid doing those things which are likely to encourage a forced and excessive growth in spending."[32]

That was Coyne's view too, and he was more than willing to keep down the growth in the monetary supply as a contribution to that end. Presumably he had Fleming's tacit support, for as the minister told a British Columbia party stalwart who had written to complain about tight money, the term should be avoided. The government had nothing to gain in a dialectic or semantic sense from permitting its fiscal policy to be described as "a tight money policy. . . . As you know, we have sought to avoid being tagged with that name."[33] That was hardly rejection of the policy.

Coyne's most important and controversial address was made on October 5, 1960, to the Canadian Chamber of Commerce in Calgary. Here he dealt particularly with foreign investment, arguing that Canada was at a crossroads "when economic developments and preoccupations with economic doctrines of an earlier day are pushing us down the road that leads to loss of any effective power to be masters in our own household and ultimate absorption in and by another." That was strong stuff. So was Coyne's assault on "the unimpeded inflow of foreign capital on the part of foreign companies and investors who thought they saw golden opportunities to undertake various projects in Canada or to buy up existing Canadian companies. Massive imports of capital put the Canadian dollar at a premium and induced massive imports of goods and services. The entire economy was put under strain. . . ." What was to be done? "We should, for our own sake, live within our means and increase our means by our own efforts . . . a country which has reached Canada's stage of development can make better progress, and retain more control over its own destiny, by relying on its own savings to provide the necessary capital."[34]

The Calgary speech made an impact. Alvin Hamilton's chief political aide sent a note saying "It is *most* important you read this. . . . I cannot recall a speech made like this by anyone except P.M. in our history."[35] Walter Gordon, actively engaged in rebuilding the Liberal party, told L.B. Pearson that Coyne's was the bluntest, most devastating, and most outspoken criticism of government policies that had ever been made by a senior civil servant in Canada.[36] And A.F.W. Plumptre, no admirer of the governor, told Ken Taylor in a nine-page memorandum that Coyne was wrong about foreign investment. Plumptre maintained that there were two possible ways of dealing with it: an interventionist approach with legislation detailing things to be done and imposing controls or a market-and-institutional approach involving the development of Canadian markets and financial institutions in ways designed to alleviate the difficulties of foreign ownership. "One might expect a central banker to dwell on the latter possibilities; the fact that he does not do so seems to imply a lack of interest in them." More particularly, Plumptre said that foreign capital could not be turned on and off like a tap. "This whole field needs a much lighter hand and more refined touch than Mr. Coyne seems disposed to apply to it." Of course the percentage of foreign ownership in some industries was high, but that was not the point. The real question was "how do foreign subsidiaries actually behave? If they are behaving in ways that are contrary to Canadian interests how may these errors be corrected?" What angered him was Coyne's inflammatory phrases, as one passage from the October 5 speech demonstrated: "I prefer to put understatement behind us . . . to speak not of non-resident control but of foreign domination." That, Plumptre said, "to apply an understatement, is surprising."[37]

While not oblivious of the criticism of his speeches, Coyne was remarkably unperturbed by it. "I know [the bank board of directors] agreed with a great deal of what I said, but above all they said it was desirable I should say those things if . . . the views I held . . . [were] in the public interest . . .," he told the Senate Committee on Banking and Finance in July 1961. But in February of that year some of the directors said that Coyne's speeches were causing political controversy and that the Opposition was using them as a club to beat the government. The governor disagreed: "I do not think the Government was called upon either to agree or disagree with ideas which [I] was putting forward . . . but in view of the fact that the Government was busy disavowing any responsibility for monetary policy whatever, I can understand how some of this controversy developed. It was in this way, and only in this way," Coyne maintained, "that it can be said that my speeches became the subject of political controversy. There was nothing partisan in anything I said, and in my view there was nothing hostile or adverse . . . to the present Government of Canada. . . ."[38]

The government increasingly was feeling otherwise. But the force of the complaints against Coyne was weakened by the supplementary budget Fleming brought down on December 20, 1960. To one observer, it seemed that the government had adopted the major thrust of the Coyne position with measures directed at the inflow of capital and at the flood of imports into the country. A withholding tax of 15 per cent was imposed on dividend and interest payments to non-residents while the profits of unincorporated branches of American companies were also to be subject to a 15-per-cent levy. The minister, one commentator wrote, was clearly trying to make foreign investment in Canada less attractive.[39]

In the House, the Leader of the Opposition was quick to seize on any apparent differences – or similarities – between the minister and the governor. Under pressure, Fleming on February 21, 1961, replied to his criticism by stating that "in the field of monetary policy parliament has given the essential authority to the Bank of Canada and not to the government or to the minister of finance . . . parliament has given no power to the government." Pearson was criticizing the bank, not the government, Fleming said, even though Pearson was speaking on the pretense "for his own partisan purposes" that the government has responsibility. He himself had no right to censor Coyne's speeches. "He does not refer them to me. Why should he do so? This is a free country."[40] But as one of Fleming's colleagues noted in a message passed to him in the House of Commons, "If the Governor of the Bank is responsible to Parliament the Leader of the Opposition should move for his dismissal. We should agree. I do not consider that you should defend the Gov. of the Bk."[41]

Who was to defend the governor? The Liberals exploited the issue but did not support the policies Coyne was proposing. Walter Gordon, for example, wrote to his leader that he had been impressed by academic criticisms of Coyne and the calls for his resignation that were beginning to be heard. To Gordon it was the confusion that Coyne was producing, not to mention the apparent confusion in the government's economic policies, that was so disturbing. One day Coyne spoke out against foreign investment and the next day Fleming offered a contrary opinion. "Does this mean that Government policy has changed since Mr. Coyne made his speech . . .? Or does it mean the Government has two policies, one for home consumption and one for export?"[42]

Fleming was as aware of the contradictions as was Gordon, no matter what the minister might say in Parliament. And when he saw Coyne in mid-March 1961 he asked the governor to cease making speeches. Coyne agreed, but the damage was already done.

II

The ostensible cause of the final clash between the governor and the government was a petty one. On February 15, 1960, after a nine-month study, the directors of the bank approved a change in the pension arrangements for the governor and his senior deputy. Henceforth, the two officers would be guaranteed a pension equal to half their current salary or, in the case of the governor, $25,000. This was a very large sum indeed in 1960, but when compared to the pension schemes offered the presidents of chartered banks, for example, it was modest. As usual, the board had discussed the change, approved it, and proceeded to implementation without either publishing it in the *Canada Gazette* or formally notifying the Minister of Finance. Publication of such business had been deemed unnecessary in the past according to legal rulings from the Justice department; and the minister surely did not require notice when his deputy minister (or, as it happened on the day the pension was finally approved, his assistant deputy minister) had been present at the board meeting. In addition, one board member, J.T. Bryden, president of the North American Life Assurance Company and a Diefenbaker appointee, had discussed the pension with Fleming at a Muskoka cottage as early as August 1959.[43]

The pension was perfectly proper, but when Fleming, who had begun to believe that Coyne should be sacked, learned on March 21, 1961, that Coyne was now eligible for $25,000 a year when he left the bank, he was outraged. He had told Bryden on at least two occasions that Coyne's salary could not be raised; now he must have felt that he had been circumvented.[44] But the real reason for Fleming's anger was that after years of defending the governor against his colleagues, and with the economy in the doldrums and unemployment at its post-war peak, his patience was at an end.

On March 23, Fleming spoke at length to the Cabinet about his relations with Coyne. He had seen the governor on March 18 when Coyne had "expressed the view that the appearance of lack of unity between the Minister and himself, and the absence of any clear enunciation of the government's economic policy, had increased the difficulty of explaining monetary policy to the public." That was why he had made speeches, Coyne said, adding the opinion that Canada was "on the path to ruin." Fleming told his colleagues that he felt "placed in the equivocal position of having to defend the Governor publicly while in fact he deplored the latter's actions and disagreed with his proposals." Then, Fleming went on, Bryden had told him on March 19 that the board's confidence in Coyne had weakened and that a majority would oppose his reappointment as governor. In the circumstances, Fleming said, he sought authorization to inform Coyne privately that he would not be reappointed when his term expired in December 1961. "He would inform Mr. Coyne that no objection would be raised by the government if he should decide to proceed on retirement leave at this time. . . . Under the Pension rules of the Bank, Mr. Coyne would qualify for an immediate pension of $25,000 per annum if he completed his initial term." Significantly, Fleming had made no derogatory mention of the pension, although in the discussion that followed some members of Cabinet did ask that the authority providing for the governor's pension be checked.[45]

The pension question was again discussed in Cabinet on March 30 when the Prime Minister reported a legal opinion from the Department of Justice that approval by the Governor-in-Council was unnecessary for the pension by-laws of the bank to be operative. He added, however, "The law officers had stated verbally that they believed that pension by-laws were probably not effective . . . until they had been published in the Canada Gazette . . . but they believed this case to be weak." Despite that opinion, Diefenbaker pressed his colleagues to consider the pension matter, which "had not been communicated to the government or to the public. The by-laws had not been gazetted. These circumstances," he said, "constituted a very clear reason why Mr. Coyne should not continue as Governor." The Prime Minister suggested that the government should introduce a bill to amend the Bank of Canada Act "by providing that by-laws of the Bank would have no effect until they had been approved by the Governor in Council. The consequences of such a measure," he continued, "would also put an end to charges that the Bank was 'running' the government."[46]

What had happened, and here the Cabinet minutes leave no doubt, was that the Prime Minister had turned the pension into the crucial question, notwithstanding legal advice. When the Cabinet next considered the pension on May 1, Fleming covered the whole issue once more, telling his colleagues that "there was no real ground for an attack on the integrity of the Governor, who had not inspired the by-law amendments that had improved his pension position, and had retired from the Board meeting when this subject was discussed." That was a decent attitude, Fleming adding that the government's reasons for seeking Coyne's retirement were that he had repeatedly attacked the government's fiscal policy in public, had embroiled the bank in public controversy, and had seriously impaired the morale of the bank by his actions. Whether those were correct analyses of the Coyne problem or not, Fleming's points were at least legitimate grounds for proceeding to seek Coyne's retirement. After a long discussion that brought out once more that there was no impropriety in the pension by-laws, the Cabinet agreed that legislation should be introduced after the departure of Coyne to make clear that all bank by-laws required approval by Governor-in-Council and publication in the *Canada Gazette*; that the legislation should not interfere with the operation of by-laws passed hitherto; that the government should not ask the directors to modify the pension by-law; and that the governor should be advised as soon as possible that the government not only did not intend to reappoint him when his term expired but also hoped that the governor would retire from his post immediately.[47]

The next day, May 2, Diefenbaker told the Cabinet that "under section 14 of the Bank of Canada Act the Governor had the power to veto any action by his Board of Directors, and therefore Mr. Coyne had been involved in the decision to raise the amount of his own pension."[48] This was a spurious position, reflecting nothing so much as the Prime Minister's desire to find some way to strip Coyne of his pension increase, but the interjection was sufficient to delay further consideration until late May. The Prime Minister had also managed to cast doubt on the legality of the pension, and some of the more credulous ministers appear to have believed genuinely that some impropriety had occurred.

Still, nothing effective had yet been done to get rid of the troublesome central banker. How could this be accomplished? The problem was critical for Fleming because he was in the midst of preparing his budget for presentation in late June, the economic situation was shaky, and there was some concern that Coyne might break loose with speeches attacking the government's budget if he was still governor when it was presented. It was, Fleming said years later, impossible to concert fiscal policies so long as Mr. Coyne was in a position to damn government policies and not co-operate in planning. On May 30 finally, after Cabinet meetings on May 26 and 28 had led to calls by several ministers for Coyne's removal from office "at this time,"[49] Coyne was asked to meet Fleming that afternoon. The issue was about to be joined.

The fullest account of the meeting between Fleming and Coyne is in the minister's report to Cabinet on June 8. Fleming told the ministers that the deputy minister of finance had been present when he told the governor that "on the instructions of the Cabinet, he was asking for the Governor's resignation prior to the next meeting of the Board of

Directors . . . scheduled to be held in Quebec City on June 12th." The minutes record that "Mr. Fleming had referred to the speeches made by Mr. Coyne, to the public controversy in which he had involved the Bank, to the fact that Mr. Coyne's ideas were irreconcilable with the plans of the government of Canada, and to the consternation of the Cabinet on learning of his most unusual pension arrangement and of his failure to disclose it to the government." Coyne had then argued that the pension arrangement was legal and "he had declared that he did not withdraw any of the statements he had made in his speeches, but that he deeply regretted any embarrassment that they might have caused. He had asked whether a successor had been chosen. . . . Mr. Coyne had asked whether the government would permit him to receive the $25,000 pension following his resignation," and Fleming, according to the minutes, had replied "that the by-law was of questionable validity, and that the government had been shocked by it and had not yet reached a decision in regard to it."[50]

According to Fleming's later recollections, the meeting had been friendly and the two men had shaken hands on parting. Coyne's recollection was that 90 per cent of the time was spent on the pension,[51] but his subsequent correspondence with Fleming makes clear that other matters were also discussed. Fleming had told him that "the Government had under contemplation certain programmes which it was thought I would be bound to disagree with." This puzzled Coyne: "So far as I am aware there is no question affecting Bank policy or operations at issue between us, and the Bank has in fact always cooperated fully. . . ." Still, it was the pension issue that dominated the discussion. Fleming had suggested that the governor had acted improperly by not vetoing the pension by-law, "that I ought to have prevented the Directors from taking action in a matter of this sort, which is unquestionably within their power and responsibility. . . ."[52]

It was this slander on his integrity that so offended James Coyne. As he said years later, he would have departed quietly if he had been confronted with a detailed list of particulars; but he could not do so in the face of charges that he had acted improperly.[53] The evidence suggests that the claim of impropriety was completely groundless; so too was Diefenbaker's later remark in Parliament that Coyne "sat, knew, listened and took."[54] The government had anticipated that the governor would step down without a fuss. Fleming had prepared the board members for action, and he had a successor to Coyne firmly in mind.[55] But Diefenbaker and Fleming had misjudged their man.

The real battle was not yet under way. Coyne said nothing in public of Fleming's demand for his resignation, and the minister too kept his silence. From May 30 to June 9, Coyne sought an accommodation, tried to discover from Taylor what was happening and, despite his talk with Fleming, simply refused to believe that the Cabinet was disturbed by the pension. He also talked twice with Bryce, who later remembered that he was seeing Diefenbaker by day and Coyne by night. But there were no indications that a peaceful settlement could be arranged, and in the meantime Coyne readied himself. He realized he could not hope to win a battle with the government, but he knew he could cause it damage and perhaps prevent it from using its power against other public servants.[56] The independence of the Bank of Canada was at risk if he did not fight, Coyne believed; so too was his good name.

The bank directors had their orders from the Minister of Finance, and Fleming was confident the directors would do their duty. At Cabinet on June 8, he had told the ministers that he expected Coyne might seek a vote of confidence from the board, but "he would not get it."[57] Coyne, however, believed that if the issue really was the pension, the directors, who knew the full story, had to back him up. But he completely underestimated the ties of party loyalty, and at the board meeting Coyne soon realized that he had little support. Even the efforts to reach a compromise that would allow him to complete his term had failed. The government, Fleming told board members who urged him to relent, had reached its decision.[58]

Faced with weakness of his "helpless, hapless, thoughtless" directors – or so the *Toronto Star* characterized them on June 15 – Coyne left the meeting and, through his office, released a statement that set out his side of the case and made clear that he would not resign.[59] Then he returned to the meeting, told the board of his action, and watched the directors vote 9 to 1 on the motion "That it is in the best interests of the Bank of Canada that the Governor do immediately tender his resignation to the Board of Directors of the Bank, and further that this action and decision on the part of the Board has been taken after prolonged consideration and with regret."[60] In the House of Commons, Paul Martin, tipped off by a friendly journalist, asked Fleming if it was true that Coyne's resignation had been demanded, and watched as the minister, taken by surprise, "turned red as a beet" and stammered out a reply. It was, Martin recalled, "this whole Coyne affair that laid the foundation for the fall of the . . . Diefenbaker government. . . ."[61]

The affair was public now, and as it escalated it justified Martin's assessment. Fleming gave Parliament his version of events on June 14. The Minister of Finance referred to the deterioration in the relations of the Bank of Canada with the public and to Coyne's embroiling the bank in continuous controversy with strong political overtones. One sign was the governor's rigid attitude on the maintenance of high interest rates, something that caused difficulties because "the Government's policy is expansionist aimed at the creation of more trade, more production and more jobs." Coyne, the minister said, stood in the way of the implementation of a comprehensive, sound, and responsible economic programme. Fleming then referred to the pension, accusing Coyne of lacking a "sense of responsibility in keeping with his high office, in accepting an additional benefit worth $13,000 per annum for life without ensuring that the matter was brought to the attention of the Government."[62]

Everything Fleming said fuelled Coyne's anger, and the governor was not without resources. A flood of press releases, statements, and hitherto confidential letters and memos began to pour forth from the bank. So intense was the flood, and so devastating its impact, that Tories began to charge that Coyne had the services of an advertising agency paid for by the Liberal party, that he was misusing the bank's resources in his counterattacks, that he had had some of his letters written for him by his old friend J.W. Pickersgill, and even that he was unbalanced. "The voice of Coyne," Diefenbaker charged, "was the so-called conscience of Pearson and Pickersgill."[63] In fact, there was no advertising agency, only one public relations officer in the Bank of Canada. And both Coyne and Pickersgill deny adamantly that anything more than occasional advice was offered by the ingenious politician to the governor. Finally, Coyne was not insane; he was furiously angry. What did disturb many at the time, and now leads Coyne to admit error, was the use of confidential correspondence to make his case.[64]

Although the government had given notice in mid-June of its intention to introduce legislation declaring the office of governor to be vacant, the budget first had to be brought down. Coyne was quick to fire his first salvo at the budget before it was delivered. On June 19, he released copies of a paper he had sent to Fleming on February 16, 1961, entitled "The Requirements of Economic Policy Today." The twenty-four-page memo argued that Canada could not achieve full employment and steady economic growth without major changes in economic policy, and Coyne laid out his prescription: reduce imports with a temporary tariff surcharge of 10 per cent; mobilize capital for investment; encourage regional development and savings; develop resources and create a national highway system; raise taxes; reduce the national debt; stabilize the dollar at parity with the U.S. dollar; restrain consumer credit; and use fiscal policy for the economic purposes of the state. It was a detailed programme, and Coyne said that if it had been put into place earlier there would have been no unemployment, no balance of payments deficit, no increase in net foreign investment in Canada, and a smaller overall tax burden. Coyne felt that his plan refuted Fleming's charges that he was in favour of restrictionist policies, and certainly some of these proposals were expansionist. The *Globe and Mail*, however, was correct when it said on June 20 that Coyne's memo called for "tightening belts."[65]

The budget of June 20 was not a direct refutation of Coyne. Fleming forecast a deficit of between $600 million and $700 million for the year and said that it would help stimulate the economy, one point of difference with Coyne. His announcement of the government's intention to encourage a decline in the exchange value of the dollar, an attempt to improve the competitive position of exports, was another point of difference. But the Montreal *Gazette* was not far wrong when it noted that "the measures introduced by Mr. Fleming follow the general line indicated by Mr. Coyne with remarkable fidelity. There are variations of detail but not intent."[66] If that was so, why the urgent necessity to purge Coyne? The Prime Minister on June 21 spoke in the House about Coyne's suggestion of higher taxes and said, "A civil servant is entitled to give his views. But however exalted he must not place himself above the people's representatives. No one can be allowed to impede national progress."[67] Diefenbaker did not explain why Coyne's advice was different from that of other civil servants or how it impeded progress.

There was no doubt, however, that Coyne was impeding the Conservatives' moves to be rid of him. So too were the Liberals. Pearson said that while Coyne's usefulness as governor had ended, his party was "determined to see that Mr. Coyne gets his day in court and to see that he is not used unfairly as a scapegoat" for the government's economic mismanagement.[68]

The Cabinet discussed the bill declaring Coyne's office vacant on June 20, the ministers deciding to make no reference to the question of the amount of pension to be received by the governor. The Cabinet apparently believed that the fundamental issue, Coyne's fitness for office when he had lost the confidence of the government and the bank directors, would be clouded if the pension issue were included. "In addition," the Cabinet minutes note, "this was not an advantageous time for the government to adopt a firm position on the pension question, bearing in mind the probable attitude of the Opposition and the Senate in this respect. . . ."[69] That reasoning was probably correct; much less explicable was the decision to refuse to permit the bill to go before a House committee where the government had a majority. Diefenbaker later remarked that Coyne "wasn't entitled to that, Mr.

Fleming denied him that." It was, said the Chief, Fleming's decision and one that Cabinet had ratified: "If we had allowed him that opportunity then he would have simply said: 'Well they have decided against me and it was a plugged jury.' " Fleming, however, maintained that it was not on his advice that the Cabinet acted.[70] Whatever the origins of the idea, it was an error of the first magnitude. From the point of view of parliamentary strategy, R.A. Bell said years later, "I know of no greater black eye that any Government ever suffered."[71]

The black eye was inflicted by the Senate, which stepped in and, with its large Liberal majority, gave Coyne the opportunity to be heard before the Standing Committee on Banking and Finance. And certainly Coyne wanted that. In a letter to Fleming on June 26, a letter promptly released to the press, Coyne charged the government with trying to prevent Parliament and the people from learning the truth about the affair. "What is at issue here," Coyne said, "is the right of Canadians to know why I refused to meet the demand of the Government [to resign]."[72] Coyne then made one of his few errors when he lashed out at the Prime Minister's charges in Parliament that Pickersgill had dictated Coyne's many letters and statements. "Mr. Diefenbaker," the governor wrote, "has been the evil genius behind this whole matter. It was his unbridled malice and vindictiveness which seized on the . . . pension fund . . . as a clever stick with which to beat me, and intimidate me." Coyne was entirely correct, but that charge nonetheless briefly lost him the high ground.[73]

The bill sacking Coyne finally passed the House of Commons on July 7 after unruly debates, charges and countercharges, all fuelled by Coyne's seemingly inexhaustible files. Now it was the Senate's turn, but the Senators faced a difficult situation. It was a serious matter to reject a Commons bill, not least because Diefenbaker had threatened to make Senate reform an election issue if the Senate turned down the Coyne bill and a piece of tariff legislation.[74] On July 8, the Coyne bill was sent to the Senate Banking Committee.

"It was a hectic week," wrote Liberal Senator T.A. Crerar to his family. "For once the poor old decrepit, senile Senators were in the limelight. Everyone agreed that Coyne made a strong if not devastating case against the treatment given him by Fleming and the Government."[75] Indeed, that seemed the general response as the sympathetic Senators led Coyne, dignified and grave, through his story. The Liberals had been told by Pearson with great tact that "while they should give Coyne a chance to state his case in public, they should avoid any possible indication that they were in agreement with his policies,"[76] and the Senators did their job well. Angry Tories interrupted with objections, but Coyne outfaced them time and again, introducing his damaging evidence into the record. Yes, the by-law procedure used in the pension decision was exactly the same as that used before. No, the minister had never taken exception to the bank's policies. Yes, Fleming had asked him in March to cease public statements and, except for an appearance before a Senate committee, he had obeyed.[77] Coyne was an impressive witness, and never more so than in his closing statement on July 12. Speaking emotionally, Coyne explained his actions over the previous month:

> In the circumstances in which I found myself I felt that I had no right to take chances on the question of what procedural problems there might be [that might prevent a hearing in Parliament]; that I had to rely entirely upon my own efforts to see that public replies were made to misleading, incomplete and inaccurate statements made . . . by members of the Government. . . .
>
> I regret having said certain things, and I regret having done certain things – since May 30. I felt I was fighting for important principles, and fighting very largely alone against an extremely powerful adversary – so powerful, indeed, that it was bound to win in the end. . . .
>
> Now that the fight is almost over . . . I wish to say that I fully recognize that because of the events of May 30 and since – not because of anything that happened before that date – the management of the Bank of Canada must change. . . .
>
> A vote in favour of this bill, after this hearing, is a verdict of guilty. There can be no equivocating about that. I shall be marked for life as a man . . . declared . . . unfit to hold a high office of Parliament by reason of misbehaviour. . . .
>
> A verdict of not guilty will not prevent my immediate departure from office, but it will permit me to retire honourably and to hold up my head among my fellow citizens. . . .[78]

It was a brilliant peroration, "one of the most dramatic affairs I have ever witnessed," H.W. Herridge, an NDP M.P. wrote. "When he had finished, Senators, M.P.s, Pressmen . . . were wiping the tears away from their eyes."[79] Coyne's speech had stiffened the Senators' spines, and the committee thereupon passed a motion on July 13 that the bill should not be proceeded with and "that the Governor of the Bank of Canada did not misconduct himself in office." The same afternoon, the whole Senate accepted its committee's report. James Coyne had been vindicated, and he submitted his resignation at once.[80] The staff of the bank presented the governor with a gold medal lauding his "courage and integrity." Not all the staff agreed with Coyne's policies or actions; none, however, doubted his courage and integrity.

The Coyne affair had gravely damaged the Diefenbaker government. The administration's economic policies had been demonstrated to be in disarray. The pension question, patently phoney, was used to smear the governor, and Diefenbaker and Fleming had turned the full power of the government against one man. They had achieved the impossible – making James Coyne, an aloof and sometimes arrogant man whose policies were not even supported by the Opposition, into a sympathetic figure. John Diefenbaker may have been the author of Canada's Bill of Rights, but in this instance at least he seemed motivated more by vengeance than by justice. It was an unsavoury affair, and if it ended James Coyne's career, it also clearly revealed the incompetence and ineptitude of the government.

Who now would succeed Coyne as governor of the Bank of Canada? In the circumstances, who would want the job? Fleming had no doubts about the man he wanted – Louis Rasminsky, one of the bank's deputy governors – and he had made this clear to the Cabinet as early as June 8, 1961.[81] Rasminsky's appointment, he wrote to J.M. Macdonnell, "is one of the purposes which I had hoped to accomplish while I held this office . . . he is much more than a thinking machine; he is a gentleman."[82]

Born in Montreal in 1908, Rasminsky had grown up in Toronto. After graduating from the University of Toronto, Rasminsky had attended the London School of Economics. But he took a job with the League of Nations in Geneva before he completed his doctorate, and he stayed with the League until the war brought him back to Canada and a job with the bank. There he had risen quickly, establishing his credentials as an expert in foreign exchange and largely shaping the Canadian position for the discussions about a post-war world financial order. But in 1954 he had not been chosen for governor. Coyne's selection had come as a blow to Rasminsky, one made all the more hurtful by the rumours that swirled around Ottawa that he had been passed over because, as he was a Jew, the chartered banks would not deal with him. There were also suggestions that the Cabinet itself had worried about Rasminsky's faith in 1954, and it is worth noting that on June 8, 1961, when Fleming first broached Rasminsky's name as a successor to Coyne, the minutes record the government's resolve "not [to] be influenced by the possibility of criticism by anti-semitic groups."[83]

Rasminsky was the ideal choice for the post in 1961. But he did not want the job until matters were clarified, and the most important point was that the government had to accept its own responsibility for monetary policy. Fleming and his predecessor had evaded responsibility, and that evasion had led to the Coyne affair. The ministerial position was contrary to reality, and Rasminsky was determined to ensure that the government accepted its responsibility or he would not take the job.

The first formality was the selection of Rasminsky by the Board of Directors. That was no problem, for he was genuinely their choice.[84] Then Rasminsky had to talk with Fleming and to discuss the language of a letter he would write that would set out his position. That letter, as ultimately drafted, said things simply and clearly:

> I believe that it is essential that the responsibilities in relation to monetary policy should be clarified in the public mind and in the legislation. I do not suggest a precise formula but have in mind two main principles to be established: (1) in the ordinary course of events, the Bank has the responsibility for monetary policy, and (2) if the Government disapproves of the monetary policy being carried out by the Bank it has the right and the responsibility to direct the Bank as to the policy, which the Bank is to carry out.

The first principle, Rasminsky said, was necessary to give the bank the independence to enable it to resist day-to-day pressures from any source. But if there were serious conflicts with the government, then "the Government should be able formally to instruct the Bank what monetary policy it wishes carried out and the Bank should have the duty to comply with those instructions." The governor might have to resign in such circumstances, but at least no one could doubt where the ultimate responsibility lay. Rasminsky also added that "consideration should be given to setting up a routine procedure for regular meetings at fairly frequent intervals" between the governor and the minister.[85]

Donald Fleming had no difficulty accepting this letter. His reaction was curious, to say the least, for Rasminsky was requiring the minister to accept a responsibility he had avoided consistently. But Fleming, ultimately a pragmatist, never had much difficulty in changing positions without embarrassment, and he "swallowed three pages of crow," as the Toronto *Star Weekly* put it, to get Rasminsky.[86] The Prime Minister, however, was dubious, but when Rasminsky told him that "the job is impossible if the Government doesn't take the same view as the Governor regarding the responsibility for monetary policy," Diefenbaker went along after a few minor changes in phrasing.[87] At a stroke, Rasminsky, whose appointment was made public on July 24, had clarified the situation, and there could never be any doubt again that the bank's monetary policy was the government's.

One final note: the directors of the bank temporarily suspended Coyne's pension in the midst of the affair in 1961 with, as Donald Fleming said, "our knowledge and approval."[88] But after a review of the legalities, the directors lifted the suspension, and Coyne received the pension of $25,000 a year that had been the excuse for his firing.[89]

III

The Coyne affair had seriously damaged the government's economic credibility, and it had left Donald Fleming's reputation in tatters. Reporters speculated freely that the Prime Minister would dump Fleming, and in late December rumours of a major Cabinet shuffle swept Ottawa. On December 26, the press took it as certain that Fleming was through, but two days later the shuffle turned out to be very minor indeed. Fleming, the press agreed, had refused to go quietly, and the business community, alarmed at the spending tendencies of the government, had told the Prime Minister in no uncertain terms that it wanted Fleming to stay where he was, a brake on the profligacy of his colleagues.[90] Whatever the reasons, Fleming remained Minister of Finance, and soon he had to face a new and serious financial crisis.

In one sense, the emergence of economic difficulties in mid-1962 was somewhat surprising. The economy seemed in good shape, and the new governor of the Bank of Canada had told the minister on January 2, 1962, that the country was in the midst of "a marked upturn," the Gross National Product in third quarter 1961 being up 4.8 per cent. Unemployment had fallen to 6.5 per cent in November, and the current account balance of payments was also improving. Rasminsky then noted, however, that the recovery had been associated with "increasing government expenditures entailing a large budgetary and over-all deficit and a considerable degree of monetary expansion." In the first three quarters of 1961, government expenditures had risen by 7 per cent, compared with increased expenditures of 2 per cent for the economy as a whole. "The increase in expenditures has been such that it would not be matched by increased revenues even under very prosperous conditions." That concerned the governor, who said that in the present situation "an over-all Government deficit of the same magnitude as in 1961 – not to speak of an even larger one – would lead to a very difficult and perhaps dangerous situation in financial markets." The confidence of investors in Canada's financial stability might be impaired. Not that Rasminsky was calling for a balanced budget. That, he knew, was not possible. What he did suggest was that policy should be directed towards achieving "some reduction in this year's deficit."[91]

If only that had been possible. On February 27 the Deputy Minister of Finance sent Fleming his estimate of budgetary revenues and expenditures. The 1961-62 budget had predicted a $650-million deficit, but although revenues were slightly higher than Fleming had forecast, expenditures were up even more, with the result that the deficit was $791 million. For 1962-63, he estimated the deficit at $695 million – if there was a 7-per-cent increase in the GNP. Even in the best circumstances the deficit situation was an unhappy one.

And it was the deficits that primarily troubled businessmen in Canada and financial experts abroad. The *Globe and Mail*, for example, spoke for orthodox businessmen when it warned that "there can be an excuse for a deficit in a time of recession, but continuing deficits in a period of economic expansion can hardly be justified."[92] Abroad, the International Monetary Fund considered the performance of the Canadian economy "disappointing." Its 1961 report on Canada was very critical, not least because of the deficits and the potential for inflation. The IMF was also unhappy with Canada's "managed" exchange rate that kept the dollar at around ninety-five cents U.S. and repeatedly pressed Canada to move to a fixed par value.[93]

Fleming's budget of April 10, 1962, contained little to cheer the critics. The forecast deficit for the coming year was set at $745 million. And Fleming strongly defended the government's decision not to peg the dollar, stating that the fluctuations in the exchange rate had been small, that Canada was not being unduly pressed by the IMF, and that before it fixed a new par value, the government wanted prospects for success to be better than they had been between 1946 and 1950, the last time Canada had operated under a fixed rate.[94] About all that commentators could say in Fleming's praise was that at least he had not offered pre-election tax concessions. The voters, advised on April 18 that an election would take place on June 18, would judge.

Apparently speculators, foreign firms, and worried Canadians judged harshly. In the days after the election call, trends that were already apparent began to accelerate alarmingly. Canada's official holdings of U.S. dollars and gold had stood at $1,921 million in January 1962, but in that month and in March there had been very large losses of reserves, and after mid-April the losses increased. The total decline in reserves since the beginning of the year, Rasminsky told an IMF board meeting studying the Canadian difficulties on May 2, amounted to $460 million[95] – or about 24 per cent – and that had frightened the government.

The dimensions of the crisis had been brought home to the Prime Minister only on April 29, when R.B. Bryce told Diefenbaker that when the April foreign exchange figures were published on May 5 the market might be difficult to control. For a government in an election campaign, one already being denounced for economic mismanagement, that was bound to be frightening.[96] By May 1, the Cabinet had decided to act, and on May 2, with the Prime Minister away campaigning in Quebec, the dollar was pegged at 92.5 cents U.S. – just three weeks after Donald Fleming had defended Canada's managed rate.

The IMF was supportive and greatly pleased.[97] Canada had acted firmly and the rot was checked.

So it was, temporarily. But the government had not been unanimous in its decision to peg the dollar. Diefenbaker later said, "I was alone, and I finally agreed" to Fleming's importunities and the advice of "the so-called experts." He said he "never claimed to be an economist although that is what I took my master's in," but maintained that if Canada had not devalued the dollar it "would have gone down, nobody would have had any concern . . . nobody would have cared."[98] Others – Alvin Hamilton, for one – believed the crisis was caused by speculators in Toronto selling the dollar short, and Hamilton also argued for a peg lower than 92.5 cents on the grounds that this would be a "tremendous boost" for the campaign because of the stimulus it would give exports. And Fleming himself admitted there was no consensus in the Finance department on the rate.[99] Indeed, as Bryce noted in a memo written just before election day, he had been reminded that "par at 92½ was a compromise proposal" put forward by Fleming after hearing from his officials "all the arguments for and against various alternative proposals (5 in all) that were outlined." Bryce wrote, "Parity at 92.5 was not proposed by any official. Mr. Fleming's proposal of it was not objected to by his officials after they realized it was his choice, having heard the case."[100] The firmness of commitment was not impressive.

No one yet knew how the decision had been made, but even so the financial community was not convinced of the government's determination to defend the 92.5-cent exchange rate. That message was given to Fleming on May 31 by the Governor of the Bank of Canada who was, he said, worried by the behaviour of the exchange and bond markets. The government faced "a major financial crisis," Rasminsky said, and although he was not suggesting specific steps at the moment, "I thought it right to put [the Finance minister] on notice that if my apprehensions turned out to be right it would be, in my judgment, essential for the Government to take action immediately after the election to restore confidence by indicating its determination to deal with some of our basic problems." Fleming, faced with a difficult campaign in his own constituency, replied that "he thought that the lack of confidence [might] have been generated by the election campaign and that one was entitled to hope that the present atmosphere would change once the election was over."[101] Fleming, if not Diefenbaker, had been warned of the impending crisis.

The speed of the process increased on June 8 when Agriculture minister Hamilton told a Vancouver press conference that the 92.5-cent rate was a compromise and that he, for one, favoured a further drop to

90 cents, a "natural peg which is defensible with our negative trade balance." That remark, as Fleming later said (incorrectly), started the run.[102] Plumptre wrote on June 10 that the country's reserves had fallen by one third since January, and "we cannot go on using up reserves at this rate; urgent steps are needed to restore confidence in the Canadian dollar." Equally bad, there were signs that capital was fleeing the country, frightened by rumours in New York that the fixed rate was not to be defended or, alternatively, that foreign exchange controls would be set in place to defend it to the death. Hamilton's Vancouver gaffe had fed the panic, Plumptre said. What was needed now was a statement affirming the government's determination to defend the fixed rate. Such a statement by the Prime Minister might check matters temporarily, but in the immediate future "Canadians and foreigners with funds that can be transferred into or out of the country will no doubt be seeking some firm basis, in the realm of government action, relating to the future of the Canadian dollar."[103] That night a statement of the sort Plumptre demanded was issued, but over Fleming's signature. "I couldn't get [Diefenbaker] to come out and make a statement," Fleming said.[104]

The statement calmed the markets slightly, although the electoral wars continued without quarter. The Liberals, sensing the disintegration of the government, criticized the fixing of the new par value at 92.5 cents, attacked Hamilton for his foolish comments, and roundly and soundly denounced Diefenbaker and Fleming for the mismanagement of the economy. The Liberals even issued "Diefenbucks," green 92.5-cent dollar bills, based on a brilliant Winnipeg *Free Press* cartoon. The effect devastated the Tories and undoubtedly served to weaken confidence in the Canadian dollar. About all that John Diefenbaker could do was to say, as he did on June 14, that all was well. "The truth has been on our side. We have given you the facts. We have bared the record. We have concealed nothing and shaded nothing."[105]

IV

The government faced a difficult task in the election of 1962. The great sweep of 1958 could scarcely be duplicated again in the best of circumstances, and the circumstances, after its five years in power, were not of the best. There had to be losses, and the Conservative party's aim was to minimize them.

The party planning for the campaign was set out for the members of the National Campaign Committee at the Chateau Laurier in Ottawa on April 15. Dalton Camp, the party's advertising strategist, listed the election themes: Leadership, Achievement – Promises Kept, National Development, Program for the Future, and "The Same Old Bunch – the People Were Right in 1958." It was to be a television campaign, the first in the party's history, and the Prime Minister was to be accompanied by a field crew shooting news film each day.

The Tory strategists expected the issues raised by the Liberals to be three: "1. Get the country moving again. 2. The 'team' around Pearson. 3. With 1 and 2, the Liberals 'have the answer' to any and all problems." And, Camp said, the Liberals could be expected to fix on unemployment and the GNP, the Common Market, and relations with the United States. "This is the familiar 'Kennedy' approach which appeals to the Grits because they must seek issues designed to influence pockets of grievance wherever they are to be found. And they must also divert the campaign from 'leader' issues which they have discovered are not likely to be helpful." That, he went on, was why the Conservative campaign was to be focused on leadership, a reflection of the fact that, for all his problems, John Diefenbaker still projected a stronger image as a leader than did Lester Pearson. The Liberal "team" also provided a good target: "We can stress the heavy content of 'experts' and ex-Civil Servants on the 'Pearson Team', including, of course, Pearson himself. These were really the men who said 'No' – who couldn't find the answers."

That took care of the Grits. More positively, the Tory campaign was to stress "the broad Canadianism of the Conservative Party," the party that had named the first Indian to the Senate, appointed the first woman and the first Ukrainian to the Cabinet, and had the first Chinese M.P. ever elected. "This is not a 'team' but a national movement exclusive only in its uniqueness in Canadian politics as a Party of all Canadians." The government policy "has been universal and it has made hard decisions such as South Africa; it has stuck to principles; and it has shown an initiative and inspired direction, such as its drive in the export trade field." And, Camp said, the more the Liberals attack the Prime Minister, the better – "when they do, they are fighting the campaign on our issue, our winning issue."[106]

That was the Conservative plan, and when the election was called on April 18, the party was ready. Well financed, generally well organized (except in Quebec, where there were serious problems),[107] and equipped with an able advertising group, the government also had the country's ablest campaigner in Diefenbaker. The Chief was tired after five years as prime minister, but he had no match as a stump orator; and although his evangelical oratory was beginning to pall, particularly in urban areas, he still struck a resonant chord in millions.

But the Conservative record, the party campaign plan notwithstanding, was not all wine and roses. There was still high unemployment, and the economy, recovering from the worst days, was still shaky. There was growing tension with the United States over nuclear weapons. There was the prolonged squabble with the British over the Common Market. There was the impression that the party was "anti-intellectual."[108] And above all, there was the perception that the government was not forceful or decisive. Diefenbaker might still lead the opinion polls when people were asked to select their preferred leader, but the Chief had begun to slip in the public mind thanks to the effective Opposition campaign in Parliament and in the country. The election was no shoo-in this time.

It was a race the Liberals thought they might win. During the year or so after the shattering electoral disaster of 1958, the party had been disorganized across the country and a shambles in the House of Commons. Pearson did not seem cut out to be Opposition Leader, and many Liberals feared the Conservatives would be in power for a generation. But matters turned around slowly, issues such as the Coyne affair gave the Liberals heart, and unemployment and the faltering economy cut into government support. The party began to seek out its Liberal roots, a process that the Kingston Thinkers' Conference in 1960 and the National Liberal Rally in 1961 accelerated. And in the process good candidates began to step forward. The result, as a third-party strategist wrote in early 1962, was that "in recent months the Liberal party has succeeded in presenting to the public the image of a qualified 'team' of candidates who, if elected, would provide Canada with the capable leadership required for Government." The observer had his doubts about this, for he believed that the Liberals were in the pocket of the interests. "Nonetheless the general public will continue to be persuaded that they are astute and public spirited men."[109]

That indicated that the Liberals were getting their message across. What the party had to do was to transmit the atmosphere of confidence and competence that now characterized it and to convey the team idea. The basic issues, all worked out at the 1961 rally, were employment, purposeful government, a national health plan and a pension plan, and Canada's place in the world, and the strategy was to personalize "Mike" Pearson, to talk about socialists (not the just-formed New Democratic Party), and to criticize the Tories in a positive way so as to force Diefenbaker to respond negatively. It was, in many ways, a plan modelled on John Kennedy's, just as Camp had said. Above all, the Liberal brass were convinced that Diefenbaker, after five years in power, could not fight the 1957 and 1958 elections over again by denouncing the party for its pre-1957 sins.[110]

The opinion polls also showed that the Liberal message was being heard. An April 1962 poll demonstrated that the Liberals ranked better than the government on "dealing with the issues," and it identified unemployment as the key national concern. But, curiously, the members of the Liberal team added no strength. Diefenbaker himself led overwhelmingly on personality and ran well ahead of his party in popularity; the Conservatives also led on the strength of *their* team, although that was probably simply because ministers had built-in access to the media and patronage in a way the Opposition did not. Still, the Liberals were ahead by 40 per cent to 34 nationally, and a later poll, at the end of April, showed the lead to be 45 per cent to 38, a reading distorted by the Liberals' lead of 53 per cent to 32 in Quebec but one that nevertheless suggested at least a Liberal minority.[111]

The New Democratic Party, preparing to fight its first federal election, did not look good in those same polls, the Gallup showing it with only 9-per-cent support at the end of April, a disappointing showing for the new alliance between organized labour and the old CCF. The CCF, founded in the Depression, had never made great headway in Canada. In 1944, Tommy Douglas had led the party to power in Saskatchewan, forming the first social-democratic government in North America. Douglas had governed well and at length, but his success in Saskatchewan proved almost impossible to export. Alberta remained obstinately Social Credit in orientation, British Columbia appeared content to keep the CCF forever in opposition, and in Ontario the party always seemed to be rebuilding for a recovery that never arrived. Nationally, the high point for the CCF had been the September 1943 Canadian Institute of Public Opinion poll that showed the socialist party one point ahead of the Grits and Tories, a happy situation quickly countered by a massive free-enterprise campaign that squelched CCF hopes and by Mackenzie King's skilful theft of CCF social welfare ideas. After the war, the party had won a number of seats in each election, but it had had to be content to jostle with Social Credit for third place in the party standings. The 1958 election, however, had seen Diefenbaker's Progressive Conservatives steamroller the party, reducing it to a rump of eight seats, three from Ontario, one from Saskatchewan, and four from British Columbia, and to 9.5 per cent of the popular vote. If the idea of social democracy was to survive at the national level in Canada something had to be done.

The answer seemed to be the formation of a direct link with organized labour, which the CCF had long sought but which much of organized labour had resisted. In 1943 the Canadian Congress of Labour had endorsed the party as its political arm, but most often that pledge of support had amounted to very little of a practical nature. But in 1954 negotiations for the merger of the CCL with the more conservative

Trades and Labour Congress of Canada began, and when they came to fruition two years later (not long after the parent American Federation of Labor and the Congress of Industrial Organizations in the United States had united), the new Canadian Labour Congress brought virtually the entire labour movement under one roof. As important for the CCF, the CLC in April 1958 had called for a "fundamental realignment of political forces in Canada in . . . a broadly based people's political movement which embraces the CCF, the labour movement, farmer organizations, professional people and other liberally minded persons interested in basic social reform and reconstruction through our parliamentary system of government."[112] Shattered by the election results of March 1958, the CCF accepted the invitation and the National Committee for the New Party, jointly formed by the CCF and the CLC, was soon in operation. The farm organizations declined to participate, but New Party Clubs, open to anyone, were soon organized as a way around such opposition. "New Party clubs were intended as the vehicle by means of which both 'intellectuals' and groups of the 'general public' could come into the new party movement," a discussion group reported, but neither group had shown "any spontaneous desire" to do so.[113] The New Party was going to be very much the product of the CLC and the CCF.

That troubled many in the three years the New Party was in gestation, and there was much heart-searching within the CCF ranks. Some members of the party's tiny parliamentary caucus, men like H.W. Herridge of British Columbia and Douglas Fisher of Port Arthur, Ontario, feared the influence of big labour on the CCF's "pure" socialism and suggested that labour would deliver very little in the way of votes in return for the surrender of the CCF's existence. But the doubters were partially silenced when Walter Pitman, a New Party candidate, captured the constituency of Peterborough in October 1960, an event that persuaded many that industrial Canada was receptive to the still unorganized new alliance.

The result was a huge and well-organized New Party convention in Ottawa in the summer of 1961. The 2,084 delegates gave the party the name "New Democratic Party" and selected Premier Douglas of Saskatchewan to be the national leader, awarding him the prize on the first ballot by a convincing margin – 1,391 to 380 over Saskatchewan M.P. Hazen Argue. But the NDP, at least in its parliamentary caucus, was still divided, and there remained substantial resentment about the way the party "establishment" had ramrodded the merger with the CLC and the selection of Douglas. Herridge, who was NDP house leader until Douglas made it into Parliament, wrote, ". . . I am not very popular . . . because I do not believe in being told what I should think. . . . Never have I known so many people preaching the Brotherhood of Mankind who had so little of the milk of human kindness in their veins.''[114]

Hazen Argue in particular was unhappy, and in February 1962 he jumped ship to sign on with the Liberals. In January 1962, Argue himself had told Douglas Fisher that ''this 'Liberal' talk is amazing. I don't know where it got started. I have denied it and it keeps on,'' but he added with some evident bitterness that ''the great T.C.'' Douglas was good ''at P.R. but with no substance. . . .''[115] A month later he was gone, and the best the shaken NDP could claim was that the defection had galvanized the caucus, the party secretary telling Douglas that if the M.P.s had been ''leaderless and disjointed'' before, they were so no longer. ''Argue's defection has united the group as nothing else could have done.''[116] The NDP had potential strength in the West and in Ontario, but new leader and new party or not, it was hardly in the best of heart for the coming fray.

Social Credit was different. In the West, the ''funny money'' party had the substantial organizational and financial support of Premier Ernest C. Manning's entrenched and popular government in Alberta, and the new national leader, Robert Thompson, was a Westerner – by way of Ethiopia, where he had, among other duties, commanded the Imperial Air Force Academy and been a director of Haile Selassie's Ministry of Education. But the new action in Social Credit was in Quebec, where Réal Caouette, an automobile dealer from Rouyn, had electrified the party organization.

Social Credit had existed in the province ever since the victory of William Aberhart in Alberta in 1935 brought the party's ideas of monetary reform to public notice. But Social Credit doctrines had initially made very little headway in French Canada, and in the party's first effort to elect candidates to Ottawa in the 1940 election, its candidates were easily defeated. But a base had been established, there was a newspaper, *Vers Demain*, and over the years the Social Credit movement in Quebec perfected its message and learned how to pitch it to appeal to French Canadians. There were assurances that Social Credit doctrines were not in conflict with those of the Church, and there was a heady mix of nationalism and autonomy, including opposition to conscription during the war. By 1945, the party felt able to put up forty-three candidates in Quebec in the general election; none was elected, and the party attracted only 4.5 per cent of the popular vote.

There were soon tensions between the Quebec party and the Alberta-dominated national organization. By 1947, established Social Credit was becoming more moderate and was shedding its allegiance to the doctrines of the founder, Major C.H. Douglas; but in Quebec, the

Douglas monetary reforms continued to draw support from ardent followers, and there was a split along linguistic lines. At about the same time, as the historian of Social Credit in Quebec, Michael Stein, has noted, Réal Caouette and Laurent Legault were coming to prominence in the party. Caouette, then a salesman, and Legault, a party organizer, became convinced that the keys to success were broad, catchy slogans, personality, and effective organization. That combination had won Caouette election to Parliament in a 1946 by-election, and it was the same formula that Caouette would practise with success in Quebec early in the 1960s. Caouette in 1958 had organized Le Ralliement des Créditistes, a breakaway group from the provincial party, and had become its leader. The old-line Social Crediters had thought of themselves as a movement; Caouette wanted a political party to fight and win elections, a pragmatic organization that would allow him and his supporters to promote their beliefs through the political system. And Caouette hit on television as the way to advance his cause. Political telecasting was still novel in 1958, but the glib and silver-tongued Caouette quickly attracted a devoted audience for his talks, which were soon being seen in most of Quebec. At about the same time, Caouette linked the Ralliement to the national Social Credit party, which had been completely eliminated from the House of Commons in the Diefenbaker sweep of 1958.[117]

Thus the basis was laid for Caouette to make an impact in the 1962 election. His TV broadcasts effectively capsulized the discontents of Quebec's poor, left out of the prosperity of the preceding years, mixed with doses of nationalism into spell-binding oratory. The programmes also produced contributions that helped the Créditistes to organize the back counties, and a flood of basic political advice went out from Ralliement headquarters to candidates and supporters, most of them newcomers to electoral politics. The best advice, conveyed to all, was "NE PAS PERDRE LA TÊTE," and the organization committee president prepared a draft budget for each candidate that projected $2,150 in expenditures for his constituency.[118] On that budget, the wonder was that the Créditistes could get anywhere. But something was going on in Quebec, and at Caouette's campaign kickoff on May 6 there were more than five thousand cheering supporters in attendance. The crowd purchased ten thousand photographs of Caouette and 14,000 ball-point pens. Under their nihilistic slogan, "Vous n'avez rien à perdre," the Créditistes were on the march.[119]

No one else was marching in a lacklustre campaign. John Diefenbaker, to many, seemed at first only to be going through the motions, and his special assistant noted that he was "a very sick and nervous man . . . so irritable and suspicious and unreasonable. And he was allergic to advice." John Fisher, the publicist and broadcaster who had entered Diefenbaker's service in 1961, quoted the Chief as saying, "I've been betrayed. Nobody is helping me. I get no advice." He was at the end of his tether, Fisher remembered.[120] In part, the Chief's black mood was caused by the dollar devaluation, a decision that, if only because of its timing, the Prime Minister could see would have an adverse effect on the campaign. The Diefenbucks proved him correct.

But Diefenbaker and his supporters put the best face possible on the devaluation. A "Campaign Memo" of May 25 talked about devaluation's stimulative effects, how it helped exports and reduced imports and thus encouraged domestic production. "The Canadian consumer can buy Canadian-made goods in all of these fields and *will now be buying more of them*. Is that bad?" The Tories also professed pleasure at the quiet campaign. "A quiet campaign works for the government. The plain fact of the matter is that the contending parties have not been able to create any of the excitement or any of the issues that the Prime Minister developed so spectacularly as the contender in 1957 and 1958. If the campaign has been quiet, it's been because neither the Liberals nor the N.D.P. have been able to make it otherwise."[121]

On May 30, however, the campaign heated up at a Diefenbaker rally in Vancouver. There were seven thousand people in the arena, and while most were prepared to Follow John yet again, the audience included representatives of the unemployed, the ban-the-bomb groups, and others disaffected by government policy. The result was a near riot with fists thrown, jeers, and placards waved to such an extent that Diefenbaker could barely be heard. A leading B.C. Tory later told the Prime Minister that "we never expected hoodlums and goon squads would gang up at the Forum, particularly as your government has done so much to help the unemployed." It was the NDP that had organized it, he said.[122] Whoever organized the riot, it helped Diefenbaker, giving him back some of his 1958 fervour, and in the last two and a half weeks of the campaign, the Tories came to life. The Gallup Poll released on May 26 showed the government with 36 per cent; that on June 6 gave them 32 per cent; and the final pre-election poll a week later showed that Diefenbaker had recovered to 36 per cent.

The Liberals, on the other hand, dropped steadily, sliding from 44 to 42 to 38 per cent on the last poll.[123] "We are leading," National Campaign Chairman Walter Gordon had wired to all candidates on May 21. "Confidently expect Liberal victory," he had telegraphed on June 15. "Suggest you stress to voters the fact that only our party can win a working majority in the next House of Commons. . . ."[124] But in fact the Liberals were starting to panic about the situation in Quebec, the area where they had counted on returning to their traditional dominance. Senator Chubby Power, party warhorse and legendary Quebec organizer, had charge of the twenty-eight ridings in the Quebec City district. His initial survey on April 30 put *rouge* chances at eight excellent, five good, five doubtful and five bad, and he did not mention the Créditistes at all. On May 22, his estimates showed eight excellent, seven good, six bad and seven doubtful in an area that at dissolution had had twenty-three Conservatives and five Liberals. Again, Social Credit was unmentioned. But on June 7, his last report, the Créditistes had suddenly become a factor in fifteen ridings.[125]

Power did not know what was happening. He wrote to a friend on May 29 that up to then Liberals had welcomed Social Credit's rise on the grounds that this could only hurt the *bleus*, already badly weakened by the absence of a Union Nationale government to assist them. "Up to the present the Tories have been attacking Social Credit but our people have left them alone, but if their movement continues to grow in importance it may be necessary for our candidates to turn on them also." It all puzzled Power. "These people have very little in the way of argument that one can rebut, their whole campaign being largely based on the idea that people are disappointed in the major parties and that they might find some hope in voting for a party of the people." Even so, Power calculated that Caouette might take two seats at best. But he did add a qualifier: ". . . as you know, the damn thing snowballs, and once it gets started you don't know where it will end. . . ."[126]

The results demonstrated that Canada was to have a minority government. Diefenbaker's party hung on to win, falling 17 per cent in the popular vote and returning 116 members to 100 for the Liberals, 19 for the NDP, and an astonishing 30 for Social Credit. Caouette's Créditistes had taken 26 seats in Quebec and won more votes outside Montreal than either the Liberals or the Conservatives. His success confounded the experts and unquestionably deprived the Liberals (who won 20 of their 35 Quebec seats in Montreal) of their chance at power. In the process Diefenbaker's 50 seats in Quebec in 1958 had shrivelled to 14. In Ontario the Tory decline was almost as precipitous, the party falling from 67 to 35 seats. Only on the Prairies did Conservative strength hold, but even there the party lost 5 seats. The Liberals won 14 in the East, 35 in Quebec, 44 in Ontario, 2 on the Prairies, and 5 in British Columbia and the North. The NDP won a seat in Nova Scotia, 6 in Ontario, 2 on the Prairies, and a surprising 10 in British Columbia. Tommy Douglas, however, failed to win in Regina, a victim of the bitter battle over medicare in his home province.

The Tories were left strong in small towns and rural areas, saved by the fact that there had as yet been no redistribution in the 1960s to cut away at the rural rotten boroughs. Their supporters could be characterized as those over fifty years of age, English-speaking, and having only secondary school education; they were Protestants, non-union labour, farmers, or white-collar workers.[127]

The Liberals were pleased with their gains – the 1962 result was in truth a remarkable organizational achievement in only four years since the 1958 débâcle – but far from complacent. Tom Kent, Pearson's chief policy adviser, wrote that the party had not effectively made out a positive case for voting Liberal. "We underestimated the extent to which marginal voters, disillusioned by the Tories, would remember that a few years ago people had become tired of the Liberals. Too many decided that they might as well try something new." The voters had judged the two old parties as Tweedledum and Tweedledee, Kent said. Next time, the Liberals had to say "positively, definitely, simply, convincingly" that Canada would be different "in ways that matter to ordinary Canadians" if the Liberals were returned.[128]

The results were shattering to Diefenbaker. As early as June 1961 in the midst of the Coyne fiasco, the Prime Minister, feeling the strain, had begun to suggest to friends that he should resign. In September 1961 he had said this again to Gordon Churchill, and in January 1962, Churchill had openly accused Fleming and George Hees of being in league with Toronto businessmen in a plot to drive Diefenbaker out of the prime ministership. Now, faced with election results that Churchill called "simply appalling," the Chief was again in bleak mood.[129] The Governor General, Georges Vanier (who had been named to the viceregal post in 1959), seeing the Prime Minister after election day, noted that he was "not sure the PM is happy to be the incumbent."[130] And Lester Pearson noted there was much to be said "for leaving the responsibility for cleaning up the mess to the government which created it. Short of winning with a good majority, this situation is preferable, until we can secure a decisive victory. . . ."[131]

Perhaps that was true. In any case, the election had burst the myth of Diefenbaker – "he sagged like a pricked balloon," one journalist wrote.[132] The Chief had led the triumph four years before, but now his party and his reputation were in disarray, not least because of the shaky economy, the financial crisis, and doubts about the Chief's desire and perhaps his fitness to govern. Even strong Tories felt the change in mood. George Hogan, who had worked long and hard for the party, wrote privately that Diefenbaker had arrived at a low point earlier reached by Macdonald and King: ". . . large numbers of Canadians were prepared to believe them capable of any depth of chicanery. . . . Large numbers of Canadians have built up a hostility to their Prime Minister which makes them predisposed to believe anything critical of him, and predisposed to disbelieve the contrary." The best Hogan could foresee was that people still might be prepared to vote for Diefenbaker "if the issues were presented in the right way."[133] The Tories faced an uphill battle.

V

In terms of the fiscal and economic situation, the election results were as bad as they could possibly be. A minority Diefenbaker government might be expected to be even more spendthrift than the majority government that preceded it. And with the balance of power held by "funny-money" Social Credit, no one had much confidence in the type of deals the Conservatives might be forced to make to survive.

The officials in Finance, the Bank of Canada, and other concerned departments were aware of all this. As early as the end of May Rasminsky had begun to think of the kinds of measures that would be necessary after the election, regardless of its results, to restore confidence in the dollar. On June 12, he had produced a draft plan,[134] and he was part of an officials' committee that had a formal proposal ready on June 17, the day before the election. The officials laid out the situation, mincing few words. The exchange reserves had been cut in half in just six months, and there were fears of a flight of capital. The country could be brought to its knees if action were not taken. How had it all happened? One cause was the consistent balance of payments deficit on goods and services, aggravated by the outflow of capital. Another was the widespread criticism over the size of the federal deficits: "It is pointed out, over and over again, at home and abroad, that Government spending seems to have got out of hand" and those concerns "have been translating themselves into misgivings about the value of the Canadian dollar."

What could be done? It was risky to un-peg the dollar and only slightly less dangerous to lower the par value to 90 cents. Nor was it practical to put foreign exchange controls in place. Instead, the mandarins suggested defending the dollar at its present level and "an immediate and impressive announcement of a combination of financial policy measures designed to restore confidence in our financial situation and our ability to defend the established par value of the Canadian dollar." Measures had to be undertaken to tackle the deficit and the balance of payments, and to this end the officials proposed that Canada secure standby credits of $1 billion, cut the budget by "not less than $200 million in a full fiscal year" and preferably by more, and slap temporary tariff surcharges on a wide range of imports. The net effect, they said, would be to reduce the foreign exchange deficit by $600 million in a year.[135]

Faced with this advice and with the continuing crisis – the reserves continued their slide – the battered government had to take some steps. On Friday June 22 Diefenbaker released a statement promising that on Sunday next the government would announce measures to improve the balance of payments and reduce the deficit. There would be no exchange controls, he said, and the value of the dollar was to be "firmly" maintained.[136] But that was all that was agreed. The officials were absolutely convinced that unless the announcement of budget cuts was tied to specific departments nothing would result. Fleming was in agreement,[137] but the rest of the Cabinet began to wobble. At one point the Prime Minister called Rasminsky to urge him to announce an increase in the bank rate instead of the package of measures desired by the officials' committee. Rasminsky, terribly concerned, refused, and on June 23 he wrote to the Prime Minister to say that he was "disturbed at the information that the Cabinet is considering not publishing any details regarding the $200 million of expenditure cuts which I was informed yesterday had been decided upon . . . but instead may confine itself to the general statement that expenditures are being reduced by $250 million in a full fiscal year." How could such a measure increase confidence? How could Canada expect to get more than a billion dollars in loans and credits abroad on such a programme? It was absolutely essential that the programme carry conviction, he said, "for unless it does it cannot succeed, and the nation will have gone further into debt through the foreign borrowings which are contemplated." Rasminsky's tough letter had its effect. After another call from Diefenbaker, Rasminsky wrote again to express his pleasure that the decision to cut government expenditures by $200 million during the fiscal year was firm and that the precise cuts were soon to be settled by Treasury Board.[138]

The package was announced by the Prime Minister on June 24. His statement, Diefenbaker said, was made in response "to an increasing degree of uncertainty and instability in the last few days," and included a 5-per-cent surcharge on $2.3 billion of imports, a 15-per-cent surcharge on luxury imports, and a 10-per-cent surcharge on deferrable imports. Tourist duty exemptions were cut sharply as well. Those measures were expected to produce $300 million, and in addition the government pledged to cut $250 million in expenditures. Then the Prime Minister detailed the borrowings and credits arranged in the United States, the United Kingdom, and with the International

Monetary Fund and the Export-Import Bank in Washington. And, although this was not announced in the statement, the Bank of Canada simultaneously raised the bank rate to 6 per cent.[139]

The crisis was over. The government applied the expenditure cuts ruthlessly, ordering departments not to fill staff vacancies, to slash repair and upkeep spending, and to cut travel and supplies budgets.[140] A committee of officials was set up to plan longer-term measures such as increased hydro exports and measures to stimulate tourism.[141] By July 3, Rasminsky could write to the Governor of the Bank of England that "the pressure against us has completely disappeared and we have been able to recoup some of our losses on a modest scale."[142] Indeed, the reserves increased rapidly to $2.1 billion at the end of July, to $2.33 billion the next month, and by the end of 1962 the holdings were $2.54 billion or a half-billion dollars more than at the beginning of 1962. Interest rates also fell rapidly and at year's end were at 4 per cent, a rate that the Bank of Canada said reflected "the reappearance of an appreciable inflow of long-term capital into Canada."[143] Similarly the import surcharges were quickly dismantled. As early as August 31 some surcharges were lowered, more cuts followed in November, and all had been lifted by March 31, 1963. The revised estimates, tabled in Parliament on October 18, showed cuts in spending of $228 million, but the deficit was still estimated at $570 million, substantially below Fleming's budget figure but well above the figure projected by the government during the crisis.[144]

Despite the crisis, the economy had boomed, and the government could tell itself with some justice that it had brought prosperity through its devaluation of the dollar. Unfortunately, few now believed the Diefenbaker government when it talked about the economy, and the Liberals, echoing the press, charged that Diefenbaker had hidden the crisis until after the election. Even when things went well, the Conservatives found difficulty in receiving the credit. And, as the nuclear crisis with the United States demonstrated at the same time, few things were going well for the government by late 1962.

CHAPTER 5

The Defence Débâcle, 1957-1963

"I don't think his post will be quite as soft as he may have thought," American Secretary of State John Foster Dulles said at a ceremony in Washington marking the swearing-in of Livingston Merchant as ambassador to Canada in 1956. "The post . . . used to be reserved for people who wanted a nice summer place and not much to do." But no longer, he said.[1] Dulles was dead right, and over the course of the next half-dozen years relations between Canada and the United States reached a historic nadir.

The reasons were twofold. Merchant himself reported in July 1958 that Canadians had become extraordinarily sensitive because of their history and "their position of inferiority in power in relation to us. The last year has seen the development of a strident, almost truculent nationalism."[2] Many saw Prime Minister John Diefenbaker as the creator of that new attitude, although Diefenbaker himself told American officials that while he knew he was considered anti-American in Washington, he was not. But as the opposition painted him as "dominated by United States policy," the Prime Minister, the American government concluded, felt obliged to outdo the opposition in defence of Canadian interests.[3]

The second factor was the personal relationship between the Prime Minister and the presidents of the United States during his years in power. With Eisenhower the Canadian got on well, addressing him as Ike and being called John in return. There were occasional frictions between the two countries, but in general the pervasive friendliness allowed matters to be smoothed over and forgotten. That was not true with John F. Kennedy, however. The two leaders, so different in age and style, failed to hit it off, and as the personal relationship chilled, so too did the relations between the two nations.

The scene of the difficulty was in the area of defence. The demands of the Cold War, the escalating costs of military equipment, and the pressures exerted by the United States on an often reluctant Canada all contributed to create a tense situation. But the true cause lay in the character and make-up of the Prime Minister. John Diefenbaker was prickly and sensitive, a leader who reacted sharply to pushing from Washington or from the Department of National Defence in Ottawa alike. Even so, trouble might have been averted if Diefenbaker had been able to make decisions quickly – one way or the other – on the question of acquiring nuclear weapons for the Canadian armed forces. The delays enraged the U.S. government and led directly to the defeat of the Conservative government, left in a minority position after the election of 1962, in Parliament. It was a débâcle and a largely unnecessary one.

I

Ironically, the Conservative government's troubles with defence began because the Prime Minister made one decision too quickly. When George Pearkes, the new Minister of National Defence, brought Diefenbaker a proposal to integrate the air defences of Canada and the United States into a single command – the North American Air Defence Command – the Chief quickly agreed with his friend and colleague that the step was necessary. On his copy, Pearkes inscribed, "Discussed with the Prime Minister and approved 24 July, 1957." That was how Canada entered NORAD – without Cabinet or Cabinet Defence Committee discussion and with few ministers even aware that the decision had been taken.

There was a long history behind that day in July 1957.[4] The idea of combining the air defence forces had a military logic to it, particularly because both air forces saw themselves as organized and equipped to counter any Soviet bomber attack on North America. The Royal Canadian Air Force in particular believed it could only benefit from closer ties with the large, powerful, and technically sophisticated U.S. Air Force. Indeed, in February 1953, with Korean fighting still under way, the Canadians had proposed that a joint Military Study Group be set up to examine air defence, and later Canadian and American studies recommended a separate commander for North American air defence,[5] the need for "the integration of the two air defence systems and the ultimate establishment of a combined command."[6]

Whatever the reasons, however, the Canadian Chiefs of Staff were a bit reluctant to press ahead, and the initiative came from the United States[7] for an integrated command that left each air force separate and distinct but under joint operational control. By December 19, 1956, the Military Study Group had approved operational integration and the centralization of authority for operational control – the power to direct, control, and co-ordinate operational activities. Some care was taken to ensure that the overall commander would be responsible to both the American and the Canadian Chiefs of Staff, who were declared responsible for keeping their governments informed.[8] To ensure that Canada would not be swamped in the vastly larger American air defence command, the report specified that the commander and his deputy "should not normally be from the same nation. His staff should be a joint staff composed of officers of both nations."[9]

In effect, the military decision had been taken, and all that remained was to secure political consent. Between January and June 1957, the plan percolated its way through the committee process in Canada, being discussed in the Chiefs of Staff Committee, and being incorporated into a memo for the Cabinet Defence Committee.[10] But in the pre-election atmosphere, the process slowed. The Americans nonetheless approved the integrated command on April 11, and General Charles Foulkes, the Chairman of the Chiefs of Staff, under pressure from his American counterparts, carried a forceful aide-memoire with him when he saw Defence minister Ralph Campney on June 12, two days after the election that saw the Conservatives secure the largest number of seats. The Americans, he said, had been promised a decision by June 15 and in Foulkes's view, the St. Laurent government should decide the question. The general was the most experienced military-politician Canada had ever produced, but this was simply silly, and the chairman had to advise the Americans that the outgoing government "regretted to state that they did not consider they were any longer in a position to finalize international agreements. . . ."[11]

Foulkes was concerned at his failure to deliver, and as George Pearkes, the incoming Minister of National Defence, remembered, "from the moment I took over" Foulkes "pressed the urgency of getting a decision. He certainly gave me the impression that it was all tied up by the Liberal government, that promises had been made that it would be signed immediately after the election. . . . I do know that they [the Canadian military] were under almost daily pressure from the military in the United States." Pearkes himself was a soldier, sympathetic to seeing military necessity take priority over political considerations. In the circumstances, he agreed that the plan sounded sensible.[12]

Ordinarily the proposal should have gone to the Cabinet Defence Committee, but no such committee had yet been set up by Diefenbaker, suspicious of the military (and civilian) advisers of the old regime. That being the case, Foulkes talked with the Under-Secretary of State for External Affairs, Jules Léger, and the Secretary to the Cabinet, R.B. Bryce, about getting the integrated command approved "without setting up a Cabinet Defence Committee"; both apparently agreed. As a result, Pearkes saw the Prime Minister on July 24 and got his agreement to what was soon to be known as NORAD.[13] Pearkes's recollection was that Foulkes had also briefed several ministers. The issue, however, did not reach Cabinet until July 31 when the appointment of Air Marshal C. Roy Slemon as deputy commander of NORAD was approved.[14]

Did Foulkes stampede the new government? Foulkes himself apparently thought so, for he later said just that: "Unfortunately I am afraid – we stampeded the incoming government with the NORAD agreement. . . ." Pearkes agreed. "I am inclined to think that the Chiefs of Staff did over-emphasize the importance of signing the Agreement at an early date. Whether or not it was done deliberately I am not prepared to say," he told Diefenbaker in 1965. But Diefenbaker was not convinced, writing in his memoirs that "to suggest that we were stampeded in the early weeks of our government is to suggest that I, as Prime Minister, and more particularly, Major-General George Pearkes, V.C., the Minister of National Defence, had no appreciation of the requirements of North American defence."[15]

The deed was done, obviously with the Prime Minister's enthusiastic concurrence. But the Department of External Affairs was less pleased, the acting under-secretary complaining that he had first learned of the agreement from the United States ambassador, who had come to discuss a press release to be issued on August 1.[16] The result was a nasty little squabble between External Affairs, scrambling to catch up, and General Foulkes, and an effort, ultimately successful, by the diplomats to enclose NORAD within a web of Canadian-American treaties and committees.[17]

In addition, the question of just how – or if – NORAD fitted within the North Atlantic Treaty Organization also arose. Initially, that query had been suggested by the State department to the ambassador in Washington. The Americans were seeking "a livelier sense of partnership,"[18] but the idea was soon picked up by the Prime Minister who was already anxious that his government not appear to be too closely entwined in the American embrace. Thus Diefenbaker told the NATO Council in December 1957 that "this integrated force is an integral part of our NATO military structure in the Canada/United States region and will report . . . in a manner similar to that followed by other NATO military commands."[19] That was General Foulkes's view; it was not that of Jules Léger. Officials in his department, he told his minister, did not believe that NORAD was a NATO command in the normally accepted sense of the term.[20] Inevitably this point, and others, was raised in the House and in the press, and Lester Pearson, the Liberal leader, said that the St. Laurent government had never had any intention of approving the agreement as it stood when the government left office.[21]

The confusion in the bureaucracy and in the government over the NORAD agreement was apparent. The political consequences of NORAD had not been thought out by the incoming government, and External Affairs, while it knew some of what was happening, had not subjected the agreement to detailed analysis. The confusion that accompanied the agreement, the irregular and unusual manner followed, were indicative of the new government's total inexperience in foreign and defence policy.

NORAD's origins went back well into the days of the St. Laurent government. So too did the CF-105 Avro Arrow, the aircraft that caused the Diefenbaker government no end of heartache and no end of political unpleasantness. The story had its roots in the Korean War years when Ottawa had been forced to consider the implications of the increasing threat to North America caused by the Soviet Union's possession of nuclear weapons and development of long-range bombers. By 1953, the Chief of the Air Staff had proposed the development of a supersonic all-weather interceptor. The plan was for some six hundred aircraft, with the engines, armaments, and electronic control systems to be secured elsewhere. Only the airframe was to be developed in Canada, and two prototypes, at a cost of $27 million, were agreed to by Cabinet in December 1953.[22]

But the pace of development had to be accelerated after the Russians demonstrated a long-range bomber at their annual May Day parade in Moscow in 1954. Canada responded by deciding to produce eleven prototypes and a pre-production order of twenty-nine Arrow aircraft at a cost of $190 million. Problems were already occurring, however. No suitable engine could be found, and, with misgivings, the government agreed to support the development and construction of the Iroquois engine at a cost of $70 million. The costs were beginning to skyrocket, and the government considered scrapping the project and substituting one of the U.S. supersonic interceptors, such as the F-101 B Voodoo aircraft or the F-102. The American planes, built in large runs, would be much cheaper and Canada would be spared the development costs. But the RCAF, concerned with the difficulties of flying in the North, was certain that the U.S. machines could not meet Canadian needs, and as a result the Chiefs of Staff recommended continuing with the Arrow.

The Liberal government's decision in December 1955 was a compromise. The Arrow's development would be limited until test flights proved out the design. Eleven machines would be produced, and total costs were to be limited to $170 million over three years. After the first flight, the entire programme was to be reviewed. At the earliest, Arrow squadrons could not be in service until 1961 or 1962.[23]

The project suffered another blow in late 1956 when the United States Navy cancelled work on the Sparrow, the air-to-air missile intended for the Arrow. A new weapon now had to be found, but a harassed government simply deferred the question until after the Arrow's first flight. It also decided, early in 1957, to reduce the prototypes from eleven to eight and to limit expenditures to $216 million (significantly higher than the previous limit). This was the situation when the Conservatives came to power in June 1957.[24]

The Chiefs of Staff Committee in October 1957 considered the aircraft's fate and decided to recommend the purchase of an additional twenty-nine Arrows as well as the continuation of work on the Sparrow. The Cabinet agreed and allotted $176 million for this purpose in 1958-59. In effect, the Conservatives had revived the programme, a decision based in large part on the first successful test of the Arrow's airframe in August 1957.

But the missile age was coming to fruition and beginning to affect the argument. Why proceed with an expensive manned aircraft if a relatively cheap American-produced anti-aircraft missile was available? The Bomarc, just such a missile, was under development. Furthermore, the Soviets' successful launching of a satellite in 1957 demonstrated that the world was close to entering the era of intercontinental ballistic missile warfare. With the equation altering quickly, the Arrow, a project begun early in the 1950s before the USSR even had long-range bombers and still under development after the Soviet Union had demonstrated a nascent ICBM capacity, was not scheduled to enter service for another four or five years.

The one certainty was that the costs continued to climb. A Department of Defence Production study in mid-1958, soon after the CF-105's first flight on March 25, estimated that $300 million had been spent and that $871 million more was necessary to complete the project. The total unit cost per aircraft for an order of one hundred or so was therefore about $12 million, including development costs, an extraordinary price in the late 1950s and about fifteen times the cost of the CF-100, the last Canadian-built interceptor still in service, and six times the cost of contemporary U.S. aircraft. Where was the money to be found in a difficult financial period? And if the Arrow was built, could money be found to re-equip the RCAF Air Division in NATO, still flying obsolete F-86 aircraft, and to procure new weapons for the navy and army?

Thus by the summer of 1958, the time of decision had neared. The Chiefs of Staff had developed a number of alternative scenarios. One, costing at least $2 billion, called for completion and purchase of 169 CF-105 aircraft, for two Bomarc sites, and for installation of SAGE, the Semi-Automatic Ground Environment necessary to control the Bomarc. But cost made this impossible, General Foulkes told the Secretary to the Cabinet, "and even if we had a budget of two billion dollars we would have no room for re-arming the air division or for doing anything in regard to defence against the ballistic missile." His preferred alternative called for sixty CF-105s in RCAF squadrons and sixty more to be purchased by the USAF for use in their squadrons on leased bases in Newfoundland and Labrador, two Bomarc sites, and SAGE. Worth noting, too, was that planning for the Arrow by this stage called for use of the American MB-1 air-to-air nuclear missile.[25]

The Liberals had tried hard to sell the Arrow to the Americans, and now the Conservatives returned to the charge, George Pearkes travelling to Washington in the summer of 1958. But the simple truth was that the USAF did not like the Arrow – it was heavier, more expensive, and did not make use of SAGE as did their own new aircraft.[26] Unstated, but equally obvious, the Americans believed that their aircraft companies could use the business. The Canadians tried to argue on grounds of Allied solidarity and on the heavy imbalance in military trade between the two countries. Nothing worked. If Canada wanted to fly the Arrow, it would have to pay the shot.

In the circumstances, the decision was clear. The Chiefs of Staff Committee now came to the conclusion that it preferred to see all the services get something instead of only the RCAF getting the CF-105. In effect, as Foulkes noted, the military and economic considerations did not justify the continuation of the project. The Chiefs told the Cabinet Defence Committee, therefore, on August 8 that the Arrow should be scrapped, providing that consideration was given to securing a new interceptor for the RCAF, presumably from the United States.[27] The committee was next informed on August 21 that to cancel the Arrow probably would put the A.V. Roe Company and Orenda Engines Limited out of business, would affect the employment of 25,000 persons, and would cost some $170 million in cancellation charges. Those were political considerations of the first magnitude, and the Cabinet Defence Committee decided only that "consideration" be given to abandoning the programme.[28] At the same time, the committee recommended the construction of two Bomarc bases. This decision, as Douglas Harkness, then the Minister of Agriculture, reflected later, was taken almost cursorily: "I believe that the concern over cancellation of the Arrow occupied the minds of members of cabinet to such an extent that the significance of acquiring the Bomarc, equipped with nuclear warheads, did not make much impression and was accepted as a necessary step in order to meet our air defence responsibilities under the NORAD agreement.''[29] It was "unreasonable" to secure the Bomarc without the nuclear warhead, the Chiefs of Staff told the Cabinet Defence Committee on 14 August, in large part because of the feared adverse public reaction if Canada took the missile without the most effective warhead.[30]

Thus the Arrow was almost dead, the decision awaiting only the *coup de grâce* of Cabinet approval. George Pearkes had agonized over the decision, but he was convinced, as he told Bryce, that the CF-105 was not a wise expenditure: "It cost too much money and was, in my opinion, getting out of date."[31] But the Cabinet, worried about adding to unemployment by cancelling the project, waffled. A "careful and comprehensive" review of the requirements for the Arrow aircraft was to be completed before March 31, 1959.[32] This decision was presented to the public on September 23 when the Prime Minister announced that as the bomber threat was decreasing fewer aircraft would be necessary than previously believed. To provide defence against such bombers as did exist, the Bomarc would be installed, the CF-100s would continue in service, and the decision to begin production of the Arrow was postponed, although limited development could continue. The Sparrow was cancelled, and the Arrow was to be modified to accept an American missile and control system. In effect the political and financial considerations remained uppermost. But if the Arrow had a reprieve, it was only temporary. When the defence estimates for 1959-60 were being prepared in late November 1958, Pearkes told his colleagues that he "proposed to assume that the contract would be cancelled and to include only the cancellation costs" for the CF-105.[33]

Early in the new year, the military began the autopsy. At a Chiefs of Staff Committee meeting on February 5, Foulkes summarized the situation, saying that the Chiefs "in the light of the changing threat" did not consider that the return to be gained justified the expenditure. That was a fair summary, but the Chief of the Air Staff persuaded his colleagues that the need for a new interceptor had to be made part and parcel of any recommendation to kill the Arrow.[34] When the Arrow decision was passed to Cabinet, however, the operative clauses said only that the Chiefs had "grave doubts as to whether a limited number of aircraft of such extremely high cost would provide defence returns commensurate with the expenditure." Somehow the RCAF had been snookered, and it was 1961 before a decision was made to replace the obsolete CF-100s on NORAD duties with more up-to-date Voodoo aircraft.[35]

The government finally agreed, on February 17, to scrap the Arrow and the Iroquois engine and to notify the contractors at the same time that the public announcement was made. The Cabinet also decided to make an agreement with the United States for implementation of arrangements "on the sharing of Bomarc and S.A.G.E. installations in Canada" and, most significantly for the future, the Cabinet agreed that an announcement of the Arrow decision "and the acquisition of atomic weapons be made in the House of Commons. . . ."[36]

The Prime Minister made the announcements on February 20, and a full-scale furore erupted. The government was denounced for selling Canada and Canadian technology short and for causing the ruination of the aircraft industry. It was assailed in Toronto for creating massive unemployment and for putting all of Canada's defence eggs in the U.S. basket, not least for deciding to take the still untried Bomarc. A.V. Roe did its part by putting its 14,000 workers out on the street as soon as the government announced the cancellation.

But Diefenbaker did not back down. He had made the right decision, the only one possible in the circumstances. Despite arguments then and later about the CF-105's technological sophistication, Canada simply could not pay the costs involved in creating a modern weapons system by itself, a lesson the British and others were also learning. The only error in the government's decision was that it had not been made earlier.

II

The NORAD and the Arrow decisions had put the government into hot water. By themselves, they did not create difficulties with Washington although there was resentment at the failure of the Department of Defense to buy Arrow aircraft and at the military pressure from the American Joint Chiefs that allegedly had led the Canadian military to push the government precipitately into the air defence arrangement. But both issues fed the Canadian nationalism that was building quickly and that Diefenbaker very often seemed to be leading. There was resentment and envy in the Canadian mood, a feeling that the United States was a bully in Canada and around the world. There was also concern about American policy, a feeling that the United States was too strong militarily and too ready to use its power to achieve its ends. The mistrust was growing.

Difficulties between Canada and the United States particularly concerned Arnold Heeney, the ambassador in Washington. Heeney had served as Secretary to the Cabinet during the war, and he had joined

External Affairs at the very top, succeeding L.B. Pearson as under-secretary. He had then served as ambassador to NATO and as ambassador in Washington from 1953 to 1957, and although his auspices and friends had always been Liberal, he had managed to make the transition to service under the new Progressive Conservative government with relative ease, in part at least because of the skill with which he had served as head of the Civil Service Commission from 1957 to 1959. In 1959, Diefenbaker sent him back to Washington, and Heeney began to worry almost as soon as he took up the reins again. The problem was in Ottawa, Heeney noted in his sporadic diary, and "This 'anti-Americanism' – as it is called, but it is something less than that, and more complicated – is to be found in the highest quarters in Canada. . . ." The Canadian mood he characterized as "not ill will but combined asperity & cockiness," and the Americans he described as "generous, charming and often frightening."[37] The auguries were not good.

They soon turned bad. The occasion for the change was an air defence exercise called Sky Hawk, scheduled for October 1959. The exercise plan called for Strategic Air Command bombers, in the guise of a Soviet air attack, to attempt to penetrate NORAD defences, and in the process civilian air traffic was to be grounded to permit the employment of electronic countermeasures. Planning had been underway for at least six months when a NORAD briefing team came to Ottawa in mid-May 1959 to give details to officials of National Defence and Transport.[38]

But the Department of External Affairs, it seems, did not hear of Sky Hawk until mid-August, and the first senior official in the department to express an opinion, John Holmes, the assistant under-secretary, was mildly dubious about its necessity at that moment. Premier Khrushchev of the USSR was to visit the United States in September, and Eisenhower was scheduled to return the visit. Was it a good idea to upset matters with a large air defence exercise when efforts to create *détente* were in train? Certainly Howard Green, the new Secretary of State for External Affairs who had been appointed to the post after the death of Sidney Smith, did not think so. As he wrote on Holmes's memo, "Totally inappropriate and provocative now. Reserve right to consider proposal further."[39] This the Cabinet did, and the government decision was that Canada should withhold approval "without, however, precluding reconsideration at a later date." The reasons given were the Khrushchev visit and "the disruption which the exercise would cause in civil air traffic."[40]

Heeney was summoned to the State department twice on August 28 to hear the Americans' outrage at first hand. The Canadian decision had been received with "shock," and the U.S. officials expressed "the gravest concern" at the fundamentally opposed appreciations of the factors involved. What made the Americans furious was that the exercise had been in the works for months, had already cost large sums, and Canadian military and civil officials had been directly involved from the beginning. The Secretary to the Cabinet, R.B. Bryce, made that point to the Prime Minister, but the rejoinder was that "Sky Hawk [was] an illustration of a tendency on the part of military officers to assert authority in a field where the real authority and responsibility properly lay with the civilian government."[41] That was so, but what the affair really demonstrated, as Heeney noted, was that procedures in Ottawa had broken down.[42] By the end of August, Diefenbaker had accepted that; nonetheless, he was determined "not to have Canada 'put on the tail of the United States' in a scheme of such questionable wisdom."[43]

The Prime Minister and Cabinet stuck to their position despite the importunings of the ambassador in Ottawa and a letter from Eisenhower. The best the Canadians would offer was that if the civil air disruptions were scrapped, they would reconsider;[44] but that did not seem possible, and Sky Hawk was cancelled on September 15.

For Arnold Heeney, this nasty little business had come closer to doing serious damage to the foundations of Canada–United States relations in joint defence than any other event in his experience.[45] What Sky Hawk had demonstrated was that there was an element of capriciousness in External Affairs and in the Cabinet. It was almost as if the department had been piqued to learn of the exercise so late, and as if Howard Green's and John Diefenbaker's nationalist hubris, once involved, forbade any alteration in a Canadian position. Equally important, this was Green's first victory in Cabinet as Secretary of State for External Affairs, the first time he had managed to translate his concerns about war and the United States into policy. That he could carry the Prime Minister with him was significant.

The Americans were annoyed and puzzled, and their suspicions of Diefenbaker's government began to burgeon. Even the President was concerned, and he called Secretary of State Christian Herter on April 8, 1960, to say that "from somewhere he had heard that our relationships with Canada were deteriorating. This he said he could not understand, and suggested inviting Prime Minister Diefenbaker down to Washington. . . ."[46] Diefenbaker was invited, and the visit in June was a love feast. But it was never the personal relationship that needed repair – it was the building sentiment of anti-Americanism in Canada.

This apparently worried the Prime Minister who at the end of August 1960 spoke to Ambassador Heeney about "anti-Americanism," which was, Heeney recorded, "now worse than at any time in his lifetime or mine . . . an 'avalanche.' " The causes were the popular view that the Americans were "pushing other people around," distrust of the U.S. military, the economic aggressiveness of American interests, and Canada's adverse trade balance. Diefenbaker wanted the President to know his assessment of the gravity of the situation. Heeney did not agree with Diefenbaker's appraisal, and he was suspicious about the source of most of Diefenbaker's opinions – the Prime Minister's mail. What did worry him was the Canadian leader's dark mood and the simple fact that in January 1961 there would be a new administration in the U.S. capital. Whichever party won, Canada would be confronted by those "who knew not Joseph." They would, "for this reason and by reason of the individuals concerned, be much more difficult for us to deal with."[47]

That turned out to be true, although the opening stages of Diefenbaker's relations with President Kennedy were cordial enough. On February 20, 1961, Diefenbaker and Kennedy met at the White House. The Prime Minister described the meeting as "excellent . . . it could not have been better," and Merchant from Ottawa reported how "greatly impressed" Diefenbaker was by "the President and his top lieutenants."[48] That was true in February.

But the new administration, building on the fears of the old, was less impressed with the Canadians. Green was "naive and almost parochial," while Diefenbaker "is not believed to have any basic prejudice against the United States. He has appeared, however, to seek on occasion to assert Canadian independence by seizing opportunities for Canada to adopt policies which deviate somewhat from those of the United States. . . ."[49] Another paper, prepared prior to Kennedy's visit to Ottawa in May 1961, was blunter. Diefenbaker showed "a disappointing indecisiveness on important issues, such as the defense program, as well as a lack of political courage and undue sensitivity to public opinion."[50] With that kind of material in his briefing books, the new president, humiliated by the Bay of Pigs disaster in mid-April, was probably less sensitive to the feelings of the older man than he had been in February. The talks were blunt at times,* and Diefenbaker was incensed by a memo that had been found in a fold of a sofa after the

* Diefenbaker told a different story to his brother, Elmer: he and the President "get along very well together. The opinion I formed of him when I first met him – a brilliant intellect and a wide knowledge of world events – was not only borne out but intensified as a result of our discussions. . . ." (PAC, Diefenbaker Papers, Family Series, Diefenbaker to Elmer Diefenbaker, 18 May 1961, f.2135.)

"Unless something unexpected happens," Gordon Churchill, John Diefenbaker's key organizer at the 1956 Progressive Conservative leadership convention, said, "there is no doubt as to the outcome." Nor was there. Diefenbaker, exultant, won on the first ballot, and the defeated contenders, Donald Fleming of Toronto and Davie Fulton of Kamloops, raised the victor's arm, smiled gamely – and hoped he would forgive their running against him.

/ictorious in the 1957 election, triumphant in he 1958 cakewalk, for ı time Diefenbaker estrode the land like ı colossus. He was the overnment, he was he party, he was the Chief. Duncan Macpherson, the rilliant cartoonist of he Toronto Star, *aptured this npression superbly ith his drawing of the ory "team."*

It did not take long for issues to press in on the Tory government. One disaster was the "Coyne affair" that pitted Finance minister Fleming and the Governor of the Bank of Canada, James Coyne, against each other. The two, seen here announcing the Conversion Loan of 1958 via closed-circuit television, battled so fiercely, with Diefenbaker and other ministers egging Fleming on, that although Coyne was edged out in mid-1961, the government never recovered from the appearance of bungling.

Another crisis began for Diefenbaker when he shifted his old friend Howard Green, a Vancouver M.P., from Public Works, his ministry since 1957, to External Affairs in 1959. Seen here with the Prime Minister and Governor General Vincent Massey, as Secretary of State for External Affairs, Green proved decent and honourable, but his stubborn opposition to arming Canada's military with nuclear weapons was to bring down the government.

It was unemployment as much as anything that began the serious decline of public support for the Conservative government. These demonstrators in Toronto were protesting the pitiful Unemployment Insurance benefits available in 1961 when the rolls of the jobless were increasing quickly. The government's image was not improved by the virtual refusal of Diefenbaker to admit that problems existed, the motivation for another classic Macpherson cartoon. The Chief was forever fixed in the public memory as Marie Antoinette, telling the workers to "eat cake."

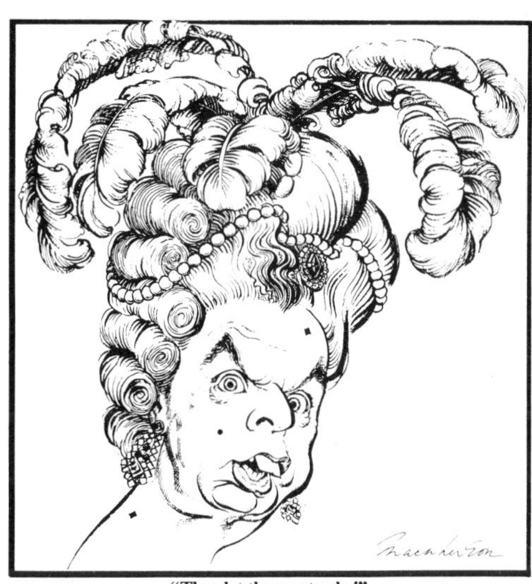

"Then let them eat cake!"

As the Tories sank in the opinion polls, the "third" parties took heart. In the hot summer of 1961 the New Democratic Party came into existence, the result of a political marriage between the Co-operative Commonwealth Federation and the Canadian Labour Congress. Wisely, the NDP selected the most successful social-democratic politician in Canada to be its first leader. Premier Tommy Douglas, portrayed just after announcement of the first ballot results that gave him the leadership, would find politics harder to master in the federal arena than in Saskatchewan.

In Quebec, hard times were encouraging an extraordinary politician. Réal Caouette, the leading Social Crediter in the province, was reaching the people through regular radio and TV broadcasts with charismatic demagoguery that made numerous converts.

The Liberals also benefited from Tory ineptitude. Bolstered enormously by the victory of Jean Lesage in Quebec in 1960, Liberal leader Lester Pearson was gradually building a team and an organization. Here Pearson and Lesage meet at the Quebec Liberal Convention in early 1963 (Madame Lesage at left).

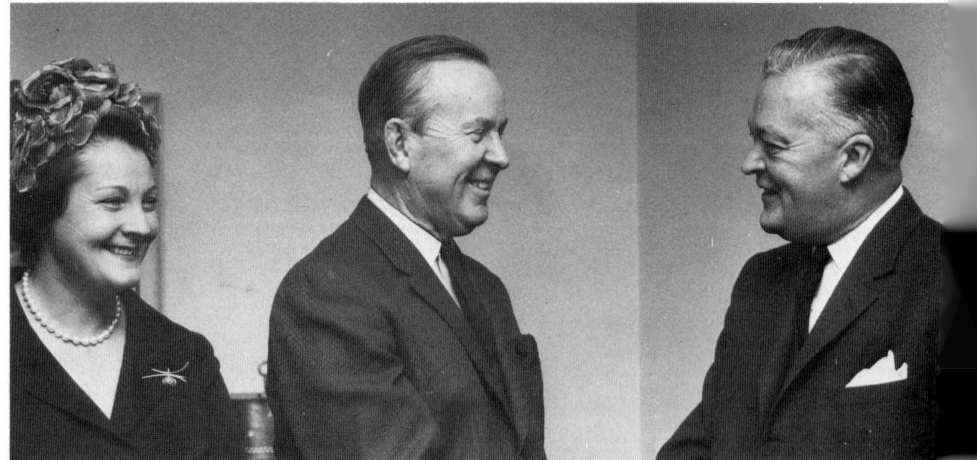

The creation of the Canada Council sparked a new interest in culture. More to the point, the council offered a crucial source of funds. Beginning in 1953, four years the senior of the council, the Stratford Shakespearean Festival brought high-quality classical theatre to the country. Operating first under a tent and then in a stunningly designed theatre, the Stratford company presented world-class actors (such as Alec Guinness, seen here) who changed the way Canadians thought of summer stock productions. This is a scene from Richard III.

The Saskatchewan struggle for medicare was one of the seminal events of the period. The NDP *government produced a plan for state coverage of doctors' bills, but when the medical profession resisted fiercely thousands of citizens, fearful of losing their community doctors, rallied round. The climax came in a great physicians' strike, and this group of marchers at a "Keep Our Doctors" rally in Regina lent it their support. The rally proved a fizzle; the strike was resolved and the province got its medicare plan. Soon medicare became a national programme.*

RCA

After the 1962 election the Diefenbaker government's days were numbered. The nuclear weapons crisis began to tear Cabinet, party, and country apart. One of the Bomarc surface-to-air missiles Diefenbaker had agreed to purchase is seen here in firing position but without the nuclear warhead he havered over buying. This delay produced in 1962-63 the most serious crisis with the United States in decades, neatly caricatured by Macpherson; it also led to wholesale resignations from the Cabinet. The Liberals' Election Colouring Book, *from which the drawing of the Cabinet meeting is taken, was a funny but vicious campaign ploy. It backfired when it made the Tories all the more determined to fight the Grits.*

This is a Conservative cabinet meeting. Oops . . . some of the ministers are missing. I wonder where they went? Colour them quick . . . before they all disappear.

BLAST OFF

The new prime minister, Lester Pearson, was a very different leader from Diefenbaker. One of his first tasks on taking over was to repair relations with the United States, and he flew to Hyannisport, Massachusetts, for talks with President John F. Kennedy, seen here with various officials including Charles Ritchie, Canadian ambassador to Washington. The Liberals quickly accepted the nuclear weapons Diefenbaker had refused to take.

Pearson soon proved almost as trouble-prone as the Chief had been. His government's administrative competence came into question. Yet the Prime Minister, despite bobble after bobble, was able somehow to snatch a victory of sorts from the jaws of disaster in a way that Macpherson encapsulated perfectly in this cartoon, "The Old Smoothie."

THE OLD SMOOTHIE

One of Pearson's concerns was to restore national unity. This included creating new national symbols that could serve to bind French and English Canadians together, and among them was a distinctive new flag. The single maple leaf design, shown here being introduced by Pearson in December 1964, emerged as the preferred choice. But the Conservative leader adamantly resisted retiring the Red Ensign with its Union Jack, seeing the new flag only as a concession to Quebec. Again Macpherson neatly summed up the Chief's position.

"A simple 'Yes' or 'No' will suffice."

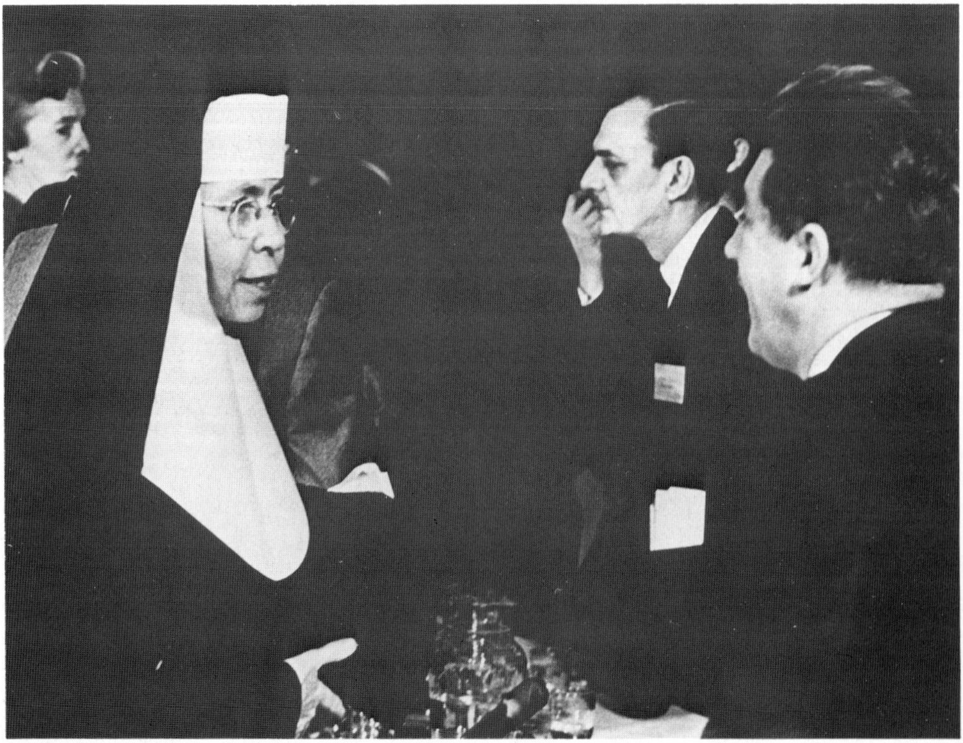

Another of Pearson's efforts for unity was the creation of the Royal Commission on Bilingualism and Biculturalism in 1963. The "B&B" commission travelled the country, holding hearings everywhere. This 1964 photograph of a meeting in London, Ontario, shows Commissioner Jean Marchand, soon to be a Liberal M.P., talking with a member of the audience. At centre, sitting pensively, is the commission's co-chairman and guiding force, the distinguished Quebec journalist André Laurendeau.

In 1965 Pearson went to the voters in an effort to get a majority in Parliament. The campaign was dominated by Diefenbaker's charges of scandal and by the NDP's effective organization, shown on facing page in a mass rally in Toronto's Maple Leaf Gardens. The result, however, was another minority government.

The cliff-hanger scenario inevitably led to further scandal-mongering, which soon brought Parliament into disrepute. The central figure was Gerda Munsinger, pictured here as she appeared on television. A German-born prostitute, she apparently had a relationship with at least one Diefenbaker government minister, a matter of some importance because the RCMP had doubts about her security status. The Munsinger affair titillated the public, but the resulting acrimony almost destroyed the effectiveness of the House of Commons.

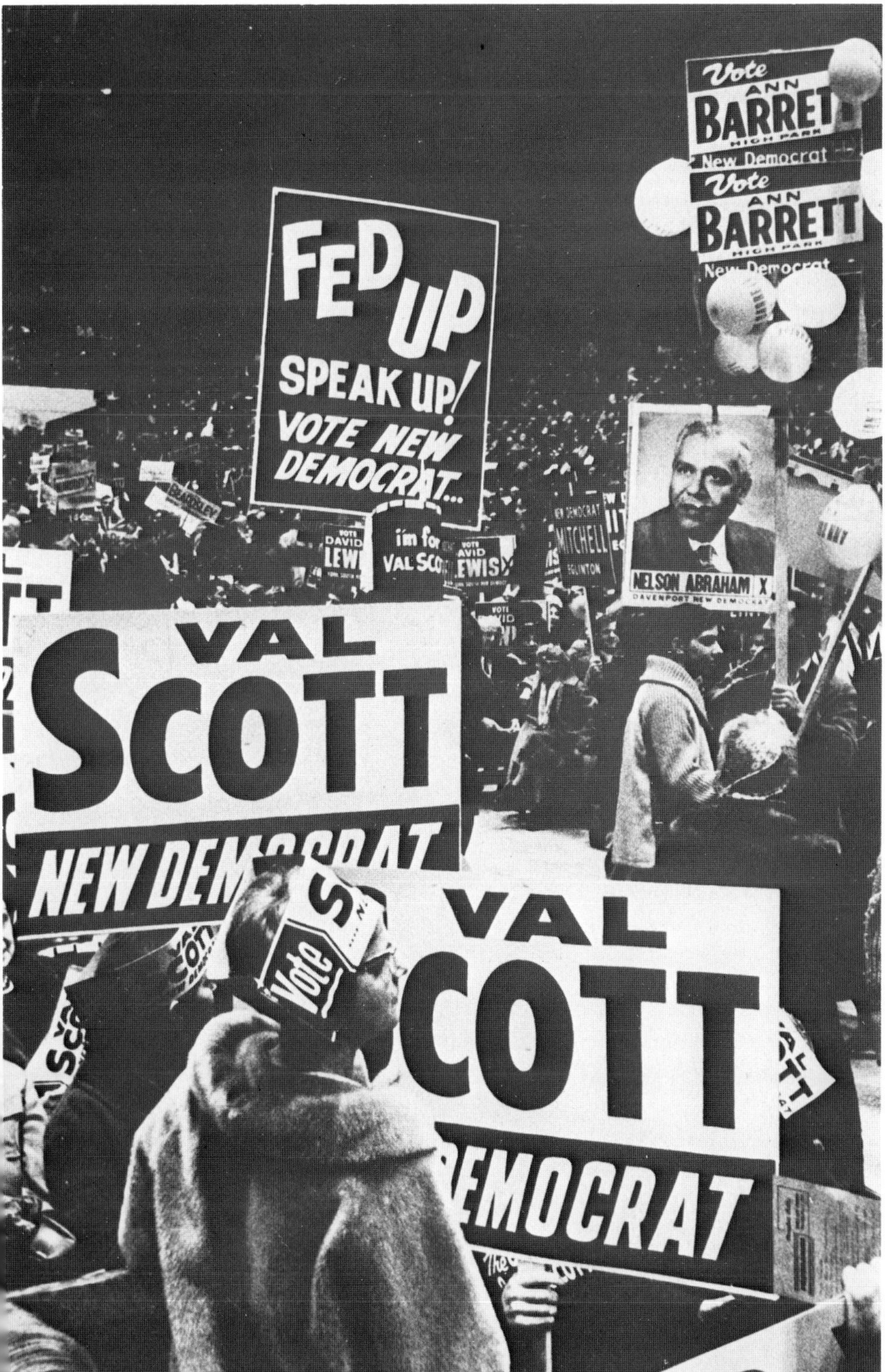
Vote
ANN
BARRETT
HIGH PARK
New Democrat
Vote
ANN
BARRETT
HIGH PARK
New Democrat
FED UP
SPEAK UP!
VOTE NEW
DEMOCRAT...
VOTE
DAVID
LEWIS
i'm for
VAL SCOTT
VOTE
DAVID
LEWIS
NEW DEMOCRAT
MITCHELL
EGLINTON
NELSON ABRAHAM X
DAVENPORT NEW DEMOCRAT
VAL
SCOTT
NEW DEM
Vote
VAL
COTT
EMOCRAT

As Parliament wallowed in scandal, the country was entering a period of overt protests. As in the United States, the Vietnam War was a major cause of unrest, notably on university campuses. A demonstration in Toronto in 1966 featured signs that made its participants' views crystal clear.

In Quebec, the issue that exercised the young was independence, the separation of Quebec from Canada. The separatists, here members of Le Rassemblement pour l'indépendance nationale, received little public support until President de Gaulle's visit of 1967 and René Lévesque's decision to leave the Liberal party in 1968 began to tilt the balance.

The Centennial year of 1967, despite Charles de Gaulle's mischief, was a time of celebration. Across the country every town had its own party for Canada, and Montreal, the home of Expo 67, the first Canadian world's fair, had the best party of all. Expo was a futuristic extravaganza featuring stunning architecture, a dazzling mini-rail ride, astonishing exhibits from many nations, and huge crowds.

Armed forces integration had seemed a winning issue for Minister of National Defence Paul Hellyer, one man who displayed toughness and determination in the Pearson Cabinet. But Hellyer began to run into difficulties when he proposed to unify the services. The leader of the opposition within the Navy was Rear Admiral W.M. Landymore, shown here during parliamentary committee hearings on the legislation in January 1967.

By 1967 the leaders who had dominated the period were at last facing retirement. Diefenbaker, characteristically, resisted his going and even tried to succeed himself. At a leadership convention in September, the Chief was hailed by a few (even some "Youth for Dief") but emphatically voted out and replaced by Nova Scotia Premier Robert Stanfield.

Pearson departed at a time of his own choosing. His successor, who made his first national impression on TV at the February 1968 Federal-Provincial Conference doing battle with Quebec Premier Daniel Johnson (at left), was Pierre Elliott Trudeau, the Minister of Justice, here flanked by Paul Martin and Pearson.

At the Liberal leadership convention in April 1968 (where he sat with Newfoundland's Joey Smallwood), Trudeau's enigmatic face and firm views on the constitution won him victory. The old order was gone.

President's departure. On it Walt Rostow, one of Kennedy's key aides, had listed a series of points on which Kennedy should "push" Diefenbaker. "The P.M. said," Heeney recorded ten months later, "he had not so far made use of this paper but 'when the proper time came' he would not hesitate to do so. . . . I have rarely if ever been so disturbed by a conversation with the head of the Can. govt."[51]

Well he might have been. Diefenbaker's favourable impressions of Kennedy were gone, replaced by a brooding suspicion of the President's motives and a certain envy of his style and youth. The Prime Minister's domestic difficulties also magnified the slights from Washington and the unanswered messages – "Not a bloody word," Diefenbaker said, in reply to one congratulatory message he had sent.[52] And Kennedy's reaction to the Prime Minister was similar.[53] All it would take now was one new and major difficulty to bring the relations of the two countries to the breaking point.

The issue was to be Cuba. The Diefenbaker government had disagreed with the American attitude to the Cuban revolution almost since Fidel Castro seized power on New Year's Day, 1958. After a brief burst of interest in the bearded, cigar-puffing Cuban leader, the Americans quickly decided that he was a Marxist bent on creating a one-party state and threatening to export revolution to the hemisphere. "We are facing a serious situation in the Caribbean," Eisenhower had written to Diefenbaker in July 1960, "which is obviously inviting Soviet penetration of the Western hemisphere."[54] A few days later, at a meeting of senior ministers of both countries at the Seigneury Club in Montebello, Quebec, the Americans went further. They were thinking of economic sanctions as a way of bringing home to the Cuban people the costs involved in supporting Castro and Communism, they said, and they wanted Canada to co-operate by blocking Cuban funds in Canadian banks. They hoped, Norman Robertson, the very sceptical Under-Secretary of State for External Affairs, wrote after the meeting, "to avoid the use of armed forces." All the Canadians present seemed to agree that American policy was wrong, destined inevitably to force Castro toward the Soviet Union.[55]

The Canadian attitude did not please Washington, nor would Canadian suggestions that Canada might mediate between Washington and Havana.[56] Thus when the new administration took over in January 1961, Kennedy's ministers and officials, generally tougher and more conscious of American power than those in the previous administration, were not well disposed toward Canadian policy to Cuba. Heeney discovered this when he sat beside Dean Rusk at a dinner and told him that Canada did not think cutting off trade would do anything except make Cuba completely Communist. Rusk "got quite hot in his response. The U.S. were simply not going to have a Communist base established in Cuba . . . and wd do whatever had to be done to prevent it including if necessary sending in troops. This was primarily a matter of the Monroe doctrine. . . . Further U.S. policy was not going to be altered because Canada didn't like it."[57] Such American attitudes had led to the Bay of Pigs.

No one expected a major crisis, however, least of all the Canadian ambassador in Moscow, who reported on October 19, 1962, that Khrushchev had told the American ambassador that "he had no intention of building [an] offensive military base" in Cuba.[58] That was three days after Kennedy had seen the first aerial surveillance photographs showing construction of a Soviet missile installation on the Caribbean island.

On October 21, two Canadian intelligence specialists who had been at a meeting in Washington returned to Ottawa with the first word of the impending crisis. The next day, Livingston Merchant, the former ambassador, flew to Ottawa to brief Diefenbaker.[59] As Kennedy wrote to the Prime Minister, "we are now in the possession of clear evidence . . . that the Soviets have secretly installed offensive nuclear weapons in Cuba and that some of them may already be operational."[60] Merchant showed photographs of the installations, explained the actions to be taken by the United States, and read Kennedy's speech that was to be delivered on television two hours later to announce the American naval blockade of Cuba. Defence minister Harkness asked about the stages of alert to which the U.S. forces were to be raised and also about the methods of blockade, and as Harkness wrote, "The Prime Minister stated that in the event of a missile attack on the United States from Cuba, Canada would live up to its responsibilities under the NATO and NORAD agreements."[61]

No one doubted that. But how was Canada to respond to the immediate crisis? As soon as Kennedy's broadcast ended, NORAD went to DEFCON 3, the middle of five alert statuses. According to Air Marshal Slemon, the deputy commander of NORAD, the expectation at Colorado Springs was that Canada would follow suit at once or within a few hours. Slemon was told by the chairman of the Chiefs of Staff Committee, Frank Miller, that the Canadian government would give the committee the authority to enable NORAD to increase the state of readiness of the NORAD forces in Canada to the same level and at the same time.[62] But this did not occur.

In fact, on the evening of October 22 when Harkness asked the Prime Minister for authority to put the forces on alert, he found Diefenbaker "loath . . . and [he] said it should be a Cabinet decision."

As Harkness noted, he and Miller discussed what actions they could order without a formal alert. But all that could be done was to man the services' intelligence and communications headquarters, to issue warning orders to field commands, and to order manning of field communications.[63]

The next morning Harkness explained to his colleagues the reasons why an alert was necessary. "I believe all the cabinet would have agreed to this," he said, perhaps underestimating the resentment of his colleagues at Kennedy's late notice to Canada, "but the Prime Minister argued against it on the ground that an alert would unduly alarm the people, that we should wait and see what happened etc. He and I finally came to fairly hot words, but he refused to agree. . . ." The Cabinet decided only that further consideration of the alert would come after the reactions of other countries, and particularly Britain, had been ascertained.[64] When he returned to his office, however, Harkness on his own ordered the Chiefs "to put into effect all the precautions we had discussed in the morning; but in as quiet and unobtrusive a way as possible." Personnel on leave were not recalled, but everything was ordered to go ahead as though an alert had been authorized. That readied the forces, Harkness observed, but it did not "reassure the United States and our other allies . . . that we were prepared to fight."[65] In other words, the Canadian forces were on alert despite the delaying tactics of their Prime Minister, an alert to which they were committed through their membership in NORAD, the alliance into which Diefenbaker had led Canadians. There were no nuclear weapons in the forces' hands, but no one could charge that Canada had let down its friends – for more than a day.[66]

What was the cause of Diefenbaker's extraordinary actions? Part of it was undoubtedly his hesitation in making decisions. Another part was the suspicions he had developed of Kennedy as a brash young man and of American policy as unsound. But part also was his support, announced in the House on October 22, for a United Nations-sponsored mission to Cuba to find out the facts. That idea had emerged from the Department of External Affairs,[67] but it was an immediate non-starter, not least because it suggested that Canada did not believe the evidence in the American photographs. It did, however, serve to delay a formal Canadian decision on implementing the alert status and to worsen matters with Washington.

On October 24, the day the American blockade went into effect, the Cabinet again refused to sanction an alert,[68] despite Harkness's shouting at the Prime Minister that "we were failing in our responsibilities to the nation and *must* act, which produced an outburst from the Prime Minister to the effect that he would not be forced into any such action." When Harkness returned to his office, he learned that the Americans had moved to a greater degree of readiness, DEFCON 2. "I at once went to see the Prime Minister . . . showed him the message and said we just could not delay any longer and, in an agitated way, he then said, 'all right, go ahead.' "[69]

The indecision had ended and Harkness's alert had been legalized. But the Americans did not forget the political delays, even though the crisis quickly dissolved when Khrushchev agreed to withdraw the missiles. Nor did the Canadian people. Public opinion was strongly supportive of Kennedy's actions – and very critical of the government's hesitancy. Almost 80 per cent of opinion sampled in a Gallup poll supported Kennedy, a fact that led a Privy Council Office official to note that Canadians felt "a fundamental alliance with the United States that is often covered over but never seriously threatened. . . . The main lesson to be drawn from all this," he wrote, "is that when the U.S. President chooses to psychologically mobilize the American people on the occasion of a serious threat to them, the Canadian people will be drawn up in the process also."[70]

That was exactly so, and in the circumstances Diefenbaker's performance was found wanting. Newspaper commentators reached for their negative adjectives – inglorious, humiliating, embarrassing. Harkness wrote that the crisis shook confidence in Diefenbaker among Cabinet ministers "and the faith in him was, I believe, never restored to what it was." Pierre Sévigny, the Associate Minister of National Defence, called the government position "vacillating" and added that it cost Diefenbaker the support of even "fanatical" Tories.[71]

Diefenbaker's defence, delivered in Parliament after the fact, was that it was too much to expect any country to react instantly when it learned of a crisis an hour before it became public.[72] That was fair, and Canada was entitled to greater consideration under the terms of the NORAD agreement. But this was a crisis of earth-shattering import, and Canada's leader had flunked the test. That was not only the view of the Americans and the Canadian public but also of some members of the Cabinet. The impact of all this was to be enormous when the nuclear weapons dispute with the United States reached its denouement.

III

The question of whether Canada would accept nuclear weapons for its armed forces should have been resolved once and for all when Canada decided to take the Bomarc missile in September 1958. Then and in the Cabinet decision that determined the Arrow's fall, the nuclear question was decided *de facto* if not *de jure* but almost in passing, so concerned were the ministers with the political fallout that was sure to come with the cancellation of the CF-105. Nonetheless, when the Prime Minister announced the decision on the Arrow on February 20, he spoke of nuclear weapons in a way that left no doubts. "The full potential of these defensive weapons," he said, referring to the Bomarcs, "is achieved only when they are armed with nuclear warheads." The government was already looking at the problems involved in securing warheads for the Bomarcs and for "short range nuclear weapons for NATO's defence tasks," and the Prime Minister did not foresee any difficulty in reaching agreement with the United States. "It will of course be some time before these weapons will be available for use by Canadian forces."[73] That delay between decision and operational readiness was to allow time for second thoughts.

There had already been some delay. The Americans had been pressing Canada to take MB-1 nuclear-armed missiles for the RCAF's interceptors at least since December 1957, and at the same time they had asked that similar weapons be stored at their leased air bases in Newfoundland and Labrador.[74] And early in January 1958, the Cabinet had agreed that "exploratory discussions" could be held between the military authorities of the two countries.[75]

In addition, in December that year at the Canada–United States Ministerial Committee on Joint Defence meetings held in Paris on explicit authority of the Cabinet there were extensive discussions between ministers of the two countries over the draft of a statement, presented by Sidney Smith, the Secretary of State for External Affairs, that would be made to announce the Canadian decision to take nuclear weapons. In the discussion, George Pearkes confirmed that the decision was to cover MB-1 rockets and nuclear depth charges for the Navy. "It was agreed by the meeting that there seemed to be no difference of principle between Canadian and US views on the matter of control to be exercised over the use of nuclear weapons. . . ."[76]

And from early 1959, Canada was engaged in detailed negotiations with NATO authorities over the replacement of the equipment of the Air Division in Europe with a new aircraft to carry out a "strike/attack" role that was defined from the outset as "referring to attacks with nuclear or conventional armament against pre-determined surface targets." General Lauris Norstad, the Supreme Allied Commander in Europe, made that point clear to the Cabinet on May 18, 1959, when he said that none of the NATO allies had been better in quality than Canada, and this quality adapted to the delivery of atomic weapons in the strike/attack role would be an important element in NATO strength. The general also indicated that he thought nuclear weapons could be made available to Canadian forces under the same type of arrangement as they were to the British. "Warheads would be made available on NATO authority in furtherance of NATO plans; they would be located on Canadian bases and guarded by Canadian servicemen; the 'key to the cupboard' would be held by a United States officer, and maintenance would be done by a small group of United States personnel. These weapons," he went on, "could be used only if both Canada and the appropriate NATO authority, acting on behalf of the United States, agreed."[77] In July 1959, Canada chose the F-104 aircraft for this role.[78]

In other words, from 1958 onwards everything in Canadian defence was based on the clear assumption that nuclear weapons would be secured from the United States for the weapons systems Canada was acquiring. The military wanted the weapons; External Affairs apparently had no objections, subject only to the terms of the agreements being satisfactorily worked out; and the Prime Minister and the Cabinet were also apparently in favour. The formal and the final decision to take nuclear weapons had not yet been made, to be sure, but all the evidence leads inescapably to the conclusion that this would be simply the final seal of approval on a decision made long before.

Equally important, the Americans assumed that the decisions had already been made. For example, in June 1959, President Eisenhower met with some of the senior members of the administration to discuss the Bomarc system, under attack in the House of Representatives Military Appropriations Committee and the subject of interservice rivalry. Eisenhower was in an accommodating mood, asking his officials if the Canadians wanted the Bomarc bases in the northern United States sited farther north to give additional protection. But the real question was whether the Bomarc's development should be continued. The Secretary of Defense commented that "if we were to go out of the BOMARC program, he did not think we could live with the Canadians, who had just recently, after long joint discussions, adopted it in preference to interceptors for their air defense." It is at least arguable that had Canada not decided to take the weapons, the Americans might have decided to cancel production. And when in 1960 the Bomarc ran into testing difficulties and new problems in Congress, administration officials went strongly to bat for the weapon.[79]

What turned this smooth and on-track situation into the quagmire it became? The first misadventure was the death of Sidney Smith in mid-1959 and his replacement as Secretary of State for External Affairs by Howard Green. A strongly partisan M.P. of long service, Green had been made Minister of Public Works in 1957 and, although he had not hitherto been known for firm views on current foreign policy, he was quick to form opinions. The prospect of nuclear war horrified Green, and he turned the search for disarmament into a personal crusade. To Green, logically enough, if Canada was to press for disarmament abroad, it could not acquire nuclear weapons for the Canadian forces. "We were advocating in the United Nations that there should be control of the spread of nuclear weapons," Green said later, ". . . and then to turn around and take them ourselves just made us look foolish."[80] In his position on nuclear weapons, Green was greatly assisted by his deputy minister. Norman Robertson was an experienced career officer who had served as Mackenzie King's under-secretary through the war and as Clerk of the Privy Council, High Commissioner in England, and ambassador in Washington after the war's end. A great, brooding man of intelligence and depth, Robertson by mid-1959 had become convinced that nuclear weapons were a direct route to "global suicide." Our efforts, he told some of his officials, "should be turned . . . to the tremendous political effort that needed to be undertaken to avoid the awesome consequences of nuclear warfare." But as a realist, the under-secretary recognized that dilatoriness on this issue would have serious repercussions on Canada–United States relationships, and would lessen Canada's ability to influence U.S. policy on important issues.[81] Robertson and Green made a formidable team inside the bureaucracy and at the Cabinet and committee tables.

Against them were the officials in the Department of National Defence. The generals wanted their men to have the best possible weapons and to them that meant nuclear weapons. The minister, General Pearkes, took the same view,[82] and after Pearkes went to his reward as lieutenant-governor of British Columbia in October 1960, the new minister, Colonel Douglas Harkness, felt even more strongly about the need for Canada to take nuclear weapons. The pro-nuclear forces had one very important ally in Robert Bryce, the one civil servant completely trusted by the Prime Minister, a position he had earned by getting massive quantities of work done well and on time and by always putting his views squarely before Diefenbaker. On defence questions, an area that Bryce knew well from his long service on Treasury Board and in Finance, he was an unfailing advocate of a hard line – and that included nuclear weapons.

In essence, with National Defence and Bryce on one side and External Affairs on the other, the struggle was for the soul and mind of the Prime Minister. And the Prime Minister's soul and mind were sorely troubled. He believed in the reality of the Communist threat, and he wanted Canada to take its fair share in the struggle against the Soviet Union. He admired and respected the United States and particularly President Eisenhower. But he resented bitterly any suggestions that Canada was being pushed around by the Americans, and he was concerned, as were other prime ministers before and after him, about the "real intentions" of the Pentagon.

By the summer of 1960, under continuing pressure from Howard Green, under the pressure of a growing Canadian public opinion that mistrusted the United States and was beginning to flirt with the idea of neutrality as a possible course, Diefenbaker was beginning to waver in his support for arming the forces with nuclear weapons.[83] On one day he could put off a Cabinet decision until such time as the Americans could present a justification for their requests of Canada; on another he could tell the ambassador in Washington that the early conclusion of a nuclear agreement with the United State was "desirable" if arrangements for joint control could be made.[84]

But whatever his own growing personal doubts, Diefenbaker seemed slowly to be moving the government toward a firm decision to accept the nuclear warheads for the Bomarcs, for the RCAF interceptors in NORAD and the CF-104s in NATO, and for the Honest John surface-to-surface missiles used by the Canadian Brigade in Germany. On December 6, 1960, for example, the Cabinet decided to support an Irish disarmament resolution at the United Nations and agreed that henceforth only the Prime Minister would speak on nuclear weapons and Canadian policy. In addition, the ministers agreed that

> discussions (or "negotiations") with the U.S. Government concerning arrangements for the essential acquisition of nuclear weapons or warheads for use by the Canadian forces, in the manners already decided, may proceed as soon as they can usefully be undertaken but the acceptance of joint control is to be a basic principle;
>
> an agreement with the United States concerning the storage of defensive nuclear weapons at Goose Bay and Harmon Field for the U.S. Air Defence forces should not be concluded until after discussions with the United States on other matters had been concluded;
>
> in the discussions at the N.A.T.O. meeting this month, Canadian Ministers should recognize that the government has agreed, at the meeting in December 1957 and at other times, and is morally bound, to supply Canadian forces under N.A.T.O. command equipped and ready to use nuclear weapons if and when they are necessary; . . .
>
> preparations should continue to enable the Canadian forces to have the vehicles, missiles, bases, training and other requirements to enable them to be ready to use nuclear weapons to be acquired from the United States under joint control arrangements if and when the adoption of these weapons is considered necessary.[85]

The paragraph of the Cabinet decision on NATO was a clear admission that Canada had made commitments to the alliance; the other paragraphs amounted to a recognition of the fact that Canada had made commitments to the United States, subject only to reaching of agreements on joint control.

But on the other hand – and there was always another hand – the Prime Minister had told the Canadian Club of Ottawa on November 24, 1960, that Canada would not make a decision on nuclear weapons so long as progress toward disarmament continued. That speech encouraged External Affairs; the Cabinet decision emboldened National Defence.[86] Nonetheless, when Harkness tried to get the Cabinet to reaffirm the Prime Minister's House of Commons statement of February 20, 1959, External Affairs was able to block the move by arguing that Diefenbaker's recent speeches could be regarded as a modification of the Commons speech, and Robertson, setting out the arguments for his minister, added that the one firm element affecting the decision on nuclear weapons was the delivery date, which was still well in the future. "It would seem reasonable, therefore, to hold to the view that a decision to acquire weapons at this time is premature."[87]

That was the situation when Diefenbaker flew to Washington to meet President Kennedy for the first time on February 20, 1961. In their talks, Diefenbaker set out the Canadian position:

> Mr. Diefenbaker [in his report to Cabinet on February 21] had stated that negotiations should continue regarding . . . storage at Harmon Field and Goose Bay, but that Canada would insist upon joint custody and control, and joint authority over use. The President had seemed to raise no objection. Regarding the submarine base at Argentia, Mr. Diefenbaker said he had stated that Canada would require joint custody, but that use should be determined by N.A.T.O. He had further stated that, so long as serious disarmament negotiations continued, Canada did not propose to determine whether or not to accept nuclear weapons for the Bomarc base or for the Canadian interceptors; but that, if such weapons were accepted by Canada, this country would require joint custody and joint control, and use would be determined in the same manner as on U.S. bases. Negotiations for the necessary arrangements should now continue on the basis of a "package" deal, no one agreement being signed before the others had been worked out. There would be no hold up if war should occur. The President had asked whether the same sort of "two key" arrangement as the United Kingdom had would be satisfactory and Mr. Diefenbaker had said it would.[88]

Matters had advanced not at all between February and May when Kennedy paid his return visit to Ottawa. Harkness and Green could not reach an agreement between themselves and their departments on nuclear policy, and the negotiations with the Americans, in consequence, continued to be stalled.[89] Thus when Diefenbaker and Kennedy talked, the Prime Minister was, if anything, more negative on the subject of nuclear weapons than he had been in February. "Prime Minister said that in view of public opinion in Cda," External Affairs telegraphed to Geneva, "it would be impossible politically at moment for Cda to accept nuclear weapons." Nor could Canada take the F-101 Voodoo fighters from the United States as replacements for the CF-100, primarily because the arrangement offered by the United States was contingent on the aircraft being armed with nuclear rockets. "He asked President to reconsider deal on basis that while aircraft would be fitted to receive nuclear arms rockets would remain in storage in USA pending a decision in Canada on nuclear weapons."[90] Whether other promises were made is unclear, although Willis Armstrong, the second-ranking officer in the American embassy, did tell a friend that Diefenbaker had pledged that he would prepare Canadian opinion for the acceptance of the nuclear weapons.[91]

But again, nothing happened until on August 3 Kennedy sent the Prime Minister a letter that went over the ground in detail and argued that the bilateral control agreements should be negotiated now to be in place when the Cabinet took the decision to accept the warheads. Diefenbaker replied on August 11, at a time of some tension between East and West over Berlin, to say that he would ensure "that final preparations were expedited for the negotiation of the agreements to which you referred." But news of the exchange of letters was leaked (in Washington), and the Prime Minister was furious. As a result, the negotiations again stalled,* and Livingston Merchant, again appointed ambassador to Canada, pressed the President to send yet another letter. He added, "I do not share apparent Canadian Government assessment that acquisition nuclear weapons constitutes issue on which it would encounter overwhelming opposition." That might have been a rather presumptuous judgement for Merchant to make had the opinion polls – one on December 1, 1961, showed a 2-to-1 majority in favour of Canada acquiring nuclear weapons – and editorials not demonstrated that he was correct.[92]

Merchant confirmed his surmise in an extensive tour of Central and Western Canada in the spring of 1962 and in secret briefings he himself conducted for the Ottawa press corps. He reported that while

* Even so, Diefenbaker told his brother in September 1961 that "the world situation is terrible and people not knowing the situation are loud in their opposition to Canada having any nuclear defence. It is an ostrich-like philosophy which, while adhered to by many sensible people, is most beneficial to the Communists. . . ." (PAC, Diefenbaker Papers, Family Series, Diefenbaker to Elmer Diefenbaker, 14 Sept. 1961, f.2213.)

there was vociferous opposition, the overwhelming majority of businessmen and other community leaders considered the possession of such weapons necessary and hence inevitable. Canadians, in the ambassador's view, "have no doubt that their destiny and even survival is indissolubly linked with ours." Although Diefenbaker would not have agreed with Merchant that Canada's destiny was linked to that of the United States, on March 8 he told the ambassador that he expected "to proceed forthwith on negotiations looking at least to initialing texts as finally agreed." And, Merchant reported, Diefenbaker seemed confident of his ability "to carry through."[93]

But events intervened. The election of 1962 decimated the Prime Minister's following in the House of Commons, and the economic crisis that preceded and followed the vote took its toll on the Prime Minister's reserves of strength. For five weeks nothing happened, not even a Cabinet shuffle. Then on July 23, Diefenbaker broke a bone in his ankle and was virtually bedridden for another five weeks. The injury did nothing for the Chief's humour, and the atmosphere of indecision around him grew almost palpable.

On August 9, however, the Cabinet was finally reorganized. Donald Fleming was replaced as Minister of Finance by George Nowlan, and the hard-working Fleming took the Justice portfolio. Davie Fulton became Minister of Public Works, and it was obvious that Diefenbaker had demoted him and Fleming. Ellen Fairclough left Immigration to become Postmaster General, and Ernest Halpenny became Secretary of State. R.A. Bell became Minister of Citizenship and Immigration and Paul Martineau Minister of Mines. The one major surprise was that Wallace McCutcheon, a key figure in Argus Corporation, a giant holding company in Toronto, became a senator and Minister without Portfolio. "Kennedy's got McNamara," Diefenbaker said, referring to the American Secretary of Defense who had headed the Ford Motor Company before going to Washington, "I've got McCutcheon." The appointment was obviously designed to reassure the financial community about the economy.[94]

Perhaps that might have worked if the economic woes, rapidly healing as international confidence in the dollar returned, had not been succeeded by the Cuban crisis of October 1962, which once again brought defence to the fore. Diefenbaker's hesitancy in supporting Kennedy had a major impact in Ottawa, on the country, and on our political history.

In the first place, Diefenbaker's own condition was in question. The prime ministerial ankle had mended but Diefenbaker's spirit had not, and throughout the fall of 1962 he was repeatedly threatening, both in the Cabinet and to his friends, to resign. Those threats inevitably led aspirants for the leadership to talk with their supporters and others to begin discussion as to how, as Gordon Churchill put it, to avoid the quicksands that might engulf the government. Late in the year Diefenbaker told Churchill, probably his closest colleague and the one most worried about his state of mind, that he was definitely going to retire. But if Diefenbaker's decision was final, it was no more final than many of his other decisions, and nothing happened.[95] The party, the Cabinet, and the country drifted rudderless.

But when the Cuban crisis was past, Defence minister Harkness was determined that the nuclear question had to be resolved. As he wrote later, "Immediately after the Cuban crisis I succeeded in getting a full discussion of the nuclear question in cabinet and it was unanimously agreed that we should at once reopen negotiations with the United States in order to secure an agreement." The Cabinet decision on October 30, Harkness said, was to accept "nuclear ammunition for the weapons in Europe . . . on the same terms as the European members of NATO had agreed to with the United States." For the Bomarcs and the Voodoos in Canada, "we were to try to get an agreement under which the nuclear warheads, or essential parts of them, would be held in the United States, but could be put on the weapons in Canada in a matter of minutes or hours." Harkness considered this to be a dubious proposition militarily, but he was so pleased to have the NATO weapons question resolved that he went along.[96]

The negotiations were to be conducted by Green, Harkness, and Churchill, and in November there was a three-day meeting with the Americans. There was, Harkness said, "no difficulty over the European nuclear warhead supply – a copy of the standard agreement on this was given to us and no objections were raised to it." But the arguments over the methods of shipping warheads or a specific missing part by air to Canada were long. To Harkness the question was simply unrealistic: "To accomplish this a large number of aircraft and hundreds of men would be required which would make it an extremely expensive operation. . . . In addition, if weather conditions were bad, it might not work." This was an "impractical" solution, and the only purpose it served was to permit Canada to maintain that no nuclear weapons were on its soil. That, however, was important to Green. By December, when Green and Harkness went to Paris for the NATO meetings, nothing had been resolved, and although the two men had discussions with Secretaries McNamara and Rusk, they made no headway. The Americans apparently went away convinced that there would be no further satisfactory progress toward Canadian acceptance of nuclear weapons.[97]

Harkness also noted that between the October 30 Cabinet decision and the NATO meeting he had repeatedly attempted to have the Prime Minister sign the papers to authorize nuclear weapons for the NATO forces. There was an element of urgency involved for it was expected that at least six months' time was necessary to bring the CF-104 squadrons to operational readiness. "He had no objection to this agreement as such," Harkness remembered, "but argued that the whole thing should be announced at one time, and would not agree to immediate action for the European end. . . ."[98]

The Liberal party was having its own problems over nuclear weapons. Under Pearson, the Grits had opposed Canada's acquisition of nuclear weapons, a position shared by the NDP. But under pressure within the party,[99] Pearson himself had been agonizing over the defence question. Early in 1962 he set out his views and those of some friends he had consulted, including Walter Gordon and Paul Hellyer. All agreed that in the changing conditions of the day, defence policy had to be flexible, although this was no excuse for refusing to take decisions, the "besetting sin of the present Canadian government." But how to be decisive? That was not easy, but Pearson did manage to set down some firm positions. The Bomarcs, he wrote, were useless against missiles and of little use against bombers if only because, as fixed installations, they were vulnerable. "These Bomarcs should be scrapped," Pearson wrote, "unless a much stronger case for their retention can be made than has been made" thus far. If circumstances changed in ways that made it necessary for Canada to provide sites for nuclear weapons, "a Liberal government will not shirk its responsibility to make a decision." For the moment, however, Pearson concluded that nuclear weapons would not add "in any substantial way to our own or collective defence. . . . Therefore we should not manufacture, or acquire nuclear weapons for Canadian forces, either under Canadian or joint Canada-US control." The one exception he made was to say that the weapons should "be made available to Canadian forces in NATO for defensive tactical purposes, if they are under NATO, and not national control."[100] In effect, Pearson was rejecting the strike/attack role of the CF-104s, and as the warheads for the Honest John would be under ultimate U.S. control, he was consigning those weapons to the scrapyard as well. Under the conditions of 1962, then, Pearson was opposed to Canada going nuclear.

But this position was under assault,[101] and Pearson began to modify his stand. His policy statements, he wrote one supporter, had always been phrased so "as not to 'require' us to use nuclear warheads, which is, of course, less definite than to say that we will *never* use nuclear warheads in any circumstances."[102] What turned Pearson around completely, however, was the word that Paul Hellyer and Judy LaMarsh, two of his M.P.s, brought back from a visit to NATO and a talk with General Norstad in November 1962. Canada was not meeting its commitments, they said, and as a result it was endangering the alliance and the country's place in it. The two felt very strongly about this and apparently indicated they would leave the party if the policy remained unaltered.[103] Hellyer in fact delivered a speech at Walkerton, Ontario, on December 8 in which he said that as Canada had committed itself to taking the weapons, it had to follow through. "I don't object to that," Pearson said, "but I would add: 'or change the commitment.' "[104] Jack Pickersgill weighed in as well, pointing out that the public saw the Liberal party as being just as bad as the government in its vacillation. "You have already decided what our position must be on existing commitments and there was no dissent in caucus," Pickersgill wrote on January 3, 1963. "But let it be said simply and decisively and without any qualifications about trying to get out of it."[105]

But before Pearson could announce his party's new defence policy, General Norstad came to Ottawa. The retiring NATO commander held a press conference on January 3, 1963, and left no one in doubt that Canada was committed: "We are depending on Canada to produce some of the tactical atomic strike force. . . . I know that they have committed the Starfighters [CF-104s]. . . ."[106]

It was not Norstad's statements that persuaded Pearson to change the Liberal position: that decision had been made at least a week before. But the general's remarks gave added potency to Pearson's new line, delivered in a speech in Toronto on January 12. "As a Canadian," Pearson told a party meeting, "I am ashamed if we accept commitments and then refuse to discharge them." What was to be done? Canada "should end at once its evasion of responsibility by discharging the commitments it has already accepted. . . . It can only do this by accepting nuclear warheads, for those defensive tactical weapons which cannot effectively be used without them but which we have agreed to use." In addition, there should be an immediate examination of the bases of Canadian defence policy. Canada should also discuss with the Americans and NATO a role "in continental and collective defence which would be more realistic and effective for Canada than the present one." But until the present role was changed, "a new Liberal government would put Canada's armed forces in the position to discharge fully commitments undertaken for Canada by its predecessor."[107]

Pearson had taken the plunge. The Tories were clearly divided on the issue and a Gallup Poll in November 1962 showed that a substantial majority still wanted Canada to have nuclear weapons. "These factors," Pearson said, "certainly did not inhibit me."[108] Significantly, and despite the popular perception to the contrary, Pearson did not say that his government would renegotiate the nuclear commitment and return Canada to atomic virginity. As Paul Hellyer later wrote to him, ". . . you never did say that we would – either immediately or otherwise – negotiate out of a nuclear role. You may have given that impression but you did not say it."[109]

For Harkness, the Pearson switch was a promising development. "I believed that this would enable the matter to be settled, and would remove it as a major question in the forthcoming election. . . ." But that was not the Prime Minister's position: ". . . to my complete surprise," Harkness wrote, "he took the position that we must now oppose the position taken by Pearson and delay any decisions on acquiring the warheads." That further strained relations between Harkness and Diefenbaker.

So too did the events surrounding the resolution on the nuclear question at the mid-January 1963 annual meeting of the Progressive Conservative Association. Eddie Goodman, a Toronto lawyer, was chairman of the resolutions committee and a strong believer in Canada taking nuclear weapons. Goodman had made up a draft resolution from the many submitted by constituency associations across the country stating that if no system of nuclear disarmament were adopted by the great powers before December 1963, Canada would accept nuclear weapons provided that those for use in NORAD were under joint control. The Prime Minister tinkered with Goodman's phrasing but ultimately rejected the resolution, saying that if the association accepted it, the party would need a new leader. Goodman, a tough man and a veteran of the fierce fighting in Normandy in the summer of 1944, refused to retreat. In the end, the resolution was emasculated when the meeting referred it back to the government for "consideration and decision." Harkness was not unhappy with that, but he was furious at the way Diefenbaker had tried to squash the resolution before the meeting: ". . . it became more apparent than ever that he was planning to back away from a nuclear position and the whole defence policy we had followed for the previous four to five years." And Harkness told his friends in the Cabinet that he would resign if the government did not take a position on the nuclear question that he could accept and defend.[110]

At the first opportunity after the association meeting, Harkness told the Cabinet that the question had to be resolved. The House was to resume on January 21, and while Diefenbaker argued that "we must continue on the line of delay and no definite policy until the election was over," Harkness said he would quit if that course was followed. The result was that the ministers decided to settle matters once and for all on Tuesday, January 22. Prior to that Cabinet meeting, Diefenbaker told Parliament that there would be a debate on defence and foreign policy on Friday of that week.[111]

Characteristically, the Cabinet on the twenty-second did not resolve matters. Instead the Prime Minister proposed to create a committee of four – Harkness, Green, Churchill, and Donald Fleming as chairman – to find an acceptable solution. Harkness agreed, but made clear that he could not accept anything short of the Cabinet decision taken October 30, 1962. Fleming's committee pored over the records of Cabinet decisions and other documents on January 22 and 23. According to Harkness, Green initially argued that the government had never made a decision to accept nuclear weapons, but the record showed "that we had definite obligations, assumed at different times and in different ways . . . there was no question that acquisition . . . had been approved of at several times." Green then backed down, and the committee members pressed Harkness to retreat from his adamant stand so that a report could be presented that might be acceptable. In the end, reluctantly, Harkness did. The result was a one-page report acknowledging that Canada had accepted a nuclear role in NATO but suggesting that recent statements by President Kennedy and Prime Minister Macmillan after their meeting in Nassau had put that role "in some doubt." It was therefore necessary for Canada "to seek on the part of NATO a clarification of her role in NATO defence plans and dispositions." That could take place at the NATO Ministerial Meeting scheduled for Ottawa in May 1963. "Should NATO reaffirm for Canada a role involving nuclear weapons, Canada will equip her NATO forces to discharge her obligation." As for the Bomarcs and Voodoos, the ministers agreed to continue negotiations "with a view to reaching agreement to secure the highest degree of availability to Canada." By this date, the Americans had made clear that it was impossible to fly a missing part into Canada. They were willing to store the parts in Canada if they could be installed without delay.[112]

The committee's report was unanimous, but Diefenbaker refused to accept it. He ranted and raved, Harkness wrote. "He said he would not be forced into any position on the matter and he complained that I had not compromised in any way to reach a settlement. I replied . . . that he appeared to regard compromise as giving in completely to his point of view, and also that I would put in my resignation at once." But again matters were smoothed over, the committee and the Prime Minister agreeing that the report could go to Cabinet on Thursday. At that meeting, after the Prime Minister had left the council chamber, the great majority accepted the Fleming report. Fleming then left to give this result to Diefenbaker, but again the Prime Minister refused to agree. Once more Harkness said he would resign, but at another Cabinet meeting at 5 P.M. Harkness was prevailed upon to hold his resignation, his colleagues urging him to await the Prime Minister's speech in the House the next day.

Diefenbaker's address on January 25 was confusing to all who heard it. On the one hand, he seemed to reject nuclear weapons: ". . . more and more the nuclear deterrent is becoming of such a nature that more nuclear arms will add nothing materially to our defences. Greater and greater emphasis must be placed on conventional arms and conventional forces." But on the other hand, the Prime Minister revealed the secret negotiations with the United States, and he did state the terms of the Fleming committee report as policy.[113] That inclusion satisfied Harkness who, as Minister of National Health and Welfare Waldo Monteith noted, said, " 'Thank you very much' and shook hands" with Diefenbaker, "said he was more than happy and could live very well with it."[114]

If Harkness was satisfied, no one else was. The press was confused by the flow of words, and on Sunday, January 27, Harkness issued a press release clarifying what Diefenbaker had said – "the definite policy of the Government." This he did emphasizing the Fleming committee recommendations.[115] Diefenbaker was appalled: "This is terrible – you've ruined everything – why did you do it?" But for the next few days nothing happened, the Prime Minister telling questioners that he stood by his speech. At Cabinet on January 30 there were further threats of resignation from Harkness, but once more the ministers persuaded him to delay. By this point, Harkness wrote, several ministers were saying rather openly that no solution could be found if Diefenbaker remained prime minister.[116]

The tenor of the debate now changed dramatically. At 6:15 P.M. on January 30 President Kennedy's Department of State issued a statement that turned the domestic struggle into a major crisis. The American document briefly detailed the weaponry that had been put into Canada, noted the inconclusive discussions that had been held, briefly corrected some of Diefenbaker's comments in the House on January 25, and then devastatingly noted that "the Canadian Government has not as yet proposed any arrangement sufficiently practical to contribute effectively to North American defense." The press release also noted that the Nassau talks had raised no question of the appropriateness of nuclear weapons for Canadian forces in fulfilling their NATO or NORAD obligations.[117]

The Americans had called Diefenbaker a liar, and in a briefing the next day, Dean Rusk took out none of the sting: ". . . we regret it if our statement was phrased in any way to give offense. The need for this statement, however, arose not of our making but because of statements which were made in the defense debate in Ottawa. . . ." The Americans were blunter still in private, telling one officer of the embassy in Washington that they "had felt obliged to set out in factual terms the status of the problem as seen by the United States in the light of [Diefenbaker's] statement of January 25."[118]

Theodore Sorensen, Kennedy's close aide, said later that the President "did not like and did not respect Diefenbaker, and had no desire to see him continue in office,"[119] a comment that suggests, perhaps too strongly, that Kennedy used the press release with conscious and deliberate effect. McGeorge Bundy, another key aide, told Canadian ambassador Charles Ritchie that the President knew nothing in advance about the State department release.[120] The new ambassador to Canada, Walton Butterworth, reported that in his view the press release required no apology – not surprisingly, for the draft had originated in his mission. It was "very useful" and "will be highly beneficial in advancing U.S. interests by introducing realism into a government which had made anti-Americanism and indecision practically its entire stock in trade."[121]

The Diefenbaker government was visibly collapsing. Although all parties in the House deplored the U.S. intervention, there was little willingness to doubt the essential accuracy of the American charges. In the Cabinet, the Prime Minister seemed even more unwilling than before to carry out the October 30, 1962, Cabinet decision or the Fleming committee recommendations, and he was, Harkness noted, determined to dissolve Parliament on the issue of the Americans' intervention. Indeed, on January 31 the Prime Minister arranged to see the Governor General the next day. No argument could sway the Chief on that – "he was convinced he could win an election on an anti-U.S. appeal and this," Harkness claimed, "to him, was all that mattered." But by the next day the Prime Minister had thought better of this idea. Vanier privately indicated how glad he was that Diefenbaker had not sought dissolution: ". . . it would be giving too much importance, too quickly, to what the State Department had said." He was also relieved; his notes indicated how reluctant he would have been to grant Diefenbaker the dissolution and a constitutional crisis – like that of 1926 – might have resulted.[122]

By this time, February 1, Harkness had persuaded himself that it was time for either himself or Diefenbaker to resign, and a number of other ministers had reached similar conclusions. But when the Cabinet met on February 2, the Prime Minister kept the members busy for three hours making appointments and then proceeded to seek a snap decision on a dissolution on the anti-American issue "without any discussion, by simply asking each member in turn to say whether he favoured dissolution or not – a straight yes or no without remark." That was unacceptable to many, and the meeting broke up without decision. The next meeting was scheduled for Sunday morning, February 3. Harkness had now definitely decided to leave if Diefenbaker did not, and he said so to the Chairman of the Chiefs of Staff Committee. Léon Balcer, the Minister of Transport, Pierre Sévigny, and George Hees all agreed that Diefenbaker had to go, and McCutcheon also said that he would support a move to force him out.[123]

The meeting of ministers on Sunday morning at the Prime Minister's residence was unquestionably the strangest in our political history. Harkness took the bull by the horns and told Diefenbaker he had lost the confidence of the country and must resign. "People of nation, Party, Cabinet and *he* had lost confidence in P.M.," Monteith recorded. "All hell broke loose – P.M. asked standing Vote of Confidence – some (saying misunderstood issue) did not stand." The Prime Minister then left the room, saying he was going to see the Governor General to submit his resignation. Green, Churchill, Hamilton, Dinsdale, and Monteith said that if Diefenbaker resigned, they would as well. In the confusion that followed, the ministers met with Howard Green presiding and Harkness repeated that he had lost all confidence in the leader. As Monteith recorded, "It was felt that Doug should leave – he did in sorrowful way [it seemed] to rest of us. . . ."[124] To Harkness, who had expected his friends to resign with him, this scene was "a failure in human courage. If the majority who felt this was necessary had been prepared to face the situation, I think there is no doubt [Diefenbaker] would have resigned." Harkness's assessment is almost certainly correct.

Meanwhile, the meeting reconvened with Diefenbaker again at the table. "P.M. and Green thought we should dissolve," Monteith scribbled. "Majority thought we should force vote and be beaten."[125] The meeting broke up, but Fulton and Hees returned to urge Diefenbaker to resign, a request that was indignantly refused.

The next day, February 4, Harkness made public his letter of resignation. In Parliament, the Liberals moved want of confidence in the government, deliberately framing the resolution so as to attract Social Credit and NDP votes. The decision would come on February 5.

In the interim, George Hees and Wallace McCutcheon separately saw the Prime Minister, urged him to step down, initially in George Nowlan's favour, and apparently promised him the office of Chief Justice if he did so.[126] There was also a "secret meeting" in Hees's office to which a number of ministers were invited,[127] and the NDP were offered assurances that if they supported the government in the

February 5 vote, Diefenbaker would be gone in forty-eight hours.[128] It was the Social Credit M.P.s who held the balance of power, however, and they were badly divided. Robert Thompson, the leader, and his Western supporters did not want to defeat the government, but the Quebec members elected in 1962, with Réal Caouette absent – "as usual," Créditiste M.P. Guy Marcoux remembered – wanted to topple the Tories, probably because Diefenbaker made no move to offer them anything in exchange for their support. "We've got to have an election. Our electors are fed up with compromises," they said. When Caouette learned of the decision, he tried vainly to reverse it, but it was too late.[129] And the NDP, also fed up with the government, decided to vote with the Liberals. "It wasn't a government worth supporting any more," York South M.P. David Lewis said. "The issue didn't count. It was a carcass; it wasn't a government."[130] The result of the vote was 142 to 111 against the government. John Diefenbaker's government had been defeated, and an election, the second in less than a year, was inevitable.

But the bizarre events had not yet ended. At a Conservative caucus on February 6, deliberately rescheduled to precede, and not follow, a Cabinet meeting where Diefenbaker was to be ousted by rebellious ministers, the party tore itself apart and then made itself whole again. Monteith's diary tells the story:

> Caucus at 9 A.M. – Hees in chair – started in to justify innocence of private meetings his office Tuesday (how to get Soc. Cred. to support in vote). Apparent innocents at meeting Martineau, Fulton, Bell – question mark McCutcheon, Halpenny, Sévigny, Balcer – all at Hees' invitation. P.M. forced Hees to tell of his visit to 24 Sussex at 8.30 Tuesday A.M. Hees offered chief justice to P.M.
>
> P.M. gave fighting speech and offered to resign – Back benchers rose in arms to say NO. [Senator] Alf Brooks, [Senator] Grattan O'Leary, and Angus MacLean gave wonderful effort on behalf of unity. Tears in all eyes. Finally, P.M. agreed to go on if all agreed. Eventually all stood up [except Harkness and possibly Sévigny] – and Hees . . . with tears in his eyes agreed. . . .
>
> 
>
> Seemed like another united caucus and Hees went overboard to say so to press later. 100% behind P.M., etc., etc.[131]

That afternoon, Parliament was dissolved and the election set for April 8.

The spurious unity could not last. On February 8, Hees and Sévigny resigned, the former having been pressured by his friends in Toronto. On the next day, the ministers still in town were called to 24 Sussex and, as Monteith wrote, "Extensive phoning – [to find out] who still

O.K. and who not.'' Halpenny was willing to carry on if his health permitted. Martineau was willing, as were McCutcheon, Starr, and Fairclough. Balcer wavered, but Nowlan and McCutcheon persuaded him to continue. O'Hurley (Minister of Defence Production) was willing, but Fleming, for family reasons, had decided to leave. Fulton was ''ready to stay if leader,'' Monteith noted, ''– only P.M., Churchill, Green and M[onteith] really knew. . . .''[132]

On February 12, Diefenbaker brought Marcel Lambert into the Cabinet as Minister of Veterans Affairs, McCutcheon was given Trade and Commerce, and Churchill took Defence. (Later, on March 18, Frank McGee, Martial Asselin, and Théogène Ricard were appointed to the ministry.) The crisis was not yet over, however, for on February 13, after a routine meeting, ''Balcer very emotionally told P.M. in his considered opinion only one thing for P.M. to do and that was resign. Complete shock,'' Monteith wrote, '' – P.M. felt he should [resign] – others including O'Hurley and Martineau felt he should stick.'' But that crisis too blew over, and Balcer even remained in the government.

The battered Tory government, its ranks depleted and its morale shattered, headed into the election. It was clear, Jack Pickersgill wrote to a friend, that nothing like that had happened to a Cabinet since Mackenzie Bowell had to deal with the nest of traitors in 1896. That was true enough, but Diefenbaker, particularly with his back to the wall, was a far more formidable politician than the unlamented Bowell.[134] In fact, as R.A. Bell noted, the Chief was a changed man now, in good spirits and steady – ''every inch a Prime Minister.''[135]

IV

The Liberals should have been in good shape for the election. The party had been organizing feverishly ever since the 1962 vote, and there was no shortage of money. But there were disquieting signs. In Quebec, sympathetic political figures were reporting that Caouette, bolstered by the Liberals' switch on nuclear weapons, might win as many as forty to fifty seats.[136] On the other hand, opinion surveys conducted for the party before Diefenbaker's defeat in the Commons had demonstrated that unemployment remained the key issue and that the new, seemingly definite Liberal defence policy should be hammered for all it was worth, with special care taken not to qualify or amplify a phrase.[137] Those polls, however, seemed less reassuring a month later when Pearson's aide, Tom Kent, reported that there was now a good deal of sympathy for Diefenbaker in the country. In his view, this demanded a quiet campaign to keep the emotional voltage low.[138]

Probably that was good advice, and unfortunately for the Liberals, they failed to follow it. Instead Pearson's party went in for gimmicks with disastrous results. One effort was to purchase and distribute 50,000 copies of *The Election Colouring Book*, a viciously funny production that made observers blanch once they saw its effect on the public. One full-page line drawing showed Diefenbaker riding backwards on a rocking horse:

> This is the leader.
> He is trying to go two ways at once.
> Sometimes he tries to go three.
> Most of the time he doesn't move at all.
> Colour him in reverse.

Some voters laughed; more seem to have been angry that the Liberals were making fun of the Prime Minister. Even less successful was the Truth Squad, an idea first suggested for the 1962 election. The tough and combative Judy LaMarsh was given the task of shadowing Diefenbaker and issuing corrective press releases to set out the "facts." There was a purpose behind the idea, for the Conservative leader did play fast and loose with statistics and events. But at Moncton, local Conservatives set up a special and well-marked table for LaMarsh and, as National Campaign Chairman Dalton Camp remembered, "Dief was up anyway, but that really got him up. We had a marvellous time with them. . . . Dief just played them like an organ and the crowds loved it. . . ." Later in Halifax the Tory crowd turned ugly, pushing and shoving at the embattled Judy, and the Liberals cut their losses after three days, leaving LaMarsh "incensed" and humiliated.[139]

The Tories also capitalized on a *Newsweek* cover story that featured a portrait of a glowering, almost satanic Diefenbaker. The text was patently unfair, and Conservative headquarters sent thousands of copies across the country. "It is difficult to recall any American publication making a more abusive and inflammatory attack on the head of any state, friendly or otherwise," the party's covering letter said.[140] The Liberals were not to blame for the news magazine, but the cover story reinforced the growing public perception that the Liberal gimmicks were Kennedyesque in style, and in an election where American interference was a major issue, that did Pearson and the Liberals no good. As Camp recalled, *Newsweek*, the colouring book, and the Truth Squad turned the election from a rout into a real contest.[141]

The key was Diefenbaker. The Prime Minister ought to have been a broken man. Instead the Chief rebounded magnificently from the carnage, his energy restored by contact with the crowds that came to see and stayed to cheer him, particularly in the Maritimes, in the West, and in countless small towns. As he told one audience, "Everybody's against me but the people. No, I haven't got the big Toronto papers with me, but a crowd like this makes it pretty plain that the people are reading other papers."[142]

Diefenbaker's buoyancy made it hard for his followers to paint him as a martyr, but some tried. Waldo Monteith, for example, running in his riding of Perth, told one meeting that he had been shocked at some of the things that were being said about the Prime Minister. There were rumours abroad that Diefenbaker had Parkinson's disease, that he was insane, that he was a pathological liar and rabidly anti-American, to give only a few examples. "I now ask you to accept my word," Monteith said, "against the malicious slander which has been spread across this country by those who would like to destroy John Diefenbaker. . . . I know this man. I respect and honour him. I trust him." Privately, Monteith wrote to Diefenbaker to say that his constituents' biggest worry was that the Chief might resign. There was not much concern about "indecision." That drew the reply from the Prime Minister that "the question of indecision is now the new Liberal campaign. Everyone should point out that it was the Opposition that blocked us and made it impossible to get anything through," a rejoinder that neglected the nuclear question completely.[143]

That question should not have been a strong point for the Tories. The polls still confirmed Canadian's support for acquisition of nuclear weapons (although Quebec had reversed itself and was said to be against nuclear weapons in a March 1963 poll).[144] And the Tory position was extraordinarily fuzzy. As one of R.A. Bell's aides advised, "It is a simple matter to say 'yes' or 'no' to any complex problem – to render such a decision without a full appraisal of the situation – to swing with the Gallup Polls. . . . It is more difficult to say that you are not prepared to make a final 'yes' or 'no' decision – that you believe the situation to be so complex and fluid . . . that a simple 'yes' or 'no' is neither appropriate nor satisfactory. . . ."[145] That would have been a reasonable non-position – if only the Conservative government had not purchased the weapons that required nuclear warheads and had not accepted a nuclear role in NATO and NORAD.

Nor could the Tories sort out their position during the campaign. The new Defence minister, Gordon Churchill, tried to get the Prime Minister to agree to review the NORAD situation, but Diefenbaker refused: "That would mean that the Americans would immediately arm their Voodoos with nuclear weapons at their bases in Newfoundland and Labrador," Churchill remembered him saying. Even the loyal minister asked himself if the real reason for disagreement was that the Prime Minister feared he might be seen to be yielding to Kennedy.[146] Indeed, anti-Americanism was a major campaign theme of the Prime Minister's. At a rally in Manitoba he told the crowd that the United States couldn't accuse Canada of not doing its part – not after the Second World War, where the Americans had stayed neutral until December 7, 1941. "We don't need any lessons as to what Canada should do after that record of service in two world wars."[147] The Americans, watching Diefenbaker closely, confined themselves to memos that noted that "many of his speeches carry snide comments, innuendoes or other anti-U.S. overtones."[148]

This worried many Conservatives too. Bell, for example, had an argument with Diefenbaker after dissolution and told his leader that he would not be a party to an anti-American campaign, a statement that drew the rejoinder, "I will do whatever I bloody-well like and I don't care whether I have your resignation or not."[149] And Donald Fleming, sitting out the election, wrote to the Secretary of the Treasury in Washington that "the mutuality of [Canadian-American] interests is one of the most important facts in the world today," a statement that was passed to the President as an example of disgust over Diefenbaker's tactics.[150]

But Diefenbaker had the devil's own luck. Late in March, a letter purporting to be from American ambassador Butterworth to Pearson and dated January 14, 1963, fell into Conservative hands. The letter congratulated the Liberal leader on his nuclear policy, said that the timing had been perfect, and added that Diefenbaker was "unfit to continue governing the country. At the first opportune moment, I would like to discuss with you how we could be useful to you in the future. You can always count on our support." The letter was branded a forgery by Pearson and by the embassy, but some believed it to be genuine.[151]

The letter came too late in the campaign to be decisive (no more so, at any rate, than Diefenbaker's veiled references to the memorandum Kennedy had mislaid in May 1961),[152] but the Prime Minister got substantially more mileage from the release of Defense secretary McNamara's secret Congressional testimony on the Bomarc. In essence, McNamara had referred to Bomarc targets in Canada as useful only because they would attract Soviet firepower toward Canada.[153] That was not quite what McNamara said, but that was Diefenbaker's interpretation as his attacks on the worthlessness of the weapons he had purchased reached a crescendo, and the Liberals, committed to arming the Bomarcs, were put on the defensive.[154]

The travails of the Grits were in part caused by their appearance of being power hungry and unscrupulous, a party that would do anything – even reverse its position on nuclear weapons – for political advantage. The party argument for a majority government tended to reinforce that perception. Keith Davey, the Liberals' national organizer, told Pearson that there were unprecedented numbers of the undecided, a phenomenon he explained by noting that those appalled by Diefenbaker were nonetheless searching desperately for reasons not to vote Liberal. How that could be countered, particularly after the Truth Squad fiasco, was difficult to determine. Walter Gordon, the architect of the Liberal revival, was more optimistic, certain that the party would win if it got the support of the government of Jean Lesage in Quebec (which it did on March 21) and if Pearson stressed a firm agenda for action in his first ninety days in office. But "Ninety Days of Decision" did not have the proper ring to it, and soon Pearson had promised "Sixty Days of Decision," which was to be a fateful pledge.[155]

Quebec support was indeed critical to a Liberal majority. As late as March 8, reports from the province continued to predict a big Créditiste showing, possibly much bigger than in 1962. Liberal surveys showed Caouette's troops sharply denouncing nuclear arms, with a strong appeal to men and the young, while Liberals generally were supported by women and older people.[156] But in fact the national Liberal situation was not bad, in large part because of the massive media support the party was drawing. The big city newspapers hammered at Diefenbaker daily while businessmen, afraid of the consequences of an anti-American policy, threw their money and support to the Grits. Some openly called for a majority government and sent letters to their employees urging this, implicitly a plea to vote Liberal.[157] The results showed in the Gallup polls that had the Conservatives stuck at 32 or 33 per cent for the entire campaign, the NDP at 12 to 14 per cent, and the Social Credit fluctuating between 11 and 16 per cent. The Liberals, however, dropped from 44 per cent early in February to 41 per cent two months later. The Chief's achievement was to have prevented a total Conservative collapse; Pearson's failure was to have allowed an early Liberal lead, one sufficient for a solid majority, to dwindle.

The result was a Liberal minority victory. Pearson's team won 129 seats, a gain of 29; the Conservatives held 95, a loss of 21, including 7 ministers. The NDP took 17, not benefiting much from its clear position of opposition to nuclear weapons, and Social Credit lost 6, again confounding the experts, to end at 24 seats. The Liberals won 41.7 per cent of the popular vote, gaining in all provinces, to the Tories' 32.8 per cent. Pearson picked up seats in Quebec (from 35 to 47), in Ontario (from 44 to 52), and in the Maritimes (from 14 to 20), but in the West won only a single seat on the Prairies and 3 in British Columbia. The Conservative vote again was concentrated among the elderly and the rural, the poor and the Protestant. The Liberals were the party of the cities, the professionals, the educated, and the Catholic. They were also the party of the Armed Forces, drawing 70 per cent of the service vote.[158]

Pearson's victory produced great sighs of relief in corporate boardrooms and city editorial offices. The public service in Ottawa was delighted at the return to sanity, as so many saw it.[159] And the Americans too were pleased. Ambassador Butterworth wrote to Walter Lippmann, the great columnist, that the election had been about fundamentals. "That is why facing up to them was so very serious and why the Pearson victory . . . was so significant." There was no doubt that Canada's place in the world and with the United States was the key issue, he said, and that place had now been settled. "At any rate, the outcome holds salutary lessons which will not be overlooked by future aspirants to political office in Canada."[160]

CHAPTER 6

Culture and Scholarship: The First Ten Years of the Canada Council

During the long Liberal heyday that extended from 1935 to 1957, the federal government had begun to intrude into new sectors of the polity. The Depression had produced a great crisis, and belatedly Ottawa had begun to consider unemployment insurance and housing policy as necessary to meet the needs of the people. The Second World War had speeded the process, and the federal government went into the business of building and operating industries to produce war materiel; it also intervened massively in areas of provincial jurisdiction with family allowances, and its proposals in the Green Paper of 1945 represented the federal bureaucracy's attempt to reorder the Canadian constitution to suit the realities of the new Keynesian era. That attempted federal "grab" for power, or so some of the provinces saw it, was an indication that post-war Canada was going to be vastly different from the laissez-faire state of the pre-war years. The federal government had become fully conscious of its power and obviously intended to use it, and the Cold War and the Korean War provided all the justification that Ottawa needed to continue its interventionist approach.

Not even culture, hitherto the least important and least developed area of Canadian civilization, was denied its share of federal beneficence. In a sense, the creation of the Canada Council was the most striking of the many examples of the use of federal power, simply because culture had been so patently an unwanted orphan before 1957. Culture was European, foreign, not Canadian, and the idea that the national government should offer funds to help opera singers or long-haired professors was virtually inconceivable. But the Canada Council changed all that, and the state put up the money to help foster education and create arts of high quality in Canada. It was a daring step, and almost no one in 1957 realized that eventually the state would begin to impose its priorities on the arts and on the academy.

I

The two men walked to work together each morning, striding from Rockcliffe to their offices in Ottawa's heart. John Deutsch, the Secretary of the Treasury Board, was a long way from the Saskatchewan farm that had given him birth, but he still looked fit enough to take the plough. His companion, J.W. Pickersgill, was the Minister of Citizenship and Immigration, a former political adviser to Mackenzie King and Prime Minister Louis St. Laurent and once the senior public servant in the land as Clerk of the Privy Council. Pickersgill had been raised on a Manitoba farm, and that circumstance, along with their years of working together in Ottawa, had helped to make the two men into friends.

"It's a shocking thing to think that we're going to get a hundred million dollars of unexpected revenue out of two estates," Deutsch remarked out of the blue one day in mid-1956. Times were still good in Canada that year, and the federal government was in surplus yet again; now even fate had smiled on the government with the death duties that would bring a huge windfall from the very large estates of Izaak Walton Killam and Sir James Dunn, two Maritimes entrepreneurs. That windfall pleased Deutsch, the man in charge of saying no to departments asking for money for their programmes and plans. But it didn't please him that the $100 million would be "just piddle[d] away" on ordinary expenditures.

Pickersgill was equal to the task of spending the money more creatively. " 'John' he said, 'how would it be if we persuaded the government to provide 50 million of this 100 million to meet these capital needs – or some of them – of the universities? And another 50 million to provide an endowment for the Canada Council. . . .' He thought this a pretty good idea." As Pickersgill now recalls it, Deutsch passed that suggestion on to Maurice Lamontagne, the economics adviser in the Privy Council Office.[1]

Lamontagne had been pressing the Prime Minister for some time to move toward the establishment of the Canada Council, but all his efforts had been blocked by the lukewarm attitude of St. Laurent to things cultural and, it was said in Ottawa, by the opposition of C.D. Howe, who sat at St. Laurent's right hand. According to Lamontagne, he and Deutsch had discussed the $100 million in succession duties, and Lamontagne, asked by the Prime Minister to suggest things he might say to the National Conference on Higher Education in November, listed the doubling of federal grants to universities and, he remembered, "vous pouvez annoncer la création du Conseil des arts avec une dotation de $100 millions."

St. Laurent looked at him as if he had "devenu fou." But when Lamontagne explained the availability of the succession windfalls, "le visage du premier ministre commença alors à s'éclairer." St. Laurent said he would discuss the question with Howe, and a few hours later he called Lamontagne, told him that he and Howe were agreed, and asked his adviser to begin preparing the speech for November.[2]

There can be little doubt that Deutsch, Pickersgill, and Lamontagne were present at the creation, all trying as good bureaucrats and public servants should to make their prime minister do what he ought. And with great success.

In fact, the true origins of the council go back farther, to the European national experiences with support for the arts and, particularly, to the Arts Council of Great Britain, set up in 1945 as an "arm's length" agency, funded by the state but virtually independent of it in day-to-day operations. The Royal Commission on National Development in the Arts, Letters and Sciences, established in 1949 under the chairmanship of Vincent Massey, the former Liberal Cabinet minister, envoy to the United States, and High Commissioner in London, had produced a wide-ranging report in May 1951 that recommended the establishment of a "Canada Council for the Encouragement of the Arts, Letters, Humanities and Social Sciences," largely as an attempt to overcome a small population, great distances, and the overpowering presence of the United States that had combined to stifle development of a national culture. Responsible to Parliament, it would be in no way an arm of government. The contemplated Canada Council was also suggested as the generator of scholarships in the social sciences and humanities.[3]

"I had hoped," Massey wrote in his memoirs, "that the Canada Council would be established several years before it was."[4] But there had been difficulties. For example, when on January 4, 1955, St. Laurent brought Massey, by now Governor General, a copy of the Speech from the Throne prepared for the new session of Parliament, he commented:

> I expressed my disappointment over the omission of any reference to the "Canada Council". He proceeded to explain why it had been left out. It was thought that it might have an unfortunate effect on the present issue between Ottawa and Quebec. I said that it was impossible to placate Duplessis. The P.M. agreed but said that moderate opinion might be affected adversely if they thought the "Canada Council" was a centralizing instrument. We talked about it at some length and I expressed the deepest regret. I said it would disappoint many to find the project dropped. The P.M. suggested that those interested would not be very numerous. I said that their importance could not be measured by numbers or by material strength. . . .[5]

The Quebec issue, behind which St. Laurent was sheltering, was a serious one involving the near total breakdown of communications between Duplessis's autonomist regime and the federal Liberals. A year later, however, nothing had changed and the new Throne Speech still lacked any reference to Massey's project. The Governor General "wasn't surprised," he wrote in his diary. "However I avoided any discussion of the subject. . . . as usual the P.M. seemed shrouded in an impenetrable veil of politeness."[6]

Pickersgill, Lamontagne, and Deutsch had torn the veil aside, and when Massey met St. Laurent on September 22, 1956, "he told me that the Cabinet had decided to introduce legislation on the Canada Council. This time I think it will happen. An endowment of $100,000,000 is to be given the new body!" A month later, the Prime Minister said that "he had asked Brooke Claxton to head the Canada Council and that he had accepted. Gave me the names of others to be asked to join the Council. Wonderful!"[7] So it was, and at the head of the list of names of the council's founders must stand that of Vincent Massey. It was his greatest contribution to Canada.

"Speaking in his most patriarchal, and self-confident manner," or so Claude Bissell described it,[8] St. Laurent duly informed the National Conference on Higher Education on November 13, 1956, that his government intended to establish the council with $50 million so that it could finance "its activities from the annual income to be derived from the investment of that capital." In addition, the astonished educators heard that the Canada Council would receive a further $50 million with which to make capital grants to the universities equal to 50 per cent of the cost of specific building or capital equipment projects. The Prime Minister was not yet finished, for he added the announcement that he was doubling the fifty cents per capita grant for university education.[9] It was a day of miracles, and Bissell later wrote that a "new age had dawned . . . the days of poverty and self-justification were over." At last Canadian intellectuals and artists had achieved a measure of state support. "They had attained, in fact," Carl Berger wrote, "the intellectual parallel to the system of bounties that other social groups and classes had received since the inauguration of the National Policy."[10]

The Prime Minister moved the resolution that led to the establishment of the council in the House of Commons on January 18, 1957, and the subsequent bill passed second reading on February 13 with only the Social Credit M.P.s opposing it.[11] He was not against culture or the stimulation of cultural activities, Socred leader Solon Low wrote to a supporter, but he did object to the fact that the government was spending $100 million for a non-essential when it was doing nothing for old-age pensioners or veterans.[12] Nor did Social Crediters alone feel that way. Senator T.A. Crerar said, "I fancy an Opposition could make a good play of this – taking $100 million for culture and starving the country's schools."[13]

As those remarks suggest, the word "culture" made some Canadians reach for their guns. And Brooke Claxton, the long-time Liberal politician and the first chairman of the Canada Council, ruefully wrote a private note to himself after the 1957 election had turned the Liberals out of office: "To the list of causes of the defeat of the Liberal party must be added the establishment of the Canada Council. . . ." Although the opposition in the House had been slight, "there was not much enthusiasm and it is doubtful if any elector voted for the Liberals because of this measure," which had added to the complex of issues that made voters feel that the government was arrogant and inconsiderate. A great believer in the Canada Council and a patron of the arts himself, Claxton concluded that the council's creation in 1957 was "premature," just another element in building up sentiment hostile to the government.[14] That is probably a slightly exaggerated assessment, although there is certainly little doubt that many people, less concerned with the state of culture than they were with the increasing centralization of power in the federal government, saw the creation of the council as just another intrusion of Ottawa into places where it had no business. But if Claxton's comments were correct, they were a sad commentary on the Canadian electorate in 1957. There were much better reasons to drive the St. Laurent government from office than its support for the arts.

II

The Canada Council's Act enjoined the new body to "foster and promote the study and enjoyment of, and the production of works in the arts, humanities and social sciences." This was a sweeping task but one that was completely undefined, and how the council was to proceed was left equally unclear. The new organization was obliged to report to Parliament each year and its finances were subject to the examination of the Auditor General; on the other hand, its employees were not subject to public service regulations or to the rules and procedures of the Treasury Board, and it was also able to accept gifts and donations and carry money forward from one year to the next. The council, then, was in some ways a public agency and in others a private foundation – it was a distinctively Canadian hybrid.[15]

The council began its work in April 1957 in temporary quarters of the best sort – the prime minister's offices in the Centre Block of the Parliament Buildings.[16] With an election campaign about to begin and with Parliament dissolved, St. Laurent had handed his office space over to the new body and its first four permanent staff: the director, Dr. A.W. Trueman, formerly president of the Universities of Manitoba and New Brunswick and chairman of the National Film Board; Eugène Bussière, the associate director; Lillian Breen, the secretary of the council; and one stenographer. There was also the Chairman of the Canada Council, Brooke Claxton.

In the first days, Claxton was everywhere. He took an interest in finding the council its office space, in the furnishings, in the staff, and eventually in the policies on grants, scholarships, and fellowships.[17] The vice-president and general manager for Canada of the Metropolitan Life Insurance Company, Claxton had more than enough energy to run the Canada Council too – and without pay. The order-in-council setting up the organization had provided $5,000 a year for the chairman, but Claxton told the Prime Minister that he was "most anxious that there should be no honorarium even authorized for him much less paid to him."[18] A good Liberal, Claxton had probably assumed that his term of five years would proceed uninterrupted under the Grits; the voters decided otherwise on June 10, 1957. Concerned about the propriety of his occupying the chairman's post, Claxton asked the Governor General privately if he should resign. Massey said no: "It would be as much as to say that the chairmanship of the Council and the Council itself were political. Diefenbaker would probably be embarrassed by any such action. . . ." If the new prime minister wanted a change, Massey said, a hint would suffice to produce a vacancy.[19] That was good advice, and Claxton stayed at his post until his death in June 1960.

Under Claxton was the vice-chairman, Father Georges-Henri Lévesque. The best-known social scientist in Quebec, revered by some and reviled by others, Lévesque had given Laval University a major reputation. His term was for five years. The members of the Canada Council, all appointed by order-in-council, numbered nineteen, of whom six were to serve for two years, six for three years, and seven for four years. Included were some well-known academic figures – Francis Leddy, N.A.M. MacKenzie, and W.A. Mackintosh; well-off businessmen – Samuel Bronfman and E.P. Taylor; cultural figures – Vida Peene and Sir Ernest MacMillan; and public figures – Leonard Brockington and Georges Vanier. Four of the members were French Canadian and four were women, while one only – Bronfman – was of neither British nor French descent, and there was at least one representative from each province. In other words, the membership was balanced, in the

Canadian tradition. Claxton in fact declared, "Work on getting the Canada Council set up was worse than forming a cabinet; this is really the damnedest place for people to disagree whenever anyone suggests the name of someone for anything."[20]

All the members were acceptable to the Liberal government that appointed them: that had to be expected. Inevitably, in the first group of members, and especially in the subsequent ones, some were not particularly competent to judge questions concerning the arts or learning. They could hardly be, being appointed more for political than for scholarly or artistic reasons. As one author noted acidly, there were suggestions at one point that one member wanted to reduce the grant to the Stratford Shakespearean Festival "on grounds of the immorality of its actors." And one scholar of note argued that "the list of members of the Council contains [in 1963-64] not a single name of a social scientist, distinguished or undistinguished." Even Claude Bissell, the chairman in succession to Claxton, wrote to Trueman to say how impressed he was by the council's officers: ". . . this, I assure you, is no malarkey. Thank goodness we have this rock to fall back upon, since I can't honestly say that the Council collectively is as wise and informed as it is handsome and amiable."[21]

At least the council's money was in good hands. An investment committee chaired by Graham Towers, retired Governor of the Bank of Canada, and with James Muir, the chairman and president of the Royal Bank, and J.G. Hungerford, the president of the National Trust Company, handled the council's $100 million. The treasurer of the council was Douglas Fullerton, a civil servant who had worked in the Finance department and more recently with the Royal Commission on Canada's Economic Prospects. Under the terms of the act, the University Capital Grants Fund of $50 million had to be invested in bonds of or guaranteed by the government. That limited flexibility, but by careful stewardship Fullerton was able to report in 1963 that the fund had produced a return of 5.83 per cent, substantially more than the 4-per-cent average return of Canada bonds over the same period. The Endowment Fund of $50 million was somewhat less restricted, and Fullerton and the committee initially put the fund's money into short-term Canada bonds and treasury bills, then gradually replaced the short-term paper with holdings in bonds and National Housing Act mortgages. Over time, Fullerton noted, changes were made in the portfolio "basically because we follow the investment philosophy that the Fund should be managed actively, that is, that bonds should not be bought and put away but rather that the changing spreads in the market between different types of securities should be exploited." This was important, for the council's operations were wholly financed by the income paid by the Endowment Fund's investments. That income, Fullerton said, had increased from $2,369,000 in the first year to an estimated $3 million in the 1962-63 fiscal year, a return of 6 per cent. Fullerton added that the fund's bonds had returned 7.5 per cent and its stocks approximately 9 per cent. Given the interest rates of the period, such returns were very good.[22]

Thus the council's operations had a secure base from which to proceed, and the officers set about creating the basic programmes. The key man was Trueman, hard working, amiable, an experienced academic bureaucrat, and one who knew his way around Ottawa. His judgement was good, a matter that was to be tested at each council meeting – in the early years every request for money carried Trueman's assessment, his yea or nay. Should a playwright be given support for the writing and staging of a play about Champlain? Competent Quebec assessors were dubious and so was Trueman. The plan was unrealistic, and there were doubts about the author's competence. Should a request for money for a university student conference on world affairs be granted? No, the money was mainly for travel. Could a society's book be subsidized to the tune of $10,000 so that the cost to purchasers could be kept down? No, the manuscript was ragged; but the council could help by buying 300 copies for $1,800.[23] Trueman's good sense helped set the basic patterns for the council's grants.

Trueman was also able to draw on the experience of major American foundations. Indeed, a guest speaker at the first meeting of the council on April 30 and May 1, 1957, was Dean Rusk of the Rockefeller Foundation (and later Secretary of State under Presidents Kennedy and Johnson) along with representatives of the Ford and Carnegie foundations. His advice was sound. "There would never be enough money available to deal with [all the] legitimate proposals," Rusk said, "and the Council would probably find it necessary to decide between competing projects." The Rockefeller Foundation accepted one project for every seven to ten it declined to support. It was particularly important, Rusk added, that no reasons be given for decisions and that the council recognize that its choices were bound to be arbitrary. All the foundation representatives present agreed on that, and all warned that "no immediate results of philanthropic activities could be expected for, perhaps, five or ten years." Rusk noted as well that organizations would say they were certain to collapse unless they were assisted, but "this imposed no claim upon a Foundation, and that a Foundation should not regard such misfortunes as operating principles." Examples of that sort of emotional blackmail were destined to appear soon.

Rusk also said that if, of fifty grants, ten turned out well, twenty indifferent, and twenty unsatisfactory, "this would be a pretty fair average."[24]

However good this advice, the foundations were not the same as a Canadian organization funded by government. The peculiar status of the council forced it to apply slightly different standards. Excellence was the goal, but regionalism was a fact of Canadian life. This became clear in the first few months of the council's operations as complaints arose over the way the grants were being parcelled out. Council member N.A.M. MacKenzie, president of the University of British Columbia, wrote to Trueman to protest that "a concentration of interest on Toronto and Central Canada" was certain to discredit and destroy the council. He liked Toronto, MacKenzie said,

> but it is already wealthy – sometimes because of Markets in the rest of Canada and it is reasonably well off culturally compared with say New Brunswick. The fact that Toronto has been given the bulk of our grants to date – while not a cent goes west of Winnipeg is well designed to develop instant bitterness and criticism. I know the problems – but the rest of Canada will not calmly accept the further enrichment of Toronto while they get nothing. The "Quality" argument of Toronto's productions are all very well – but say what they will about tours etc. the fact remains that they provide enjoyment primarily for the people of Toronto.[25]

The council meeting a few days before MacKenzie's letter had seen a request for support from the Vancouver Festival Society delayed and an application from UBC for assistance in arranging a seminar in Tokyo referred to a committee for consideration. UBC had, however, received $700,000 from the University Capital Grants Fund. Nonetheless, there could be no doubt that MacKenzie was correct – the council had to spread its largess across the country, but it could not be bound to ensure that each province received strict "rep by pop." The dilemma was as clear as it was unresolvable. Claude Bissell later said, "We believe that our resources should go to the support of full-time professional artists and organizations that are likely to achieve some degree of national prominence and to efforts to create an audience for first-class performances." Such a policy caused political problems for the council.[26] While there was no resolution possible, neither was there malice.

MacKenzie's complaints were political, and the council was subject to other political pressures as well, not least the questions of appointments and salaries. Claxton had recognized this when he wondered if he should volunteer his resignation in 1957, but Diefenbaker had not hinted that he wanted it. Quite naturally, when Claxton died, there was substantial concern at the council over his successor. There was much delight, therefore, when Diefenbaker selected Claude Bissell, the president of the University of Toronto, to finish Claxton's term, an appointment that council officers greeted with satisfaction, and, Trueman wrote to Bissell, "for your private ear . . . with a profound sense of relief."[27] Bissell immediately endeared himself to Trueman and Bussière by asking them if their salaries were sufficient, by getting a motion for an increase put through the council, and by going to the responsible minister, in this case the Prime Minister, for approval. Bussière's increase was routinely approved, but Trueman's was limited to a thousand dollars. After some time the reason was discovered: "Mr. Diefenbaker said, 'Trueman's a Grit and his son Peter's a Grit, and writes columns in the Montreal *Star* criticizing me and my government. Why should I raise Trueman's salary?' "[28] The sins of the son were visited upon the father, and Trueman's salary was not adjusted until the government changed in 1963.

Apparently, Diefenbaker also contemplated replacing Norman MacKenzie when his term expired in 1960, for the UBC president was well known as a friend of Opposition Leader Lester Pearson. When word of the Prime Minister's intention got out, however, Leon Ladner, the influential B.C. Conservative, objected. MacKenzie's replacement three years before he was due to retire as UBC president "would have serious political repercussions in the province and elsewhere," Ladner wrote, adding that MacKenzie did not get on well with Premier W.A.C. Bennett, a plus, and did with all the Conservative ministers from British Columbia in Ottawa. The representations had the desired effect.[29]

The council's supporters, however, could not mobilize enough clout to persuade Diefenbaker to increase the Endowment Fund. Faced with a growing need to provide more scholarships and more support for the arts, the council sent the Prime Minister a request for more money in November 1960. "The income of the Endowment Fund for the current fiscal year is estimated at approximately $2,900,000," the brief stated. "The Council sees the need, therefore, of raising its income as rapidly as possible to $3,400,000, and respectfully urges the Government of Canada to take the necessary steps. . . ."[30] Unfortunately, to boost the income by $500,000 required increasing the endowment by up to $10 million, and the Clerk of the Privy Council, R.B. Bryce, told Diefenbaker that it was hard to get public support for such an increase when the primary need was for expenditures to produce immediate employment.[31] The Prime Minister returned a dusty answer when he saw the council's representatives on December 6,* and Bissell's subsequent suggestion that the endowment might be increased by $2 million a year was equally unsuccessful.[32] But it is worth noting that Diefenbaker generally treated the council well, despite the coolness of some Opposition figures in 1956-57 when the organization was created. Evidently culture was beginning to be looked on with some favour, one sign that élite attitudes in Canada were changing.

The Canada Council later made an appeal to the Pearson government on March 3, 1964, for additional money. The request now was for an additional $10 million for the Endowment Fund in each of the next three years.[33] The Liberal government responded positively on March 19, 1965, but not in quite the way the council had wanted. "The government has decided that the Council's income should be increased," Pearson told the House. "We believe that the best long-term method of achieving this result would be to increase the endowment fund, because it fully protects the independence of the Council. We feel however that it would be unwise to take this course under present circumstances." The circumstances were that a major study of university financing, under Professor Vincent Bladen, was under way, and suggestions had been heard that the humanities and social sciences should be taken from the council and put in the care of a new agency. Pending a resolution of these two problems, the government therefore chose to make a donation of $10 million, intended to be spent over an unspecified period of time, instead of an addition to the endowment.[34] The council's officers were overjoyed at the new money, and Trueman wrote to Bussière to report that Diefenbaker, now Leader of the Opposition, "is said to have expressed the view that this item would find general agreement among the members. This unforced sweet accord must establish something of a record for John G."[35]

The possibility of dividing the council was troubling. The idea had first been raised in Parliament by the Secretary of State, Maurice Lamontagne, on November 3, 1964, and the council's executive committee was called together immediately to consider a response. Its conclusion, "after having studied with the utmost objectivity the proposal," was unanimously against any split. Such a change so soon after

* Bissell later recalled that "when we appeared before Diefenbaker to present our brief for money, he suggested that the Council might take over sports and thus get more money and win wider recognition. Trueman and I refused to take this suggestion seriously, but Bronfman . . . whispered hoarsely to me 'Tell him, we'll do it.' " (Letter to author, 26 March 1984.)

the Council's creation could be seen as a repudiation of the Massey Commission report of 1951. It would destroy the interrelationships between the arts and the humanities and social sciences. It would mean the creation of new bureaucracies when the council was able to do the job well. It would frighten all those who had objected to the creation of the Canada Council in the first place as an intrusion of Ottawa into the arts, and it would confirm their worst fears. It would lead academics to believe that the government was going to interfere with their ability to do research where they chose. And the real problem was not one of organizational alteration but one of money. Then, with unblushing style, the council seized the opportunity to ask for $15 million in additional income over the next three years.[36] For the moment, at least, the spectre of division was banished; it would return some years later and lead, as Trueman wrote in his memoirs, "to loss of the independence which supposedly the social scientists crave, and to a political determination of the nature and extent of research in the social sciences and humanities."[37] If the government was to put up the money, as it began to do on a regular basis after 1967, clearly it could be expected to attempt to impose its priorities on the Canada Council (without much success) and on the Social Sciences and Humanities Research Council.

III

If the Canada Council had priorities when it began its work in 1957, one of the most important was to determine what could be done to improve the level of the country's cultural life. No one could have claimed that culture, difficult to define as it was, flourished in Canada. The arts were underfunded and parochial in outlook, yet they aped the metropolises of New York and London, and lacked audience support. Theatre companies in the major cities generally languished, and only the Stratford Shakespearean Festival seemed able to produce first-rate drama on a regular basis. Outside of Toronto, Montreal, and Vancouver there were usually only amateur performances and occasional tours by road companies from the United States or Britain. Orchestras existed in quantity, but the quality was poor and good performers had to leave Canada to be trained and to practise their craft. Outside the National Film Board, the film industry was virtually non-existent, and while a large number of painters were producing work of quality, their reputations at home greatly exceeded their recognition abroad.

This was the bleak situation when the Canada Council appeared, bringing with it the promise of money and attention. In the first year, the council awarded $749,000 to encourage dance, music, theatre, the visual arts, and writing; the next year, the total almost doubled; and in 1966-67 the council spent $4,297,000 in support of the arts.[38] The effect throughout the decade was almost miraculous – theatre companies blossomed across the country, orchestras improved mightily, and artists left their garrets at last. The change was not entirely attributable to the Canada Council, of course. The country had grown in population and maturity; people were travelling more and had broadened their horizons; the country was better off and had more time to devote to leisure; and provincial institutions like the Province of Ontario Council for the Arts, founded in 1963, were becoming increasingly important as sources of money and encouragement. But it was the Canada Council that put up most of the money required to get the arts under way, it was the council that set the example for other levels of government and private benefactors, and it was the council that, more than any other entity, deserved credit for starting Canada on the road to artistic maturity.

But the road was never easy, and there were obstructions along the way. Although each of the arts had its own special problems, many of the difficulties were common to them all, and something might be learned by examining the council's efforts to assist ballet, only one example among many. Over the council's first ten years, support for dance rose from $130,000 in 1957-58 to $571,000 in 1966-67. Substantial sums indeed, but in percentage terms the support declined over the decade from 17.4 to 13.3 per cent of all council money devoted to the arts.[39] That decline was in part a measure of the development of other sectors such as theatre and the visual arts, both of which greatly increased their claims on the council in these years. In some ways, however, the decline was probably a reflection of the problems with ballet: no area of the arts had more intractable financial and artistic problems and no area posed more serious political problems.

The difficulties became apparent at the very first meeting of the members of the council. The minutes detail the opening ceremonies, the passing of by-laws, the arrangements for a secretary and a corporate seal. But then they begin to recount discussion on the "financial difficulties of the National Ballet Guild of Canada." The National Ballet was nearing bankruptcy, and it needed immediate help to survive. To their credit, and perhaps because the council had just heard the representatives of American foundations urge the new body not to be panicked by the pending collapse of artistic organizations, the members decided that they "could not come to the aid of the Ballet Guild at this time or [at least not] to the extent suggested. . . ." The chairman and director were instructed to inform the guild that no grant could be made before an adequate study was completed.[40]

But the problems of the National Ballet resurfaced at the first meeting of the council's executive committee on June 18. Since its beginnings in 1951-52, the guild had accumulated a deficit of $112,000. If it was unable to get a commitment from the council of $50,000 a year in grants it would go into liquidation in a matter of days. Again the members refused to be stampeded, agreeing only to put the National's case to the whole council.[41] By August 19, the next council meeting, some of the basic planning for arts grants had been completed, and this time the members agreed to give the guild $50,000 in 1957 and promised a further $50,000 the next year, provided that the company tackled its deficit, held a major fund-raising campaign, and arranged and contracted a national tour. That was a satisfactory resolution, demonstrating the council's ability to insist on conditions being met before giving a grant. But as the council at the same meeting gave the Royal Winnipeg Ballet $20,000 and indicated its willingness to consider an application from "the Montreal Ballet," Les Grands Ballets Canadiens, then just beginning its first professional season, it was evident that the dimensions of the ballet problem were only beginning to come into focus.[42]

What was the problem? The Massey Commission had surveyed ballet's growth from three companies in 1939 to more than twenty in 1951, and it had carefully detailed the festivals and films that had helped popularize dance in Canada. The report had added wisely that "in the ballet, as in surgery, there can be no amateur status," and pointed out that strong public support, rigorous training, and skilled instruction were the keys to the development of a great company.[43] None of these existed in 1951, and none existed in February 1958 when Trueman travelled to New York for advice. His report quoted the dance critic of the *New York Times*, John Martin, as saying that the National was "not yet a really good company on the international competitive scale." That view was generally agreed to by the editor of *Dance News*, Anatole Chujoy, who did say that the National "had reached a very good standard indeed." The Royal Winnipeg was another question entirely, and the editor said he saw "almost no hope" for it, suffering as it was from the loss of key personnel who had helped found the company in 1949 and from divided counsels.[44] "While they were better at the outset than the National Ballet," Trueman was told, "they have long since lost this position."[45] None of Trueman's contacts mentioned the new Montreal company.

This omission was corrected in the fall of 1958 when, after awarding new grants to the National and Winnipeg ballets, the council commissioned Kenneth LeM. Carter, a leading Toronto chartered accountant, to undertake a survey of the financial conditions and problems of the three companies. Carter reported on January 28, 1959, in the fullest exploration of the financial state of any of the arts ever made in Canada to that time. The total expenditures of the three companies in 1957-58, he said, were $728,508 as against earned revenues of $463,227, leaving an operating loss of more than a quarter of a million dollars. This had been met by $130,000 in Canada Council grants, by grants from municipalities, fund-raising efforts, and membership dues. The Royal Winnipeg had an accumulated deficit of $1,847 and the National Ballet of $109,986.

Carter also reported that the three companies employed seventy-six dancers and that they had given 110 performances in Canada and 99 abroad before audiences totalling 283,657. If those figures were small in comparison to the costs, Carter explained the discrepancy away by noting the high costs of touring, the need for orchestras, settings, and costumes, and generally sky-rocketing production costs. The National, for example, toured with an orchestra, which cost it $124,798 compared to the $80,680 paid the dancers. The minimum union rate for a musician was $155 a week; for the unorganized dancers, the basic wage was $77.50 a week including allowances on tour in Canada.[46]

Carter had also been asked to give an answer to the key question: should Canada try to support three companies on a national scale? He responded by observing that the National Ballet had become "an international company, and, to a certain extent, a Canadian travelling showpiece." It was the only company staffed to perform full-length grand ballet, and while it had to rely on grants and donations, it was nonetheless recovering a higher percentage of its costs from box office receipts each year. "As a long-term investment for Canada," Carter said, "this company should be supported until it is self-supporting on tour." The two other companies were less important in Carter's Toronto-centric approach: they should be encouraged to tour their regions, they could live on modest budgets, and before any increase was made in their grants, "their achievements and plans should be reviewed."[47]

The Carter report lent substantial support to the National Ballet's claim to be the national company, a claim that was acknowledged by a grant of $80,000 made at the May 1959 council meeting. But by August the National was back for more, asking now for a minimum of $125,000 a year. This new request caused some consternation, prompting Trueman to say in his assessment of the application that "from the figures before us" it appeared that Canada could support only one ballet company with the possibility of development to international standards. But, he added, a decision to support the National alone "would in effect place the future of professional ballet in the hands of its artistic director and might make original contributions to the art of ballet from elsewhere in the country extremely difficult." Perhaps that comment was behind the tart note in the council minutes that "concern was expressed by some members at the continued pressure which this organization brought to bear on the Council with each application." Nonetheless, the National got an additional $20,000, even though the minutes recorded complaints that the company was receiving almost 10 per cent of the total arts budget for 1959-60.[48]

Thus the Canada Council was faced with a perennial dilemma. Was it best to sink all the available money into one company that had a chance to become a world-class ballet (if, indeed, the National had that prospect)? Or was it better to recognize the political and regional nature of the country, to satisfy different clientele and interests in Quebec, Ontario, and the West, and to subsidize each of the three companies on a more or less equal basis – and thus probably ensure that none would reach truly professional standards?[49] The answer given in August 1959 was equivocal, an understandable response. As the president of the National Ballet Guild was Edwin A. Goodman, the Toronto lawyer and key Progressive Conservative organizer, however, that equivocation was perhaps more courageous than it might seem at first. But there was no doubt that the council was troubled by the importunate demands for funding from Toronto. W.A. Mackintosh told Brooke Claxton in a half-jocular fashion that everyone at the meeting was "sobered and depressed by the insoluble problems of the ballet. I am tempted to suggest propaganda to convince people that this is a decadent form of art and a sinister deviation from our Canadian way of life." Claxton was similarly vexed, replying that he strongly opposed anything more for the National "except on the basis of some specific new plan of financing which showed it breaking even with not more than $50,000 a year from us."[50]

But no new financial scheme emerged, and matters went on as before. In May 1960, the council's officers recommended an allocation of $145,000 for ballet, with the National to get $85,000 and the Winnipeg and Les Grands Ballets dividing the rest, about two thirds of the sums requested by the companies. "Your officers," the council members were informed, "have previously warned . . . that the problems entailed by the maintenance of three ballet companies . . . would become rapidly aggravated. It would now appear that some radical decision must be taken since we cannot support the companies at the level they require; nor do we see in the circumstances how we can abandon any of these companies since each has a unique quality."[51]

The next year, Trueman tried a different tack in his efforts to make the council grasp the nettle. In a memorandum to the members, he reported that council officers had been concerned to note that the National Ballet's recent Ottawa performances showed "what appeared to their admittedly non-professional eyes . . . some considerable deterioration in the standards of performance. . . . The Company appeared to lack discipline and that indefinable 'élan vital' which makes dancers of quality." Similar opinions had been expressed by Montreal critics and by an expert consulted by the council. Trueman's suggestion now was that the council consider inviting a distinguished foreign expert to come to Canada to offer a considered opinion.[52]

The state of the National was also of concern to Claude Bissell, the council's chairman. In a letter to Peter Dwyer, the council's Arts Supervisor, the University of Toronto president argued that it was "not simply a question of whether or not we come to the rescue of a given ballet company; it is a question of whether we are prepared to support a national ballet." That was the question, but given the criticism of the National, was that company the only one to rely on? Bissell was worried by this, and he wrote that he knew "that I sound as if I were trying to defend the mediocre. But, in the blinding glare of international artistic standards, aren't we doing this for all of the activities we support? We have, it seems to me two enemies to guard against – those who would ridicule any artistic activity – and, in particular, the ballet – [and those who believe that culture] is not really part of the stalwart Canadian character. I think there is a very real danger of these two forces coalescing to kill the National Ballet."[53]

Bissell's strong letter may not have been conveyed directly to the council at its meeting on May 23-24, but its message almost certainly was. Even so, the National's position was precarious. Once again the company was on the verge of bankruptcy, its deficit now $180,000; once again, the council was asked to make an emergency grant of $75,000 to reduce the deficit and to pledge a future grant in the spring of 1962 comparable to the support given in previous years. But after lengthy discussions and after an *ad hoc* committee had considered the situation, the council agreed not to become involved in paying off accumulated liabilities, "particularly in view of grants made by the Council since 1958, amounting to $385,000." Instead, an offer of a grant of $100,000 for 1961-62 operating expenses was made. In addition, the Royal Winnipeg Ballet was awarded $40,000 and the Montreal company $30,000. The total was $170,000, and the council firmly pledged "that at no time in the future would the Council make grants in excess of $150,000 per annum for ballet in Canada." It was also decided to bring in an expert to assess the whole scene.[54]

In August 1961, Peter Dwyer approached Lincoln Kirstein, the founder and general director of the New York City Ballet, about coming to Canada. Kirstein, quite familiar with the Canadian situation, suggested a small commission of experts. As eventually constituted, the commission consisted of Kirstein himself, Richard Buckle, the ballet critic of the *Sunday Times* of London, and Guy Glover of the National Film Board.[55]

Kirstein's report offered a sweeping look at the three companies. The first point that concerned him was the companies' choices of name. It was unfortunate that the Winnipeg ballet had a royal charter which "somehow calls forth expectations of true merit corresponding to regal quality."[56] The National Ballet, despite its name, was artistically "the least representative" and Les Grands Ballets Canadiens was "not very great or big." Those were only the opening shots. "While purely national criteria may be currently sufficient," Kirstein said, "the Canadian people as a whole are not blind to absolute levels. . . . Lacking taste, talent, and esthetic efficiency, much is forgiven on the basis of dollars and cents knowhow; but what is known how to do? Persistence or existence are no ends in themselves." To Kirstein, Les Grands Ballets Canadiens was "miles ahead of the other two companies" in stage decoration, music, and lighting, good local support, a strong director, and the least provincial attitudes. The Winnipeg company was neatly trained and had a not undistinguished musical basis. But its visual taste was haphazard and its artistic direction weak in authority and experience. "The atmosphere," he said, "is hopeful but not one crammed with potential." The National drew Kirstein's sharpest comments: the company "has aims to represent a nation but is the least native in style or repertory" with its overall tone that of "a dowdy step-sister of the Royal Ballet. It is the largest Canadian company but mere numbers have neither contributed to elegance or flair. . . . Its execution is undistinguished; its visual and musical taste alarming. . . . The artistic direction suffers as much from complacency as from ignorance. . . ."

Buckle's comments on the National Ballet were much the same. He found it a company that performed works that appealed to the unsophisticated, that lacked discipline, and that was striving to be a copy of the Royal Ballet. The National had to continue, Buckle said, but some means had to be found to improve its atrocious standards of design, to give it a more creative artistic policy, to improve the company's schooling, and to force it to present first-rate modern works. Unlike

Kirstein, however, Buckle found the Montreal company worthy but in precarious health; to him, the Winnipeg ballet was "perhaps the most satisfactory single company in Canada and the general standard of dancing is probably higher than in the other two." Direction he found good and devoted, the musical standard high, and only design seemed to be lacking.

Neither man held out much hope for what Peter Dwyer had characterized privately as "Ballet Canada," a truly national company that would combine the best talents of the three companies. The country was too big, the local loyalties too strong for that, even if such a solution was a favoured bureaucratic one.[57] That assessment the council had to accept, and the 1961-62 *Annual Report*, drafted by Dwyer, made the point that the Kirstein-Buckle surveys had been made "only to ensure as best as possible that our audiences can in the future enjoy in increasing measure the true beauty of the dance." To make this point clearer still, Dwyer, a man of wide culture, quoted from Mallarmé's *L'Après-midi d'un Faune*: "Ces nymphes, je les veux perpétuer."[58]

At the council's spring 1962 meeting, the officials proposed that grants to ballet for the year might total $165,000[59] – what had happened to the air-tight ceiling accepted the previous year is unclear – but once the council had a chance to digest the surveys, the mood stiffened, a subcommittee concluding frostily that "the Council should not make any drastic change that would put the National Ballet immediately into bankruptcy." Instead, the National would receive $75,000 while Winnipeg received $45,000 and Montreal $40,000. The two smaller companies got their large increases in response to the experts' praise; the National's cuts sprang from the assessors' criticism.[60]

The next year, the waves caused by Kirstein and Buckle had passed. The three companies were back for their annual dollop – and the council officers recommended dividing $160,000 among them on a 50-25-25 basis, with the National getting the largest share. Perhaps this was a reflection of the "general consensus among critics that there has been a slight, but noticeable improvement in this company."[61] Trueman added the comment that the difficulties of the three companies "reflect in an acute form problems which are becoming general to the majority of arts organizations in Canada. A growth is taking place very fast which makes demands upon our resources which we are quite unable to fulfill. We do not see any remedy . . . except an amalgamation of the three companies and . . . this solution is not at present a feasible one."[62] The council also saw data on the companies' finances. Costs were $957,887, up almost a quarter of a million dollars from five years before; earned income had increased to $513,030, up only $50,000. But donations had risen to 47 per cent of costs, and total revenues for the companies were $1,000 above the costs – the National, in fact, had revenues 104 per cent of costs.[63]

One point that worried the council's officers was the low earning capacity of and the small number of private donations that Les Grands Ballets received. The pattern of corporate and private giving in Quebec was different, and Trueman also made the comment, "This is no doubt partly caused by social considerations which make French Canada slow to accept classical ballet." But the Massey Commission earlier had commented that the Anglo-Canadian attitude to ballet had long been shaped by the maxim, "no sober man ever dances," and a 1982 history of the Canada Council by two francophones observed that English Canadians had discovered with surprise "que le ballet n'est pas un art exclusivement réservé aux pays slaves et latins."[64] There were perceptual differences at work in Canada in culture as well as in politics.

The problems of the ballet companies seemed by 1963 to be largely over. The Royal Winnipeg visited the Jacob's Pillow Dance Festival in Massachusetts in 1964 at the invitation of the great Ted Shawn and won glowing reviews in the New York papers. "That's where we became famous," the Winnipeg's artistic director said. The National had a good season in 1962-63, and by 1967, equipped with a new version of *Swan Lake*, it was drawing plaudits everywhere – and large audiences.[65]

Thus by the end of the council's first ten years, there had been substantial gains in ballet and the performing arts. This is best illustrated by the account offered in the *Annual Report 1966-67* by a council official, undoubtedly Dwyer, of his travels in March 1967. He had seen a performance of *Twelfth Night* in Ottawa by the Stratford company; in Toronto there was the National's highly original *Swan Lake*; two days later he was in Vancouver to hear the Vancouver Opera's *Lucia di Lammermoor*. The next night at the Vancouver Playhouse, he saw *Anything Goes*, and a day later Britten's *War Requiem* performed by the Vancouver Symphony Orchestra. Then it was back to Ottawa for Le Théâtre du Nouveau Monde's *Le Bourgeois Gentilhomme*, and while there he saw in the press that three Canadian singers had the leads in *La Bohème* at the Royal Opera House, Convent Garden. There were no Canadian works in that list of productions, and that was still unfortunately typical, although destined to change by the end of the 1960s. Even so the range of choice – and the employment offered by those productions to Canadian dancers, singers, musicians, and actors – was extraordinary; the certainty is that nothing like it would have been possible in 1957 when the council began its operations, and the same explosion in quality and quantity (as can be readily discovered in the entries in the *Oxford Companion to Canadian Literature*, 1983 edition) was taking place in the writing of novels, short stories, and poetry, in painting and sculpture, and in virtually all areas of the arts. The same *Annual Report* noted that over the first decade, earned revenues of Canadian companies in the arts had risen from $2.6 million to $7.5 million; that attendance had increased from 1.5 million to 3.5 million; and that budgets had gone from $3.6 million to $14.5 million. Culture had begun to matter, and the Canada Council's existence had helped push the provinces and municipalities into the act as well. The arts in Canada were entering a new phase,[66] and the Canada Council had laid the groundwork for the development that was to follow.

IV

University education was also entering a new era. Half the money given to the Canada Council in 1957 was to be used to assist universities with capital costs. This $50 million, intended to be expended within ten years and not to be renewed, was a gesture by a government that recognized the increasing public demand for higher education, the financial weakness of the provinces, and the unwillingness or inability of corporate or private donors to meet the regular shortfalls in income that most institutions suffered.

Certainly the demand for places in the universities had increased. In the 1920s about 3 per cent of those in the appropriate age group went to university; by 1959 the proportion had reached one in ten of all persons between eighteen and twenty-one years of age or some 102,000 full-time students. Projections in 1959 by the National Conference of Canadian Universities and Colleges were that by 1970 there would be 241,000 students, a flood that would completely swamp existing facilities. The universities estimated that $180 million in new construction was necessary.[67]

There were precedents for federal assistance, even though education was clearly a provincial responsibility. There had been grants for technical and agricultural instruction since the era of the Great War, and the great influx of veterans into the universities after 1945 (doubling the university population from 40,000 in 1944-45 to 83,200 in 1948) had been largely financed with more than $140 million from the Department of Veterans Affairs. In 1952, the government offered an annual per capita grant of fifty cents for university education, and that grant was doubled in the same speech in which St. Laurent announced the council's establishment. By the end of the 1950s, therefore, federal aid to the universities of Canada had reached $38 million a year, a four-fold increase over a decade.[68]

Now the Canada Council was also in the field. The University Capital Grants Fund was to help provide the money for expansion, and the council's act provided that the $50 million was to be divided among the provinces on the basis of population as determined in the last census. Thus Alberta was to receive $3,499,000, Ontario $16,838,000, Nova Scotia $2,165,000, and Prince Edward Island $309,000.[69] The interest and profits earned on the balance of the fund owing to each province each year was to be allocated in a similar fashion.[70] On the advice of the National Conference of Canadian Universities and Colleges, the council also decided to distribute the money within each province so that the allotment to any institution would bear the same relationship to the provincial allotment as the registration of that university to the total student enrolment in that province.[71] In other words, each university could calculate its entitlement with some precision. The final qualifying phrase in the UCGF regulations was that the council could provide no more than 50 per cent of the cost of any project, the rest to be found from the provincial government, private sources, or the university's revenues.

The UCGF was expected to last ten years, and although the council in a sense was only a trustee and administrator for the money, there were nonetheless difficulties. Were the arts, humanities, and social sciences fostered if the UCGF was used to build student residences? The Auditor General had some doubts, but a legal opinion cleared the way: ". . . provided the proposed residence to be established and operated is more than a mere rooming or boarding house, so that its existence and operation may fairly be said to be in furtherance of the Council's objects. . . ."[72] That was sufficient for the council – and by March 31, 1960, grants amounting to 34 per cent of the almost $22 million awarded to that time were for residence construction.[73]

Another problem was that the rigid formulae in place tended to favour the larger and well-established universities at the expense of the newer and struggling. At a council meeting in October 1957, General Georges Vanier supported complaints raised by colleges affiliated with the Universities of Manitoba and Sudbury, arguing that the "unlimited expansion of the large universities was not necessarily a good thing . . . and that there was a very real danger that the large institutions might benefit at the expense and to the detriment of the smaller ones." Vanier feared that the Sudbury university, located in an area far removed from other institutions and with only a small percentage of area students going on to higher education, might falter. Such smaller schools, he said, were "a safeguard against the danger of a regimentation of thought in a few centres." N.A.M. MacKenzie countered by saying that if the larger universities failed to get their full share, "thousands of the best young people would be denied access to the humanities and the fine arts. The larger institutions might become more and more interested in scientific activities if they were not encouraged to promote programs in arts, letters, and humanities." Inevitably the big battalions won.[74]

Yet another difficulty was caused by Quebec's insistence that its universities refuse to accept UCGF money. Such grants, Premier Maurice Duplessis maintained, violated the provinces' rights in the field of education. But after the Liberals under Jean Lesage came to power, the past was swept away, and at the May 23-24, 1961, meeting of the council, McGill University applied for grants of $1.75 million. This provoked Marcel Faribault, the president of the Trust Général and a council member since 1959, to an extraordinary statement. He had accepted a position on the council in the expectation that some special agreement could be made between the federal and provincial governments to resolve Quebec's concerns. That had not occurred, and he had concluded that the UCGF "was clearly and unequivocally unconstitutional. . . . Now to most people of common law experience I would say that the matter of unconstitutionality is something which is merely inappropriate. To a man bred to civil law," he went on, "it is something illegal, and therefore much more than inappropriate, something morally wrong and practically sinful." Such difficulties, he was convinced, would be resolved over time, and Canada's constitution was altering through evolution. Nonetheless, the Quebec government was being "penny-wise and pound-foolish" in letting its universities take the council's money "because it endangers the recovery of its taxation powers which it needs so acutely." Faribault's remarks were praised on the council – and disregarded. McGill got its money, and soon every university in Quebec got its share as well. As a *Canada Council Bulletin* – subsequently withdrawn from circulation because of these comments – put it, "it was largely to avoid the dilemma posed by the BNA Act that the Canada Council was established in 1957 as a non-governmental agency."[75] Faribault and others could not see the distinction, but this incident – and Ottawa's intrusion into Quebec's jurisdiction – upset many.

These concerns aside, the UCGF was a successful device, one that helped the universities prepare for the 1960s. The earlier projections turned out to be drastically understated – instead of 241,000 students in 1970 there were actually to be 309,469 full-time students and 142,206 part-time students[76] – and had the UCGF not been in place, those numbers could not have been housed.[77] Had there not been Canada Council scholarships and fellowships the students would have had no Canadians to teach them.

V

Before the Canada Council's creation, aid to scholarship had not been in the Canadian tradition. In 1938, there were twelve scholarships or fellowships in the social sciences for the whole country, fourteen in the humanities, and ninety-six in the natural sciences.[78] Twenty years later there were 3,600 awards available – of which 1,700 were in Public Health and Hospital Service and awarded by the Department of National Health and Welfare; the remainder covered all the disciplines, and the best estimate was that approximately one sixth were in the humanities and social sciences.[79] For a country with university enrolment nearing one hundred thousand, contemplating a doubling or tripling of that enrolment over the decade ahead, and anxious to participate fully in the burgeoning technological revolution, those figures were simply pathetic. The Canada Council's task was to help redress the balance.

The nature of the problem was pointed out at the first meeting of the council at the end of April 1957. Brooke Claxton said that while there was a shortage of space in which to accommodate students, there was an even greater need for professors to teach them. "It might well be that in the three fields of the arts, humanities and social sciences, the Council might give a high priority in programs of fellowships, scholarships and sabbatical leaves, subsidies for travel and publications, and the like, particularly at the pre-doctoral and post-doctoral levels. . . ." There was agreement that this must be a high priority and that the council should not get into loans or university entrance scholarships.[80]

The basic guidelines, largely developed by Trueman, were laid out at the next council meeting in August. There were to be ten types of scholarships: pre-Master's degree (worth an average of $1,200); pre-Doctor's degree ($2,000); Senior Fellowships ($4,000); Junior Arts Fellowships ($2,000); Secondary School Teachers' grants ($2,000); Short Term grants ($2,000); Arts Teachers' grants ($2,000); Short Term grants ($300-$700); Non-resident fellowships ($5,000); grants for Journalists and Broadcasters ($3,000); and a category designed for senior scholars and artists whose requests did not fit the other categories. Adjudication, surprisingly but sensibly, was farmed out to the Canada Foundation, the Humanities Research Council, and the Canadian

Social Science Research Council. The Canada Foundation had been formed during the war to help airmen from the British Commonwealth Air Training Plan learn something of Canada; after the war it had turned its interest to fostering the arts. The two research councils were academic bodies and grant-giving agencies, well qualified to assess the merit of professional applications for assistance. The Canada Council got a bargain – the estimated cost of processing applications was ten dollars in the humanities and social sciences and five dollars in the arts; the appraisal of manuscripts for grants in aid of publication was estimated to cost $150; and the Canada Council agreed to pay $5,000 to each of the three bodies for this work and to increase that if the work load warranted it. It also reserved to itself the right to refuse recommendations made to it and to seek additional advice if it so desired.[81] Those were good beginnings, and by December 1957 the council was ready to print its forms – and even to make a few preliminary awards out of applications already on hand.

By late March 1958, the results of the first competitions for pre-M.A. and pre-doctoral grants were complete. The pre-M.A. program had not attracted very satisfactory candidates, only 274 applications being received for 100 awards. That was not the case with the pre-doctoral competition, where 333 applicants sought 60 awards and where the competition was fierce. As a result, with typical flexibility, the council reduced the number of M.A. awards to 70 and increased the senior awards to 89. At the same time, the council increased the funds available for short-term research grants from $40,000 to $75,000.[82] The total value of scholarships and grants awarded was $640,000, and awards in the next few months raised the total to $955,400 for the first council year. The next year $1,215,000 in awards were distributed, 38 per cent in the humanities, 37 per cent in the social sciences, and 25 per cent in the arts.[83]

After the first few competitions, the council had its procedures in hand. The appraisal of applications, still contracted out, worked well,[84] but there were new questions to be decided. There were more applicants in the humanities and social sciences than in the arts, for example, but arts organizations drew heavily on council funds. Did that mean that funds should be diverted so that more scholarships could be given to humanists and social scientists? Or was there already more outside support for those areas than for artists for whom the council was the only granting agency? In the circumstances, Trueman in January 1960 recommended dropping the awards for journalists and film-makers: "The applicants are few, and not outstanding, and almost all who apply under Broadcasting and Film-making are from the CBC and the NFB." Similarly, the director recommended the elimination of non-resident grants in the arts: "The state of art education in this country is not yet sufficiently advanced to justify granting scholarships to people from other countries. . . ."[85] Most important, Trueman urged that the pre-M.A. scholarships be dropped and that the money saved be devoted to the pre-doctoral competitions: "There are 7000 [professors] now, but well over 16,000 will be needed in 1970-1, if the present ratio of teachers to students is to be maintained."[86] That last recommendation would not be accepted until the end of 1964.[87]

In the meantime, there was another problem raised by the Canada Council's vice-chairman, Father Lévesque. Widely acclaimed as the *Père de la Renaissance Québécoise* (the sub-title of the one biography of Lévesque),[88] the Father was widely respected in the country and on the council. He expressed concern, however, that French Canadians were not getting their fair share of scholarships. This was causing criticism in the province and was personally embarrassing to him. "On the one hand," he wrote to Brooke Claxton on April 1, 1960, "I have been trying for many years to strongly support the federal institutions and this has led our parochial nationalists and politicians to consider me as a centralizer, a traitor, etc. On the other hand, if they are given by the Canada Council the slightest opportunity to attack its policy, everything I have done until now to promote federal spirit and friendly understanding between our two ethnic groups would become, I fear, rather useless."[89]

Lévesque then sent a memorandum to all the council members setting out his concerns and pointing out that the Canada Council as "a bicultural and bilingual institution, which must in all fairness promote the interests and serve the needs of the two main cultural groups of our country" should provide roughly one third of its assistance to French Canada. To achieve this, Lévesque urged that the Humanities Research Council and the Social Science Research Council be encouraged to set up linguistically based panels to deal with applications. To bolster his complaints, Lévesque attached some statistics showing that at the February council meeting only 8 of 44 grants in the humanities went to French Canadians and only 33 of 124 in the social sciences. "Strangely enough," he added of the humanities results, "throughout the whole of Canada one keeps hearing that it is in that particular field that French Canadians seem to excel."[90]

Lévesque's memorandum drew a quick rejoinder from MacKenzie: the Lévesque formula would lead to balkanization. What should be done instead, the UBC president argued, was to bring the council's programmes more forcefully to the attention of Quebec universities and to advise selection committees "to keep in mind the necessity of special consideration being given to applicants from the outlying areas of Canada and, in particular, to those whose language is French. This can perhaps best be done by insisting that competent individuals, whose mother language is French, are included in the personnel of these committees."[91]

The result of Lévesque's initiative was the establishment of a Special Committee on Scholarships, composed of Lévesque, MacKenzie, and W.A. Mackintosh, and the collection of data by the council's officers. The data were inconclusive. In the first year of competition, French Canadians won 39.2 per cent of pre-doctoral awards, substantially more than might have been anticipated, given that only 28.7 per cent of the applicants were French speaking; in the third year, 24.8 per cent of awards went to francophones although only 17.5 per cent of applicants were French Canadians. In all, the council officers noted, French-speaking candidates had won 26 per cent of the scholarships and fellowships in all categories over the first three years of the Canada Council's existence. The data also showed that when awards were categorized by region, Ontario did better than it should have in proportionate terms, the Maritimes got their just deserts, the West did not, and that Quebec ordinarily did well.

The statistics seem to have allowed the debate to peter out. But the council's officers began to pay visits to Quebec universities to hear comment and complaint, some of which was devoted to attacks on the anglophone bias of adjudication panels.[92] The problem Lévesque had raised was an important one, one that cut to the heart of the council's operations. If grants could be awarded to French Canadians on a pro rata basis, then British Columbia could demand similar treatment and so would every ballet company in Podunk with aspirations to rival the Royal Winnipeg. A point of principle was at stake, and Lévesque was wrong in his position. In a speech in 1963, Trueman said proudly that the council "makes no attempt to distribute the income of the Endowment Fund in accordance with provincial or regional population." The money was awarded in competition – it had to be that way.[93]

But would there be enough money for the council to do its job? In a submission to Prime Minister Diefenbaker in November 1960 asking for an increase in the Endowment Fund, the council argued that applications had increased dramatically while the number of awards had scarcely increased. In the pre-doctoral competition, for example, applications were up a third over three years, but the council could give grants only to one in four; the adjudicators said that half the applicants merited a fellowship. This was important, the council brief argued, because new faculty had to be found at an annual rate "rising from 1000 in 1960 to 2000 in 1970," and half those faculty had to be in humanities and social sciences. To give the scholarship programme sufficient money, the council maintained that it needed $255,000 more each year.[94] The government did not come through.

Nevertheless, the council began to shift its priorities. The beginning of the 1960s saw an explosion in demand for university faculty – and the construction of York, Trent, Brock, Waterloo, Simon Fraser, Calgary, the Université de Québec system, Lethbridge, Regina, and other universities. How could these institutions be staffed? The council's budget for pre-doctoral awards in 1962-63 was $295,000,[95] but actual expenditures were $373,700; the budget for 1963-64 was $400,000; for 1964-65, $450,000; for 1965-66, $1,083,500; and for 1967-68, $6,575,000.[96] In substantial part the increases after 1964 were made possible by the Pearson government's decision to give the council $10 million in 1964, a decision consciously made because of the perceived necessity to staff the universities.[97]

The problem was serious. A report by Eugène Bussière, the associate director, on the state of graduate studies in 1964 made depressing reading. Canadian students went abroad to study because Canadian universities lacked facilities; in the United States, in particular, Canadian graduate students were often taught by expatriate Canadians who had earlier emigrated.[98] A survey by the council in 1966 found that of 431 persons granted pre-doctoral awards in that year only 127 expected to secure their degrees in Canada. Of the remainder, 165 expected degrees from American universities, 69 from British, 54 from French, and 16 from universities in other countries. Of those working in Canada, 55 expected to take the doctorate at Toronto, 13 at Laval, 14 at UBC, 10 at McGill, and 9 at Montreal.[99]

Did those who went abroad to study return to Canada to teach? The council addressed this question in a major survey of award holders from the first seven years of the pre-doctoral programme. There had been 809 successful applicants from 1958-59 to 1964-65, and of those located 588 or 87 per cent replied. Two hundred and forty-one had completed their degrees, 318 expected to do so within one to five years, and only 29 reported that they had abandoned their studies for reasons ranging from marriage to "Ph.D. nausea." The median age at graduation was thirty-two. Of the group with completed Ph.D.s, 221 were teaching in a university, as were 50.6 per cent of those whose degrees were not completed. Almost two thirds of those who had abandoned the degree were also employed in teaching. In all, 87 per cent of the respondents were university professors, and 26.7 per cent of the respondents had Canadian degrees or expected them soon, 41.3 per cent had or expected U.S. degrees, and 32 per cent had or expected European degrees. Of the group that had studied in the United States, 77 per cent had returned to Canada and of those who had studied in Europe, 90 per cent had returned; the combined repatriation rate was 80 per cent, and for francophones it was 92.5 per cent. Others who were working abroad hoped to return as well, and the data suggested that the country had good value from the council's awards.[100]

The data notwithstanding, the council as early as 1963 had begun to cut back the number of award holders who were allowed to go abroad. By trimming travel grants the council hoped to reduce the number to 50 per cent abroad, and by asking applicants to give reasons for study outside of Canada, it hoped to encourage more to study at home. The intent was partly to save money on travel and thus to increase the number of awards; equally, the council wanted to forcefeed Canadian graduate schools.[101]

The Canada Council's research grants programmes were also forcefeeding the development of scholarship. For the first time, money was readily available to fund travel to the sources, for example, for historians, and to assist with typing, research assistants, computer time, and the like. In the first four years of the council, $356,500 in short-term grants was made available, and in the 1964-65 year, $123,100 was awarded for ninety individual projects, along with $13,800 for group projects.[102]

Perhaps it was good sense that prevented the council from attempting to measure the success – or failure – of these projects. The council could measure success in pre-doctoral competitions simply by counting the number who persisted and ultimately received their degrees; but it was difficult to measure the success – or even the completion – of academics' research projects (an area for which the Canada Council assumed full responsibility, taking over from the Humanities Research Council and the Social Science Research Council in 1959). One example that revealed the difficulties was an application received in 1958 from the distinguished historian W.L. Morton, of the University of Manitoba. Morton wanted the council's support for a multivolume history of Canada, "The Canadian University Series: A History of Canada," that was to involve sixteen of the country's ablest historians. Indicating that he and Donald Creighton would be the editors, Morton sought $68,000 for travel and research costs, clerical expenses, and honoraria for the authors. His estimate was that it would take seven or eight years for the sixteen volumes to be completed and the books to be published by McClelland and Stewart of Toronto. The request was recommended for partial support by Trueman (who frugally deleted the honoraria), but the council effectively refused it, indicating instead only the willingness to support individual authors who sought assistance.[103]

Four years later, some research and writing having been done, the Social Science Research Council and the Humanities Research Council jointly approached the Canada Council on behalf of the Morton project, this time seeking $7,600 a year for five years.[104] The series was still expected to be completed by 1967. Over time, the number of volumes grew to nineteen, the name was changed to the Canadian Centenary Series, and the original authors dropped off the list with a frequency that suggested plague had struck the nation's history departments. A series that was to have taken seven or eight years in 1958, that was projected in 1962 to require five more years, by 1985 still had gaps in its ranks.[105] The only lesson was that academic research can be painfully slow – with or without research support.

Perhaps it all was the way Dean Rusk of the Rockefeller Foundation had put it at the first meeting of the Canada Council in 1957: of fifty grants made, twenty would fail, twenty would produce indifferent success, and only ten would turn out well. To hard-line economists and bottom-line accountants, such a success rate probably is too low. But in culture and scholarship, in the world of the Canada Council in its first decade, a 20-per-cent success ratio was probably sufficient. And there can be no doubt that the council succeeded in its mandate. The growth of the arts, the increase in scholarship, the survival and development of companies such as the National Ballet were proofs of that.

CHAPTER 7

Medicare: Saskatchewan Moves the Nation

The social welfare state that had begun to take shape in Canada with old age pensions in the 1920s and continued with unemployment insurance and family allowances during the Second World War remained incomplete in the mid-1950s. There was still no pension scheme – without a means test – that could reasonably be expected to give the elderly the opportunity to live without privation. As important, there was no plan to provide coverage for the crippling expenses ill health could bring, nothing to assist with hospital bills and nothing to pay for doctors' bills. Those bills, even for people covered by private plans that were relatively expensive, could be ruinous, and every Canadian, it seemed, knew a family that had lost its house and savings supporting a father or mother through a lingering and costly illness.

Other countries had dealt with the problem. In Great Britain, particularly, the Labour government led by Clement Attlee had created the National Health Service in a deliberate and conscious effort to reduce the costs of medical care and to improve the health of the people. The costs of the NHS to the state were high, and there were often line-ups at doctors' offices and crowding in hospitals; but the great majority of the British people were receiving better medical care at lower cost than ever before. That experience had its impact in Canada on governments and on the national and provincial medical associations.

The advent of serious interest in health and hospital insurance in Canada coincided with the beginnings of a great shift in power in Canadian federalism. During the war and continuing into the reconstruction period, Ottawa had seized control of tax powers to prosecute the war and had spent billions with rapidity. The federal government had the money and the power, and it also had the politicians of skill and the bureaucrats with ideas: the C.D. Howes and the

Clifford Clarks were the architects of Ottawa's power. But in a federal state, power is never fixed for all time, and over the years the provincial governments either began to demand more money to carry out their plans, as was the case with Quebec, for example, or to create programmes that were so attractive that they virtually forced Ottawa to replicate them across the country. The leader in introducing programmes was the CCF government led by Premier T.C. Douglas of Saskatchewan.

I

When the CCF won power in the Prairie province in 1944, the victory came as a stunning shock to the old parties and to their supporters in the business and financial community. The CCF was avowedly socialist, and its Saskatchewan triumph marked the first electoral success for social democracy anywhere in North America. That frightened many in case the 1944 election presaged a federal CCF victory the next year; as it turned out, however, the CCF was checked at the polls by Mackenzie King's suddenly populist Liberals and by a virulent anti-socialist campaign. But Tommy Douglas, the forty-year-old Scots-born Baptist preacher and Member of Parliament (1935-44) from Weyburn, did turn his province into a social laboratory with the government trying a variety of approaches, many of which did not succeed, to give the people of Saskatchewan their due share of Canadian prosperity. His was a government that believed in planning, one that refused to accept the idea that politics had limits. As a direct result, the provincial civil service attracted able, innovative officials. They came to Regina with freshly minted degrees, and the best were sent to Harvard and elsewhere to improve their qualifications. The process was open and fresh, motivated by Douglas's Social Gospel idea that government was an instrument for positive change and social good. And the people responded, returning Douglas's CCF government to power election after election.

As socialists, the CCF worked to a fixed agenda, and inevitably that produced clashes with elements in the province who found their natural outlet in the Liberal and Conservative parties. John Diefenbaker and the federal Conservatives owned Saskatchewan after the 1958 election, but that control scarcely penetrated to the provincial level where the Tories, saddled with past history and weak leadership, did not manage to elect more than a single M.L.A. between 1956 and 1964. Wiped out federally, the Liberals nonetheless kept their provincial vote above 30 per cent and always won seats. Even so, the CCF was so dominant in the province that opposition was almost forced to take shape outside the confines of party politics and the legislature.

One such opposition group was the Saskatchewan College of Physicians and Surgeons [SCPS], the organization that represented the province's 922 doctors.[1] Saskatchewan physicians' net earnings in 1958 were on average about $12,000, a very substantial income in the 1950s, and the highest earnings in the nation for doctors. By comparison, in 1957 58 per cent of Saskatchewan breadwinners earned less than $2,500 a year and more than a third made too little to pay income tax (which began at $2,000 for the married.)[2]

Like those of almost everyone else in the province, the doctors' attitudes had been shaped by the Great Depression. The 1930s had devastated Saskatchewan. Drought dried up the crops and the unceasing winds blew the topsoil away in great dust storms. Wheat prices dropped to the lowest levels in centuries, and some farmers were reduced to eating gophers and living on the charity – infrequent – of their bankers. Even doctors, their patients reduced to penury, had been forced onto the welfare rolls, and in 1942, when the war was beginning to bring a measure of relief to the province, the SCPS had come out in favour of "state-aided health insurance on a reasonable fee-for-service-rendered basis," provided that "the administration of such an arrangement is put in the hands of a non-political independent commission on which the medical profession is adequately represented. . . ."[3]

This progressive attitude meant that Douglas's government had relatively little difficulty when, in its first days, it passed the Saskatchewan Health Services Act as a first step toward hospital insurance. Coverage for hospital charges began in 1947 (and in British Columbia and Alberta two years later), and by 1957 payments for hospital insurance were $24.3 million against receipts of $23.4 million. In Canada, of course, jurisdiction between the provinces and Ottawa is intertwined in many areas, and Paul Martin, the activist Minister of National Health and Welfare in the St. Laurent government, had long been pressing for Ottawa to move into hospital insurance. The result, just before the Liberals were defeated in June 1957, was the Hospital Insurance and Diagnostic Services Act, legislation that held out the promise of a federal contribution of 50 per cent of hospital costs – once six provinces representing a majority of the population agreed to Ottawa's terms and conditions, a qualification that blocked the act from coming into force. Prime Minister Diefenbaker called the first dominion-provincial conference of his administration in November 1957[4] and, responding to requests from Premier Douglas, announced that the six-province requirement was to be eliminated. Diefenbaker's decision allowed Saskatchewan (and the four other provinces that qualified under the act) to get federal assistance for the costs the provincial coffers alone had borne.[5] In 1959, as a result, Saskatchewan received $12.2 million from the federal government under the act, and by 1961 all the provinces had signed up for hospital insurance, a tribute to the effectiveness of the Douglas example and the federal largess.

Federal aid for hospital insurance freed enough provincial revenue to enable the Douglas government to begin to think of legislation to cover medical care costs. Medicare had been a CCF priority since the beginning, part of the 1944 platform that brought Douglas to office. But economic development took precedence, and medicare was not seriously considered until 1951 when the CCF had to conclude that the province was unable to carry the costs without federal assistance. In 1954 Douglas told a correspondent that once Ottawa picked up part of the costs of hospital insurance, the government could provide health insurance within a year.[6] That was too optimistic, but the Douglas administration was anxious to move ahead as soon as it could.

There were already private and voluntary medical insurance plans operating in Saskatchewan, as elsewhere. Medical Services Incorporated (Regina) had come into existence in 1939 and by 1950, under the name Group Medical Services, covered 87,000 people. Another group, Medical Services Incorporated (Saskatoon), had begun after the war and by 1959 had spread across the prairie to enrol 204,000. Costs averaged eighty dollars a year for a family. An additional 70,000 Saskatchewan residents were covered by other private plans. Municipal doctor plans (which used tax revenues to cover part of the costs) gathered in 107,000 more; members of the armed forces, the RCMP, native people, and others were covered by federal programmes; and public assistance recipients had their costs covered, as did another 53,000 people under the "Swift Current Plan." In 1946 the government had designated the lightly populated and under-doctored area of some 10,000 square miles around Swift Current as Health Region No. 1; it had created a twelve-person regional board with authority to supervise health services and made it responsible to a Health Services Planning Commission in Regina. Physicians were paid on a fee-for-service basis with moneys raised by a per capita tax and a small land tax. Was that socialized medicine? To some in the Canadian Medical Association [CMA], the conservative national organization of doctors, it was, and proposals to use the Swift Current model elsewhere in the province met SCPS opposition.[7]

All in all, in Saskatchewan by the end of the 1950s 610,000 persons or just about two thirds of the population were covered by some form of prepaid medical care insurance. Was provincial medicare necessary in these circumstances? To Tommy Douglas there could be no doubt about it. Private plans charged each family seventy-five to ninety dollars a year, regardless of family income, and he said, "It seems to me that this is inequitable and has no relationship whatsoever to the individual's ability to pay and as health services become more complex and as costs go up, these per capita premiums will go up with the results that there will be more and more people who are unable to participate." To the CCF it was better to have a government plan with a premium that the average family "can afford to pay." Premiums alone could not pay the costs of medicare, but general tax revenues, taking most from those best able to pay, would meet the remainder.[8] It was, in other words, CCF ideology that drove Premier Douglas towards a head-on clash with the individualistic, free-enterprise beliefs of the province's physicians.

Work on a medicare plan began in earnest in November 1958 when Douglas's government met for its Cabinet Conference on Planning and Budgeting. At these innovative annual sessions, the government's ministers and officials presented their "forward planning proposals" for the next year, and at the 1958 meeting medicare was discussed. The ministers realized that they faced major negotiations with the SCPS and considerable resistance had to be anticipated. In theory, the cabinet believed the doctors should be salaried, but no one doubted the unacceptability of this to the college – unless the salary was sky-high. In the circumstances, a recommendation for a pooled fund and a fee-for-service basis of payment was adopted.[9]

That was the beginning, and on April 25, 1959, just after a Cabinet Planning Board conference had set up an interdepartmental committee to study medicare, Premier Douglas told a by-election meeting in Birch Hills that he looked to a "complete health-care program" operating in a way similar to the hospital insurance plan. No date was fixed, and Douglas added that it was likely medicare would require universal coverage and a premium paid by individuals.

The SCPS was quick to react, pointing out that no one had asked the doctors of the province their opinion about medicare.[10] At a council meeting later that year, the SCPS decided to seek a "private audience" with the Premier to find out what he had in mind. At the same time, the council agreed to employ writers, economists, and public relations experts to prepare a campaign "should the Provincial Government come out with a health scheme."[11]

What Douglas had in mind, or so he told the SCPS representatives on October 14, was to bring in legislation in 1960 and to put medicare into operation the next year. "At present," as the College's minutes tell the story, "the thinking was that doctors would be paid on a fee for service basis" and there would be no ceiling on their incomes. Most important, the Premier offered assurances that "he would not put any plan into operation without consulting the profession and obtaining their cooperation." But when the SCPS council met the representatives of the CMA on October 18 and 19, the provincial body was urged to proceed cautiously and to resist medicare by establishing a policy of its own, by carefully preparing publicity, perhaps by suggesting a plebiscite to the people, and by supporting the existing voluntary prepaid plans. Moreover, the SCPS should "by all means keep up the negotiations, so that the profession might be able to practise under Government plans if and when brought in." That did not sound very militant, and Dr. E.W. Barootes of Regina, a council member, "emphatically" argued that "the profession must not surrender to Government sponsored and controlled compulsory prepaid medical care. . . ."[12]

The doctors of Saskatchewan evidently had changed their minds since the Depression and the resolution of their college in 1942. Twenty years of prosperity had removed the fear of economic uncertainty from the profession, and fifteen years of socialist government had helped to create a defensive mentality. The physicians saw themselves as individualists, self-made men who worked hard, saved lives, and had earned their position of prestige in their communities. Now the Douglas government was prepared to overlook their needs and to ram the regimentation of state medicine down their throats. Moreover, the SCPS Council declared at a special meeting, medicare would have serious negative effects:

1. There is over-demand for services.
2. Paper work involved robs the doctor of valuable time.
3. By example: the standards in countries where such plans have been brought in, are not so good.
4. It would violate the doctor-patient relationship.
5. Doctors practising under this hardship would tend to leave the area and go where they could practise under more favourable conditions. . . .
6. There would be possibility that some of the leading men would leave. . . .
7. This climate (under a plan) would be less attractive to doctors who were seeking a new location.
8. The doctor's satisfaction in his work would be missing.[13]

Essentially, the doctors believed that standards were certain to deteriorate because demand would swamp resources. They worried that specialists might leave the province and that they would become paper-pushing bureaucrats. And they feared that their province might get a system like that of Britain's National Health Service, which, according to the SCPS, meant assembly-line medicine. Moreover, the doctors argued, there were already needs of much greater importance than medicare, notably care for the chronically and mentally ill and the requirements of existing hospitals.[14]

But to the government, in receipt of its interdepartmental committee report in late November 1959, medicare was to be "a major objective of a new term of office . . . a social and political instrument for achieving a better integrated, co-operative society and a wider acceptance of the social and moral values inherent in the concept of community responsibility for individual needs."[15] The government also set up an advisory planning committee to study medicare further, and on November 27 Dr. W.P. Thompson, president emeritus of the University of Saskatchewan, agreed to be chairman. "The Government will accept the full responsibility for the decision to proceed," Douglas told Thompson, adding, "I am convinced that if we can make such a program operate successfully in Saskatchewan, within ten years it will be copied in almost every other province in Canada."[16]

Douglas went to the people with his detailed proposals in a radio talk on December 16. Five principles had to govern any plan, he said. First was prepayment – medical care should be paid on an insurance basis. Next, there must be universal coverage, and third, a high quality of care. Fourth, the programme had to be government-sponsored and administered by a public body responsible to the legislature. Finally, and ultimately of most importance in the struggle to come, Douglas said that the programme must be "*acceptable both to those providing the service and those receiving it.*" The advisory committee, he added, would include three representatives named by the medical profession and three by government; there would be three representatives of the general public and one appointee from the university's medical school.[17] The announcement was popularly viewed as a prelude to an election. The government had last gone to the polls in 1956, and a 1960 election, after Douglas's broadcast, was certain. The medicare issue would be fought out in the campaign.

II

The SCPS initially was dubious about the Thompson advisory committee. Douglas had made clear that the committee was to produce a plan that fitted his guidelines and protected the interests of doctors and patients. In other words, the effective decision to proceed with medicare had already been taken. Not unnaturally, that upset the college, and the doctors were loath to participate. Suspicion about the government's good faith was growing, and one strategy of the SCPS, in keeping with its earlier statements about more pressing areas of concern, was to demand that the advisory committee study the whole field of health care, which Premier Douglas eventually conceded in writing on March 15, 1960. The Deputy Minister of Public Health warned Douglas, "As I see the strategy of the profession it is to delay action on a medical care program."[18] That was the strategy; nonetheless, on March 29 the SCPS named its three members to the Thompson committee.

Meanwhile the college was raising the money for a major public relations campaign against the government. The SCPS council voted to make $20,000 available to a special committee on public relations for the next six weeks and decided to levy a special assessment of one hundred dollars on each college member. When word of this leaked out, the college president declared that there was no political purpose behind the move – the sole aim was to fund a Medical Information Centre in Regina where "medical data is being researched, compiled and co-ordinated prior to distribution to responsible individuals and organizations" and to employ a full-time public relations officer. The council minutes were more frank – the levy was to be used to "resist Government-controlled medicine." All in all the levy raised $60,411. Moreover, the CMA was asked to match dollar for dollar the money raised in Saskatchewan, and the national body eventually contributed $35,000.[19]

The college's special committee, chaired by Dr. John Leishman, was responsible to the council, and its first act was to prepare a statement of policy. The people of Saskatchewan, the committee draft affirmed, must have the right to determine if they wished to prepay the cost of physicians' services, to choose the insuring company, and to determine the comprehensiveness of coverage. Moreover, the citizen had to have freedom to choose doctor and hospital, the right of recourse to the courts in all disputes, and freedom to choose the method by which he prepaid or paid for medical care. And the individual doctor had to have the right to choose the location of his practice, freedom to accept or reject a patient, and freedom to choose to participate in any insurance plan or not, as well as to determine his method of remuneration.[20]

More practically, the Leishman committee was creating an organization. A central committee was to direct the battle and provide direction to the public relations experts. A medical relations committee was to establish liaison with the private medical plans in the province and with individual doctors, using a "key-man" set-up that allowed rapid mobilization. A community relations committee was established to work with ethnic, religious, fraternal, and church groups and to provide doctors who could use persuasion on leaders of such groups. A publicity committee had as its main task, the special committee chairman noted, "to suppress information in the Press or debate in the Press." As the election, scheduled for June 1960, approached, the publicity committee's function changed to press liaison and to considering the possibility of buying TV and radio time. There was also an economics committee that was to collect data and prepare pamphlets for distribution through doctor's offices. Finally, a special projects committee had a variety of tasks, one being to unify the medical profession. "We must remember," the special committee chairman said, "that one of the main weapons which the Premier uses is to divide and conquer. . . . He will try to divide the rural practitioner against the general practitioner . . . the specialist against the general practitioner." The SCPS had to prevent that.

The SCPS saw its task as to "once again establish a democratic way of life in this Province. It is important the the rights of minorities be protected. It is important that government centralization, government power and government bureaucracy be removed." That was a clever tack, playing on fears about the coercive power of socialism, for the college was in difficulty attacking a medicare scheme still on the drawing boards. "The fact that the organized body of the Profession cannot wage a war against the scheme . . . does not prevent the profession . . . from coming out and supporting the idea of abhorrence of government bureaucracy, government centralization of power and government disrespect for the wishes and rights of minorities."[21]

For all their organization and planning, the province's doctors failed to take control of the election campaign issues or even to influence the political struggle decisively. A TV debate took place on March 20 between Premier Douglas and Dr. Barootes, the ablest medical spokesman in the province, but although the doctor set out the case against medicare, he was hampered, as he admitted, by the difficulties "of a doctor inexperienced in political debate or public speaking" in following the "polished oratory of a gifted speaker" such as Douglas.[22] There were radio and newspaper advertisements, mailings to all householders, TV panel discussions between doctors opposed to medicare, and letters sent to selected opinion leaders and women asking them to think what "state Medicine might mean to you and your family," what it could do to "your personal relationship with your personal doctor,'' and how it could affect ''your personal household budgets.'' A kit was also given the newspapers: ''What will happen if British doctors pull out of the province en masse?'' one flyer in that kit asked. ''They will have to fill the profession with the garbage of Europe.'' Another said that ''a government-controlled plan offers a latent but potential threat to certain dogmas of the Catholic Church,'' a hint that Tommy Douglas's medicare might enforce birth control and allow abortion on demand. These campaign tactics undoubtedly hurt the doctors and helped the government. So too did the SCPS Council's vote to ask doctors ''to refuse to service'' medicare if it passed the legislature, even though the doctors also agreed ''to continue to serve the patient as we do today. . . .''[23]

The doctors' hopes were diminished further by the position of the Liberal party. Led by Ross Thatcher, a lapsed CCFer, the Liberals did not oppose medicare. Instead the leader said that ''if the people want it, a Liberal government will establish [medicare] immediately, universally, for all the people.'' All Thatcher would concede was that a plebiscite could be used to determine the will of the voters. That was cold comfort for the SCPS. So was Tommy Douglas's assault on the SCPS campaign as ''abominable, despicable and scurrilous.''[24]

Douglas won the election handily, the CCF being returned with more seats than in 1956, an undoubted mandate to proceed with medicare. In the June 8 poll, Douglas took thirty-eight seats to the Liberals' seventeen, and the CCF won 41.3 per cent of the popular vote, a very good showing in a four-party race (Liberals, 33.1 per cent, Conservatives, 14.1 per cent, and Social Credit, 11.2 per cent). The victorious premier was quick to tell the press that earlier suggestions by the media that the government would not proceed with medicare unless it got a majority of the popular vote were incorrect. ''No such statement was ever made by me. . . . The CCF shall have the largest number of seats in the new Legislature and we shall take this as a mandate to proceed with the program upon which we were elected.''[25]

That was an unassailable statement in the light of parliamentary practice, and even some doctors seemed to agree. The General Secretary of the CMA, Dr. Arthur Kelly, said that as there could be no doubt about the result, the CMA would cease its opposition to medicare in Saskatchewan. ''This is democracy,'' Kelly said. ''The C.M.A. accepts the decision in this light. Our efforts will now be bent on avoiding the defects we see in government plans elsewhere.'' But the SCPS was not moved by the result of the election or Kelly's comments: the college remained ''unalterably opposed'' to medicare.[26] The battle was just beginning.

III

If there were splits between the CMA and SCPS positions, they were quickly papered over. The CMA met in convention at Banff a few days after the election and, after upbraiding Kelly for his comments, adopted a fourteen-point statement on medical services insurance that noted that "a tax-supported comprehensive program, compulsory for all, is neither necessary nor desirable." The CMA's principles, however, did not rule out state medicine as long as it adhered to the organization's demands: the right of doctors to choose their patients; the right of recourse to the courts in all disputes; the separation of the administration and financing of medicare from other programmes and the fiscal autonomy of any agency set up to run medicare; and the right of doctors to determine their method of payment.[27] The SCPS representatives had no difficulty in accepting the CMA principles, a decision probably helped by the national body's promise of continuing financial support. The SCPS estimated its expenses to the end of 1960 at $110,000, of which $46,000 was to cover costs of preparing a brief to the Thompson committee. Expenses for 1961 were estimated at $81,000, and the CMA, expected to match the money raised in Saskatchewan, came through, agreeing to put up $95,000.[28]

In fact, the college's special committee wound up operations in July 1960, probably because its propaganda during the election had attracted so much criticism in Saskatchewan and around the nation. To continue its work, the SCPS created a steering committee of four, headed by Dr. J.F.C. Anderson and including as a member Dr. H.D. Dalgleish, the new SCPS president.[29]

By the fall of 1960, echoing a long-standing CMA policy, the college had recognized that some Saskatchewan residents could not afford medical care. As a result, "the profession would welcome a decision by Government to pay for these" through the existing voluntary plans.[30] That was recognition of the difficulties the indigent caused the medical profession. But to suggest that the government pay the tab through the private plans was certain to be contentious, particularly as the SCPS proposal meant an increase in doctors' incomes at government expense. The press, however, cheered the doctors, the Regina *Leader-Post* noting that the recommendation met the government's desire to help those who could least afford medical care without creating a "grandiose state edifice which would saddle taxpayers with a heavy financial load."[31]

There were also pressures of another sort on Tommy Douglas. The proposal to create a new political party from a merger of the CCF with organized labour had been gaining support since 1959. But there was serious concern from those who feared labour's influence, and this opposition was particularly strong in Saskatchewan, the province with the most vigorous farmers' organizations. The infighting was fierce enough that Douglas felt obliged to ask CCF stalwarts around the country in March 1960 for a moratorium on the intraparty fights until after his June election. That request was largely successful, but once the decision was made to create a new party, Douglas, the most successful socialist politician in Canadian history, came under immediate pressure to become leader. Although Douglas's instinctive response was to stay in Regina, by March 1961 he was beginning to change his mind, and on June 28, he announced that he would seek the leadership.[32] In August, Douglas was the overwhelming choice of the delegates, the first leader of the New Democratic Party. There were a few months to wrap up in his work in Regina, but an era had ended in Saskatchewan.

Part of Douglas's wrapping-up was medicare. Indeed, critics had begun to charge in the spring of 1961 that medicare was simply an issue that was being used to propel Douglas to the national stage.[33] In June, the Minister of Public Health, J.W. Erb, asked the Thompson committee, slowly studying the whole field of health care, to submit quickly an interim report on medicare. But, as Erb's deputy minister told him, medicare could not be in place before July 1, 1962.[34]

The interim report was handed to the minister on September 27. The majority called for a general comprehensive and prepaid medicare scheme, administered by a public commission responsible to the government through the Minister of Public Health. The plan was to be universal in application, financed by premiums, and doctors were to be paid on a fee-for-service basis with patients being responsible for a small portion of the fee at the time of service. The administrative commission was to have a chairman and from four to six members. Subject only to the approval of the Lieutenant-Governor-in-Council, the commission was to have the power to draft regulations for the plan.

A dissenting report, filed by the SCPS representatives and another committee member, argued that the majority's plan would result in a state monopoly that would worsen the quality of medical care. The labour representative on the committee also filed a dissent, calling for doctors to be salaried, a proposal even more objectionable to the doctors than the majority recommendation.[35]

The government had already worked out the cost of medicare. Provincial Treasurer Woodrow Lloyd told the government caucus on September 28 that the plan was to be financed by the premium (twenty-four dollars a year for a family), a 2-per-cent sales tax increase, a 6-per-cent increase in personal income tax, and a 1-per-cent increase in corporation tax. The total to be raised was $21.1 million to which could be added the $900,000 spent on medical payments by the social welfare and health departments. Medicare, in other words, was to cost $22 million a year.[36] The government bill to create the plan was introduced on October 13 – without any previous direct consultation with the SCPS – and, with a few changes, it closely followed the Thompson committee recommendations. There was no utilization fee, and the method of paying the doctors was unspecified, both matters being left to the soon-to-be-established Medical Care Insurance Commission [MCIC] to determine by regulation. The Liberals in the legislature supported the bill in principle, voting for it on second reading, but the Opposition objected to details of the bill and to the government's unwillingness to accept amendments and voted against medicare on final reading. With only this limited resistance, medicare passed into law on November 18, 1961.

The SCPS was unshaken in its determination to resist. A college newsletter to members noted that while some aspects of the Thompson recommendations looked attractive, there was no guarantee they would be maintained. "In fact, many of the so-called concessions made by committee members may be regarded as temporary expedients to ensure acceptance of a plan which can be modified after our acceptance. . . ."[37] That did not indicate any willingness to trust to the good faith of the government. And at the SCPS meetings in October, the steering committee chairman summed up the Thompson report and the medicare bill as imposing "A State monopoly of medical services, Rigid State control of the Commission" and providing no assurance that the voluntary plans could survive, no enactment of fee for service, and no assurance that "medical care will be free from political interference and influence." The college's membership quickly voted to reiterate their refusal to accept medicare. The doctors of Saskatchewan would not co-operate with the plan; they would continue to give service to their patients, but they would sign no individual contracts to service an overall medicare plan.[38]

On November 7, Woodrow Lloyd was sworn in as Tommy Douglas's successor. A teacher, an able and experienced politician although not one readily able to compromise, Lloyd lacked Douglas's oratorical skills and, what was more important, did not have his predecessor's sense of political timing. Lloyd was able and decent; that he was not as sure-footed as his mentor was a misfortune.

The new premier's first task was to get the SCPS to the bargaining table. At the end of November, W.G. Davies, Lloyd's choice to succeed Erb as Health minister, talked with Dr. Dalgleish on the telephone, only to be stalled. Moreover, as Davies recorded, the SCPS did not wish to talk about the act. "It would have to be some program 'within our principles.' "[39] The SCPS was equally firm in its private discussions, the council deciding just before Christmas that the repeal of the Medicare Act was a *sine qua non*, a message conveyed to Davies.[40] The stalemate continued.

Dr. Dalgleish added a new element when he told the press in January 1962 that many of the province's doctors were being made aware of opportunities elsewhere. There might be difficulty replacing them with others trained in Canada, he said. This was the first time that the possibility of an exodus from the province had been raised. There was in the statement a muted suggestion that only foreigners would come to Moose Jaw to replace the departing native born and the hint that the quality of medical care would decline or might even become unavailable if the emigration turned into a flood. Significantly, at the time Dalgleish spoke to the press, the SCPS had no hard data on the likely number of departures. Five months later when data were finally gathered to demonstrate that only a small number were seeking work outside the province, the scare campaign, far from ceasing, intensified.[41]

Meanwhile, the opposition to direct negotiations continued. The college remained adamant, refusing offers of meetings in December 1961 and with the MCIC in February 1962. Not until March 2 when the Minister of Public Health again sought a meeting, this time stating that the government "is willing to discuss the Act and to consider specific changes if it can be demonstrated that they are required to protect the medical profession's legitimate interests" was there the slightest break in the SCPS's cold front. Dalgleish said the college was willing to meet if the changes contemplated would "permit the implementation of our recommendations" to eliminate medicare. They were not, but Davies, on the instructions of the Cabinet, called a meeting for March 28: "It is proposed that the agenda be left open. Attendance at this meeting would be without prejudice to the previously stated positions or conditions on either side."[42] On that basis, the government and the SCPS met at last on March 28, 1962, in Regina.

The college arrived determined to force the withdrawal of the act. Dalgleish presented a proposal that called for the use of the existing voluntary plans for self-supporting citizens and the provision of assistance from public funds for those who were not. Such a plan, the doctor argued, satisfied the five conditions laid down by Douglas in 1959, most notably the last about acceptability to those receiving and providing the service. According to the SCPS summary of the meeting, Deputy Premier J.H. Brockelbank said that the act "could be discarded and new provisions prepared if the Government's principles were not violated.''[43]

That seemed a ray of hope, and when the college council and steering committee met on March 31, a detailed outline of the doctors' proposals was accepted. The doctors carried this with them when they met with the Cabinet once more on April 1, not the most appropriate of days. The ministers listened, then presented their own memorandum as a basis for discussion. This paper detailed changes in the legislation to enhance local participation, provide additional safeguards to the profession, and establish a mechanism for payment of the doctors. The ministers also said they could change the composition of the MCIC. But Dalgleish brushed aside the government proposals on the grounds that they included retention of the act, which remained completely unacceptable. When the Premier suggested that, as July 1, 1962, was the start-up date for medicare, some interim arrangement should be implemented, the doctors, while unenthusiastic, at least did agree to look at detailed proposals.[44] The parties decided to meet again on April 11.

There had been some movement, but thus far it was all on the government's side. Allan Blakeney, the Provincial Treasurer, scribbled a query to himself to ask, ''Do we accept the principle that the plan be acceptable to the doctors?'' His answer was: ''We accept our obligation to strive to arrive at a plan acceptable to the doctors. We cannot accept the proposition that the College has the right to veto any plan on the grounds that it is 'not acceptable' without defining *with precision* the reasons *in full* as to why the plan approved by the Legislature is not acceptable.''[45] That suggested that the government's patience was not unlimited.

The SCPS came to the April 11 meeting with an eight-point proposal that was, government officials observed, ''even less satisfactory than the original'' because it gave the voluntary plans the right to determine the premium to be charged the indigent, the aged, and the chronically ill, over and above the government subsidy. The college brief also argued that the Medicare Act controlled the physicians, and the Premier took sharp exception to that, adding that the SCPS position did not satisfy the government's principles. After an adjournment, Lloyd returned to the conference room to say that the SCPS proposals were inferior to the service provided by the voluntary plans and therefore inadequate. ''It is the intention of the Government to proceed to introduce a Medical Care Insurance Plan designed to meet the needs of our citizens.''[46] As Health minister Davies noted, the government had little choice. To accept the college plan meant that the best features of the act had to go. There could be no control of costs or of expanding administrative structures, and it would be a betrayal of the federal NDP's policy and of the concept of public health. At the same time Davies did not underestimate the SCPS. To refuse the doctors' demands meant a long struggle that might be lost and that could endanger the government's position.[47] That appraisal was essentially correct, and certainly the provincial newspapers assailed the Lloyd government for the collapse of the negotiations. "This is a matter in which the Freedoms are involved," the *Star-Phoenix* said on April 18. "One could ask, who's next for the guillotine? This fear is concerning other groups in Saskatchewan."

Both sides continued to press. The SCPS called a special meeting of members for May 3 and 4. The government amended the Medicare Act, giving the MCIC the right to take legal action on behalf of a beneficiary in a dispute about payment and to offer payment to a doctor providing services under the act. The amendments also permitted patients to "contract out" for a "particular insured service" but did not relieve them of the necessity to support medicare through premiums and taxes. The net effect, according to the SCPS, was "a further tightening of the control measures on patients and physicians" and, the college newsletter argued, "Some have claimed these amendments mean 'complete conscription of doctors' . . . [and] 'vicious compulsion'. . . ."[48] The government position was that the amendments were necessary to protect patients by preventing doctors from billing them and boycotting the plan.*

The SCPS special meeting on May 3 and 4 was attended by more than six hundred doctors and began with an address by the Premier, who had asked for the privilege of playing Daniel in the lion's den. Lloyd was received politely for most of his talk as he traced the origins and intentions of the act. But when he said that attacks on the integrity of government as an institution could undermine the foundations of liberty, there was jeering. Lloyd also spoke of Douglas's principles of 1959 and the promise that the plan would be acceptable to the doctors, saying, ". . . neither you nor the Government, or the news media

* The billing question was critical. A representative of the Quebec College of Physicians and Surgeons testifying in 1962 before the Royal Commission on Health Services set up by the federal government talked of the doctor-patient relationship involved in direct billing. "What contact?" Commissioner Emmett Hall asked. "Taking a dollar from his pocket and giving it to the doctor?" It was hard to explain, the doctor said. It was a matter of sentiment, of harmony between doctor and patient, which must be continued. "What if the patient merely mailed the cheque?" Hall asked. "The very gesture would be important," was the reply. (*Montreal Star*, 14 April 1962.)

can, in conscience, look at one of these principles or at part of one of them while ignoring all the others.'' Lloyd asked that the college give medicare a fair chance, but the doctors were not accommodating. Bolstered by the announcement, apparently timed to coincide with Lloyd's speech, of the resignation from the Cabinet of the former Health minister, J.W. Erb, the college was in no mood for concessions. At the end of the Premier's address, Dr. Dalgleish asked the members at the meeting ''who opposed the M.C.I.A. and its amendments and do not intend to participate under the Act'' to stand. ''The assembly rose and applauded. Dr. Dalgleish then asked those that approved of the M.C.I.A. . . . to arise. Several members stood.''[49] The Premier could be in no doubt of the mood of the doctors.

After Lloyd had left, the doctors got down to the serious business of deciding what to do when the act came into operation on July 1. Many resolutions were discussed, but the central one, carried with only two opposed and three in abstention, said that the implementation of medicare ''will prevent all doctors from providing services to patients from that day forward.'' The doctors had voted for a strike, their only concession to the needs of the people being a decision to ''set up arrangements to provide emergency services for patients.''[50] If the province had broken its pledge to produce a plan acceptable to the doctors, the doctors now were violating their promises to continue to care for their patients. The council also urged all doctors not to speak to the press, particularly as a federal election campaign was under way and the medicare question was important in all Saskatchewan ridings and especially in Tommy Douglas's Regina-City constituency. The paradox, as Ralph Allen noted in *Maclean's*, was that doctors, furiously rejecting ''dictatorship'' from without, ''accept dictatorship from within. They'll only talk when authorized.''[51]

The federal election increased the tension in the province. The press, still markedly hostile to the Medicare Act, increased its attacks, and citizens' groups were being formed to ''Keep Our Doctors.'' (By July there was also ''Save Our Saskatchewan,'' a response by businessmen, Opposition political figures, and ordinary people to the fear that hundreds of doctors might leave.) The threat of a doctors' strike greatly increased the concern. About all the Cabinet could do to avoid adding to Douglas's difficulties and those of the national party was to urge caucus members to stress that medicare was ''a question of the rights of people versus monopoly.'' The MLAS, caucus was told, should start urging their supporters to withdraw from the voluntary medical plans. At the same time, Cabinet struck a committee to manage the confrontation with the SCPS. Four tired men, Lloyd, Davies, Brockelbank, and Blakeney, were to carry the load and to decide, among other things, which of the many mediators offering to resolve the dispute should be heard. The Cabinet agreed that the act could not be withdrawn, although additional "safeguards" for the doctors remained possible. But although that sounded firm, Lloyd may have been beginning to wobble. In a memo to his MLAS and federal candidates, the Premier asked, ". . . how much punishment can the people take? How much can we justifiably expose them to? How much of the severe local criticism can you take?. . . In the face of [the threat of a doctors' strike] do we still stand where we said we did?"[52]

The federal election results on June 18 increased the wavering. The Diefenbaker government, although battered nationally, held sixteen of seventeen seats in Saskatchewan while the Liberals took the other. Douglas was beaten in Regina, his new party shut out in the province, and the NDP popular vote fell by 6 per cent from the total the CCF had received in the disastrous year of 1958. It was a rout, a sure sign, the doctors crowed, that the public was with them.

Yet the impact on medicare was surprisingly slight. Despite the election débâcle, the government stayed firm, bolstered by the markedly unfavourable reaction the doctors' position was receiving across the country if not in the Saskatchewan media.[53] To the *Leader-Post* the government was "power drunk," but to *Saturday Night* in Toronto, "the doctors look to be determined to protect privilege more than principle and if they think their presently closely-guarded profession is above the will of the people, they are in for a rude shock."[54] In essence, those were the positions, sharply different, of the press inside and outside the province.

Meanwhile, the SCPS prepared its emergency service plans. While doctors' offices were to be closed after July 1, patients in need of emergency service could go to twenty-nine hospitals where one of the 239 physicians required to run the emergency service would see them. Patients were to be charged no fee for this service, and the doctors were to draw $450 a week and an accommodation allowance for their work in the emergency service. The emergency hospitals, as well as the ninety-five that were to be shut during the strike, would have to send patients home or make special arrangements for those who could not be released. In other words, discretionary medical services and elective surgery were to cease well before July 1.[55] The strike was certain to pose a major crisis for the province, and the government sent Dr. Samuel Wolfe, a member of the MCIC, to recruit doctors in England.[56] The CMA, scenting victory after the federal election results, urged the government to renew negotiations with the SCPS (which Lloyd had tried to do on June 7) and said that the passage of the act had already "resulted in serious impairment of medical care . . . implementation will accelerate this deterioration to disastrous proportions." The act was "completely unacceptable to the doctors of Canada," the CMA said, announcing that it had set up a fund to assist Saskatchewan physicians. The general secretary, Dr. Kelly, did call for "give and take," suggesting that the SCPS would "be reasonable in making an agreement which would not completely cause the Government to lose face."[57] The CMA evidently did not intend to play a mediatory role.

The government and the SCPS met from June 22 to 25 in a last attempt to find a way out of the crisis. The college's position remained unaltered – the Medicare Act had to be scuppered and replaced with new legislation based on the doctors' plan, although the SCPS now was willing to agree that medicare, provided it were run through the voluntary plans, be available to all residents on payment of a premium. The Cabinet said that while each and every section of the act was open to discussion, it still did not know precisely what amendments were thought necessary by the college. If the negotiations did not succeed by July 1, Lloyd said, "then we suggest that the College withhold its proposal to have its members withdraw their services and we will continue the process of mediation and negotiation."[58]

Over the four days of discussion, the government made changes that would allow doctors in private practice to bill patients directly, and it offered additional professional safeguards. It specifically conceded the right of physicians to practise outside the plan.[59] But the SCPS rejected these olive branches, which had been part of their own position in April, saying that their legal adviser had indicated that it was "virtually impossible" to work outside the act. The doctors clearly believed that the government was on the run; if they could keep the strike threat alive, the Lloyd government would have to cave in and withdraw the act.

Despite last minute mediation efforts by representatives of the Saskatchewan Urban Municipalities Association,[60] the two sides failed to arrive at a settlement. How could they? The government, while weakening, was committed to retaining the act; the SCPS was committed to its elimination. On Sunday, July 1, therefore, doctors' services ceased to be available except in the designated emergency hospitals. And when Canadians picked up their newspapers on the day after the Dominion Day holiday, front-page stories reported the death of an infant after his parents had driven ninety miles in a search for medical help. "They knocked in vain at hospitals and surgeries closed by the 900 doctors who have suspended practice . . ." the newspapers said.[61] And when the province's pharmacists tried to mediate, the SCPS rejected further talks until "this unjust and monopolistic act is withdrawn."[62]

Thus each party waited for the other to crack. There were government gestures on July 6 when Deputy Premier Brockelbank told the press that "if the doctors would resume practice . . . the Government might be willing to discuss revising of the law" and to recall the legislature. Dr. Kelly of the CMA responded by saying that a special session of the legislature was "a step in the right direction," but that it could not change the situation "unless it is preceded by discussions to make amendments satisfactory" – and that had to be preceded by the suspension of the Medicare Act. That was not exactly conciliatory; nor was Brockelbank's letter to Dalgleish on July 6 that summarized the concessions the government had made at the end of June and added, "I am puzzled as to why your Council cannot see fit to recommend to your members that medical services be restored immediately. . . ."[63]

While both sides dug in, the out-of-province comments grew more critical of the SCPS and its CMA ally. The *Globe and Mail*, not ordinarily a supporter of socialist governments, lashed out at the doctors for their demand that the act be repealed. "This is a dangerous stand. . . . Were the Government to suspend the Act, which was properly passed by a properly elected Legislature it would be denying the responsibility of government in a democracy, and yielding to the pressure of a special interest group." A few days later, the Toronto paper defined the issue: ". . . not medicare but democracy."[64] The newspaper was precisely correct.

The government was under pressure too, and from within the province. In the first place, there were the ordinary people, frightened of what might happen to their families and friends in the event of a medical emergency. The farms and small towns were especially vulnerable with available emergency care often far away. Replacement doctors or doctors operating under the act – there were ninety-seven on July 9 – were being denied hospital privileges or, if from the United Kingdom, being made to wait for certification from the SCPS, a necessity before they could practise.[65] There was the added pressure that even faithful NDPers often looked to the family doctor as a wise counsellor, and there was a tendency to believe that the doctor knew best. The Keep Our Doctors organization issued a call for a mass rally at the legislature grounds on July 11. The KOD told the press that it could get from 30,000 to 50,000 people out, and if it had been able to carry that off, it is highly possible that the government might have had to sue for peace. But the KOD rally was a great disappointment to its organizers, no more than 4,000 showing up to wave placards and shout at the Lloyd government – a hard blow to the SCPS and its supporters who maintained that the people were with them.[66]

Still, the strike weighed on the Cabinet. There were suggestions that an impartial royal commission be set up to look at the whole matter, and among the suggested names for commissioner were Vincent Massey and Louis St. Laurent.[67] There were self-appointed mediators shuttling between the two sides, including Dean Otto Lang of the university law school.[68] There was the sentiment among some members of the Cabinet strategy committee that the government had to stand firm and reject mediation. But this, ministers noted, "would require a careful calculation of our ability to provide adequate medical services (over and above the emergency services) for what could be a relatively prolonged period."[69] That could not be guaranteed, and at best, the ministers decided on July 9, they had ten days to two weeks.[70]

At this stage the name of a possible adviser/mediator surfaced. This was Lord Taylor, a British labour peer and medical doctor who was friendly with Graham Spry, Saskatchewan's representative in London, and who had expressed some views on the act to Spry. "I had not even heard that there was a doctors' strike impending," Taylor wrote later, "and he sought my advice on the Act. . . ." One clause offended Taylor and he told Spry so. " 'Put it in writing,' he said, 'and send it to the Premier of Saskatchewan.' I did so and thought no more about it. Then a few weeks later I received an invitation to visit Saskatchewan and advise the Government on what ought to be done."[71] Taylor had been involved in planning Britain's National Health Service, but he had criticized aspects of it sharply in recent years. In a curious way, therefore, he was acceptable to both sides, but at best the peer was operating with an uncertain mandate.

The wild card was needed nonetheless. As late as July 9, the SCPS was still demanding that Premier Lloyd withdraw the act, although Dalgleish now proposed that a mediator "work towards a type of Medical Care Insurance Program and Act which each could accept . . ." and which would permit the voluntary plans to continue to enrol subscribers. That was almost no concession at all, something Lloyd pointed out in his reply, again noting that doctors were not obliged to practise under the act.[72] Dalgleish returned on July 14, significantly after the KOD fiasco, to suggest that the act be suspended "for a limited and specified time" to allow negotiation, probably for a month. But Lloyd saw the flaw: "What would happen if no agreement were reached at the end of the specified time period?" The college would ask for an extension, and that could stretch *ad infinitum*. "The Government is concerned," the Premier added, reiterating the strongest point in the province's favour, "that your members have not accepted the fact that they are free to practise privately. The Government is publicly committed to take whatever steps are necessary to guarantee and safeguard that right.'' But the SCPS legal advisers, including Dean Lang, had told Dalgleish that doctors outside the act were still subject to the control of the MCIC because of its discretion in paying bills. The changes to the act made in June, Dalgleish said, were ''really meaningless.''[73]

Meanwhile Taylor arrived in Regina on July 16 to find charges and counter-charges in the press on the subject of the harassment by striking physicians of outside doctors working in the province. A few days earlier Lloyd had announced his intention of setting up a royal commission to investigate these charges, and one American doctor claimed that the SCPS threatened him with jail. ''I thought I was complying with the law and the Government assured me I was within my rights,'' he said. ''I came to help people. . . .'' Lloyd publicly apologized to the doctor. For Taylor, it must all have been very puzzling. He told the press there was nothing in the act to make the practice of medicine more difficult. ''But I could be wrong. I want to see what the doctors say about it. I am trying to be impartial. . . .''[74]

Perhaps it was Taylor's presence that led Dr. Dalgleish to appear at the NDP provincial convention in Saskatoon on July 18 to address the delegates. The SCPS president defined the issue as freedom and claimed majority support in the province, a position that was much less credible after the KOD rally on July 11. But he did suggest some crucial modifications in the college's position. No longer was there a demand that the act be scrapped, hitherto the critical point. Now the college wanted specific changes to allow the medicare plan and the voluntary agencies to exist together. Doctors, Dalgleish said, had to be guaranteed the right to practise outside the act, and medical services provided by such doctors should not become insured services until the beneficiary applied to the MCIC for a refund. In addition, the beneficiary should have the right to assign this payment from the MCIC to a voluntary insurance agency that would also be recognized as a collector of premiums. That was a major breakthrough.[75]

Over the next five days, the two sides bargained through Taylor who shuttled back and forth between the Cabinet and the college. ''My first job,'' Taylor said, ''was to get the doctors' confidence. . . . The theory I was working on was don't let these chaps meet because if they do there will be misunderstanding. . . . So I had to keep them apart. I had to keep in my head the thought of what each side was saying. . . . It was by this time perfectly clear what the issues were and what the points of division were. They weren't really very big by now. . . .'' As Taylor knew, a clear, written document was essential. After a few days of cut and paste, Taylor had a draft that he showed to the Cabinet and then to the SCPS. ''I wouldn't let them get hold of this thing. . . . I knew if anybody held it other than me they'd start mucking about and worrying it. I read it to them . . . fairly quickly so they could see it was beginning to be sense and then I took it paragraph by paragraph." The SCPS objections then went back to the ministers. By now it was Saturday, July 21, and Taylor told the college negotiators he was through. "I'm fed up with this, I'm utterly fed to the teeth. Either you agree or I'm off. They begged me to stay," and Taylor conceded, agreeing to one more day. The next day it was virtually settled, thanks to Taylor's temper tantrum. "I swore and raved and then had to apologize . . . for the scene I had made."* The so-called Saskatoon agreement was signed on July 23.[76]

The settlement gave the SCPS most of the points Dalgleish had asked for in his address to the NDP convention, points Lloyd could accept because they were ones that fitted within the act. The one difference was that the SCPS won the right to have the voluntary plans continue to operate in partnership with the MCIC, even if the doctors did not secure the private agencies the right to collect premiums. But that too was satisfactory, as Blakeney wrote, because there was only a minor place for the agencies and the final agreement put the government "in a better position than we were in immediately after our reimbursement offer of June 25th."[77] The SCPS proudly told its members that the Saskatoon agreement allowed them the right to practise "completely *outside*" the act, permitted the continuation of the voluntary agencies, and that amendments to the act would remove the "major control sections."[78]

Both sides had won, or so they seemed to believe. The *Globe and Mail* felt that the settlement gave the doctors more than the government and "might be viewed as a complete victory for the doctors except that it establishes that to which they were most opposed – the first government-sponsored medical insurance plan on this continent."[79] That was the key, and there could be no doubt that Lloyd's government had triumphed.

If the crisis was over, the struggle was not. The legislature was called into session to pass the amendments to the act agreed to in Saskatoon. But there was a battle across the province as the doctors sought to use the voluntary plans as a new vehicle to oppose the MCIC. It had been a gamble for Lloyd to allow the private plans to continue, but the

* "Oh shit, Al," Dalgleish said to A.W. Johnson, the Deputy Provincial Treasurer, who was involved in the negotiations, "that man is so irritating. How did he get here? He threatens us with going home and we're trying to persuade him not to. We didn't invite him. . . ." (Johnson interview, 21 March 1983.)

Premier was banking on the fact that simple administrative convenience eventually would encourage doctors to take their payment directly from the MCIC. But as one of Lloyd's aides noted, "every day sees more evidence of the doctors' determination to practise outside the Act and to intimidate their patients into enrolling with G.M.S. and M.S.I.," the voluntary plans.[80]

The government had its own weapons. The doctors' strike had led some communities to set up co-operative community health clinics where doctors operating under the act and billing the MCIC provided services to patients. By mid-August, sixteen associations were incorporated or in the process of incorporating, and preparations were under way, with government assistance, to recruit British doctors for the clinics. This upset the SCPS doctors, one of whom told a national CBC programme that "it would take a great many years for me to overcome my resentment at the . . . scab labour – which is what most doctors feel towards these immigrants."[81]

That suggested the depth of resentment among the province's physicians. Undoubtedly some left the province in disgust. The SCPS *Newsletter* of April 16, 1963, reported that 284 doctors in private practice had left (or died) between the beginning of 1962 and March 1, 1963, figures that were immediately challenged by the MCIC, which noted 201 new registrants in the same period. A later study in the *CMA Journal*, covering an additional year, found that the number of doctors in Saskatchewan had increased and the physician/population ratio had improved from 1:1037 to 1:980. The figures, however, showed a decline of thirty-five in the number of specialists and from 66 to 56 per cent in the ratio of doctors trained in Canada with a corresponding increase in those trained in Britain and elsewhere from 35 to 44 per cent.[82] That was serious, although scarcely the mass exodus foreseen by the SCPS.

More trying for the government, the number of doctors willing to accept payment from the MCIC increased very slowly. On July 10, there were 26; on September 21, 92; by May 30, 1963, 142; and by September 26, 1963, 175, or well under a fifth of the profession.[83] Perhaps that was behind Lord Taylor's private comment, "I am quite sure that our friends are harming themselves in the long run by their stupid attitude. There will always be a few diehards. . . . But as time goes on they cut less and less ice." That was true – by 1978 the private plans processed only 6 per cent of medical claims.[84]

The political potency of medicare also dwindled. Although delegates at the SCPS convention in October 1962 talked about exercising their influence in the next provincial election, the doctors played no great part in the 1964 contest. The Liberals agreed that medicare would not be threatened, an indication of the plan's popularity (as well as a sign that the national party's support for medicare limited the provincial possibilities), and Ross Thatcher won power on April 22, 1964, taking thirty-three seats to the NDP's twenty-five and the Conservatives' one. The NDP had lost, although its popular vote held up, and a shattered Woodrow Lloyd said that medicare "worked for us on the whole. At the same time it did much to activate and strengthen the efforts against us."[85] After twenty years, the voters had decided it was time for a change and, with medicare not an issue, they voted for the Liberals.

Significantly, the Thatcher government did not tamper with the medical care plan. "I think medical insurance is here to stay," Thatcher said in 1966,[86] and while the government modified some provisions of the act, the principle had become sacrosanct. Medicare was something the people of Saskatchewan wanted, and they received good quality care for the minimum amount of money. The governments of Tommy Douglas and Woodrow Lloyd had taken on the entrenched medical establishment of the province and country and had won. In the process, the CCF/NDP government of Saskatchewan, despite the terrible struggle of July 1962, had greatly advanced the cause of social justice in Canada. All that remained was to translate that success into a national programme.

IV

The Saskatchewan experience did not frighten off all the national parties. John Diefenbaker's Progressive Conservatives, who had probably benefited from the issue in the 1962 federal election in Saskatchewan, did not count medicare among their platform pledges, but the NDP did. Led by Tommy Douglas, the party could scarcely have done otherwise, but medicare was in fact a long-standing CCF pledge. Insurance against illness was an age-old Grit promise too, dating back to the 1919 convention that had chosen Mackenzie King as leader. But despite years in power, the Liberals had not proceeded with legislation, although the issue had been studied closely, particularly during the great wartime burst of interest in social legislation. Douglas's decision to proceed with medicare in Saskatchewan in 1959-60 had finally forced the Liberals off the fence, and in the 1962 and 1963 election campaigns the Pearson-led party had promised to implement medical insurance. But there was little immediate effort to redeem the pledge as the Pearson government after 1963 devoted its reformist energies to creating the Canada Pension Plan.

In June 1964, however, the first volume of the report of the Royal Commission on Health Services was tabled in Parliament. The Chief Justice of Saskatchewan, Emmett Hall, and his fellow commissioners had been appointed by Diefenbaker three years before to study the delivery of health services, in part at least as a way of delaying pressures building up in the Department of National Health and Welfare for major and costly federal actions in the field, not excluding medicare.[87] Hall had tackled the task with thoroughness and zeal, retaining an able research staff, dealing extensively with the CMA to ascertain the profession's position, and holding hearings.[88]

His report was startling to almost everyone. The large volume dealt with all aspects of medical and dental care and pharmaceutical needs, but what drew most attention was the commission's call for joint federal-provincial action for the provision of physicians' services. In effect, this was Saskatchewan-style medicare, and as Hall later recalled, the key point in his report was the call for universality.[89] Predictably, the CMA objected. The general secretary, Dr. Kelly, told Hall that his organization agreed with "85% of your proposals" but refused to accept that what was needed was a series of Saskatchewan-type plans, and the CMA's retiring president denounced the commission's recommendation as compulsory, monopolistic, and providing no guarantee that doctors could practise outside the plan.[90] It was almost as if Saskatchewan medicare had never happened. What the Pearson government would do with the report was uncertain.

In 1964, after the Saskatchewan election that toppled Lloyd and the NDP, a number of key civil servants in Regina began to look elsewhere for work. One was Al Johnson, the Deputy Provincial Treasurer, who was enticed to the Department of Finance in Ottawa by R.B. Bryce, now the deputy minister. Bryce had intended to use Johnson on federal-provincial fiscal questions, but when his minister, Walter Gordon, realized that Johnson had been involved in the medicare issue, he quickly assigned the new recruit to work on a federal medicare programme, a policy that could become a very useful part of the next Liberal election platform. Bryce was unhappy about losing a strong addition to his federal-provincial team; he was also upset that medicare, with its potential for high costs, was likely to be on the federal plate at a time when new programmes and rising expectations were straining the federal budget. The minister won out, and Johnson started work while federal officials began a series of discussions with their provincial counterparts.[91]

The Prime Minister was deeply interested in medicare as well, and he set up a Privy Council Office committee, chaired by Gordon Robertson, the Clerk of the Privy Council, with Tom Kent, Pearson's chief aide, and Donald Cameron, the deputy minister in National Health and Welfare. Johnson was an alternate member of the committee and did the basic work. Drawing directly on his Saskatchewan experience, he determined that four principles were critical: coverage had to be comprehensive and extend to virtually all physicians' services; the plan had to be universal in coverage; the provinces had to take responsibility for the administration of their plans; and benefits had to be portable.[92] The committee agreed, and Pearson made his government's proposals for medicare as a new shared-cost programme the centrepiece of a federal-provincial conference that opened on July 19, 1965. The Prime Minister told the premiers that to qualify for federal financial assistance they must adhere to the four principles. The estimated per capita cost for 1967 was twenty-eight dollars; of that, Ottawa would pay half or fourteen dollars (and it promised to keep its contribution up to 50 per cent if costs rose) to provinces that qualified.[93] Pearson said that he hoped the national programme could be in place by July 1, 1967.

The government's resolution to introduce medicare was brought forward in the House on July 12, 1966, by the Minister of National Health and Welfare, Allan MacEachen. Judy LaMarsh had been switched from the Health portfolio after the 1965 election on the grounds, she explained later, that Pearson wanted to proceed with medicare without controversy, which might be more likely with a less abrasive minister in charge. LaMarsh had been reluctant to go: "I argued with him that Allan MacEachen was lazy and that he just wouldn't do what was necessary."[94] Perhaps that was true, but an even more significant change had been made in the Cabinet when, after Walter Gordon's departure, Mitchell Sharp became Minister of Finance. Sharp was not overtly opposed to medicare, but he was acutely conscious of the fiscal pressures on the government and of the continuing opposition to medicare from the CMA and the insurance companies. The Sharp message was to make progress very slowly.

The MacEachen bill nonetheless adhered to the four Johnson principles, and the minister defined universality as 90-per-cent coverage at the outset, rising to 95 per cent over time. The NDP supported the bill, but the Tories were tepid, Davie Fulton criticizing the measure in detail and in principle. Premier Manning of Alberta, the sharpest provincial critic of the scheme, considered the measure financially unsound and of dubious constitutionality.[95]

The Minister of Finance, generally conservative, agreed with Manning on the financial quicksands of medicare, and in September 1966, in an atmosphere of fiscal uncertainty and rising expenditures, Sharp won Cabinet approval for the postponement of a number of programmes, including medicare, for a year. The much more liberal MacEachen was unhappy, considered resignation, and was apparently assuaged only by the promise that, if economic conditions permitted, medicare could take effect before July 1, 1968. There was a vigorous assault on Sharp at the Liberal party's policy convention in October 1966, but the minister defended the postponement on the grounds that the costs of the plan would have fuelled inflation.[96] Leftist Liberals were furious. Nevertheless, the Sharp version of the medicare bill passed Parliament in December 1966. The vote was 177 to 2, with only two Social Crediters against. Medicare was politically potent; no one could afford to be seen as opposed.

But as the start-up date drew closer, hesitancy increased. In the summer of 1967, Colin Brown, a London insurance agent, published advertisements in the newspapers urging those opposed to medicare to let their M.P.s know.[97] Davie Fulton in the Conservative caucus continued to oppose the universal and compulsory aspects of the act. "That is not welfare," he told a correspondent, "it is a handout."[98] And there were rumblings that the Prime Minister, disturbed by the objections of the provinces that continued everywhere except in British Columbia and Saskatchewan, was weakening. Walter Gordon, back in the ministry as President of the Privy Council, wrote to the Prime Minister in November 1967 to urge that it was "most important that you should not give the impression that you personally are ready to reconsider it. I do not think there is anything that could do more damage to the government."[99] At Cabinet on November 20, ten days before a "mini-budget," Sharp tried to get the starting date pushed back, but Gordon and others managed to beat off the persistent Finance minister. As a result the budget statement on November 30, while it said nothing about a delay, did make the point that new taxes would be necessary to pay medicare's bills.[100] Sharp was not yet through. Egged on by some provincial finance ministers, he raised the issue again in Cabinet on January 18, 1968, only to be rebuffed once more.[101] The race for the Liberal succession was under way, and Sharp, a candidate, was running as the fiscally responsible alternative.

The start-up date, however, survived the Liberal leadership campaign, and on July 1, 1968, medicare came into effect. British Columbia and Saskatchewan, provinces that satisfied Ottawa's four principles, instantly became eligible for federal payments to meet half the costs of their provincial plans. By the end of 1968, Manitoba, Nova Scotia, and Newfoundland had indicated they would join in 1969, and New Brunswick was also moving toward acceptance of the Ottawa principles. Ontario and Alberta remained aloof, but the promise of federal moneys ultimately forced them to enter the plan. Although

Quebec would have preferred to stay out, it could not but made a fight for the revenues collected in the province before its plan went into effect.[102]

Thus medicare was in place on a nation-wide basis by the beginning of the 1970s. The social welfare state was complete at last, the culmination of a process that had been under way since the mid-1920s. The federal Liberals deserved the credit for persevering with their plan, but there was no doubt that Tommy Douglas and Woodrow Lloyd had shown the way a decade before in Saskatchewan. The CCF/NDP government had identified an area of genuine popular concern and public need, and it had acted with courage and determination to meet it. So powerful had its example been that Ottawa and the other provincial capitals were virtually compelled to follow.

Twenty years before, a lead such as that provided by Saskatchewan would have been inconceivable. Then the provinces had complained and grumbled, but they almost always knew their place and confined themselves to blocking federal initiatives where and when they could. No longer. By the beginning of the 1960s, as medicare demonstrated, the initiative had begun to pass from Ottawa to the provincial capitals. Here again, Douglas's Saskatchewan led the way, a direct result of the ability found within Douglas's visionary cabinet and within his small but effective public service. The day of the C.D. Howes and Clifford Clarks had passed in Ottawa; the hour of the provinces was at hand.

CHAPTER 8

A New Nationalism? Symbol vs. Reality

The narrow Liberal election victory in April 1963 brought Lester Pearson to power. The new prime minister was probably the best-known Canadian in the world. Indeed, to many at home and abroad, Mike Pearson seemed the representative Canadian, the rational man whose instinct was to compromise rather than to fight, the hybrid of the best of the British and American temperaments, the friendly and affable leader. Pearson was all of those things, but he was also much more. No one who had worked his way up through the bureaucracy as he had, rising to the pinnacle of his profession in twenty years, could have accomplished that on charm and a winning personality alone. No one who had become Secretary of State for External Affairs and filled that portfolio with great distinction for almost a decade was a man without a strong inner core. And no one who had manoeuvred so that the Liberal party's leadership fell into his hands and who had led the Opposition for five years, in the process bringing down the government with the greatest majority in Canadian history up to that time and learning how to be effective in Parliament, was a man without resource.

Lester Pearson was a much tougher and harder-working politician than he seemed. He had enormous ambition and revealingly he referred in his memoirs to being passed over for the under-secretary's post in the Department of External Affairs in 1941 as his most painful experience. Until then, Pearson had always got what he wanted; after that, he always got what he wanted, too. He enjoyed office and all the perquisites of power, and with his sometimes frightening and total self-confidence, he believed that he could resolve any problem given sufficient time. The difficulty about politics was that choices had to be made, some of which, in most undiplomatic fashion, did not readily lend themselves to compromise. And for Pearson, compromise was always the goal, and once it was found it became his position. His old friend and fellow diplomat Hume Wrong once said that "Mike is like Houdini – put him in the middle of a crisis and he will get himself out of the mess, and in the process will help others to get out of it too."[1]

That was true enough, and Pearson had never had much difficulty in dealing with people, such was the overwhelming power of his personal charm and manner. People liked Mike Pearson and wanted to be close to him. But there were difficulties here. Walter Gordon, for example, was an old friend, the man who had raised the money to allow Pearson to risk leaving the public service in 1948 for the vagaries of politics, the man who had put together his leadership campaign in 1958, the man who had directed the rebuilding of the Liberal party after 1960 and organized the elections of 1962 and 1963 that destroyed Diefenbaker and brought Pearson to power. But when Gordon became a liability, Pearson gradually withdrew his support and Gordon was gone from the Cabinet by the end of 1965. Every prime minister always views his own survival as the greatest good, and Pearson was no exception to the rule. To his credit, he felt sad about the necessity of doing in his old friend, and Gordon, who fought with Pearson and ultimately felt betrayed by him, nonetheless retained much of his feeling for the man. Just before Pearson died, Gordon went to see him for their first real conversation in four years. The talk was easy, and Pearson said that he regretted that they had drifted apart. He also spoke about how shabbily Guy Favreau, his Minister of Justice, had been treated by politics. "It was," Gordon wrote, "the closest I have ever seen Pearson go in saying he was in the wrong – or . . . admitting guilt."[2]

That is shrewd observation. Pearson was a man who believed that everything he did was right and necessary. People could be hurt, ministers might be hung out on the line to dry, but it was always considered to be necessary if the greater good was to be served. And even on his deathbed, Pearson might feel twinges about some of his actions, but he could not openly admit that any of them were wrong. It was that certainty about his own star that made Pearson such a success and so attractive a personality. Even those who were hurt, like Gordon and Favreau, could never hate him.

Pearson was a great success as a diplomat. He was not, however, a great success as a prime minister. His Cabinet leaked secrets like a sieve, his organizational talents were limited, and he was not forceful enough to direct firmly the work of his government. Nor was he a man with much capacity for abstract thought. But leaders need not be intellectuals. On the other hand, as Paul Hellyer, one of his ministers, reflected, Pearson was a man whose ideas led not to action but only to the next idea. Moreover, Hellyer complained, Pearson was influenced too much by the last person he saw.[3] Those were not ideal prime-ministerial traits.

Even so, Pearson's time in power saw great problems tackled and some resolved. Among them were the Royal Commission on Bilingualism and Biculturalism, the Canada Pension Plan, medicare, and the flag. Each of those was a genuine achievement, and none could have been tackled without Pearson's sense of where he was going and his knack for deciding how to get there. And yet the disorganization and chaos that surrounded Pearson and his team were such that the ultimate statement on Mike Pearson as a politician probably remains Duncan Macpherson's superb *Toronto Star* cartoon of the Prime Minister as a baseball player trying to catch the ball, repeatedly fumbling it, and yet somehow making the grab before the ball hits the ground. The caption – "The Old Smoothie" – says it all.[4]

One of Pearson's main aims on taking power was to restore Canada's relations with the United States to their pre-Diefenbaker condition. The Prime Minister believed that Canada had to repair the links to the Kennedy administration that had been destroyed by the bitter wrangle over nuclear weapons in 1962-63, and he was confident that his sunny ways could return the relationship to the relatively happy state of affairs that had prevailed when he had been Secretary of State for External Affairs. For Pearson, this was essential because he recognized that Canada could never win a one-to-one fight with the United States on issues that genuinely affected the defence interests of Canada's superpower neighbour; indeed, even to get into such a fight was foolish. But he also looked back to the immediate post-war era when Canadian nationalism had received a healthy fillip from the successful practice of internationalism. The nation's success in aiding its friends and allies with loans and grants after the war, in helping to found NATO, and in playing useful roles in producing a Korean armistice and resolving (if only temporarily) the Suez Crisis had helped to make Canadians more conscious of their worth in the world and hence more proud of themselves at home. That mattered for a country that for too long had been a colony and sometimes still acted like one in its querulousness. Positive internationalsim, in other words, could help tie Canada together, or so Pearson's Liberals believed.

For the Liberal government, therefore, particularly with the Quiet Revolution in Quebec in full bloom and with strains growing between French and English Canadians, pan-Canadian nationalism was an important question. Pearson was convinced that Canada had to have national symbols of its own and that gestures had to be offered to French-speaking Québécois and to those new Canadians who had come from central and southern Europe and from Asia. Similarly there had to be a political and economic accommodation with the United States.

But neither course proved easy to follow. Finding distinctive Canadian symbols turned out to be a highly emotional and divisive exercise, and it was no easier to discover ways to increase domestic control over the economy in an interdependent continent and world. Moreover, the United States, soon caught up in a brutal Asian war, proved a difficult, often pushy neighbour. Canada's problems somehow had become much less simple, much more intractable, than they had been a decade earlier.

I

The Liberals had taken office with a pledge to introduce a distinctive Canadian flag within two years. A national flag was a question with which the country had been grappling off and on for decades. The House of Commons had discussed it on several occasions in the 1930s, and in 1945 Mackenzie King had set up a joint Senate-House committee to study the subject. But nothing emerged, the politicians agreeing that the issue was still too highly charged emotionally to be resolved. Nonetheless, there was substantial sentiment for a new flag, and even the Conservative party felt it; their national association in 1959 passed a resolution that urged the Diefenbaker government to adopt a flag and anthem as soon as possible.[5]

Pearson had come to believe that the country needed a flag of its own during the Suez Crisis of 1956. Egyptian diplomats at the United Nations had told Canadians who were trying to get the Queen's Own Rifles infantry battalion into the U.N. Emergency Force that their people would not understand that the soldiers were not British – the uniforms were similar and the Canadian Red Ensign had the Union Jack in the corner. That entirely reasonable complaint made an impression on Pearson. So too did the Quiet Revolution in Quebec, which had brought *nationaliste* sentiment to the boil and put all traditions under siege. With the English-Canadian presence in the province under attack as French Canada sought a new role for itself, the survival of Canada seemed at stake. One indicator of Pearson's concern was the Royal Commission on Bilingualism and Biculturalism; another was the search for truly Canadian symbols,* images that seemed to grow more important as Ottawa's relations with the Lesage government in Quebec worsened.[6]

Pearson himself favoured the maple leaf as the central motif of a distinctive flag. On May 14, 1964, the Post Office had released a three-maple-leaf stamp with the words "United Uni" beneath it, and that was the tip-off to Pearson's preferred design. He told his office to leak five possible designs to the press and to ensure that they were well drawn to counteract the scrawny and unimpressive designs beginning to appear. "Our flag policy," Pearson said, "could be destroyed by leaving the field to the Red Ensign supporters who are now well organized. . . ."[7]

Certainly the Ensign's supporters were well prepared, as Pearson discovered when he addressed the Royal Canadian Legion's national convention in Winnipeg and had his remarks on the need for a new flag drowned out by a chorus of boos from the veterans. Another group of opponents included Donald Creighton, W.L. Morton, and other professors. The Canadian historians argued that a new flag was necessary but, they said, "we protest that the maple leaf flag . . . is innocuous . . . that it can therefore be adopted without any display of strong feeling whatever. We have a despairing feeling that this insipid flag, instead of promoting national unity, will produce only an indifferent response, and in doing so will subtly undermine the Canadian will to survive." What was needed, they maintained, was a flag that recognized the symbols of the past.[8] There was little doubt that the academics had identified the point that would be the centre of controversy nation-wide. Union Jacks and fleurs-de-lys? Or beavers, armorial bearings, or crossed hockey sticks and pucks rampant?

For the next half year the flag issue dominated the House of Commons, disrupted it, and led many to despair of the future of the country. The reaction of some in English Canada was to accuse the Liberals openly of "pandering" to French Canada. "This is a banner not of compromise," the Vancouver *Province* said in an entirely typical cry of full-throated bigotry, "but of surrender of principles to cheap political expedients."[9] John Diefenbaker, leading a hardline crew of Red Ensign supporters, was no less adamant, accusing the government of dividing the country with the flag: "If the government had calculated a means whereby division could be secured in this nation, they could not have gone about it in a more effective manner."[10]

---

* "Do you realize that this country hasn't even got a flag?" someone asked the American comedian Mort Sahl in Toronto in 1961. "That's a start," Sahl replied. (Quoted in Mordecai Richler, *Home Sweet Home: My Canadian Album* [Toronto, 1984], p. 150.)

The debate in the House on the government's proposal for a Canadian flag began in June and then continued from August 12 to September 11, through a hot Ottawa summer. Once the basic positions had been staked out there were few new arguments to be made. A Red Ensign supporter could go on about how the Canadians in the Second World War had fought and died under the Ensign, but that was always countered by those who noted that the gravestones of servicemen all featured the maple leaf. Traditionalists insisted that the Jack and the fleur-de-lys should be on the flag, perhaps with a maple leaf as well. But that approach was challenged by others such as Paul Hellyer, the Minister of National Defence, who wrote to one critic that "those of us of English stock, whether we like it or not, are in the minority in this country . . . about one-third of the population." Many who wanted a new flag preferred one that represented Canada and "not one country of origin of Canadians."[11] The arguments were repeated over and over as the Tories tried – with great effect – to delay government business by filibustering the flag. In exasperation, J.W. Pickersgill, the Liberal House Leader, sent his Conservative counterpart a note: "If this performance is going to continue, please, please get a new speech writer who is not so boring and repetitive."[12] By the end of August the country had come to agree.

The Conservative aim, as Diefenbaker wrote to Gordon Churchill, was "to get the Liberal Party to vote against the Red Ensign, otherwise when the flag is chosen they can say we never gave them the opportunity."[13] The government aim was to escape from the parliamentary morass in which the Tories had mired the House. The debate could not go on after the third week in September, Walter Gordon wrote to the Prime Minister. Parliament was being made to look ridiculous, and the government was being blamed for it. He had expected Diefenbaker to relent earlier because of the pressure of public opinion – the press was crying for the Commons to get back to work – but he had underestimated Diefenbaker's willingness to divide Canada. The government's only options, the Finance minister said, were a committee to study the flag question, closure, or withdrawal of the bill until next session.[14] Pearson's choice, announced after a meeting of the party leaders on September 10, was a committee to report within six weeks. But there was no doubt in the Prime Minister's mind about the result: "We are going to have a new flag by Christmas. It's going to be a distinctive national flag and it will be based on this historic and proud emblem of Canada, the maple leaf."[15]

Pearson was correct, but it was a narrow squeak. The committee of seven Liberals, five Conservatives, and one each from the NDP, Créditistes, and Social Credit, began its work on September 17, and for forty-five sessions the members wrangled over symbols. The committee got down to voting on October 22. A motion by Waldo Monteith of the Conservatives for a plebiscite on any new flag was defeated 9 to 5. A second vote, that there should be only one national flag, carried 14 to 0. The third motion, put by Conservative Hugh John Flemming, was that the Red Ensign be the national flag, and that lost 10 to 4. Then the members voted on three different flags, one being Pearson's three-leaf design, another being a single red leaf flanked by two red bars, and the third a design that retained the Union Jack and fleur-de-lys. The past was eliminated first, and it was then a choice between the two remaining designs. Expecting the Liberals to support Pearson's flag, the Conservatives decided to oppose it and to their surprise found themselves joined by the entire committee. Pearson's flag was rejected 14 to 0, and that left the red maple leaf flag as the choice, even though the Conservatives voted against it. The Conservatives had been mousetrapped, and the flag committee had a choice to present to the House of Commons and the nation.[16]

The struggle in the House then began anew. Diefenbaker was not prepared to accept the design which he described as "the Peruvian flag, almost entirely a replica excepting in one case you have a maple leaf and in the case of the flag of Peru a representation of some coat of arms and at a distance of 100 yards you wouldn't know which was which." But the Chief's vehement opposition to the flag was beginning to split his caucus. Léon Balcer, the senior Quebec M.P., issued a statement on October 29 calling for the adoption of the new flag and warning against a long debate, which would be "fatal" to national unity. Two other M.P.s, Gordon Fairweather and Ged Baldwin, also indicated their unhappiness, and all the French-speaking *bleus* indicated that their preference was for a flag with neither a Jack nor a fleur-de-lys. They could live with the committee choice, they said.[17] The question at issue became a limit on debate, and Diefenbaker, supported by most of his party's M.P.s, simply refused to accept any restriction. From November 30 through to December 17, the House debated the flag endlessly and repetitiously. On December 11, its patience at an end, the government announced that it would resort to closure, responding to an appeal from Balcer for just such a measure on the grounds that more debate would "prejudice the rights of parliament and the higher interests of the country." The motion carried, with the Liberals winning the support of almost all the Créditistes and Socreds, half the NDP, and four French-speaking Conservatives; one Liberal, Toronto maverick Ralph Cowan, voted against closure. A Conservative amendment that the Red Ensign be the nation's flag was defeated 162 to 80, and early in the morning of December 15 the maple leaf flag was adopted 163 to 78 with one Liberal, one NDP, and three Socreds joining Diefenbaker's party in opposition. On December 17 the Union Jack was adopted as the Commonwealth flag, and the great debate was over. There had been 308 speeches in all.

The flag question had exhausted the country and severely tested party loyalties. The Quebec Conservatives in the caucus had become virtual outcasts, at odds with all but a handful of their colleagues. The NDP split in two, and Social Crediters of both persuasions were sharply divided. National unity was equally shaken. If Pearson's desire for a distinctive flag had been a concession to French Canada, the value of the gesture had been lessened by the vehemence of the Anglo-Canadian reaction. But if Diefenbaker had sought to mobilize English Canada in opposition to Quebec and the Liberals, he had failed. His inability to keep his own party together, the resentment and anger at the waste of parliamentary time, and the growing fury over the Chief's tactics had weakened his hold on the country, other than in virulently francophobe quarters, and on his party, except for a dwindling band of loyalists. Few had gained from the terrible debate.

And yet when the new flag was flown for the first time on February 15, 1965, there seemed to be a new mood. Paul Hellyer wrote in his diary that "there were thousands of people on the Hill, the most since the end of the war. At 12 noon the red ensign was lowered with appropriate ceremony and the new flag raised. When the flag went up on the tower a cheer went up from the crowd. This," he concluded, "will be Pearson's greatest achievement."[18]

Perhaps his assessment is correct. The flag marked a new direction for Canada, a step into independence that ranked with the Statute of Westminster and the later patriation of the constitution. The maple leaf flag was a deliberate gesture to Quebec that its aspirations could – with difficulty – be accommodated within Confederation and a signal to the rest of the country that great efforts were necessary to keep the nation together. The Diefenbaker supporters could never accept that reasoning and continued for some years to sneer at the flag's design as more suitable for a beer label than a national symbol. But within a few years the flag was everywhere, accepted and honoured, and Canadians abroad wore maple leaf pins in their lapels or, if teenagers (hitch-hiking and trying to show Europeans that they were not Americans), on their jean jackets or knapsacks. The maple leaf flag quickly became *the* Canadian symbol, and the divisiveness of the debate that gave it birth was largely forgotten.

II

If the flag debate ultimately came to a happy ending, so too did the government's initial effort to reach an economic understanding with the United States. One area that disturbed the Pearson administration, as it had Diefenbaker's before it, was the country's balance of payments deficit, and particularly the deficit in automobiles and auto parts. In 1962, for example, Canada had imported $642 million in autos and parts and exported only $62 million; the deficit in this sector alone amounted to more than two thirds of Canada's total trade imbalance in that year. Put another way, Canadians used about 7.5 per cent of all North American auto production but produced only 4 per cent. To bring those figures more into balance was the goal. The Liberal government's solution, announced in the summer of 1963 by Industry minister C.M. Drury, was an auto export incentive scheme that allowed Canadian automobile companies to import parts duty free to the extent each increased exports. The object was to raise exports by at least $200 million over a three-year period and create employment.[19]

The ideas in the plan had first been considered by the Royal Commission on the Automotive Industry, which had reported in 1961, and they had been discussed in the Diefenbaker Cabinet in the dollar-crisis summer of 1962. They were also raised with the United States in October 1963, when the American government expressed strong opposition to Drury's plan and indicated that countervailing duties might have to be slapped on Canadian exports if the Drury scheme was deemed a bonus or subsidy to Canadian producers.[20]

Thus both sides had set out their positions. The Canadian aim was to get more production and more jobs north of the border, and by definition that seemed a threat to the American parts manufacturers and the United Auto Workers and hence to Congressmen and the administration. Moreover, American law was such that a demand for countervailing duties could be initiated by any individual, even if the government chose not to proceed.[21] What was the answer? According to an *ad hoc* committee headed by Simon Reisman of the Finance department, the matter should be resolved through a broader negotiation with the United States that would guarantee Canada a specified share of the market and see both countries agree to cut tariffs on autos and parts. In effect, the committee was arguing that the auto industry be rationalized on a continental basis, and Cabinet gave its approval to this approach on June 11, 1964. The Americans were advised that talks were in order.[22]

The negotiations began the next month. The United States was unwilling to commit itself to giving Canada a fixed share of the market, and that chilled the process. But in September the Canadian team entered into agreements with the auto manufacturers to bind them to achieve "output targets" similar to those Ottawa had hoped to achieve through the export incentives. That arrangement was to be tied to a free trade regime in autos and parts. The Americans could agree to the first part of the proposal and the second part was in accord with their own position. The basis for a deal was in place.[23]

The one remaining point that concerned the Canadians was the American ability to deliver: could an auto pact be passed by Congress? Even before the final terms had been drafted, the White House and interested departments were meeting to calculate the odds, trying to get "sufficient advance Congressional assurance that the legislation will be adopted to be able to ground Canadian agreements solidly on such assurance."[24] The assurances must have been secured, for the Cabinet approved the draft agreement on December 21, 1964, and the final text was signed by Pearson and Martin for Canada and by President Johnson and Secretary of State Rusk for the United States at the LBJ ranch early in January 1965.

The agreement was a triumph for the Pearson government. It held out the promise of thousands of new jobs and a reduction in the trade deficit. But it also rationalized a crucial sector of the economy. "I did not like this in principle," Walter Gordon, the Cabinet's leading nationalist, later said, "but as three companies dominated the industry on both sides of the border, this acceptance merely acknowledged the existing fact."[25] The Americans drew similar conclusions, the *New York Times* reporting, to the satisfaction of the White House, that "the auto plan means that Canada had abandoned the thought of creating a distinctly national and fully diversified automobile industry. It is willing to specialize."[26]

The agreement eliminated duties on Canadian cars, trucks, buses, parts, and accessories for assembly admitted to the United States; Canada eliminated the tariff on the same American goods, but in recognition of the higher costs and prices of cars in Canada, only manufacturers meeting specified criteria could import duty free. The results initially were all that the Pearson government had hoped. By June 1967, according to U.S. figures, trade had expanded such that autos and parts formed the largest single item in Canadian-American trade. American exports rose from $660 million to $1.3 billion and U.S. imports from $75 million to $900 million between 1964 and 1966. New investment in the Canadian industry was estimated at $500 million, Canadian vehicle production was up by 35 per cent and employment by 27 per cent. Half the cars and trucks produced in Canada were now being sold in the United States.[27]

So favourable to Canada was the Auto Pact that a resentful President Johnson complained to Charles Ritchie, the ambassador in Washington, "You screwed us on the Auto Pact." The Canadians generally agreed, Paul Martin pointedly adding that everyone was careful to avoid saying so to minimize the Johnson administration's difficulties.[28] But the balance of trade in auto parts still remained tilted in favour of the United States, and Canadians eventually began to wonder about the merits of the Auto Pact of 1965.

III

The Auto Pact was one of the first results of the Liberal government's new policy toward the United States, but Pearson soon found himself in hot water with President Johnson. The major cause of tension between Canada and the United States during Pearson's five years as prime minister was the war in Vietnam, and that bloody conflict in Asia proved to have a corrosive effect on the relations between the two North American nations. At the same time the war sparked domestic dissent in both countries and contributed to quite startling changes in society.

Canada's involvement in Vietnam dated back to 1954 when, at the request of the Great Powers at the Geneva Conference, the St. Laurent government had sent a large team of diplomats and military officers to help monitor the truce in Indochina. In this difficult and unpleasant task the Canadians found themselves locked into the tripartite International Control Commission with refractory Poles and cautiously neutral Indians and burdened with heavy duties involving the separation of combatants and the repatriation of civilians. Canada was on the ICC as the Western representative, and the government knew all too well that the United States was unhappy with the Geneva accords. That alone caused some strain, and when the civil war in Vietnam began to heat up and the United States began to pour military aid and advisers into South Vietnam, the pressures on Canada increased still more. Although the Canadians on the ground in Vietnam generally agreed that North Vietnam had stepped up the pace of the war and generally accepted the necessity for the United States to assist the South,[29] their obligations required them to be as impartial as possible in the circumstances.[30] That was difficult, not least because Ottawa's policy was to share with the United States the information garnered by Canadians in the ICC.

This was the background to the visit to Ottawa by Secretary of State Dean Rusk at the end of April 1964. Rusk's mission was to persuade Pearson "that the very best possible Canadian should be assigned to the ICC team in Vietnam with the specific mission of conveying to Hanoi both warnings about its present course and hints of possible rewards in return for a change." Pearson was willing, Rusk reporting that the Canadians readily agreed that Blair Seaborn, senior Canadian diplomat on the ICC, would spend much more time in Hanoi than his predecessors. Seaborn was to ensure that Ho Chi Minh's government realized the extent of "U.S. determination to see this thing through. He should draw upon examples in other parts of the world to convince them that if it becomes necessary to enlarge the military action, this is the most probable course that the U.S. would follow." That was the stick. The carrot that Seaborn was to offer was American recognition of North Vietnam's need for trade, and especially food, and the hint that such needs could be fulfilled if peaceful conditions were to prevail.[31]

While the Canadians were willing to act as conduit for that type of message, the Americans worried about Ottawa's goodwill. When the U.S. ambassador in Saigon urged that Seaborn's message be blunt – "they will be punished" – Rusk replied that "in light of present Canadian attitudes we tend to see real difficulty in approaching the Canadians at this time with any message as specific as you suggest . . . might lead us into a very difficult dialogue with the Canadians as to just what our plans really were." But when President Johnson met with Pearson in New York on May 28, there were few problems. Johnson indicated that his policy was carrots and sticks, and the Prime Minister "stipulated that he would have very great reservations about the use of nuclear weapons"; but, according to the American record, Pearson said "that the punitive striking of discriminate targets by careful iron bomb attacks would be 'a different thing'. He said he would personally understand our resort to such measures if the messages transmitted through the Canadian channel failed to produce any alleviation of North Vietnamese aggression. . . ."[32]

The Seaborn mission to Hanoi stretched out for more than a year. The Northern leaders listened, offered careful responses, and ultimately remained unshakeable in their belief that they would prevail.[33] But by spring 1965, as the Americans launched their "Rolling Thunder" campaign of bombing against the North and increased their troop commitment, Pearson began to have doubts about U.S. policy. The criticism in the press and public of Johnson's war was growing in Canada, and Pearson soon persuaded himself that Vietnam was the wrong war in the wrong part of the world.

That, at least, was the impression the Prime Minister conveyed in an address at Temple University in Philadelphia on April 2. "There are many factors which I am not in a position to weigh," he said. "But there does appear to be at least a possibility that a suspension of such air strikes against North Vietnam, at the right time, might provide the

Hanoi authorities with the opportunity, if they wish to take it, to inject some flexibility into their policy without appearing to do so as the direct result of military pressure." Pearson knew the response his remarks would elicit from the White House. His own Secretary of State for External Affairs, Paul Martin, had threatened resignation if the speech were presented as drafted, arguing that the call for a bombing halt would destroy Seaborn's credibility in Hanoi by persuading the North Vietnamese that Canada's usefulness in Washington was over. Pearson had riposted that he was a political leader, that many Canadians were disturbed by the American bombing, and that he had to say something. Unhappy, Martin stayed. And Pearson instructed the ambassador in Washington not to pass a copy of the Temple speech to the White House in advance of delivery. "It was quite deliberately held up," Charles Ritchie said. "It was Mike's own doing. He knew there would be a blow-up."[34]

So there was. Pearson had been greeted on arrival in Philadelphia by a letter of welcome from the President and an invitation to visit Camp David. When he arrived at the presidential retreat the day after the speech, he found a fuming Johnson. The address had been "bad," "awful," one that lent support to his domestic enemies. He was tired of advice from foreign visitors, who should realize the efforts that he, the President, was making to keep his hawks on a leash, the people who wanted to blast Hanoi back into the Stone Age. At one point in this furious monologue, Johnson apparently grabbed the Prime Minister by the shirt front and pursued his harangue nose to nose.[35] Pearson was naturally shaken by the assault, but in his diary wrote only that "the President is tired, under great and continuous pressure, and . . . is beginning to show it." What offended the White House most was not so much what Pearson had said as that he had said it in the United States. Resentment over this persisted for the next three years, and virtually every Canadian visitor to Washington was given the same message from Johnson: "Give Lester my best . . . and tell him that if he's got any more speeches to make on Viet Nam, please make them outside the United States."[36] There was some justice in Johnson's reaction.

Meanwhile the war in Vietnam went on. And with it came a swelling protest on the campuses and main streets of cities and towns all across the United States – and Canada. Canadian young men did not face the prospect of conscription for the Vietnam War, but the startling images brought by television each night into virtually every home in North America made critics out of many, perhaps most, of the young. Each night, the small glowing screen showed American aircraft dropping napalm canisters on straw huts and paddy fields or huge bombers spewing their loads of destruction into Vietnamese cities and towns. Many of the newly politicized young, largely the children of the privileged middle class rebelling against the standards and authority imposed by their elders in a wide spectrum of social and political issues, made Vietnam their focus.[37] The war seemed to be an unfair contest between a technologically advanced superpower and a small, struggling peasant society; it seemed to be motivated more by fanatical anti-communism than any rational assessment of the American national interest; and it was very easy to paint it as Lyndon Johnson's war, for the big, crude Texan who had succeeded the assassinated John F. Kennedy on November 22, 1963, was never as popular – in Canada – as his martyred predecessor. Johnson's bombing attacks against the North and the brutality implicit in such things as "free fire zones" stirred many Canadians to participate in protest marches before the American embassy in Ottawa and consulates across the country. Others demonstrated on campuses against recruiters from companies, such as the napalm-manufacturing Dow Chemical, that produced war materials for the lucrative American military market (to which Canada had won access as a result of the Defence Production Sharing Programme, negotiated between Prime Minister Diefenbaker and President Eisenhower in 1958). Still others, professors and students alike, gloried in revolutionary rhetoric and shook their fists in teach-ins against the evils of capitalist American policy in Vietnam and around the world and what was seen as Canadian complicity in it.

The university population had more than doubled in size between 1957 and 1967 as the children of the post-war baby boom began to reach their late teens, and the war protest soon changed direction and turned into demands for curriculum reform, for "relevance" in the courses offered, and for an end to "élitist" honours programmes. The university protests also encompassed demands that students share the power in the administration of the university. At the University of Toronto, for example, the president, Claude Bissell, was startled when student leaders, assembled to hear an address on world affairs, complained about his chair being placed at the head of the table: "What does he think he is, a school teacher lecturing kids?" Soon after this and other incidents, Bissell recommended that students be added to the President's Council, and for the first time, once the students began attending, the council began to publish minutes, a reaction to the widespread student protest against secrecy of all kinds.[38]

There were other changes in the universities, too. Segregation of the sexes in residence halls collapsed as the idea that the university had to act *in loco parentis* fell out of favour with astonishing speed. The old rule that males could visit rooms occupied by the other sex only so long as the door remained open and one foot was on the floor disappeared. Now the dormitories were integrated and doors were firmly closed. Students had greater sexual freedom than in any previous generation, the women largely relieved of the fear of unwanted pregnancy by the arrival of safe (or so they seemed at the time) methods of contraception. Both sexes were also beginning to experiment with drugs, including the widely available marijuana (which could be cultivated in balcony flower pots or in garden plots), "uppers" and "downers," and the more exotic and much more dangerous LSD. For a time in the late 1960s, the campuses with their long-haired students seemed to be a hotbed of social *and* political revolution. Adult Canadians looked on with astonishment, secretly envious of the availability of casual sex, frightened by the drugs, and openly affronted by the long-haired males and the bra-less females flouting the norms of conventional society.

Almost as upsetting to adults was the prevalence of rock music, invariably played at ear-shattering volume, and its almost total displacement on the radio of the sentimental ballads and love songs favoured by older generations. Elvis Presley and the Beatles seemed to have started the rot, but the British group's beautiful tunes soon were joined by the harder-edged lyrics and harsher sounds of singers like Jimi Hendrix, Jim Morrison, and Bob Dylan, who became cult figures. Some Canadians as well were making an impact in music in this period, the folk-singer Joni Mitchell and Galt MacDermot, the son of a Canadian diplomat and the composer of the rock musical *Hair*, being notable examples.

Like parents, governments did not know how to deal with the nation's youth, and the best idea that Ottawa could come up with was the creation of institutions such as the Company of Young Canadians, first mooted in the Speech from the Throne in April 1965, a domestic copy of the United States Peace Corps. If the CYC had been intended to co-opt the radical students by putting them to work with disadvantaged Canadians, it largely failed. Conservative critics charged the organization with advocating political and social revolution along the lines advocated by the New Left, and the CYC, some of whose members were found with their hands in the till, quickly became an embarrassment to the government that had set it up and funded it.[39]

Protests were not confined to the universities and the young. New organizations sprang up and the old ones were revivified among Canadians of all ages: the Voice of Women and the Toronto Committee of Clergymen for Vietnam were only two examples. The war had mobilized concerned men and women across the country as had nothing since the Spanish Civil War during the 1930s.[40]

The distress south of the border helped create a trickle of draft evaders and deserters slipping into Canada, and by 1967 that trickle had become a small flood, enough of a public concern that early in 1968 a *Manual for Draft Age Immigrants to Canada* sold 25,000 copies in a few months. Immigration officers gave some evaders a difficult time at border crossings, but there were support networks for those thousands who secured entry. The highly visible protest, however, was not the sum total of Canadian opinion. A Canadian Institute of Public Opinion survey of September 28, 1966, found only 31 per cent of Canadians saying the United States should leave Vietnam while 18 per cent wanted the Americans to maintain the same level of fighting and 27 per cent called for stepped-up attacks on the North. Like the Americans, Canadians were sharply torn about the war.

In the face of those divisions, government actions were cautious. The Pearson government tried to work behind the scenes to get negotiations started, and early in 1966 Paul Martin sent Chester Ronning, a retired diplomat with long experience in the Far East, to try a mediatory role in Hanoi. There was little success. Outwardly, however, the government was generally polite and supportive of the American position. Even so, Pearson told Parliament on May 10, 1967, of his increasing anxiety about Vietnam and said that "the possibility of early negotiations has receded and a quick military victory is not possible, nor a military solution." All that Canada could do, he added, was "to bring our worries and anxieties to the notice of those who are more immediately and directly involved in the hope that our advice and counsel will be of some help to them. I am thinking particularly of Washington. . . ."[41]

Walter Gordon, who had rejoined the Cabinet in January 1967, was heartened by Pearson's words. In a speech in Toronto three days later, Gordon called for an end to the bombing of the North, a halt to American offensive operations in the South, an American statement of willingness to negotiate directly with the Viet Cong, the rebels in South Vietnam, an internationally supervised cease-fire, and the withdrawal of all foreign troops. If Canada failed to do everything it could to press the Americans, Gordon said, "we must be prepared to share the responsibility of those whose policies and actions are destroying a poor but determined people. We must share the responsibility of those whose policies involve the gravest risks for all mankind."[42]

Many of his colleagues and some members of the press felt that Gordon had overstepped the bounds and broken Cabinet solidarity. Paul Martin was very unhappy, and Mitchell Sharp, Paul Hellyer, and others wanted Gordon's head.[43] At the Cabinet meeting on May 17, Pearson read a statement on "our policy" and was, Gordon wrote, very critical and obviously angry. Gordon allowed that he could live with Pearson's statement. But after several ministers had expressed themselves critically, he noted, "I said I did not regret making the speech and that I meant every word of it – would do it again." He added that he would not resign. "If P.M. wished to dismiss me that would be his prerogative." That ended the matter in Cabinet, but in the party caucus and to the press Pearson was much more critical than he had been before Gordon and his colleagues.[44]

For Gordon it had been worth it. He accompanied Paul Martin to the NATO meetings in Luxembourg in June, and he was impressed with the way Martin tried to get the Vietnam issue discussed and offered his opinions.[45] Martin himself had reached such a point by 1967 that he could write, after a meeting with President Johnson, that he had been given "the usual apologia pro mia guerra."[46] Perhaps Gordon's outspokenness had stiffened the government stand, and Gordon himself said that "we can now hold our heads up which is worth something in itself."[47]

IV

Walter Gordon was also the Liberal who raised difficult questions about foreign investment. His views were already firm when he became Minister of Finance in 1963, and the difficulties he had fallen into over his first budget had not altered his opinions. But Gordon's fall from grace did allow the government to change its priorities and stop any serious attempt to control foreign investment. Gordon had been the chief proponent of economic nationalism in the Cabinet and in the Liberal party, and when his position was weakened, Pearson's attention moved elsewhere.

The fate of the Canada Development Corporation was one indicator of this. In his book *Troubled Canada*, published in 1961, Gordon had called for the creation of a government agency "to sponsor and invest in large economic undertakings that may not be expected to pay returns for a considerable period." Canada lacked the large pools of private capital that the United States could call on for such purposes, and "as a result," Gordon wrote, "many of our more imaginative undertakings in the past have had to be promoted and financed by foreigners." In May and June 1963, that type of development corporation seemed a live idea, a measure certain to be passed into law.[48] But after the budget, the CDC went on the back burner, there to sit for years.

When Gordon rejoined the Cabinet, he found that the question of the American takeover of the Mercantile Bank, an issue that had first arisen in 1963, was still alive. At the same time that Gordon's first budget was being roasted by the Canadian financial community in the spring of 1963, officials of the First National City Bank of New York were meeting with the Governor of the Bank of Canada, Louis Rasminsky. Citibank was proposing to buy the small Dutch-owned Mercantile Bank and to begin operations in Canada, and the bankers wanted to know the government's attitude. Conscious of the political dynamite involved in having a powerful U.S. bank operating in Canada, Rasminsky urged R.P. MacFadden of Citibank to see Gordon before proceeding further, and he drew to MacFadden's attention the Finance minister's views on foreign ownership in the banking system. According to what MacFadden told the American embassy in Ottawa, Rasminsky had also warned that "purchasers would be taking risk of unfavorable Canadian action."[49] Gordon gave the same impression to Citibank when he saw its officers. The government opposed foreign investment in the financial field, he said, and a department official noted that the Bank Act could be revised to remove the charter from any bank and thus force it out of business. "In conclusion," the Canadian record observed, "the Minister said that if National City proceeded with its plan, it might tend to encourage restrictive legislation." James Stillman Rockefeller of Citibank replied to this by noting that if his bank decided to go ahead, "it will be at our own peril." That, Gordon said, sized up the situation exactly. Nonetheless Citibank decided to complete the purchase. As MacFadden told Rasminsky and the American embassy, they had given the question serious consideration and concluded they should proceed.[50]

For Gordon this was a challenge that could not be refused. When the Bank Act came up for its decennial revision, therefore, provisions were included to restrict Mercantile's growth so long as Citibank retained more than a 10-per-cent interest in it. Pressures were brought on the government by Citibank and by the American government, but they ceased when Gordon pointed out that the bank had gone ahead despite the clearest of warnings.[51] The Bank Act revisions died on the order paper when Parliament was dissolved for the 1965 election, however, and when the smoke cleared after the vote, Gordon was gone and in his place as Minister of Finance was Mitchell Sharp, a very different sort of man.

As a result when the revisions to the Bank Act were presented to Parliament in June 1966, the Mercantile issue came alive once again. The U.S. Secretary of the Treasury and the Undersecretary of State both made strong representations to the Canadian ambassador in

Washington,[52] and the pressures to give Mercantile a freer hand mounted. A few months later, when a Liberal policy convention featured a struggle between the Gordon and Sharp wings of the party over the financial relationship with the United States, the nationalists were badly battered.[53]

At this time Gordon was trying to decide whether he should resign his seat and leave politics or whether he should accept Pearson's offer to rejoin the ministry. When he met the Prime Minister on December 22, 1966, to discuss this, Gordon said he could not return unless something was done about the foreign investment question. After a further talk, Gordon wrote that "Mike realizes the importance of the foreign control issue (he has always been a nationalist at heart). . . ." What Gordon said he wanted was "the preparation of a White Paper on 'Monopoly Control of the Economy' to be prepared under my direction – to be debated and then followed by legislation. We would have to mean business – and we would have to hurry if we are to offset the NDP and the Tories on this issue."[54] By January 9, 1967, his terms having been met by Pearson, Gordon rejoined the Cabinet as President of the Privy Council. The small committee to investigate foreign control was set up shortly thereafter and a group of economists under Professor Melville Watkins of the University of Toronto hired to do research. Its report was not completed until January 1968.

Meanwhile Gordon had talked with Sharp in an effort to ensure, as Gordon wrote, that there were no "areas of conflict." Gordon first raised the matter of the Bank Act; "I said I assumed from what I had read that there would be no compromise on the subject of the Mercantile Bank. Mike and Sharp agreed." The Finance minister added that he was working on amendments to close the loophole that allowed Mercantile to sell shares to Canadians who would agree not to vote their shares.[55] That seemed satisfactory to everyone.

The agreements soon began to collapse. On January 18, Gordon met Pearson, Sharp, and Robert Winters, the Minister of Trade and Commerce and a strong supporter of more American investment; the President of the Privy Council then discovered that Winters had not been aware of the terms on which he had rejoined the Cabinet. Neither Sharp nor Winters wanted Gordon to head the study of foreign investment, and Sharp actually suggested that the Prime Minister head the study. "This would be ridiculous," Gordon later said, adding that Sharp and Winters were opposed to doing anything and that "Mike will renege if he can (perhaps I am being unfair)."[56]

That last remark seemed only just when the Mercantile Bank question came to the forefront in February. On the ninth, Pearson told Gordon that Sharp wanted to give the bank three years to sell stock to

Canadians. Gordon was appalled, arguing that the matter should be settled now and that Mercantile should be allowed no increase in its capital until Citibank's share of ownership was reduced to 10 per cent. The Cabinet subsequently agreed with Gordon's position, but Sharp nonetheless struck a deal with the bank that violated the Cabinet decision. The "doublecrossed" Gordon threatened resignation and Sharp was again forced back to the agreed position.[57]

In the Caribbean for a holiday after these tussles, Gordon discovered that the agreement with Sharp had again come unstuck. The result, after his hurried return to Ottawa, was "a flaming row in Cabinet" on March 7 at which time Gordon set out the full story, chapter and verse, and won his colleagues' pledge to hold their position. When the Bank Act came before the House a few days later, Gordon's position carried the day.[58]

Gordon had won this round, but the fight was not yet over. This was very clear when the Liberals held a special caucus conference in late September 1967. When the foreign investment issue was discussed, Robert Winters led off by pointing out that "nothing scares money away more quickly than legislation," and he also noted that 70 per cent of Canadian workers were affiliated with American unions, with half their dues going south. Gordon countered by citing opinion surveys that showed that 80 per cent of Canadians wanted their country to remain independent and 94 per cent of students agreed. The caucus went along with Gordon, deciding, as the minutes put it, "That Canada should remain independent."[59] But it was a long way from that pious hope to effective legislation.

CHAPTER 9

Unification: The Politics of the Armed Forces

Defence issues had caused the downfall of the Diefenbaker government because they directly involved Canadian-American relations and called into question the decision-making capacities of the Prime Minister and his government. But surely questions of defence organization could never provoke such controversy. Who in the 1960s could get exercised over such arcane questions as the colour of a military uniform and the design of buttons and badges? Who would oppose sweeping plans designed to reduce waste, save money, and secure the armed forces modern equipment? Who could object to the integration and then the unification of the Navy, Army, and Air Force into one distinctively Canadian force?

As it turned out, large sections of the public, press, and Parliament resisted some or all of those things, and the unification of the armed forces turned into a highly contentious issue during the Pearson government's years in office. Integration made Defence minister Paul Hellyer's reputation and unification effectively eliminated his chance to succeed Pearson; unification abbreviated the careers of a plethora of admirals, generals, and air marshals and accelerated the rise of others, and it demonstrated that, given a determined minister, change could be pushed through Parliament in the face of organized, vocal, and powerful opposition inside and outside the Commons.

The first post-war attempt at a consolidation of the armed forces had been made by Brooke Claxton. Appointed Minister of National Defence by Mackenzie King in December 1946, Claxton had the mandate of eliminating the triplication of functions that had resulted from the existence of a separate government department for each of the services. Such a division could be justified in wartime, but it was too extravagant in peacetime, and Claxton took over responsibility for the Army, Navy, and Air Force. Under him was the single National Defence Headquarters that controlled the services, each of which had a roughly similar organization at NDHQ and theoretically co-ordinated its activities with the others through interservice committees. At the top of the military organizational ladder was the Chairman of the Chiefs of Staff, a post held through most of the period to 1958 by General Charles Foulkes. Under Foulkes were the professional heads of each of the services, the Personnel Members Committee, and the Principal Supply Officers Committee. The Chiefs of Staff Committee brought together the chairman, the three service heads, and the chairman of the Defence Research Board to advise the minister on matters of defence policy and to co-ordinate "the efforts of the Armed Services in fulfillment of a single defence policy."[1]

To some extent, Claxton's structure worked. Under it all the research for the services was handled by the Defence Research Board; the Royal Military College and the other services colleges became tri-service; the medical services were co-ordinated; and a variety of specialized functions were handed to one service to run for all three.[2] But the urgency of the Korean War and Canada's overseas commitments to NATO tended to force the Department of National Defence away from any further efforts towards integration. When the Conservatives came to power in 1957, General George Pearkes took over the portfolio, and on his second day in office, Foulkes remembered, the new minister was handed a plan to continue the process of unification. Foulkes's scheme, prepared in the spring of 1957, proposed three stages. The first looked to the amalgamation of all common functions. The second stage called for the operational part of the services to become functional groups, and the final stage was the tidying up of the Policy and Co-ordinating Group or a restructuring of the top levels of command.[3] But Pearkes did not have the energy to tackle such a programme, and he told Foulkes that while he was interested in the concept he did not expect to be minister long enough to see it through. Nonetheless, Pearkes did advance or set in motion the unification of the medical services, the procurement of food, the postal services, and the chaplains' services. And, Foulkes recalled, there were plenty of difficulties in accomplishing even that.[4] If matters were to go farther, a different type of minister would be required.

Paul Hellyer became Minister of National Defence when the Liberals returned to office after their six years in the wilderness. Born and raised on a farm near Waterford, Ontario, Hellyer had graduated from the University of Toronto in 1949 (while simultaneously running a women's clothing store with his wife) where Keith Davey had been a classmate and friend. In that same year, he won election to Parliament for Toronto-Davenport. At twenty-five, Hellyer was the youngest M.P.

in the House, and while he was a careful and concerned representative for his polyglot ethnic riding, he also engaged in real estate and property development and quickly made his own fortune. If he was a businessman and a politician, Hellyer was also a deeply religious man who taught a Bible class and tried to live a moral life in the worlds of politics and business.

That was sometimes very difficult to do. It was Hellyer who had felt compelled to persuade Opposition Leader Pearson to change his position to one of support for nuclear weapons at the beginning of 1963 because the young M.P. was convinced after a visit to Canada's NATO contingent in the fall of 1962 that the country had accepted commitments and then failed to meet them. "If we do not fulfill our commitment," Hellyer told Pearson, "there will be intense pressure on us to withdraw and turn the [air division's] facilities over to others. Our influence in NATO will be reduced to negligible."[5] The ensuing controversy had destroyed the Conservative government, and Hellyer was entitled to his reward – even though, Hellyer still remembers, Pearson always saw him as having been cool to his candidacy in the Liberal leadership race in 1958. Nonetheless, Hellyer was offered Defence, after Pearson had canvassed opinion from Paul Martin and Keith Davey, among others. The Prime Minister, in fact, "definitely had in mind the process of unification that ultimately came to be identified with Hellyer's administration," Paul Martin remembered. That "was the reason that Pearson gave to me for his picking Paul as his Minister of National Defence."[6]

Hellyer's own views were still unformed. He had served in the Royal Canadian Air Force during the closing stages of the Second World War but had been mustered out even though there was a serious shortage of reinforcements in the Army at the time. When he had then joined the Army, he had been obliged to take all his medical shots and his basic training over again, a time-wasting experience that made a lasting impression upon him. In the closing days of the St. Laurent administration, Hellyer had been named Associate Minister of National Defence, another experience that taught him something of the way the department and its officers operated and thought. Equally important, Hellyer was close to John Gellner, the former RCAF wing commander who had become the country's leading defence commentator. Hellyer had persuaded Gellner to draft a paper on defence policy for the Liberals in December 1962, and when he sent it on to Pearson on the last day of the year, he told his leader that "we are in basic agreement in respect of the means, objectives and aims."[7] This was important, for Gellner had proposed, among other things, a fairly radical restructuring of the defence organization that included the virtual unification of all higher headquarters and the reorganization of service roles by functions. In effect, Gellner argued, "This unification and reorganization at the top levels would streamline the armed services, which have suffered in the past from a surfeit of 'planners' in relation to the number of 'doers', and from too much administrative tail for the available fighting strength." But Gellner had also argued that unification should take place at the top, not "on the subordinate levels, for the ever increasing complexity of the tasks to be performed on the working plane naturally leads to specialization rather than unification. This does not apply to the supporting services which should be unified. . . ."[8] Whatever position Hellyer had reached at the time he took power, it appeared that he had at least been thinking about the need to restructure defence organization.

I

The minister's thinking quickly hardened into certainty. As Hellyer said, "I soon became aware of the problems of three individual services, each with individual direct access to the Minister, making plans and presenting projects which were often quite unrelated to each other. There was no strategic unity," Hellyer maintained, "there was no unity of planning and no adequate machinery for setting priorities with respect to roles and missions, and the equipments necessary to fulfill them." There was, Hellyer claimed, no coherent war plan, each service having its own idea of the possibilities. Planning for one was based on a five-day nuclear spasm, for another on a protracted war, with a slow mobilization for a third. Of course, the Chiefs of Staff Committee was supposed to sort out conflicting claims and establish priorities, and the service chiefs always claimed that this took place. Not so, Hellyer said. The Chiefs' committee was a club ruled by mutual back scratching, and the senior officers of one service never sat down with the top brass of another. The confusion in decision making shook him. "In addition," Hellyer said, "I soon became aware of the increasing proportion of the total budget being devoted to operations and maintenance costs. In fact, a simple projection indicated that in a few years, unless the budget was substantially increased, little money would be left for new equipment. I felt that I could not justify such a large increase in the Defence budget until I had explored all means of reducing operational and maintenance expenditures."

When Hellyer came to the department, defence spending was $1.57 billion a year or 24 per cent of all federal expenditure, a sum and a percentage down substantially from 1956-57, for example, when spending was $1.76 billion and 36.3 per cent of government expenditures. The National Defence slice of the pie was shrinking in the face of rising commitments at home, and Hellyer believed that changes had to be made if there was to be any money at all for desperately needed new equipment. The brigade groups in Europe and Canada had no armoured personnel carriers, a necessity on the atomic battlefield, and tanks and weaponry were obsolescent; the RCAF's Air Division with NATO had, as the 1963 Special Committee on Defence had told the House of Commons, no weapons whatsoever, either conventional or nuclear; the Air Force generally had little transport capability; and the Navy, with its total concentration on anti-submarine warfare, could not carry Canadian troops to Europe – or anywhere else either.

There was another area that concerned the minister. He wanted to introduce "modern management methods into the Canadian Services. I knew that in many cases the hardware and software required . . . could be purchased more economically if acquired for the Forces as a whole rather than on a single service basis."[9] Hellyer's intentions were to remake the Department of National Defence, and as a result he simply refused to sign anything during his first thirty days in office. The breathing space let him get his bearings and prevented the Chiefs from hornswoggling him while he was still green.[10] Considering the way Foulkes had whipped the NORAD agreement through in the first days of the Conservative government in 1957 – and considering the impact of that event on the course of the Diefenbaker government – Hellyer's was a wise precaution.

The key question for Hellyer was finding a way to achieve the changes he wanted. Initially he established a number of departmental study groups to examine all facets of defence policy. The most important of these was one under Dr. Robert Sutherland of the Defence Research Board that had been instructed to study the entire field of Canadian defence policy and to examine all major alternatives.[11] But even before this committee had finished its work, Hellyer had sent the Prime Minister a letter setting out the terms of reference under which the department was preparing a new long-range defence policy. That policy, the Defence minister said, had to be compatible with the aims of Canadian foreign policy, had to be based on alliances to which Canada's contribution should be equitable, had to consider the financial position of the government and the needs of Canadian industry, and where possible had to be independent of unforeseen actions on the part of other nations.[12] There was no suggestion of unification of the forces. Nor was there much more than a dismissive paragraph on the subject in Sutherland's report. As he told Hellyer, Sutherland initially had been in favour of what he called "triphibious" forces, but he had changed his mind when he could not fit such forces into the likely scenarios where Canadian policy might require their use.[13]

That did not discourage Hellyer. In October 1963 he visited Washington and talked with Secretary of Defense Robert McNamara about methods of reorganization.[14] In the meantime, the Department of External Affairs in August had suggested an interdepartmental review of defence policy in the light of a forthcoming NATO study.[15] These discussions and interdepartmental pressures led Hellyer by late fall to the view that he should prepare a White Paper on defence. This was essential, he believed, because it had been years since the last clear statement on defence policy was made; even more important, as he was going to propose changes in defence policy, a White Paper was essential. This effort was unusual, however, in that Hellyer set out to prepare the draft himself, doing the job in longhand in the first two weeks of December 1963. He drew on Sutherland's report "where it fitted what I wanted to do," but much of the draft was purest Hellyer.[16]

The major portion of Hellyer's first draft – but not his sections on organization – was passed to the members of the Chiefs of Staff Committee for comment. The chairman, Air Chief Marshal F.R. Miller, told Hellyer that he recognized the Sutherland touch "and I think much of it was good." The Chief of the Naval Staff, Admiral H.S. Rayner, said that he was "very impressed. It paints a wide picture with far horizons in broad strokes." The Chief of the Air Staff, Air Marshal C.R. Dunlap, had only a few quibbles, and the Chief of the General Staff, General Geoffrey Walsh, thought it well done.[17] More critical comments came from Secretary of State for External Affairs Paul Martin, who objected to the haste with which his department's views were being sought and quarrelled with what he saw as oversimplification.[18] Hellyer also sent a copy of the draft to Prime Minister Pearson on December 27, and in a covering letter referred to the impact his proposed organizational changes would have. They would increase civilian control, he told Pearson, and they would reduce waste, extravagance, and duplication; in addition, they would make the services work together more efficiently. And, he added, "Integration of forces and long range plan will put Canada out in front in respect to innovation, while at the same time maintaining and increasing our effectiveness. Canadian force will attract world-wide attention." For Pearson, looking for ways to enhance national unity and concerned with finding symbols that worked toward this end, that paragraph was probably attractive.[19] At the same time, copies of the draft White Paper went to other departments, and

Hellyer told the Chiefs of Staff that while he was open to changes in detail, the general point of view in the draft was not open to discussion.[20]

Meanwhile, Hellyer put the final touches to his organizational paragraphs and met with the service chiefs on February 7, 1964. His proposal, he wrote in his diary, was "to integrate in full the Armed Forces of Canada" and to replace the existing service chiefs with a single Chief of Defence Staff and the service councils with a single Defence Staff. "The object is complete unification of the three forces into a single force with resultant improvement in efficiency and tremendous savings." The reaction of the Chiefs, Hellyer noted, was predictable. The chairman of the Defence Research Board was favourable, and General Walsh was not difficult to convince. "Dunlap was apprehensive and Rayner very much so. They were every inch the gentlemen, however, and did not lose control of their emotions. All in all it was not as dreadful as I had feared." The next day, after a meeting with Miller, Hellyer wrote that he had had great difficulty controlling himself. "It is the issue of who is going to set military policy – the military or the government. They have been unfettered so long they just can't get used to the idea of taking direction."[21]

Over the next month, Hellyer fought a series of battles for his White Paper. The Department of External Affairs wanted to send the draft to an officials' committee, and Hellyer was forced to agree to this in the Cabinet Committee on External Affairs and Defence despite fears about the number of conflicting views: "If we removed all the offending sections, there would be nothing left except the covers!" The Prime Minister himself wanted to rewrite some sections, and there were continuing tussles with the Chiefs.[22] Finally, with the draft now largely accepted – except insofar as it proposed reorganization of the Forces' structure – the Cabinet committee considered the final version on March 24. Pearson indicated his general satisfaction, and Hellyer gave the chiefs their chance by noting that there was no unanimity on the proposed reorganization. Admiral Rayner said that he favoured moves to bring the services closer together, but he was concerned that a unified force "was a jump into the future with little preparation before take-off." The operational effectiveness of the Navy, he said, would suffer if Canada's forces were unified and those of others were not. The Chief of the Air Staff expressed similar fears and spoke of the morale problems that such a reorganization would create, while the Army representative generally indicated his service's support for the minister's plan. So too did the chairman of the Defence Research Board and, with a few qualifications, the deputy minister of Hellyer's department, Elgin Armstrong. But the Cabinet committee as a whole accepted the draft White Paper and passed it to the full Cabinet for consideration.[23] Approval was a formality, and Hellyer had the go-ahead on March 25.

The White Paper as published argued that Canada's armed forces had never been successfully co-ordinated. The Glassco Commission (the Royal Commission on Government Organization, which reported in 1962-63) had pointed to the size of the administrative "tail" in comparison to the "teeth" – the fighting elements – and had commented unfavourably on the proliferation of committees at Defence Headquarters and at the power each service chief had over the operations of the Chiefs of Staff Committee. But Hellyer rejected Glassco's solution – the transfer of executive control to the Chairman of the Chiefs of Staff. That did not go far enough.

> Following the most careful and thoughtful consideration, the government has decided that there is only one adequate solution. It is the integration of the Armed Forces of Canada under a single Chief of Defence Staff and a single Defence Staff. This will be the first step toward a single unified defence force for Canada.

That was all the White Paper said on unification – it was all Hellyer thought he could get, given the military's hostility. "It was probably enough to include the single sentence," he wrote later.[24]

The White Paper predicted that integration and unification would reduce the headquarters and training establishments and cut costs. It would free money for purchase of equipment – the percentage for this had fallen from 42.9 in 1954 to 13.6 in 1964 – and Hellyer stated that his goal was to see 25 per cent of the defence budget spent on capital goods. And the White Paper also gave some notice to the critics who had worried over the effects on morale if unification took place and who also feared that the healthy competition between the services might be diminished. "Neither of these objections will stand against careful scrutiny," Hellyer argued. "There is no thought of eliminating worthwhile traditions" and competition would not be lost but contained at the service level. The minister also said that he had no preordained plan, that everything would be worked out in practice, and he pledged to introduce a management system for planning and controlling major defence programmes at the departmental level.[25]

In its assessment of the roles of the Forces, the White Paper pledged continued support for Canada's alliances and an expanded role in support of United Nations and other peacekeeping efforts. To do this, the Hellyer document in essence called for the creation of an "intervention force" capable of operating anywhere. In effect, Hellyer was trying to turn the Forces away from their fixation on fighting a major nuclear war, a concentration that tended to paralyse innovation, toward a new focus on mobility and firepower. There was a heavy emphasis in the paper on peacekeeping as a Canadian role, but this was not peacekeeping of the Suez or Congo type. Instead, the intervention force was to be able to move quickly to serve the government's ends; if the United Nations wanted such a unit, it could be provided; if NATO wanted it, well and good. It was a radically different role that Hellyer proposed.

But this role drew sharp criticism from inside the services. Peacekeeping was not universally popular, many officers seeing it as a distraction from the task of preparing to fight Russians in Central Europe. And many feared, as one Navy officer later wrote, "that the concept of unification would alter the roles which had developed since 1950 . . . would conflict with the possibility of continuing alliance commitments."[26] That was not Hellyer's intention at all, and his equipment purchases should have made that clear. Nonetheless the minister would spend much time over the next three years arguing his case: "If that were the objective, why on earth would we have launched a 1.5 billion dollar, 5 year re-equipment program?. . . For [a UN] role alone, an order of blue berets and billy-sticks might suffice. . . ."[27]

The initial response to the White Paper was positive, however. In the House, Hellyer received qualified support from the Opposition, and the service chiefs sent messages to their service men and women, urging co-operation with the government's plans. Admiral Rayner in fact told a Halifax audience that the minister was "vigorous . . . filled with fresh ideas and great determination." Yet the admiral did assure the Navy that the minister was not interested in a single uniform for his unified force. "We have no immediate plans to consider this matter, it is not on the priority list."[28]

Public response was similarly warm. Not unsurprisingly, John Gellner supported the ideas he had pressed on Hellyer a year earlier, and he waxed enthusiastic about Hellyer's ideas of an expanded peacekeeping role. The newspapers were lavish with their adjectives – courageous, forward-looking, realistic, imaginative, pragmatic, revolutionary – and the *Montreal Star* foresaw Canada being able to play a world military role without a big power budget. Above all, Hellyer was hailed for laying down a clear policy after years of drift. That was a major achievement.[29] The most important critical comment came from Leonard Beaton, a Canadian at the London Institute for Strategic Studies. Beaton said nothing about Hellyer's reorganization proposals, but he did blast the minister for ignoring the strategic issues and for failing to question whether Canada's commitments to NATO were necessary. To Beaton, U.N. peacekeeping was the ideal role for Canada. Despite his criticisms, the consensus of opinion was that Hellyer had scored a triumph, and the Minister of National Defence was obviously emboldened to press on.[30]

II

Hellyer's task now was to get his reorganization implemented. On April 16, 1964, a committee completed a study on a new organization for "a Canadian Forces Headquarters" that proposed a defence council, a chief and vice-chief of the Defence Staff, and a variety of functional posts.[31] These suggestions were refined during the next few months. The Act to Amend the National Defence Act was passed through Parliament on July 16, and the positions of Chairman of the Chiefs of Staff, Chief of the Naval Staff, Chief of the General Staff, and Chief of the Air Staff were eliminated. At the end of July Hellyer saw a stream of senior officers one after the other and informed them of their new duties.[32] The new structure had Air Chief Marshal Miller as Chief of the Defence Staff, a four-star post; under him were five three-star officers: Vice-Chief of the Defence Staff, Chief of Personnel, Comptroller General, Chief of Logistics and Engineering Development, and Chief of Operational Readiness. Hellyer scribbled in his diary on August 1, "First day under the new system. All quiet."[33]

The next stage was explained to the senior officers attending the Chief of the Defence Staff's Conference for Senior Commanders in November. "I gave them a 30 minute welcome," Hellyer said, "in which I suggested they get enthusiastic about the program, the change in policy and integration or turn in their badges and take special benefits."[34] That was a bald but not inaccurate summary of Hellyer's remarks.

The minister had told his audience, virtually every senior officer in the Forces, that his policy was designed to create a more balanced force, a move made necessary by the probable nature of future conflicts. The new force would have "a closer association of the sea, air and land elements" and Hellyer admitted that he proposed "radical change. This change was brought about by reverting to first principles, that is by determining what we would do if we were starting to organize the Canadian Armed Forces from the very beginning. . . ." The government's objectives were fourfold: a single recruiting organization; a single basic training organization; a single basic trades training organization; and a full integration of headquarters and commands. "If," Hellyer said, "in achieving these objectives, a single unified Defence Force for Canada is clearly the logical end result, then such a unified Defence Force will be established." There could be no doubt that Hellyer meant what he said: ". . . this is where the Canadian Defence Forces are going and all concerned must realize this fact. . . ."

Mistakes had been made, the minister admitted, and undoubtedly more would follow, but progress had been good to date. He was conscious of the dangers reorganization posed to morale: "In this respect all Senior Commanders have a responsibility to be enthusiastic and positive in dealing with the personnel under their command and must provide the leadership necessary to promote the concept of integration and help overcome morale difficulties during this interim phase."

The questions that followed showed uneasiness but no outright opposition. This continued even when the Chief of the Defence Staff explained plans for a cut of ten thousand men in the Forces' strength, "an arbitrary 20% reduction of the 50,000 personnel that are estimated as being employed in the supporting roles throughout the three Services." In addition, there was to be a 30-per-cent reduction at Canadian Forces Headquarters. The cuts could be accomplished in a reasonable period of time by attrition, but if that route were followed promotions would slow down. "Therefore premature releases are being used to a small extent . . . to preserve some degree of promotion." Those who retired early received what came to be known as the golden bowler, a special cash benefit intended as compensation for lost earnings and reduced pension benefits. By late 1966, 3,344 servicemen had drawn the "bowler," and a total of 26,300 had left the Forces from mid-1963 to the end of 1965.[35]

But there were some sweeteners for the Forces. On December 22, Hellyer announced his Christmas present in the form of a five-year $1.5-billion equipment programme. The Army was to get armoured personnel carriers, new self-propelled artillery and mortars; the Navy would receive four helicopter-equipped destroyer escorts and new supply ships; and the RCAF was to take on strength new transport aircraft. That at least indicated that Hellyer was serious about his talk of new roles.

The equipment did not ease the sting for those who valued the Forces' symbols. On December 31, 1964, the new Canadian flag, to be adopted in February 1965, was declared to be the Armed Forces flag. "I couldn't get any agreement at this stage on a single service ensign," Hellyer said in his diary, "and therefore the above solution seems to be the best of the alternatives." But that solution demanded that the Navy strike its White Ensign, and this provoked outrage. Commodore Robert Hendy, a Toronto lawyer and naval reservist, protested to Hellyer that the White Ensign "was and is the means of identifying in a personal way the Queen's ships'' and his letter contained phrases such as ''British tradition,'' the ''navies of the Commonwealth,'' and ''long-standing tradition.'' Hendy was on a first-name basis with the minister, but his approach was not one calculated to win either Hellyer's or the Prime Minister's support.[36]

Meanwhile the process of carrying out the reorganization at headquarters proceeded apace. The comptroller-general branches of the three services, created between 1955 and 1963 and similarly patterned, came together in a unified branch to control accounting and establishment functions. A new Personnel Branch was formed, designed to handle postings and the careers of all the officers and men of the Forces. Hellyer soon discovered, he said later, that integration had not worked in this branch. The Chief of Personnel, a sailor, insisted on consulting the Chief of Logistics, an airman, about all senior air appointments and the Vice-Chief of the Defence Staff, a soldier, about army appointments. Because of this, Hellyer said, personnel aspects were still being considered on a three-service basis.[37]

Other branches also posed problems. The Technical Services Branch in particular caused difficulties, primarily because each service had its own system and used different terms. But the public relations directorates combined easily – and personnel was reduced from 237 to 76. The construction engineering staffs at headquarters and in the field were also unified with personnel savings of 30 per cent, and the creation of an integrated recruiting organization was largely completed late in 1965. The work on a common trades structure also proceeded through 1965, with the result that some 350 classifications in the three services were cut to 97 in the new system. Similarly, the pay system was unified and computerized, the intelligence branches were combined, and a new Canadian Forces Communications System came into operation on April 1, 1965.[38] There had been difficulties in forcing the three service headquarters into one, but even if he had done nothing else Hellyer would still have been remembered – and favourably – for that major achievement.

The second stage of integration called for a radical revamping of the field commands. The basic structure was agreed to by the Defence Council on March 29, 1965,[39] and details were made public on June 7. The eleven major commands for the three services in Canada were reduced at a stroke to six: Mobile Command, Maritime Command, Air Defence Command, Air Transport Command, Training Command, and Material Command. The Canadian forces in NATO continued to report directly to CFHQ, and the militia and other service functions were to be handled by small regional offices reporting directly to headquarters.

The new structure, fully operational by 1966, was essentially functional in organization. Mobile Command was composed of two infantry brigade groups and tactical air units. Maritime Command consisted of the sea and air maritime units on both coasts, and Training Command was charged with personnel selection and with providing individual training from basic to advanced levels. All in all, the new structure was logical, and Hellyer was pleased. "The command structure has been *very* well received," he noted on June 7, "both internally and externally. I think it makes a lot of sense and the reduction from eleven to six will save us a lot of overhead and money." The next day he added that "our solution seems to have very general support. It is interesting that we can do this and pull it off so smoothly without even referring it to cabinet – in contrast to some of the silly things that have to go to the cabinet because of their political consequences."[40] The political consequences of unification were still to come.

While reorganization proceeded, Hellyer was doing his best to change the way the Forces planned, budgeted for, and secured their major weapons systems. His solution was to support the Air Force-style Integrated Defence Program, a method of planning, formulating, selecting, and controlling all major aspects of defence activities in order to assist top management in decision making.[41] Money was already tight, and some such scheme was necessary, for Walter Gordon was proposing to cut back defence spending even if, as he told Pearson, "this would require changes in existing international commitments."[42]

One of the first measures of the new system – and one that critics argued was a complete failure – was the selection of an aircraft to provide tactical support for the "intervention force." In September 1964 Hellyer talked to the Prime Minister and the Minister of Defence Production, C.M. Drury, about the need for a new aircraft and, Hellyer noted, it was "clear the Boss was on my side."[43] But that was only the beginning. On October 27, Hellyer and Miller had a confrontation over the RCAF's attempt, as Hellyer saw it, to tamper with cost figures so as to rule out one of the contending aircraft, the Northrop F-5.[44] Over the next ten months the wheels in the department ground slowly as the effort to fit an aircraft to the operational characteristics desired by the minister – and the different ones wanted by the RCAF – got under way. On February 19, 1965, the evaluation process concluded that the A-7 aircraft was best, followed by the A-4. The relatively cheap F-5 was pronounced unsuitable. But the F-5 was the minister's choice, not least because of its cost, and new criteria were prepared; on July 9, the F-5 was recommended to Cabinet, and six days later the public was informed: $238 million was allotted for a "new plane for a new role," a single-seat tactical support airplane (with a few two-seaters as trainers).[45]

Hellyer had forced his choice on the airmen, who preferred a fighter-bomber that cost far too much. Unfortunately, by the time the CF-5 (so designated to indicate the Canadian version of the F-5) was taken into service between August 1969 and September 1971, the priorities of the Forces had changed and the tactical support role had been cut back, so that the CF-5 was of use only as a trainer. The lead time of five to seven years had turned out to be longer than the lifetime of the tactical support role – or the political life of Paul Hellyer.

III

By the end of 1965, Hellyer had imposed his will on the armed forces in the form of a drastic reorganization of Canadian Forces Headquarters, a reshaping of the services' field organization into a tri-service, functional basis, and a new management system for his department. Now, as he told a meeting of the Defence Council on December 21, 1965, it was time to consider the ultimate shape or form of the Canadian forces so that all could "see clearly in which direction we are going and to ensure that there are no ambiguities." This was essential, Hellyer added, because "the lack of clear and unequivocal answers to questions being asked is having detrimental effects on morale."

The discussion that followed, Hellyer wrote in his diary, was "most fascinating." The "two stars [major-generals]" gave their views, "some straight forward – some equivocal," but "all the three stars [lieutenant-generals] are opposed" except for one who was "just confused."[46] In fact, the minutes suggest an emerging consensus that unification should press ahead. The deputy chief of Technical Services, for example, told his peers that "the forces must unify. To integrate and stop short of unification would only lead to confusion." The deputy chief of Operations, a sailor, said that the "process of unification had started and cannot be stopped. There should be a unified force and a collective name for it." Some parts of the new force, this admiral added, could not be unified – it would not be sensible to unify the operating elements and make the personnel interchangeable. That led the minister to say that it had never been his intention to create "universalists. The forces will always require technically trained specialists to undertake specialist missions on land, sea and air and there should be no apprehension about this. . . . The question is whether this can best be accomplished with forces as separate legal entities and with separate identities or as one unified force." That satisfied the admiral, who said that he favoured keeping the present rank designations but that he did not consider the problems of uniforms too important.

The admiral's comments were entirely typical of the two-star opinions. Perhaps it was because Hellyer, the man with power over their careers, was present, but virtually all of those who spoke expressed support for unification. To some that meant that the operating arms of the forces remained untouched while support elements were combined; to others, the questions of names, titles, and loyalties were a difficulty.

But as Hellyer had observed, there was opposition. The comptroller-general, Lieutenant-General F.J. Fleury, argued that integration had already disrupted morale in the field, and "it would be premature to take another major leap forward now. If the soldier is off balance now, are we going to improve things by jolting him again?" The chief of Personnel, Vice-Admiral Kenneth Dyer, also urged an evolutionary process and vehemently rejected the idea of a single uniform for the forces. The vice-chief of the Defence Staff, Lieutenant-General R.W. Moncel, posed the questions "if, when and how. . . . He said we should not rush into unification with a few notes on the back of a cigarette package. When an announcement is made on unification we must know where we are going. We will be getting down immediately to practicalities – issues of badges, caps, ranks, careers, etc." Nothing, Moncel added, "has been done so far in integration which inhibits us proceeding to resolve these practical issues with the existing machinery and without the need for legislation on unification." It was the practicalities that concerned this able officer who argued for "a single designation which would encompass multiple families that do certain things. . . . It was possible to perpetuate the single bits that have no civilian counterpart and retain the great names that go with them. The [army] Corps names were meaningful to personnel and should be retained. In the same way it was important to continue to allow people to join the Air Force and the Navy."[47]

Probably Hellyer should have heeded the caution lights that Fleury, Dyer, and Moncel had flashed. If the top officers at headquarters were opposed to unification, they had the capacity to delay matters, to stall, to wait out the minister. Politics is a most uncertain profession, and even though Hellyer had survived the November 1965 election and retained his portfolio (despite Pearson's offer of another one if he wished),[48] he could be shuffled or promoted at any time. Time was on the side of the military chiefs. Hellyer knew this all too well, but he was not disposed to place undue weight on matters such as cap badges, corps loyalties, and other service curiosa. His decision was to press on, and in all likelihood that had been his intention since the White Paper.

There was also an additional motive in Hellyer's mind. He had aspirations to succeed Pearson as Liberal leader and prime minister, and Pearson's retirement, particularly after the indecisive election of 1965, could not be long delayed. Given the drift and confusion that seemed to characterize the Pearson administration, Hellyer knew that his air of vigour and decisiveness was his strongest asset. On the other hand, the minister must have known that unification with its emotional baggage would make him enemies. He had integrated the forces, saved money, and created a high profile for himself in a portfolio that usually buried its occupants; the returns were starting to diminish as he pressed on with unification, but plunge ahead he did. The decision was a fateful one for Hellyer and for the Armed Forces.[49]

Hellyer wrote to the Prime Minister on January 27, 1966, to suggest "that integration has advanced to the stage where a decision on the final stage of unification should now be taken. The effectiveness of integration," he argued, "is being impeded by the problems associated with maintaining the three services within an integrated organization" and the developing uncertainty in the forces could be eliminated by a clear statement. As Hellyer told his leader,

> The concept of unification essentially is a single force, with one name, one uniform, one set of rank designations and one career management policy. Integration was basically unification of management and policy direction and the reorganization of headquarters and commands. Unification will have a more direct impact on individuals than integration and will raise emotions associated with the change of names and traditions and in these circumstances a decisive approach is essential. There is a broad base of support within the services and I believe the public in general for this concept of unification, founded on an entirely new single force, although opposition can be expected from various quarters. . . .

In reply, Pearson agreed that Hellyer could proceed to prepare the necessary legislation. But the Prime Minister added that he felt strongly that the sentiments and traditions associated with the organization of the defence forces in the past should be retained to the maximum possible extent. Hellyer had his go-ahead, but Pearson had also signalled him to exercise caution.[50]

So far the whole process of integration and unification had proceeded with quite astonishing smoothness, but the roof was about to fall in. In February 1966, Hellyer presented his department's estimates for 1966-67 to the House of Commons, and under the provisional Standing Orders then being used, his estimates were referred for detailed consideration to the Standing Committee on National Defence. The committee deliberations, as the ablest student of unification noted, showed that there was substantial unease among Opposition members regarding the publicity Hellyer was garnering and because they suspected that the savings from integration were illusory. There was also a growing desire among M.P.s to hear from serving officers. Hellyer ultimately agreed to allow officers to appear, and that gave the opposition to unification within the department a focus.[51]

In his own testimony to the committee on May 12, Hellyer said, "We have now reached the stage for final steps toward a unified force, as forecast in the White Paper." That statement, one that could scarcely have come as a surprise to the senior officers at CFHQ, somehow seemed to force the issue and to convince the doubters that Hellyer was going too fast. There were personal reasons mingled together with questions of policy. General Moncel, the vice-chief, expected to succeed Air Chief Marshal Miller as Chief of the Defence Staff in mid-July 1966; indeed, Miller had confidently told the general that the job was his. But Hellyer had realized just how cool Moncel was to his plans, and he was determined not to have another chief like Miller to obstruct, delay, and always advise caution. As Hellyer wrote, Miller "was always strongly opposed from the outset . . . and may have thought that as Chief of Staff of the integrated force he could prevent unification from taking place. I have no doubt that had he outlasted the Minister he would have succeeded in that objective." Miller's view, in turn, was that "the thinking of the Minister on the matter of unification puzzle[s] me completely, – generally I found him quite sound but on this subject he is hard to fathom."[52]

In the circumstances, Hellyer wanted a supporter as Chief of the Defence Staff. His choice was General J.V. Allard, the commander of Mobile Command and a francophone. That last quality, particularly in the context of the mid-1960s, was a positive asset, as was the simple fact that Allard was less wedded than many English-speaking Canadians to the British customs and traditions of the Forces.[53]

Faced with Allard's promotion over his head, and apparently fearing that Hellyer's rush to unification could not be checked, Moncel decided to retire. He was joined by Fleury and Dyer who also took early retirement (although Hellyer agreed to dismiss the officers so that they would receive their full pensions, and that technicality, of course, made their departures seem all the more shocking to nervous officers). Apprehension in the Forces was not at all eased when Hellyer promoted Commodore R.L. Hennessy directly from one-star to three-star rank and made him Chief of Personnel. Hennessy was the author of a report that found ways to overcome the major difficulties involved in unifying the enlisted ranks of the services.

Matters were compounded by the extraordinary actions of Admiral W.M. Landymore.[54] Commanding on the Atlantic Coast, Landymore believed that unification would destroy the efficiency, effectiveness, and morale of his beloved Navy. He made no secret of his views to his officers and men, and he also told the Standing Committee on National Defence as much. Landymore's formal statement to the committee had been sent to the minister's office for clearance (along with those of other officers testifying) and Bill Lee, Hellyer's executive assistant, had made some changes in Landymore's remarks on personnel matters. Landymore made no protest at the time and delivered the revised statement; he also responded to the committee's questions on the Navy's attitude to unification by noting that there was unrest among the officers and quite a number of the senior men: "In this sense, I would have said the morale is bad."[55] Hellyer and the admiral talked privately after that meeting, and Landymore repeated that unification would be a disaster. With the admiral apparently unwilling to carry out the minister's policy, the outcome was clear. But Landymore was not sacked immediately. That would occur after the mini-exodus of Fleury, Moncel, and Dyer, after General Allard's appointment, and after a substantial number of senior officers also decided to take early retirement. They would do so in July and August wholesale.[56]

On July 12, Landymore learned that he was through, and the admiral decided to go public. This he did, telling reporters that integration had failed, that the costs involved in a new single-service uniform were high and wasteful, and that unification had demoralized the officer corps. It was, he said, his "responsibility to make clear to the Minister the feelings of my officers. . . . I do this because I have a loyalty to them as well as to the government and the country."[57] Hellyer learned of Landymore's revolt en route to Edmonton on July 15, and as soon as he landed he exploded. "I don't pretend that support for any integration policy has been unanimous. I never expected it to be. The problems are from the very senior people only." There might be more resignations, he said, but there were plenty of good people below the top levels. The law of the land, the minister stated, "puts the military under civilian control and this is the way it's going to be run for a change." The issue, in other words, was civilian control. Hellyer added that he was surprised that Landymore had not blown up in public before; he said, "I know that they are out after my head. . . . I only hope they don't become martyrs." The senior officers, the minister concluded, had never really believed that unification would go ahead. "Suddenly they have discovered we are serious and it is going to happen."[58]

The fat was in the fire, and the Prime Minister was quick to tell Hellyer that it was not the headlines that upset him so much as "the possibility of unfriendly politicians and opponents of integration being able to exploit the situation in a bad way." Pearson added that he shared Hellyer's belief in "integration" – it seemed significant that he did not say unification – "and will continue to back you fully in bringing it about. I am anxious, however, as I have already told you, to preserve as many of the service traditions and as much of the old distinctions between the sea, land and air components of an integrated service as is consistent with the achievement of the basic objective." What did Pearson have in mind? "I am thinking of such things as identification of army units by their historic names, uniforms which will associate the wearers with the traditional services . . . rank designations, etc." Such concessions "would dampen down controversy and remove anxieties, genuine or manufactured, if it could be made clear that changes of this kind would not be made without good reason and only on the recommendation of the service members of the Defence [Council]."

There was little doubt that Pearson was backing away from the fight. His diplomatic instinct for compromise as the answer always pushed him in that direction, particularly when it was the interests of one of his ministers – and not his own – that were at stake. But Hellyer was not one to back away, and he replied that "the final responsibility must rest with the civilian head of the department. An abrogation of this principle would be both unconstitutional and an undesirable precedent." Angry as he was, Hellyer still managed to close his letter by noting that Pearson's confidence and support from the outset of the reorganization and through the controversy had been appreciated, a courteous reminder that the Prime Minister had been consulted at each and every stage.

Hellyer's letter temporarily outflanked Pearson who replied that naturally he would "continue to support" unification but now the problems "are not in the field of strategy so much as tactics." The Prime Minister agreed that ministers had to assume responsibility for their recommendations to government. "My thought – which was too carelessly expressed – was that it will help to secure public and Parliamentary acceptance for recommendations . . . to have it known that the senior serving officers support and even initiate such recommendations. That is all I had in mind." The Prime Minister was on side again; how long he would stay there was unclear.[59]

While Pearson and Hellyer exchanged letters, the opponents of unification were organizing. At the end of June 1966 the Navy League of Canada, the Naval Officers Association of Canada, and the Royal Canadian Naval Association had formed the Committee on the Maritime Component of the Canadian Defence Force. The purpose was "to consider implications of present and indicated policies of Defence Department on matters relating to maritime force," or so a telegram to David Groos, M.P., the chairman of the House of Commons Standing Committee on National Defence, said. What the sailors wanted was a full inquiry into the organization of the forces before further steps towards unification were taken.[60] After the Landymore revolt, another organization began to take form – TRIO, the Tri-Services Identities Organization. This group was founded on July 12 by a group with naval antecedents, and it was formally organized after a meeting at the Toronto Club on July 28 convened by Colonel Robert Hilborn, a militia infantryman with substantial business interests. Hilborn had asked his guests, a group that included a large number of "responsible and respected" retired officers in the Toronto area, if the "actions of those in the Navy tradition [are] reasonable and worth supporting?"[61] The answer was yes. TRIO's aims were clear: to stop the unification process, at least until a full inquiry was convened.

TRIO began its public work in mid-August. The Toronto group was the sparkplug of the operation, but eventually thirty-five branches, spread across the country, were in the field. It was not without its problems. Many of the members were militia officers fearful that they might offend the Chief of the Defence Staff and the minister and thus hurt their units; others were businessmen who feared for contracts or lawyers who worried that they might not get government work. The Royal Canadian Legion was chary of commitment, perhaps a reaction to the roasting it had taken because of its neanderthal rejection of the new Canadian flag. French-Canadian support was weak, not least because General Allard supported unification. And the recently departed generals and admirals hung back because they were on retirement leave and technically serving officers. Nor could TRIO even secure wholehearted support from the Conference of Defence Associations, the omnibus organization that brought together reservists from all three services. TRIO's leaders blamed the Liberal allegiance of CODA's president, but that only suggested that TRIO itself was Tory in cast. And, given its lack of support from retired enlisted men, TRIO was vulnerable to charges that it was a brass hats organization.

TRIO was, however, able to get sympathetic press coverage – Brigadier R.S. Malone of the Winnipeg *Free Press* and the Sifton papers, for example, lent his influence – but the simple fact was that TRIO did not have public support. A Gallup poll of February 18, 1967, showed 48 per cent support for unification and only 33 per cent against, a good showing for Hellyer after months of a bad press. Thus, if TRIO caused Hellyer and the government a few bad moments it did not seriously threaten unification's implementation.[62]

What really threatened was the possibility that no senior officer could be found to take Landymore's post in Halifax. On July 18, 1966, Hellyer tackled this problem, first meeting with the RCAF second-in-command to Landymore, an officer who briefed the minister in detail on the admiral's secret meetings with Navy officers. Then the minister met with Commodore J.C. O'Brien, on whom Hellyer's hopes were riding: "If O'Brien will take the command we should get everything under control – if not we may be in real trouble." O'Brien was very nervous, Hellyer wrote. "I told him the reasons for unification and he was most attentive. He said there were certain points he would like clarified. It sounded like bargaining but when I heard the substance there were no requests that were not in accordance with policy and I could agree in clear conscience." The next day O'Brien agreed to take over the post of Maritime Commander Atlantic and to accept promotion to rear admiral.[63] He left for Halifax at once, and the immediate crisis had passed.

Now Hellyer's task was to steer the amendments to the National Defence Act necessary to implement unification through the committee process. On August 2, the Defence Council considered the draft. "What a contrast with the 'old' Defence Council," Hellyer exulted. "All of the discussion was 'pro'. Only the details were considered at length. . . . What a pleasant atmosphere to have everyone working together to the same goal."[64] At last the minister had a group of officers around him who accepted his goals – but the cost in senior officers had been high.

A week later, the draft bill went to Cabinet committee and the minister presented the case for unification. Hellyer wrote in his diary: "To diminish the loyalty to and identification with a single environment. The practical application being related to representation, establishments, seniority and objectivity. The policy was approved by the committee and referred to the cabinet for approval. Good!"[65] Hellyer later noted, "It is basically a question of whether the defence interests of the country will be better served by having Service personnel, particularly officers, identifying themselves primarily with the total Canadian Armed Forces aims or with the narrower desires of one service and a single environment." What he wanted was decisions "based on what is right for the nation and the forces as a whole," and that could only come through unification.[66] The Cabinet accepted the final draft early in the fall of 1966. Hellyer introduced the unification bill in the House on November 4.

To the minister's surprise, Pearson went to bat for unification when the Opposition tied up the House in a filibuster during a debate on interim supply. The Conservatives wanted to get the bill to the Defence Committee before second reading and, as Gordon Churchill said, they would fight like hell for this.[67] But the Liberals hung in. On November 9 Hellyer wrote, "It is really a war of nerves. Who will capitulate first?" The caucus, he said, was "united – more so than on any other issue! The only exceptions were a few of the ambitious" who either intended to seek the leadership or were trying to hurt Hellyer's own chances. The next day Hellyer wrote that he was delighted when the Prime Minister spoke "in full support! He was great! He backed me up all the way and then told the House that we had enough money to pay the mid-month salaries and that the debate could continue as far as the government was concerned. . . . He really pulled the rug out from under *them*." The Tory filibuster dragged on for several days more, but with the opening of the PCs' annual meeting in Ottawa and with John Diefenbaker's Calvary there, the pressure was off.[68] The bill went into second reading.

Hellyer spoke on Bill C-243, the Canadian Forces Reorganization Bill, on December 7. His address, carefully prepared "by more people than any speech given by an MND in recent history" and "checked more times by more serving officers than you would believe," was massive, sprawling over twenty pages of Hansard and taking 105 minutes to read. "A few brave souls managed to stick it out to the end," Hellyer wrote.[69]

The Prime Minister's support during the filibuster and Hellyer's performance on second reading had obviously disheartened unification's opponents. Commodore Hendy, one of the TRIO founders, told a friend that "I am afraid I detect a hardening of the government's approach . . . and this will leave us with the hope that the new Bill C-243 will run into long opposition when the full debate on second reading gets under way and will also be subject to long scrutiny by Defence Committee."[70] But Bill C-243 passed second reading on February 2, 1967, by 98 votes to 62. The focus of action once again had shifted to the Standing Committee on National Defence.

The committee, chaired by David Groos (a former naval officer whose brother was heading a West Coast TRIO branch), began its three-a-day hearings on February 7 with the intention of reporting by the end of the month. The hearings turned into an all-out effort to derail unification as the Conservatives, on occasion assisted by the NDP, fought tooth and nail to reject each and every clause.

The highlights were the performances of Admirals Landymore and Jeffry Brock. An officer with a distinguished fighting record, Brock had been sacked in September 1964 and had been working actively with the Conservatives against unification, passing them queries and lists of names of officers to call as witnesses. In his own testimony Brock said that he could not believe anyone would want unification. In other countries the idea had been advocated only by crackpots and discarded. As for his dismissal, it had been done to inhibit the criticism of others.[71] Landymore's appearances on February 15 and 16 featured three written briefs and full testimony. The briefs offered his version of his campaign against unification, his relations with Hellyer, and the way his earlier brief had been censored. But Landymore slipped into farce when he charged that Mobile Command was not only too big but "dangerous to our democracy. If ever a commander of that Command decided to set himself up to control this country of ours, he has a ready made organization to achieve it."[72] That laid the admiral open to ridicule from which he never recovered, and Hellyer exulted, writing that Landymore had "bombed." The public reaction "is that he must be out of his mind."[73]

But Hellyer too was to make a major gaffe. When he testified on February 23, as he wrote later, "All went beautifully until about a quarter to ten [at night]. Then Forrestall [Conservative M.P. from Halifax] said did I wish to say why Landymore had been fired and apologize to him. By 9.45 I was physically and emotionally exhausted. I asked Forrestall if he was willing to accept responsibility for the question and when he said yes – I blurted out the truth. I said Landymore was fired for 18 months consistent disloyalty to the policy of the people he was paid to serve."[74] The next day Hellyer added, "It was really too bad that I opened my big mouth last night – otherwise I think we had them licked. Now the news is all Landymore and we have a first class diversion."[75]

So it was. Hellyer accused Landymore of holding secret Navy meetings and excluding Air Force officers in his command from them. That was the basis of his charges, and after a committee row, Hellyer offered to apologize if Landymore could say that there had been no such meetings. On February 27, the minister said that he did not feel there had been any "conscious disloyalty to Service or Country" on Landymore's part. The next day, with Landymore again on the stand, Hellyer seized an opportunity to withdraw his charge completely. "I think it was the right thing to do," he said in his diary, "because of the military connotation of the word disloyal and also the only way to get [the Committee] back on the rails."[76]

By March 1 Hellyer had taken a beating in the committee and from the press. Now it was Pearson's turn. The Prime Minister told Hellyer "there was some question of the Bill being put through this session," and there were rumours abroad that a deal had been struck with the Conservatives to end the session at Easter and thus effectively kill C-243.[77] But when Cabinet discussed the idea the next day, Hellyer was pleasantly surprised to get the support of Paul Martin, Robert Winters, and C.M. Drury, three of the senior ministers, and the decision was to proceed.[78] As was usually the case, however, nothing was ever final in the Pearson Cabinet, and rumours persisted that the bill would not be brought to a vote before the summer recess. After the funeral of Governor General Vanier at Quebec City, Hellyer seized the chance provided by their returning on the train together to beard Pearson. If the bill was not passed before prorogation, he told the Prime Minister, "you will have to find a new minister." He got his way – "You're serious about that, aren't you?" Pearson said – and Judy LaMarsh, Hellyer's friend and by then openly contemptuous of Pearson's weakness, said loudly in the House, "What the hell did you do to him? Pour concrete down his back?"[79] Bill C-243 was on the agenda after Easter.

The debate was long and heated in the House, but there were few new arguments. Finally the government resorted to the guillotine on April 18 to cut off the endless debate – but not before a further seven days had been allotted to it. The Social Credit and the NDP, not entirely happy with unification or with Hellyer (who was called "demagogic and autocratic" by Harold Winch), nonetheless largely voted for the bill,[80] and unification passed on April 25 on a vote of 127 to 73. The Canadian Armed Forces were officially unified on February 1, 1968. Paul Hellyer had won.

It was a pyrrhic victory. The Minister of National Defence had achieved sweeping alterations in his department. He had created a policy for a force that had hitherto not had clear conceptions of its role; he had integrated the headquarters and made it more efficient; he had established functional commands in the field; he had tried, unsuccessfully, to get more money for equipment. But he had also tampered with the uniforms, badges, rank styles, and traditions of three fiercely proud services – "military fuss 'n feathers," John Gellner called it. Hellyer was certainly correct when he said that what was needed was some loyalty above service loyalty. But service loyalties were very important to men whose job it was to risk their lives for their country and who, while never expecting public acclaim in peacetime, did believe in their own arcane rituals as a necessary substitute. Had Hellyer stopped before putting the Canadian Forces into a single uniform, he might have been remembered as one of the greatest Defence ministers in our history.[81]

But he did not and he is not. Instead, Hellyer is remembered as arrogant and inflexible, the man who foisted green uniforms on the services. That is unfair, of course, but public perceptions and politics are unfair. Hellyer had achieved much, but he would not capture the leadership when Pearson stepped down early in 1968.

CHAPTER 10

What Does Quebec Want?

In the middle 1950s, Quebec seemed to have been standing still for many years. Maurice Duplessis's Union Nationale controlled politics in the province more completely than ever, and electoral districts that did not vote for Le Chef had their roads left unpaved, their bridges unbuilt. Big business remained largely an English-speaking preserve, and scarcely a major corporation with its headquarters in Montreal operated in anything but the English language, however many of the secretaries or maintenance staff were French speaking. Quebec was no longer a society in which lawyers, notaries, and doctors were the only professionals, but that old saw still had enough validity to make a francophone engineer or technician a rarity. And French Canadians earned much less on average than English Canadians in Quebec. That situation was starting to concern some people who feared that Montreal could never progress, could never catch up to Toronto or New York or Paris so long as the society remained under its existing leadership and fixed in its current direction.

Just as worrisome for many French-speaking Canadians were the attitudes of the province's and the country's anglophones. In 1956, for example, André Laurendeau, the editor of *Le Devoir*, and Murray Ballantyne, the son of a distinguished political and business family and a CCFer, began to prepare an exchange of letters for publication. The intent was to raise a "Canadian Controversy," a dialogue on French-English relations. In the course of a few months, the gulf between the two men, between the two solitudes in Canada, became all too clear. Ballantyne was exercised by the response of the Quebec press and public to the proposal of the Canadian National Railways to name its new Montreal hotel "The Queen Elizabeth/Le Reine Elisabeth," a tiny issue of very limited significance but one that had somehow focused Quebec attention. "Suppose," Ballantyne began, "you start by telling me why so many of your people seem to believe that the name of our

Sovereign is not good enough for a hotel being erected by our national railway system." Laurendeau replied that the CNR choice was one that could be found in Sydney, Singapore, or any British African colony, and he asked, with genuine puzzlement, why the controversy disturbed Ballantyne so much: "Votre enfance 'imperialiste' remonte-t-elle à la gorge? Les chinoiseries du protocole paralysent-elles vos réflexes habituels?" The exchanges between the two friends grew heated enough so that the project was abandoned, itself a minor matter but a revealing one. The two cultures were separated from each other by more than language, and Laurendeau, an intellectual with a wide experience of the world, simply could not comprehend why the Crown, "une idée froide, un concept de juriste," seemed so important to Ballantyne, a man whose roots in Canada went back for generations.[1] Each culture remained *terra incognita* to the other.[2]

A change had begun in Quebec, nonetheless. In October 1959, Laurendeau's newspaper published a letter by a "Frère Untel" or "Brother Anonymous," a teaching brother who propounded what seemed to be almost heretical views on education, language, the religious bureaucracy, and personal freedom. Frère Untel subsequently produced a book, *Les Insolences du Frère Untel*, to which Laurendeau provided a preface, and the book became a runaway bestseller. The winds of change were beginning to blow, but the Church resisted fiercely. Cardinal Léger, Archbishop of Montreal, wrote privately to *Le Devoir* to complain about "la polémique" of Frère Untel which opposed "l'intervention de la Hiérarchie du Québec à la bonté et à la compréhension du Pape Jean XXIII." The brother had been severely admonished by his superiors, and the hierarchy had been led to believe that the attacks upon it would stop; moreover, Léger said, he had told his colleagues that *Le Devoir* had promised fidelity, but "vous avez manquer vos engagements." *Le Devoir* often wrote of the fear that stultified religious life in the province, but Léger said he had been in Montreal for ten years, and where was the evidence? He was convinced, the Cardinal concluded threateningly, that the Holy See might have to intervene to show Catholics in Quebec the path to true Christianity.[3]

How was this only slightly veiled attack on the freedom of *Le Devoir* to publish to be handled? A few years earlier, the newspaper might have knuckled under, but not in the fall of 1960. After agonizing over his reply, after trying to avoid "tout sucre et tout miel, de cacher sa pensée derrière des formules," Laurendeau noted that there was widespread support for and interest in Frère Untel, and although the voice of the people was not always the voice of God and the Church was not a democracy, "un livre comme les *Insolences*, il me semble, doit être en partie jugé par les résonances qu'il éveille dans le public." The book wasn't dangerous, Laurendeau argued; what was dangerous was the reaction to it of the religious authorities.[4] Even though Frère Untel's order sent him into exile (to study in Rome), even though the Church ostensibly retained its hold, the episode was revealing and important, not least for the way Laurendeau and *Le Devoir* had fought for the freedom of the press. And even Cardinal Léger, no ogre, was soon caught up in the wake of the affair. In Rome in late 1961, he told Frère Untel that the average Quebecker "rejette violemment le cléricalisme mais on ne rejette pas l'Eglise."[5] That was probably a correct assessment of the situation in Quebec at that point – clericalism was being rejected even if the Church and its teachings were not. But soon even that adherence was to change, and one of the most startling demonstrations was the decline in the birth-rate in Quebec from twenty-eight per thousand in 1959 to fourteen per thousand, the lowest in Canada, just twelve years later. The contraceptive pill had effectively ended the power of Church dogma for the women of French Canada.

What had happened to open the floodgates? The starting point was widely believed to have been the death of Maurice Duplessis in November 1959. Reforms in church and state, in business and the professions, in culture and academe that had been percolating almost unnoticed suddenly blossomed forth into public view. The Liberal victory in the provincial elections of June 1960, a stunning upset, accelerated the process of change markedly as Premier Jean Lesage and his able crew of ministers began to question the established verities. The electoral system was unfair? The gerrymandering that had kept the rural regions of the province in control of the legislature (and under the control of the Union Nationale) was reversed at a stroke, and Montreal at last received the representation it had been denied. Hydro-Québec was run by English-speaking technocrats? Why not have Québécois in charge? Soon they were, and the remaining privately owned electricity companies in the province were nationalized to boot. Quebec needed a department of education to lift the dead hand of the Church from the schools? By 1963 it would have one. And the federal system? Could it meet the province's needs? If not, perhaps separation was the answer, and soon there were a number of *indépendantiste* movements in the field and some ministers in the Lesage Cabinet who obviously sympathized with the goal of independence – unless Quebec could get what it wanted from Ottawa.

The major concerns hinged on the demographic situation of the province and of French Canadians in Canada generally. According to the 1961 Census, 12,284,762 Canadians spoke only English, 3,489,866 only French, and 2,231,172 were bilingual in French and English;

232,447 spoke neither of the two principal languages. In terms of mother tongue, 10,660,534 claimed English and 5,123,151 French, and the gap between the number citing French as their mother tongue and the number indicating they spoke only French worried those Quebeckers concerned with the creeping anglicization of the province and fearing the disappearance of the race. The figures for Quebec alone did nothing to ease the fears. There, 608,635 spoke only English, 3,254,856 spoke only French and 1,338,878 professed themselves to be bilingual. Of those numbers, 697,402 claimed English as their mother tongue while 4,269,689 claimed French, thus seemingly demonstrating that very few English-speaking Quebeckers learned French and that almost all the *bilingues* came from the francophone community. The revenge of the cradle had not succeeded; indeed, the spectre of assimilation seemed a real possibility.[6]

The Quiet Revolution, a phrase just beginning to be heard in Quebec and out, provided a focus for all the concerns in the province. There seemed to be very little that Quebec could not do on its own, so confident did the Lesage government seem. The sterile pro-autonomy rhetoric that had characterized the Duplessis years was gone; in its place was tough talk and an apparently genuine willingness to go it alone if the federal government did not change the rules of the federal game to benefit the province.

The ferment puzzled and alarmed English Canadians used to regarding La Belle Province as full of clerics, hockey-playing *habitants*, and political corruption. "What does Quebec want?" – a question beginning to be asked with increasing frequency – expressed the mood. Student groups began holding conferences, editorialists began viewing with alarm, and the pundits set to work. Eugene Forsey, a leading constitutional scholar, noted that the English-Canadian reaction to the idea that Quebec might separate from Canada was first of all profanity, secondly, a silence of mystification or hope that if Quebec was left alone the idea would disappear, and thirdly, a "grovelling acquiescence in what any group of French-Canadians want."[7] The note of growing exasperation was pronounced.

Perhaps it was with those English-Canadian attitudes in mind that André Laurendeau on January 20, 1962, proposed an inquiry into the condition of bilingualism in Canada, an idea instantly and characteristically dismissed by Prime Minister Diefenbaker.[8] The next month an informal committee on French-English relations met in Montreal with about fifteen in attendance, including Laurendeau, Maxwell Cohen of McGill University, Pierre Trudeau, then a law professor at the Université de Montréal, Claude Ryan of *Le Devoir*, and Frank Scott, the constitutional lawyer, professor, and poet. Meeting in private at McGill, the conferees agreed that the talk of separatism in the air was an indication of the seriousness of the situation, even though they noted "a certain amount of separatism in the heart of every French-Canadian." But they also agreed that the root of the problem was economic – there would be no talk of independence if people believed that Confederation had paid off in jobs and wealth. More theoretically, the meeting agreed that Quebeckers had a sense of themselves as a nation while English Canadians, with their emotional tie to England, still saw Canada and themselves as fundamentally British. That was probably still true in 1962, though the British tie was fading rapidly in the post-Suez years. The francophones at the meeting also pronounced the idea of Quebec as a rural Arcadia dead and buried, something the census data had long shown; they would use the powers of the state to catch up to the rest of Canada. And, they argued, Quebec was not a province like the others.[9] Given the people present at that meeting and the fact that one became a Cabinet minister and then prime minister and that two were later royal commissioners, there was a certain importance to those few hours spent laying out the problems.

Still, the English Canadians who had participated were untypical of their compatriots. Much more typical was the editorial writer in the *Globe and Mail* who noted on December 21, 1962, that Quebec was in good hands under Premier Jean Lesage. "If we have patience, the discovery already made by [Quebec's] leaders, that English is the language of commerce and is as essential to Quebec as to the rest of us, will spread throughout the rest of the populace. We will find wider areas of agreement. French-speaking Canadians will retain their culture, as the Welsh and Scotch have done. We will be able in time to find the unity we seek."[10] Speak white and assimilate seemed to be the Toronto newspaper's message.

The *Globe* did not yet realize that Quebec was not a province *commes les autres*. Abbé Groulx, the old warhorse of Quebec nationalism, did not forget that when he wrote to André Laurendeau in late April 1962: "Il faut établir de façon claire et nette l'existence de deux nations au Canada, un traitement d'égalité pour les deux d'un bout à l'autre du pays; traitement d'égalité dans les faits plutôt que dans les textes." Moreover, Groulx argued, Quebec had to get the revenues necessary to finance itself as a sovereign state or it would find itself facing a fatal choice. If the federal state turned out to be only a "*duperie*," it could not contain Quebec's secessionist forces.[11] That did not sound very different from the tough rhetoric coming from Lesage and his cabinet.

The battle between French and English Canada was heating up, made fiercer by the Diefenbaker government's total inability to comprehend what was taking place in Quebec. The Liberals, however, were trying to understand, and on December 17, 1962, Opposition Leader Lester Pearson made his first attempt in Parliament to define the crisis that had begun to rack the country. The bargain of 1867, he said, had "meant the rejection . . . of the American melting-pot concept of national unity . . . it was an understanding or a settlement between two founding races of Canada made on the basis of an acceptable and equal partnership." But, he went on, there were two different interpretations of the Confederation bargain. To English Canadians, the "French fact" was limited to Quebec alone; to Quebeckers, Canada had been intended to be and should be a bilingual and bicultural nation from sea to sea. And now with Quebec in the midst of a "social revolution," all Canadians were beginning to realize that Quebeckers were "determined to become directors of their economic and cultural destiny in their own changed and changing society." Pearson added that the province was demanding "equal and full opportunity to participate in all federal government services, in which their own language will be fully recognized."

The Liberal leader refrained from pledging that his party would meet all French Canada's demands, but he did pick up Laurendeau's idea and call for a great inquest into the state of bilingual and bicultural relations, a royal commission that should seek provincial co-operation in its task.[12] His was an important speech, one particularly well received in Quebec, and after he became prime minister in April 1963, Pearson quickly created the Royal Commission on Bilingualism and Biculturalism with Laurendeau and Davidson Dunton, a former public servant and the president of Carleton University, as co-chairmen. Other commissioners were Frank Scott, Gertrude Laing, a Calgary volunteer worker, Jean Marchand, the Quebec labour leader and president of the Confederation of National Trade Unions, and five others. The commission was charged with reporting on the state of "B&B" in Canada and on the condition of the partnership between the two founding races, and with "taking into account the contribution made by other ethnic groups to the cultural enrichment of Canada and the measures that should be taken to safeguard that contribution." That last reference to what would soon come to be known as multiculturalism was clearly an afterthought, as was the inclusion among the commissioners of two "ethnic" representatives.

The commissioners were also instructed to investigate the practice of bilingualism in government departments (something the Glassco Commission had reported on only a few months before); to report on the role of public and private corporations, including the media, in promoting B&B; and to discuss with the provinces the ways in which

Canadians could be taught to be bilingual.[13] That was a tall order, but the Liberal government was already convinced, as only a very few Canadians outside of Quebec were, that Canada was in crisis.

I

What did André Laurendeau – and moderate Quebec opinion – expect of the royal commission? Laurendeau set out his aims in a brief, undated note. The nation should be bilingual with autonomous provinces in which the rights of the minority were recognized. That was a formulation much like that offered a half-century before by Henri Bourassa, a country with "nationalisme à bonne conscience" in which the English Canadians would offer the French Canadians in other provinces what French Canada gave English Canadians in Quebec. Laurendeau wanted that, but many in Quebec, equating the province with the French-Canadian nation, rejected the ideal of bilingualism across the country as an unrealizable chimera. Laurendeau was not finished yet. The federal government had to be bilingual in composition, action, and administration, and French and English had to be recognized as official languages. That meant practical equality of language in Ottawa, in Parliament, in the courts, and in the public service. It meant that federal institutions such as the CBC and the CNR must be bilingual. It meant that the Armed Forces had to be bilingual. And it meant that French had to be the language of instruction in schools in provinces where numbers warranted it. That was a large menu and to achieve it all, or even a large part of it, was to challenge the ingrained and age-old prejudices of the majority.[14] Perhaps it was appreciation of this that lay behind the sardonic note Laurendeau received from a friend who wrote that Laurendeau-Dunton would rank in the history books with Cartier-Macdonald or Baldwin-Lafontaine. "On parlera de vous dans les manuels d'histoire. En bien, si la confédération survit; avec ironie, si elle crève."[15]

The royal commission's work began in earnest in the summer of 1963. The commissioners met and mingled, getting to know each other. Letters were sent to 2,636 institutions and associations inviting briefs and submissions.[16] The provincial premiers were contacted by Prime Minister Pearson and their co-operation asked. And a gigantic research plan was put in train.

The commission's research was crucial if its work was to have a sound base and lasting importance. Michael Oliver, a young professor at McGill University who had done his doctoral research on Quebec nationalism, wrote to the commission to propose a plan of organization, and at the end of 1963 he was hired to implement the scheme he had suggested, after a number of others declined the honour and the work.[17] With the assistance of Léon Dion, the Laval political scientist, as special counsellor, and of four senior scholars and a consultative committee of fifteen, a large in-house research organization was created. There were to be eight divisions: statistics and demography; institutional studies; behavioural studies; Public Service studies; social studies and economics; educational studies; popular communications; and linguistic and cultural studies. Each division was to be headed by a ranking scholar who would act as supervisor for the reports prepared within his division and for those contracted out to researchers in the universities. Each report had its contract, title, project definition and objective, method, duration, and personnel specified, and almost all were scheduled for completion in 1965.[18] By the fall of 1964 the commission was employing forty-eight researchers on a full- or part-time basis, eight short-term consultants, thirty-four senior scholars working under contract, and twenty-three summer students; in addition, three attitudinal studies were in process.*[19] The Royal Commission on Bilingualism and Biculturalism was far and away the largest research organization in the country.

The commissioners meanwhile were holding hearings and sorting out their views and impressions. Dunton was the organizer, the commission's administrator-in-chief. Laurendeau was the idea man, the one commissioner that the researchers talked to about their work and the one most deeply interested in the data being produced by the research teams. Frank Scott was a major figure at the beginning, but as the realization gradually dawned on everyone that the situation in Quebec was never going to return to the status quo ante, the place of Anglo-Quebeckers began to seem less important and Scott's role diminished in turn. One key figure among the commissioners was Gertrude Laing, very concerned about the national crisis and deeply committed to finding a solution.[20] The two ethnic representatives played a small role but did serve as a constant reminder that there were Canadians other than those of French and English origin.

The commissioners' meetings were useful in conveying a sense of what the country felt and thought about questions of race (a word that the commissioners decided should not be used)[21] and language. There

* There was even a project, commissioned but never completed, to have Pierre Trudeau do "a study of the possibility of accommodating cultural claims through a Bill of Rights." (Fonds Laurendeau, Royal Commission files, Research Report, 18 June 1964, doc. 324E.)

were meetings with the media, with the Fédération des Sociétés Saint-Jean-Baptiste du Québec, with ethnic leaders in Toronto, with the Canadian Manufacturers Association, and with ordinary citizens in a large number of regional sessions.[22] Most important perhaps were the visits by the co-chairmen to the provincial premiers. Laurendeau kept a diary of those trips and of the first seven months of 1964, and the impressions of that acute observer provide a snapshot of the national mood.

The Laurendeau-Dunton interviews began in Winnipeg on January 20. Premier Duff Roblin impressed Laurendeau as liberal in attitude but conservative in his belief that constitutional problems had to be resolved through federal-provincial negotiation. On the subject of Manitoba's francophones, Roblin was sympathetic ("parce qu'il est homme cultivé et d'esprit assez libéral"), worried about the juncture of French-language education and Roman Catholic education, and fully aware that his people were far from being as generous on these subjects as he was. Two days later, after talking with other Manitoba leaders, students, and journalists, Laurendeau and Dunton were in Edmonton to see Premier Ernest Manning – very much the preacher, Laurendeau observed, without even an ashtray in his office. There was no meeting of minds there, although the premier did pledge official co-operation. While he recognized the crisis in Quebec, Manning, in Laurendeau's opinion, did not seem willing to hear any views but his own. At Regina, Premier Woodrow Lloyd seemed more a sympathetic chairman than a leader, and the impressive figure was Allan Blakeney, the Minister of Health, who had "*l'esprit ouvert.*"

After a few days on the road, Laurendeau had already begun to shape some conclusions, to be impressed by the forces of regionalism and provincialism. How could he fail to be? But even so, as he later told his colleagues, English Canadians did have certain things in common – a sense of a shared past, a certainty about the primacy of the English language, and a marked lack of the preoccupations that obsessed French Canadians. In the West, in particular, the concept of bilingualism and biculturalism seemed a threat to the delicate balance that had been constructed over time among the diverse ethnic groups that had settled the prairies.[23]

The road show continued. Premier Lesage warned the co-chairmen that Premier W.A.C. Bennett of British Columbia was the most anti-French Canadian and most separatist leader in the country, but Bennett in person proved polite if uninformed. John Robarts of Ontario, after telling the commissioners that there was less interest in his province in their work than six months earlier, offered the opinion that if there should be a recession in Canada at the same time as a boom in the United States, he was not at all certain that Canadians would favour remaining separate from their neighbours to the south. When Laurendeau spoke on the nature of the Quebec crisis, he wrote, Robarts regarded him as a man pleading a cause, and the premier's rejoinder was concern over the "Buy Quebec" campaign under way in the province and its potential effect on Ontario manufacturers' sales. Robert Stanfield of Nova Scotia was the most intelligent and concerned of all the premiers, while Louis Robichaud of New Brunswick struck Laurendeau as "*très Acadien*," faithful and ready to compromise on everything except his vehemence at the term "*Etat du Québec*," then coming into widespread use. To Robichaud, separatism was a plague, a direct threat to the existence of the French in New Brunswick who were, in his view, at last making forward strides.

It was all an education, even in Prince Edward Island, which Laurendeau saw as "*un anachronisme*" without influence in Canada, and in Newfoundland, where Joey Smallwood greeted the co-chairmen in an office decorated with a Union Jack and two photographs of the Queen – but also with great courtesy and sympathy. And even if the Gallup polls found that a third of the population of Ontario and the West considered the royal commission unimportant, there were still two thirds of the total population who believed its work very or fairly important. In Quebec, 50 per cent considered the Laurendeau-Dunton Commission very important and 31 per cent believed it fairly important; that left no doubt that Quebec believed much was at stake.[24]

For Laurendeau, the net result of his travels was the conclusion that Canada was a country "*très malade*" not only because of French-English problems but also because of Canadian-American problems.[25] To him, and to the commissioners generally, "la situation actuelle du pays est non seulement difficile mais grave," with the split between French and English Canada serious indeed. Quebec was becoming more and more impatient, and the divisions were increasing. It was essential that the country understand the extent of the danger, become aware that Confederation was in jeopardy, and realize that certain elements might resort to violence.[26] In Laurendeau's opinion, one of the truly useful men in waking up English Canada was René Lévesque, the most vigorous of Lesage's ministers and the most vocal in his complaints. We have more to give Canada than Canada has to give us, Lévesque told the *New York Times* in February 1964, and such comments, Laurendeau wrote in his diary, were an absolute necessity to upset those with closed minds, to make self-satisfied English Canadians aware of the revolutionary sentiment that was growing in

Quebec.[27] The commissioners themselves got a taste of that sentiment in Quebec City on July 16, 1964, when separatists packed a public meeting of the commission, attacked the commissioners vigorously as *vendus,* and achieved the result of welding all the commissioners together and giving them a sense of the urgency of their task.[28]

The sense of crisis was the genesis of the royal commission's preliminary report. There was no doubt that the commissioners felt that the English Canadians had to be awakened to the national problem. Gertrude Laing told her colleagues at a meeting early in September that a preliminary statement was necessary for the West "where people are not familiar with the questions and do not feel a sense of crisis." Dunton opined that "the greatest service may be in what we teach English Canada about itself and about French Canada." And although one commissioner feared that it was impossible to write a report without "causing panic in the present context of Canadian affairs," there was general agreement to produce a report that would be strong enough to catch people's attention. And when the commission's research director asked if there was yet enough evidence to demonstrate that the situation was worse than it had been ten years ago, Laing and Dunton rejoined that "the cumulative and unique experience of twelve people across the country is a body of conviction and evidence just as valid as a scientific fact."[29]

That was the tenor of the preliminary report – the experiences and responses of a group of well-intentioned and able men and women who had been commissioned to assess the mood of the country. And their conclusions were alarming: "Canada, without being fully conscious of the fact, is passing through the greatest crisis in its history." The source was in Quebec. "But although a provincial crisis at the outset, it has become a Canadian crisis . . . *it would appear from what is happening that the state of affairs established in 1867, and never since seriously challenged, is now for the first time being rejected by the French Canadians of Quebec.*"[30] Those phrases, as well as the commissioners' judgement that English Canadians, even those of good will, had an attitude of superiority to the French-speaking among them, achieved the desired shock effect. So too did the commissioners' call for "equal partnership." The issue lay not between a majority and a minority but between two majorities, one French-speaking, in Quebec, and the other English-speaking, across the country. In a sense, by writing as they had, the commissioners had gone beyond the traditional role of a royal commission in collecting data and offering recommendations; instead, they had involved themselves in the process and had become, in fact, *animateurs.*[31]

Perhaps that was responsible for the hostile tone apparent at the commission's public hearings in late 1965. English-speaking Canadians, frightened and upset by the changes that the preliminary report presaged, reacted critically to the commission's very existence, seeing it as part of the problem. The idea that the French and English languages should have equal status outside Quebec was denounced in the West, as was the notion of a bilingual public service and French-language instruction in the schools. To some, the whole problem was caused by a neurotic Quebec; to others it was a dark Catholic plot to win by stealth what had been lost on the Plains of Abraham two centuries before.[32] And some observers believed that the election results in the fall of 1965, when the Liberal government was denied a majority, had been shaped by a backlash against the Pearson government's perceived "soft" attitude to Quebec. If the Grits were soft, the Tories were not, and in the West, at least, it seemed that the backlash was real. And Commissioner J.B. Rudnyckyj told his colleagues that this backlash existed among ethnic Canadians who objected to a government that spoke of the "two founding groups."[33]

In a sense, much of the royal commission's work was now concluded. The public hearings had ended, and the commissioners merely had to await the completion of research reports so the drafting of their final report could commence. The staff was still large – 210 full-time and part-time employees in January 1966 – and the costs were high – $6.96 million to the end of the 1966-67 budget year.[34] The first volume of the final report did not appear until October 1967, more than four years after the commission's creation. The volume offered a general introduction to the whole problem of bilingualism and biculturalism, and the bulk of it was devoted to the official languages. The commissioners noted that language did not reach the underlying causes of the divisions between Canadians – a true enough statement at a time when the debate in Quebec was already focusing on fundamental questions of power – but it was important nonetheless. It recommended that French and English be declared official languages of Parliament and federal institutions; that New Brunswick, Ontario, and any other provinces where the minority language group reached 10 per cent recognize both languages as official in their legislatures and in local governments and provide services in French for the minority; that bilingual districts be established wherever the minority group was 10 per cent of the population; that all parents have the right to educate their children in either language; that the national capital district be declared officially bilingual; and that the federal government and the officially bilingual provinces adopt an official languages act and appoint a commissioner to supervise and enforce it.[35] That was a good list of recommendations and one that approximated very closely to Laurendeau's earlier private statement.

The reaction was generally favourable. The *Globe and Mail* noted that while the general response to the preliminary report had been that the commission was unduly alarmist, now "perhaps the B&B Commission was right," a view shared by columnists Douglas Fisher and Harry Crowe: "The Commission was right. The rest of us were wrong." On the other hand, the Winnipeg *Tribune* remained unrevised and unrepentant – the early report was a "horror comic" and Book I was no better. While the *Globe and Mail* offered "unswerving support" to all the recommendations, other newspapers quibbled in detail. Continentalism made bilingualism unnecessary, some said, others that bilingualism would make second-class citizens of the unilingual.[36]

Whatever the papers might say, however, the commission had become almost irrelevant to the debate by 1967. Opinion polls showed that Canadians believed that relations between French and English were worse than they had been five years before. Only in Quebec, where 34 per cent found matters better as against 28 per cent who found them worse, were the national trends reversed. Perhaps the royal commission had demonstrated that someone was listening; perhaps that had helped.[37]

The remaining volumes of the report appeared at intervals, followed by a vast flood of research reports. Book II on education appeared in May 1968, Book III on the work world in two volumes in September 1969, Book IV on the cultural contribution of the other ethnic groups in October 1969, and Books V and VI on the federal capital and voluntary associations in February 1970. The intention had been to have a volume on constitutional questions, but by the time work was ready to proceed on it, Pierre Trudeau was in office, a prime minister with limited interest in the advice of others on constitutional questions. The volume was cancelled on budgetary grounds, a useful excuse. In fact, the commissioners, divided among themselves on constitutional solutions, were probably happy to be freed of that difficult burden.

The Royal Commission on Bilingualism and Biculturalism had been a great examination of the Canadian psyche. Its contributions in detail were not great; what it did do was to help prepare English Canadians for the necessity of change. That was a major achievement, immeasurable as it might be. Had the preliminary report not painted the dimensions of the crisis as it did, English Canadians might have been slower to react; and had the commission not provided the groundwork, the task of the Pearson and Trudeau governments in setting Canada on the road to official bilingualism, a necessity if the nation was to survive, would have been far harder than it was.

II

While the Laurendeau-Dunton Commission did its work, the federal government was attempting to introduce bilingualism into its operations. In this there was a job of work to do, for historically the public service had been effectively and solely English speaking. The mandarins were all of English mother tongue – and most did not speak French – and the bulk of the service at the officer level was similarly English speaking; only in the junior ranks, in the clerical positions and in the local staff working in Quebec, was French spoken. A study prepared for the Glassco Commission in 1961 made the point very clearly when it observed that "an administration to which 25 or 30% of its subjects remain strangers and with which, as a result, they have no wish to cooperate" was bound to be ineffective.[38]

The problem was primarily attitudinal. Clerk of the Privy Council R.B. Bryce was no bigot, but as late as 1959 he could write of a candidate for the chairmanship of the Tariff Board that "he is not perfect but he is better than any other French-Canadian that I know to be available or who might be available for the job. The job is important but rather a drab one. It is desirable to have a French-Canadian there."[39] And given that that attitude was pervasive, the recruitment of Quebec candidates was slow. In the Department of External Affairs, for example, a prestige department with ample overseas postings in its gift and the ministry with the best record on bilingualism in the public service,[40] only 80 of 368 officers entering over a nineteen-year period were French speaking; even after the Quiet Revolution alerted English Canada to the fact that something was happening in Quebec, only 20 of 107 recruits were French speaking from 1960 to 1964.[41] It was almost enough to justify André Laurendeau's comment in an address in Kingston, Ontario, in 1962: "I know French Civil Servants who are separatists, and they probably are separatists because they are civil servants." The members of the government, he went on, "speak, write and work in English, on ideas and projects which originated in English minds. . . . French is a foreign language."[42]

The Pearson government came into office committed to doing something about this lamentable state of affairs. The Glassco Report had pointed to the problem, and now a series of committees of officials were directed to consider remedies. Their recommendations were straightforward and precise and on Pearson's desk by June 1963:

a clear statement of the equality of the two languages in the public service; a directive requiring all departments to be organized in such a way that they could deal with documents in either language without translation; the organization of programmes to ensure that an increasing proportion of senior and intermediate officers could read both languages; the establishment of language training facilities; the appointment of language officers in each department; and pay incentives for those who were bilingual.[43] Moreover, it was imperative, as the Under-Secretary of State for External Affairs told his minister the next month, that "the Cabinet Committee on Bilingualism should begin to operate and be seen to operate *tout de suite*."[44]

The spirit was willing, but the flesh was prey to difficulties. One was cost, a subject of importance at a time of relative austerity in the aftermath of the dollar crisis of 1962.[45] Another was the large bureaucracy necessary if civil servants were to be tested for language fluency. In December 1963, for example, the Department of National Defence issued instructions on bilingual testing, calling for proficiency tests in speaking, writing, and reading French and English, and promising that the possession of bilingual qualifications "will be a factor in determining suitability for employment and hence career advancement."[46] That was a long-overdue step, but the thousands of man-hours of work necessary to implement it were difficult to come by in an understrength and over-tasked force. Nor was it always easy to find the right people in Quebec for the public service. Walter Gordon, the Minister of Finance, found that only two people in the senior and intermediate posts in his department were French speaking. He wanted to do better but did not know where to get the desired senior officials. The best he could suggest to the Prime Minister was that he appoint an associate minister of the department who should be a francophone. This would have been a positive step (although Pearson did not follow it up) but not one that would resolve the imbalance in numbers of civil servants.[47]

The reason for Gordon's difficulty was clear: French Canadians did not want to move to Ottawa to work in an English environment and raise their children in English, particularly when the Quebec public service after 1960 was vibrant and exciting. An officer of the Civil Service Commission put it simply: "French Canadians seem reluctant to move from Quebec. One factor is the attraction of the Lesage government. Another is that people seem eager to get back into their home environment . . . this seems to be a national trait."[48] The results could be devastating. For example, when the post office workers in Montreal went on strike in 1965, Ottawa had great difficulty finding an appropriate civil servant who could negotiate with the francophone posties in their own language. To Gordon Robertson, the Clerk of the Privy Council, "this episode epitomized perfectly one of the root problems we have in making the federal government appear to be something other than an 'alien' government to the people of Quebec . . . this is also the reason why almost no one from Quebec considers that the federal government speaks for him or Quebec; it is the provincial government that is recognized as doing that because it is a government that 'speaks French' and seems to belong to the people."

After two years of work, a depressed Robertson said, "almost no progress" had been made on bilingualism, and for all the French courses run in Ottawa probably no more than a dozen people had been made bilingual. What had to be done, he urged, was to make Ottawa more attractive for the French speaking, to begin seriously to train officers to be bilingual – Robertson suggested sending three or four deputy ministers, five or six assistant deputy ministers, and ten senior officers of promise to Université Laval for an academic year – and to set out to counter the impression that every Québécois who came to Ottawa was a *vendu*.[49]

But if Pearson agreed with Robertson, and he did, not everyone went along. Some ministers were unhappy. One Ottawa M.P. wrote to the Prime Minister to object to the bilingualization of the public service which, he argued, was undermining the merit principle.[50] And R.A. Bell, the Conservative M.P. for Carleton and one of many bilingualism critics in his party, said that he had received a large number of complaints from "senior and intermediate research, technical and professional personnel indicating that they saw no course but to go to the United States. . . ."[51] The issue was politically dangerous, and Pearson found it necessary to give a severe reprimand to one of his Quebec ministers who had told the press that he would resign if the civil service wasn't made bilingual quickly. "Resignation will be only academic," Jean-Luc Pepin, the Minister of Mines and Technical Surveys, had said, "for I won't have to resign – Quebec will do it for me, with what will be its utter disregard of Ottawa."[52]

In the circumstances, it was courageous of Pearson to press ahead and to make a statement in the House on April 6, 1966. Beginning in 1967, he said, bilingualism would become a factor in recruiting. In those parts of Canada where both languages were spoken, procedures were to be put into effect so that within a few years executive and administrative posts would be filled by bilingual officers. And the government would send twenty senior civil servants to Quebec and ten senior francophone officers to English Canada for a year of immersion. The plan was good, and perhaps to the Prime Minister's surprise, the moves received a good press. The *Globe and Mail*, trying to make amends for its past views, headed its editorial "Toward Bilingual Justice," and in Quebec the general response was summed up in *La Presse*'s editorial, "Premier pas d'une longue marche."[53]

The government had come a long way in three years, but there was indeed still a distance to go. Gérard Pelletier, a new Liberal M.P. in Ottawa, wrote in his column in the *Montreal Star* in 1966 that "it might be that in three or four years I will be accustomed and won't notice any more the fact that the capital city of a supposedly and officially bicultural country is about as bilingual as Kitchener, Ontario or Edmonton, Alberta. . . ." It was ludicrous, he said, that "in order to represent a French-speaking riding of a French-speaking province in the Parliament of my country, I am forced to live in a unilingual city where I get unilingual summonses when I disobey unilingual traffic signs; where I have to appear before an English-speaking court if I were to plead not guilty; where there is not a single public school in which my teen-age sons and daughters could pursue their studies in their own language. . . ."[54] The federal government had begun to change, but Pelletier's complaints made the point that provincial and municipal governments also had to adapt to reality.

Nonetheless a year later, as bilingualism became more entrenched if not more popular in the public service, new concerns had appeared. When Léo Cadieux, the Minister of National Defence, proposed to create French-speaking units at Valcartier, Quebec, that would include the Royal 22e Régiment, an artillery regiment, an armoured regiment, and associated combat and support units "whose cadres will be filled with French-speaking personnel" along with a francophone CF-5 squadron at Bagotville, Quebec, the response from two of the brightest young officers in the Prime Minister's Office and the Privy Council Office was striking. Marc Lalonde told the Prime Minister, ". . . we should avoid very carefully the concentration of these French-speaking Forces inside Quebec. . . . We have to think here of the problems that such a concentration could cause in the case of a very serious political upheaval in the Province of Quebec." Lalonde added, "I don't want to sound unduly pessimistic, but we should avoid providing the Government of Quebec with a ready-made Army at its disposal." And Michael Pitfield noted that Cadieux's proposal was "one of the most potentially dangerous decisions that the Federal government could ever take. . . . I submit that . . . unilingual French-Canadian units concentrated in Quebec could – in the circumstances of our times, and with the trends that are likely to become even more powerful in the future – irrevocably lay the groundwork for an exceedingly dangerous situation. . . ."[55] If the officials were correct, the relations between Quebec and Canada were at or near the breaking point by 1967.

III

The nexus of the problems was in that murky area of Canadian life, federal-provincial relations. The Liberals had come to power determined to restore good relations with the provinces, and particularly with Quebec. Under the Diefenbaker government, tensions had been built up with almost all the provincial administrations, and the resentment across the country at being told what Ottawa was going to do, after the decisions had been taken or, quite often, not taken, was almost palpable. George Nowlan, one of Diefenbaker's ablest Maritimes ministers, summed up the usual course of dominion-provincial gatherings under the Conservative government as "prayers, piety and a declaration we believe in God and Mothers and adjournments while we 'gave consideration.' "[56] That was the way it had been, but Prime Minister Pearson was determined to achieve a new "cooperative federalism" – an overall statement of attitude that implied consultation before federal policies were formed, collaboration in drafting those policies, and co-ordination in their implementation. The policy, in another word, was co-operation.[57]

In practice, however, co-operative federalism, while a well-intended method for dealing with the provinces, came under sharp assault, not least from the Quebec government of Jean Lesage. Lesage's narrow victory in June 1960 and his triumph in November 1962 had rid Quebec of the tired and corrupt remnants of *Duplessisisme* at the same time that it was bringing the Quiet Revolution that had been under way socially and intellectually in the province for some years to full public awareness.[58] The provincial government believed that Quebec, like all provinces short of money to carry out their responsibilities, had to have control of enough fiscal resources to become master in its own house. If the Ottawa Liberals had expected that their old colleague Lesage would be easy to deal with, they were soon disabused. The Quebec ministers, and most notably René Lévesque, the Minister of Natural Resources and a former Radio Canada TV broadcaster who had been radicalized by the producers' strike in 1959,[59] were unfailingly polite but obdurate in their demands for more – more money, more powers, more of everything. Even more extraordinary, the Quebec government's bureaucrats came to meetings with carefully drafted, often brilliantly conceived plans that frequently put Ottawa's officials to shame. It was not the same ball game any more, and as early as March 1962 Pearson had told a friend of his "fear and uneasiness . . . about the direction Jean Lesage feels he must go in order to cope with some of the pressures to which he is subjected."[60] As Prime Minister, Pearson's fear and uneasiness would mightily increase.

The first critical struggle between the federal government and the government in Quebec City took place over the mundane if important subject of pensions. The Diefenbaker government had commissioned a major study of pensions in 1958, and Professor Robert Clark produced a two-volume report entitled *Economic Security for the Aged in the United States and Canada* the next year. The Cabinet began considering the subject in November 1960, but it was not until a year later that serious work at devising a practical scheme was begun, largely by the Clerk of the Privy Council. The Conservative plan was to have contributory pensions but, as R.B. Bryce told Diefenbaker, the scheme was "pie in a rather distant sky as far as the man in the street is concerned." Contributors would pay for their benefits at the time but would not collect them for many years.[61] Perhaps that was why the Tories failed to pursue the idea.

The Liberals, however, had also been looking at pensions, and in the 1963 election they campaigned on the promise to introduce a national contributory pension plan, which, along with medicare, would be a cap-stone of Canada's structure of social security. And after their narrow victory in April, it fell to Judy LaMarsh, the new minister of National Health and Welfare, to put those promises into legislative form. LaMarsh was an able lawyer, a fast-talking, sometimes loose-tongued politician of great energy, and she and her officials quickly produced an unfunded pay-as-you-go plan that would begin to pay benefits ten years after its commencement.[62] That was modified pie-in-the-sky. But the government plan came under attack from those who demanded that old age pensioners receive an immediate ten-dollar-a-month increase, from the insurance companies, which feared the plan would cut into their lucrative private pension packages, and from the Conservative government of Ontario, which had passed legislation in the spring of 1963 requiring employers to establish private, portable plans.[63] Most critically, Quebec denounced Ottawa's proposals because they were pay-as-you-go, not funded, and did not create a large pool of capital that Quebec and other provinces could draw on for public investment projects. Beginning in the summer of 1963, the Lesage government began working on its own pension proposals.[64]

When the federal and provincial governments met in conference at Quebec City on March 31, 1964, to consider Ottawa's third draft of its pension proposals, Lesage dramatically presented his plan to the country's political leaders. The Quebec plan, better in virtually all respects than Ottawa's, proposed to create huge amounts of capital through pension contributions, a total of $8 billion to $10 billion over ten years, that would be under the control of the provinces. For Lesage, the glittering prize of pension revenues offered the opportunity for his province to catch up with Ontario in living standards and his people to become truly "*maîtres chez nous.*" Just as stunning to the federal team were Lesage's demands, first made in April 1963 just before the federal election, for 25 per cent of the personal income tax revenues raised in Quebec, 25 per cent of the corporation taxes, and 100 per cent of the succession duties; he also made it clear that the province was going to withdraw from many joint federal-provincial programmes and wanted $150 million in compensation for the revenues Quebec had not received during the Duplessis years. And Lesage said that if Ottawa refused, Quebec would have to impose double taxation on its people in the forthcoming provincial budget, for which Ottawa would be blamed.[65]

The Ottawa reaction to this blow-up in Quebec City was not dissimilar to that of the man who watched his best friend run off with his wife and his clothes. The Clerk of the Privy Council wrote to Pearson that Quebec had been placed in isolation by the conference – "Nothing can be more helpful to the extremists or more weakening to the friends of unity" – and that Lesage had been reduced to threats to achieve his fiscal objectives. Worse, as Gordon Robertson said, to yield now would be interpreted in the rest of the country "as demonstrating that extreme conduct *is* the way to get results."[66] Tom Kent, Pearson's closest adviser, put the problem in a broader perspective, telling the Prime Minister that the whole government programme was on the verge of going into a tailspin and a "coup" in the area of federal-provincial relations was desperately needed. On pensions, Kent argued, "we must find some formula whereby the Quebec plan will not be entirely separate from ours (and therefore Ontario won't have an excuse to go it alone)." Could a deal not be worked out in private negotiation with Lesage?[67]

Pearson agreed that it was worth a try and secretly sent Kent and Maurice Sauvé, the Minister of Forestry in his government, to Quebec City to meet Claude Morin, the deputy minister of Federal-Provincial Relations and one of the draftsmen of the Quebec pension plan. A flurry of visits between government offices and hotel rooms in Quebec City and Ottawa followed as the two sides endeavoured to put together a deal that could satisfy some of Quebec's demands while leaving Ottawa with sufficient powers and revenues to act as a federal government must. The resulting package saw Quebec agree to modify its pension plan, making it to some extent co-ordinated with the federal scheme. The funding provisions of the Quebec proposals, essential to Lesage, were retained, and Ottawa's scale of contribution and ten-year vesting prevailed. "The plan was really a monument to Dominion-Provincial relations," Judy LaMarsh (who had not known that her department's draft was up for grabs in the Kent-Sauvé-Morin negotiations) later wrote.[68] In addition, Ottawa agreed to double the rate of its withdrawal from the personal income tax field, giving Quebec and all the provinces 21 per cent instead of 19 in 1965 and 24 per cent instead of 20 in 1966, and to give Quebec an extra 3 per cent in lieu of the federal student loans and extended family allowances programmes from which Quebec was opting out. It was a victory for co-operative federalism but a costly one, for Quebec received an additional $200 million and the opting-out formula was enshrined as policy. Pearson wrote to Lesage that the deal could be a "turning point" so long as Ottawa retained the strength necessary to meet new challenges.[69] And J.W. Pickersgill, the Secretary of State, wrote to the Quebec premier that well-disposed but concerned English Canadians "want to be assured . . . that there is an influential voice in Quebec demanding the maintenance of a strong and united Canada. . . . " If that voice were there, "it will be far easier to get the necessary practical adjustments made that are essential to the preservation of your government in Quebec, and to a healthy federal state."[70]

But was that voice there? The uncertainty for Ottawa was that while Lesage was seen as a man with whom one could deal, René Lévesque was not, and Lévesque seemed to be making the running. Mitchell Sharp, the Minister of Trade and Commerce, told André Laurendeau that the federal government believed Lesage negotiated in good faith, but then "Lévesque le force à rétraiter, ce qui rend tout negociation sérieuse à peu près impossible." Laurendeau argued that Lévesque, an old friend, was not a doctrinaire and that he, too, was being pushed by strong nationalist opinion.[71] A few days later, and after the Ottawa–Quebec City deal had been signed and sealed, Laurendeau and Lévesque talked. The minister indicated that he was pleased with the bargain – Quebec had got what it needed and had had to make few concessions. Then, with "*ses yeux pétillant*" Lévesque said, "*Maintenant*, what's next?"[72] Lévesque's message seemed clear – there would always be another demand, another test to find the limits of co-operative federalism. And if those limits were found? Lévesque's own views were becoming clear. In May 1963 he had declared himself first and foremost a Québécois and "with a rather growing sense of doubt" only secondly a Canadian. He added that if Canada was a bad bargain, "the only thing you can do . . . is to get out of it."[73] Lévesque and others were already talking of associate statehood for Quebec, or special status, or independence – the rhetoric was getting hotter.[74]

But some in Quebec were opposing the trend. In May 1964, *Cité Libre*, a small but influential periodical, published "An Appeal for Reason in Politics," a "Canadian Manifesto" by Pierre Trudeau, Marc Lalonde, the economist Albert Breton, the sociologist Raymond Breton, and others. The manifesto noted that although the Quiet Revolution had achieved much, it was in many sectors just a "waving of symbols" and in others had ground to a halt. The reform movement seemed exhausted, the authors argued, deviating now into emotionalism and racial appeals. Nationalism was no answer. To use it as the yardstick for deciding policies was "both sterile and retrograde," and that stricture applied as much to Walter Gordon's June 1963 budget as to the actions of Lesage's government. "We are not any more impressed by the cries in some English circles when American financiers buy Canadian enterprises, than we are by the adoption in the Province of Quebec of economic policies based upon the slogan 'maîtres chez nous.' " The manifesto's authors argued that federalism was the best political structure for Canada, but they admitted to dissatisfaction with its practice. Joint programmes were essential where the constitution directed that powers be shared, and both the provinces and Ottawa needed the fiscal powers to carry out their responsibilities. "But, one thing is certain: the kind of haphazard political expediency which has inspired so many sharing schemes and federal subsidies for so long has got to stop."

Trudeau and friends argued that the British North America Act was not the cause of the nation's problems. "The obstacles to economic progress, to full employment, to an equitable welfare scheme, or even to the development of French culture in Canada, are not principally the result of the Canadian Constitution. The restraints are not juridical but social and economic in nature." In other words, Canada could be made to work under the existing system. "To confess one's inability to make Confederation work," the manifesto proclaimed, "is, at this stage of history, to admit one's unworthiness to contribute to the universal order."[75]

Published at a time when Canadian Army troops were keeping watch over armouries in Quebec to prevent further thefts of weapons and not long after separatist terrorists had exploded bombs in mailboxes and federal buildings,[76] the manifesto did not create a perceptible ground swell of support. Nor did Trudeau's sharp-tongued but intellectually rigorous assault on "Separatist Counter-Revolutionaries" in the same issue of *Cité Libre* in which the manifesto appeared. Denouncing those who wished to hive Quebec off from Canada as a new clerical party, as anti-democratic, as persons who wished to destroy individual freedom for the sake of some vague collective ideology, Trudeau concluded in phrases as vitriolic as any in our political literature: "Separatism a revolution? My eye. A counter-revolution; the national-socialist counter-revolution."[77]

Trudeau's attack on the separatists was characterized in his diary by André Laurendeau as more of that "*dogmatisme antinationaliste*" that had characterized *Cité Libre* since its founding at the beginning of the 1950s.[78] But among English-Canadian intellectuals, seeking some solution to the troubles that gripped the country, Trudeau was beginning to be a rallying figure. Eugene Forsey, for example, fully agreed with the Montreal lawyer that the BNA Act was a workable document, and he was worried, as he wrote to friends after attending a conference on French-English relations in Banff in June 1964, that "many English Canadians seem in effect to have lost the will to live." By that he meant that many seemed to have decided to agree to whatever Quebec sought. But not Forsey. At Banff, the "three leading French Canadian spokesmen . . . were completely crazy. . . . If these people speak for Quebec, then the jig is up. As I told them in so many words, the response of English Canada can only be Cromwell's 'In God's name, go!' "[79] Forsey's vehemence was not going to resolve the crisis, but Trudeau's fiery rationality at least suggested to concerned Canadians that there was no unanimity of opinion in Quebec.

Nonetheless, for the moment the separatists had the ball. When Queen Elizabeth II visited Quebec City on October 10 and 11, 1964, the streets were largely deserted as a forlorn royal convoy drove by, the interested frightened off by threats of violence. And when students protested the visit, Quebec City police charged into the demonstrators with nightsticks flailing, giving the day the name of "le samedi de la matraque." The students, shouting slogans like "Vive Elizabeth . . . Taylor" were clubbed into submission and martyrdom, and many who refused to agree with their ideals could share their rage.

Meanwhile the federal government and the provinces were making yet another attempt to patriate the BNA Act. All previous attempts to have the constitution domiciled in Canada had foundered on provincial concerns about the procedure for amendment, and Canada, a dominion for a century, an independent state since the Statute of Westminster in 1931, had to endure the humiliation of petitioning Westminster to alter the basic national document. When he was Diefenbaker's Minister of Justice, Davie Fulton had tried to cut the Gordian knot at conferences with the provinces in 1960 and 1961, but the Fulton formula failed to get past the objections of the provinces. Saskatchewan, with its CCF-NDP government, objected to the entrenchment of provincial jurisdiction in social and economic fields, an objection that the federal government's Deputy Minister of Justice noted "goes to the very root of the conflict between the concept of decentralization of political sovereignty and power implicit in federalism, and the practical requirements for central planning which modern economic and social conditions make increasingly desirable."[80]

Early in August, Premier Manning, chairman of the Fifth Provincial Premiers Conference, privately advised Pearson that his colleagues had held informal, confidential discussions on the constitution and were, he said, generally agreed that the formula that had emerged in 1960 and 1961 was acceptable.[81] Guy Favreau, the Minister of Justice, seized the opportunity, and the subsequent Fulton-Favreau formula that was discussed at conferences in Charlottetown and Ottawa in September and October 1964 appeared to win agreement.

The formula proposed to give each province a veto on amendments in certain areas exclusively within provincial jurisdiction. Simultaneously, the formula provided that the provinces could delegate powers to Ottawa or vice versa with the agreement of the federal government and at least four provinces. Favreau had originally proposed that powers could be delegated at the request of a single province, but there was strong opposition to this from Pearson's inner circle of advisers. Favreau took his position so that Quebec could deal with lotteries, but as R.B. Bryce, the Deputy Minister of Finance, wrote to his minister, while "it is technically correct that the Government and Parliament of Canada have control of the delegation process . . . if we agree to delegation for one, we are accepting that as a principle, and I think it is undesirable that we should accept it as a principle."[82] The objections carried the day, and after the Ottawa conference even Jean Lesage was gratified by the results.

But the opposition to the Fulton-Favreau formula began to grow, not least from John Diefenbaker and members of his caucus. Although Fulton told his leader that the formula did not differ substantially from his original plan, the Chief nonetheless attacked the constitutional package as an attempt to balkanize Canada, an attempt to allow Quebec to become an associate state. Léon Balcer, the Conservatives' senior Quebec M.P., left the caucus on this issue and sat in Parliament as an independent, but Balcer's gesture could not check the rot. Bora Laskin, probably the country's leading constitutional theorist, denounced the formula as "an unmitigated constitutional disaster," and the New Democratic Party attacked it as prescribing "constitutional futility and absolute rigidity."[83] The federal government counterattacked with a White Paper in March 1965,[84] but although all the English-speaking provinces – including those with Conservative governments – formally accepted the package, Quebec was having second thoughts. The Leader of the Opposition, Daniel Johnson of the Union Nationale, attacked the formula, and although the press in the province largely supported the constitutional patriation formula, Lesage allowed the resolution accepting it to die on the order paper. In January 1966, he told Ottawa that he was postponing consideration indefinitely.[85] The Fulton-Favreau formula was dead and patriation had to wait for another day – and another leader.

That future leader, Pierre Elliott Trudeau, had been elected to Parliament in the 1965 election as the Member for Mount Royal. As he rose in the party, the emphasis on co-operative federalism that had characterized the government's approach began to alter. As parliamentary secretary to the Prime Minister from January 7, 1966, to April 3, 1967, and as Minister of Justice after that, Trudeau was in an ideal position to press his views on Quebec nationalism and the constitution on Pearson. The results soon began to show.[86]

In early 1966 Lesage indicated in the Speech from the Throne opening the Legislature that his province intended to take over the entire field of social legislation from Ottawa. René Lévesque had been saying in speeches since 1964 that Quebec should control the distribution of family allowances, a challenge both to federal jurisdiction and to the one direct link between Ottawa and the hundreds of thousands of Quebec mothers who received baby bonus cheques each month. What was new in this ploy was that the family allowance programme was not a shared cost programme of the sort from which Quebec was opting out. Instead, Ottawa paid the whole shot for family allowances as for Lévesque's other targets, unemployment insurance and old age pensions, and the Quebec attack was thus a direct challenge to federal power.

On June 5, 1966, however, the players in Quebec City changed when Lesage's government was upset by the Union Nationale. The Liberals had pressed the pace of change too quickly and too far for the more conservative voters, and Daniel Johnson won a bare majority. The new premier, a Montreal lawyer and loyal Duplessis supporter, was as committed as Lesage or Lévesque to a re-ordering of the Canadian constitution. Quebeckers had not received their fair share of economic or political power, Johnson believed, a view he stressed in his book *Egalité où Indépendance*.[87] No sentimentality about Canada disturbed Johnson's mind, and if independence offered the best chance for Quebec to achieve its aspirations, then he was for independence. At the same time, for Ottawa the departure of Lesage meant that all necessity for treating politely with brother Liberals was gone.[88]

The new federal position had been evident as early as January 20, 1966, when the Prime Minister told the House of Commons that each level of government should stay within its own jurisdiction; his own government would meanwhile exercise care in agreeing to joint programmes in which not all the provinces participated. Moreover, in economic and fiscal policy, he said, the responsibility "is, and must remain, with the federal government. The provinces must not try to take over matters within federal jurisdiction. . . ."[89] That was a clear signal that the Liberals would be tough in tax-sharing discussions.

There was also a clear portent in the policy statement adopted by the Quebec Liberal Federation on March 26 and 27. The architect was, of course, Trudeau, and the resolutions Quebec federal Liberals enthusiastically adopted called for Ottawa to retain monetary, fiscal, and tariff powers, the provinces to have responsibility for social security, and the provision of facilities to make bilingualism possible across the country. Trudeau told the *Toronto Star* that "the main thing is that we rejected any kind of special status for Quebec. In essence the meeting was an affirmation that federalism can't work unless all the provinces are in basically the same relation toward the central government, and that the federal system as it was conceived by the fathers of confederation is still sound."[90] For the first time in years in the words of a federal spokesman, Quebec was a province very much like the others.

The crucial meetings took place in the autumn. At the federal-provincial Tax Structure Committee meetings on September 14 and 15, Finance minister Mitchell Sharp laid out the new Ottawa line. Both levels of government needed access to resources sufficient to discharge their responsibilities, and each government had to be accountable to its own electors for taxing and spending decisions. Equalization grants should let each province provide an adequate level of services without resort to higher levels of taxation than those of the other provinces, and in return the provinces had to give Ottawa sufficient fiscal power to discharge its economic and monetary responsibilities. In particular, Sharp said, Ottawa had to retain enough of the income tax field to achieve a reasonable degree of equity in taxation across the country. Moreover, there should be uniform intergovernmental arrangements, the uniform application of federal laws in all provinces, and machinery to allow the harmonization of policies and priorities between the federal and provincial governments. Sharp then offered a new equalization formula to be based on the "whole revenue or fiscal capacity" of the province and proposed that all provinces follow the Quebec lead by opting out of shared cost programmes over a period of years, with a 17-per-cent abatement of income tax. And last, the minister argued that as the negotiations over joint use of tax fields had become divisive, it was now time to alter the post-war approach that had seen Ottawa vacating tax fields to give the provinces entry to them. Both levels of government, he repeated, had their own financial responsibilities, and each should look to its own electors for direction on spending and taxation.

The provinces were unhappy at this sharp statement, and they probably expected Pearson to be more accommodating when the Federal-Provincial Conference met on October 27. But although Ottawa agreed to put more money into vocational and technical training and although it offered 50 per cent of the soaring costs of post-secondary education to the provinces, Pearson refused to budge on the main points as enunciated the month before. There was no alternative for the provinces other than to accept Ottawa's position as the basis of a two-year tax agreement, although none chose to opt out of shared cost programmes. Ottawa had won a victory.

The unhappiness in Quebec City was very pronounced, but Johnson, who had wanted 100 per cent of income, corporate, and succession taxes and who hinted at a referendum on Quebec's future, had few options. As Peter Newman observed, the province's finances were in ruins, provincial bonds were a drug in the market, and Ottawa had to provide half the anticipated $1.8 billion in revenues for 1966-67.[91] As a practical politician, Johnson knew he had little room to manoeuvre. At the Confederation for Tomorrow Conference in Toronto, called by Premier Robarts and attended by all the premiers in November 1967, Johnson was, in fact, reasonable and accommodating.

The next stage of the struggle took place at the federal-provincial constitutional conference in Ottawa in February 1968, after Mike Pearson had indicated that he was stepping down as prime minister and had called a Liberal leadership convention. Trudeau, now Justice minister, had headed a small group studying the techniques and implications of constitutional reform, and he had concluded, first, that federalism required a clear statement, and second, that an entrenched Charter of Rights was the proper approach.[92] The Trudeau solution put a charter into the hands of the Supreme Court, which would now become the final arbiter on the American model. To Trudeau, the key was that his charter allowed the guarantee of language rights to French-speaking persons all across Canada, and this was the one basis for the genuine federalism he was seeking. The premiers were sceptical, and the charter won few instant converts, although the conference did agree that as "a matter of equity, French-speaking Canadians outside Quebec should have the same rights as English-speaking Canadians inside Quebec."

What was most significant, however, was that for the first time Trudeau truly impressed himself on the consciousness of the public (although his amendments to the Criminal Code had earlier won notice, largely for his quip that the state had no place in the bedrooms of the nation). His skill in argument, his toughness, his refusal to back down when he became involved in confrontation with Daniel Johnson – all beamed across the country on television – made him an instant and credible candidate to succeed Pearson as Liberal leader and prime minister at the party convention in April 1968.

IV

The suddening blossoming of confidence that the Quiet Revolution brought to Quebec had a foreign dimension, too. Under President Charles de Gaulle, France itself was once again playing the politics of grandeur and looking around the world for situations that could be exploited to its advantage. The relations between Quebec and its one-time mother country were ripe for development.[93]

Ottawa was not unaware of the potential problems, and Prime Minister Pearson paid a formal visit to France in January 1964. In his talks with de Gaulle the whole question of Quebec was discussed at length and, while de Gaulle indicated a special interest in the province, he said that he had no wish to create problems. He wanted Canada to remain an independent nation for political as well as sentimental reasons, and it was, he said, in France's interest that the country remain united and strong.[94]

Even so, when Jules Léger presented his papers as ambassador to France later in the year, he felt obliged to draw de Gaulle's attention to the rapid changes that had taken place in Quebec and Canada since 1960. Those developments, he said, in remarks that apparently offended the President, could not possibly do harm to France, but they could occur either with or without France. It might be the path of least resistance for Canada and Quebec to change without France, but that was not in keeping with the deepest aspirations of Canada. In his reply, the President noted that if Canada's development occurred without France, sooner or later it would be at the price of Canadian independence, a shrewd if slightly overstressed assessment. Certainly de Gaulle seemed fully aware of events in Canada and of his own potential impact on Quebec's place in Canada.[95]

As a result, when Jean Lesage visited de Gaulle in the fall of 1964 the President suggested that Quebec was on the way to "*autodétermination*" in an irreversible process. Moreover, he would assist.[96] That was scarcely surprising, given what Jules Léger described from the embassy in Paris as de Gaulle's "conception arrogante et splendide du monde" and the fact that many Quebec intellectuals, bureaucrats, and politicians had been speaking for some time of the necessity for international recognition of Quebec's distinctive status.[97] Nor was it surprising when the shocking lack of a French-Canadian presence in Canadian foreign policy was considered. The Department of External Affairs, notwithstanding the presence of Marcel Cadieux as undersecretary and Léger as ambassador in Paris, was still almost unilingual and regularly paid far more attention to Britain and the Commonwealth than to France and what was becoming known as *La Francophonie*. One measure of that lack of interest was that in 1961 Canadian aid to French Africa was $300.[98] The problem of Quebec-France relations had never arisen in the past except in occasional flare-ups (as during the war when Vichyite influence was strong in some Quebec circles). Now the problem had become pressing, one aspect of the larger question of Quebec's relationship to and within Confederation.

For External Affairs, headed by Paul Martin, the Franco-Ontarian politician, and Cadieux, a tough and forthright man, the question of how to manage the question was extraordinarily complicated. On the one hand there was a genuine desire to make amends for past neglect by establishing firm links of aid and culture with *La Francophonie* and by forging new links with France.[99] On the other hand there was real concern about France's aims and policies. Could it be that France was supporting terrorists in Quebec? Cadieux asked his friend Léger in Paris. He was willing to give France the benefit of the doubt, but English Canadians might not.[100]

Meanwhile Quebec was seeking to expand its own links with France and *La Francophonie*, and with Ottawa's permission the province had opened a Délégation-Généralin Paris in 1964. Ottawa was not averse to co-operating with Quebec City, Martin told Pearson in early 1965, "to work out a programme of methods and procedures by which Quebec could develop its relations with the French Community and with the Specialized Agencies in fields of education, culture, aid and in any other spheres falling wholly or partly within the area of provincial competence."[101] It was better to work out arrangements for co-operation – Quebec and France had signed an *entente culturel* at the end of 1964 – for if Ottawa allowed the confrontation with the province to go on, the next step might be for Quebec to request "federal monies now used for these purposes to be put at the disposal of Quebec so as to enable the province to undertake international tasks in fields where it will have successfully asserted jurisdiction both internally and externally."[102] In other words, Ottawa insisted that its paramount position in foreign policy be recognized; if it was, and so long as it was, it was prepared to co-operate.[103] The difficulty was that, as in other areas of federal-provincial relations, while Jean Lesage might enter into commitments with his friend Mike Pearson, there was no certainty he could enforce such agreements on all his colleagues, anxious to expand the Quebec role in the world – and their own on the Paris stage.[104]

But the grand actor was at the Elysée in Paris. Léger had been writing since 1964 that de Gaulle "est sur son déclin. Le monde iréel dans lequel il vit est de plus en plus éloigné du monde réel."[105] Perhaps, but the old general remained a formidable figure, capable of awesome wrath when crossed and of great mischief. When Canada, for example, refused to sell France uranium except under conditions that the French found unacceptable or to buy French Caravelle aircraft,[106] de Gaulle's benevolent attitude toward Canada seemed to alter. It was an Anglo-Saxon nation, an American satrapy, he appeared to conclude, and hence it was of no use to France as a counterweight to America.

The troublemaking began in earnest in the months after the Union Nationale victory in 1966. Visiting federal Cabinet ministers were refused access to the President while Quebec politicians received their audiences. The French ambassador in Ottawa, François Leduc, was organizing the visits of French political figures to Canada but deliberately omitting Ottawa from their itineraries. A visit to France by Governor General Vanier was squelched. And de Gaulle's government refused to send a representative to the ceremonies marking the fiftieth anniversary of the battle of Vimy Ridge. An official at the Elysée Palace told Canadian embassy officers that "for the General the French Canadians are a very special case. For him they are of course Canadians in the first place but they are also former Frenchmen and for this reason the normal rules do not apply." When the Canadian official noted that Jean Marchand, the Minister of Manpower and Immigration, was one of the federal ministers de Gaulle refused to see, the Elysée representative had the grace to blush as he said that Marchand came as a representative of Ottawa. That was precisely the point. To receive Quebeckers because they were French speaking but to refuse to see French-speaking federal ministers was the equivalent of saying that only Quebec spoke for French Canada.[107] That, it seemed, was the new French policy.

How should Ottawa play the game with de Gaulle? From Paris, Léger was calming in his advice. Many aspects of French policy would probably last a long time, he said, but de Gaulle would not, and relations would be calmer after he was gone. Most of the current difficulties could be laid at his door, but time was on Ottawa's side. "Let us be discreet and patient," Léger said. There had already been benefits to Canada from the efforts made to improve relations with France and *La Francophonie*, "but the trend could be reversed tomorrow by one word from one man whose reputation for taking revenge when thwarted has not diminished with his years."[108]

Ottawa generally took its ambassador's advice and bent over backward to arrange the visit by de Gaulle to Canada in Centennial year. The government was accommodating to a fault, agreeing that the President could visit Quebec City first, not Ottawa as External Affairs had wanted. There were negotiations with Paris and Quebec City on every detail of the itinerary and endless discussions on the federal presence at the quay when de Gaulle disembarked from the *Colbert*, a French cruiser, and at the various functions to follow. Was Paul Martin to sit at the head table or not? On one level, the discussions were too silly for adults to waste hours on; on another, it was the relations between Quebec and Canada and Canada and France that were at stake, and those were important.[109]

Despite the protocol, Ottawa remained optimistic about the visit. Martin saw de Gaulle in Paris in mid-June and found the President looking forward to the trip. "There was no suggestion at all in anything he said," Martin recalled, "that he meant to use the occasion to overtly defend the Quebec position." De Gaulle had noted his special affection for Quebec and Martin had said, "I fully understand it, but I would not want France in any way to contribute to Canadian disunity."

"You may be sure I don't want that either," was de Gaulle's response.

From Martin's point of view, matters began to go awry as soon as de Gaulle landed in Quebec City. "When the Governor General stepped on to the welcoming platform," he remembered, "the band struck up *God Save the Queen*. Well there is nothing more incongruous especially in Quebec. . . . I think *O Canada* should be played first. . . . To me it was humiliating to be standing on that platform with the Governor General, the President of France, and the Premier of Quebec, to hear that the first song to be played was *God Save the Queen*. This was at a time when we were asserting a national character and when we were concerned about national unity. It was galling to the people of Quebec; it must have been galling to de Gaulle."[110]

The President's first formal address was made at the Hôtel de Ville in Quebec City on July 23. The speech was not inflammatory as de Gaulle spoke of his love for Quebec and the historical and current relations between his country and Quebec. But, as Martin wrote to Pearson, the speech suggested that de Gaulle was now adopting in his public statements the attitude he had been expressing privately of supporting Quebec's position on relations between France and Quebec. Still, the French leader had agreed that a solution to the problems between Quebec and Ottawa had to be found in concert with other Canadians. "As long as he doesn't go beyond that," Martin said, "let us not make a public issue of his interference [in] our domestic affairs. . . ."[111]

But on July 24, after a long and tumultuous drive from Quebec to Montreal, de Gaulle kicked over the traces. Before a large crowd including hundreds of separatists with placards calling for *Québec libre*, the general appeared to endorse Quebec separatism by ending his speech at Montreal's city hall with the words "Vive Montréal! Vive le Québec! Vive le Québec libre!" The finale drew a terrific roar from the astonished, delighted separatists; it drew a shocked gasp from Premier Johnson.

"Did I embarrass you in any way with my speech?" de Gaulle asked.

"Yes, you have just used a slogan which was exploited against me by my political opponents in the recent Quebec political campaign."[112]

Even the ordinarily imperturbable Couve de Murville, the French foreign minister, was nonplussed, one Quebec government official noting that his hair was mussed, a sure sign that he had not known what was coming.[113] The French ambassador to Canada, however, told Paul Martin, "Je ne suis pas étonné," a cool rejoinder to the Canadian's comment that de Gaulle had gone "very far."[114]

The country was outraged – "I could hardly believe my ears," Pearson wrote[115] – even if the ambassador was not. Ottawa was flooded with apoplectic telegrams, the press went wild, and the Pearson government was faced with a first-class political and diplomatic row. Although Martin tried to urge calm,[116] the Cabinet demanded action. Pearson sent a telegram to de Gaulle saying that his speech was unacceptable, and the government issued a strong statement reminding the President (who had compared his drive from Quebec to Montreal with his entry into Paris after its liberation in August 1944) that Canada and Quebec were already free and, equally important, that one hundred thousand Canadians had died to free France in two World Wars. De Gaulle then cancelled his visit to Ottawa, and the result of the incident was that France-Canada relations hit their nadir. The separatists were emboldened, and French-English relations, hitherto caught up in the euphoria of the Centennial and Expo 67, were badly bruised.

Nor did de Gaulle recant. At a press conference in Paris in November, delivered after Canadian and French officials had tried to repair the damage,[117] the President referred to the "great Quebec affair," denounced the "so-called" federal government, and said that "Quebec be free, is indeed what is at issue." De Gaulle added that he looked for the "advent of Quebec to the rank of a sovereign state and master of its national existence."[118]

Fortunately de Gaulle had only a few more months in power, and while his successors maintained their sympathy for Quebec, they were not prepared to go quite so far with their disruptive actions. Even so, a Quebec intellectual and politician such as Claude Ryan could, years later, say that de Gaulle deserved praise for understanding Quebec's "plight as a minority society."[119]

The de Gaulle affair, the new and harder Ottawa line, and the constitutional fighting were a backdrop for the emergence of René Lévesque as a declared *indépendantiste*. The former Liberal minister had been moving towards a personal break with Canada almost since the 1960 provincial election brought him to political prominence, and on September 18, 1967, he spoke to his riding association in Montréal-Laurier. Independence, he argued, was the only solution for Quebec, followed by some form of economic union between Quebec and Canada. His association then voted to support a statement of position to be presented to the convention of the provincial Liberal federation in October. Jean Lesage and Eric Kierans, his leading English-speaking colleague, opposed Lévesque's statement,[120] and Robert Bourassa, a Liberal MLA and economist who had helped Lévesque draft his position, also released a paper showing the economic dangers of separatism. At the Liberal convention, the separatist option was turned down by huge majorities as the party endorsed instead a document calling for wide new powers for Quebec over communications, immigration, manpower, and social security, together with participation in the formation of monetary and tariff policy. That plan, itself seen by observers in English Canada as a recipe for the dissolution of the country, was insufficient for Lévesque, who left the party and formed the Mouvement Souveraineté-Association. His parting shot was a promise that Quebec would have a separatist government in four years.[121]

The battle of Quebec, the battle for Canada, was far from over, and while only a few foretold a struggle between Trudeau and Lévesque for control of the destinies of Canada and Quebec, that contest was beginning to take form by the spring of 1968.

CHAPTER 11

Politics in Disrepute

The Pearson government had had some major successes. The government had begun the task of making government bilingual, and its creation of the Royal Commission on Bilingualism and Biculturalism had demonstrated its seriousness of purpose to both French and English Canada. It had put the Canada Pension Plan into place, it had given Canada a new flag, and it had begun the process of unifying the Armed Forces. Those were all major accomplishments. But somehow the government came unstuck and things went badly askew. The Sixty Days of Decision that began the new administration turned agonizingly into five years of scandal and bitter partisan controversy that left the Canadian people desperately sick of politics and both Liberal and Conservative parties searching for new leaders and fresh approaches. The general trend of a disheartening period is conveyed by the titles of articles on Canadian affairs that appeared in the *Round Table*, the British quarterly: "A Shaky Start for the Liberals" (September 1963), "Minority Government in Trouble" (December 1963), "Liberals Struggle On" (March 1964), "An Addled Parliament" (June 1964), "Futility in Parliament" (September 1964), "Faction and Scandal" (June 1965), "Government's Second Wind" (September 1965), "A Discredited Parliament Dissolved" (December 1965), and "Time for New Leaders" (June 1966). Something had gone wrong, and the Liberals, so confident, even cocky, about their managerial prowess before the 1963 election, made many Canadians aware that their country had always been difficult to govern – and not only in Tory times.

I

The government's troubles had begun with its first budget. Pearson had given the Department of Finance to Walter Gordon, the miracle man who had created the Liberals' electoral victory. Gordon was a top-rank Toronto accountant and business consultant with fresh ideas and a proven record of administrative competence stretching back over thirty years. He was a nationalist businessman, a rare bird indeed, but in April 1963, as Finance minister, he seemed the right man in the most important place. The Sixty Days of Decision that the Liberals had promised in the 1963 campaign were under way.

But it was Walter Gordon who first got the government into the political hot water in which it was to stay. Gordon had not been entirely happy with the condition of his department when he took over. The deputy minister, K.W. Taylor, had lost his administrative grip and ability to initiate. The minister wanted R.B. Bryce, the Clerk of the Privy Council, to replace Taylor, but Pearson, needing Bryce near him in the first days of the new government, refused to allow him to switch at the outset. The result was that Gordon, after a canvass of academics and others for a list of bright young economists who could come to Ottawa for a brief period to assist with the budget, selected three, asked them to take leave from their employers, had them sworn in, and used their talents in the budget drafting.[1]

The budget was hurriedly prepared and, after some criticism by the permanent civil servants in the department, was cleared with the Prime Minister and its bare bones presented to Cabinet.[2] It was a nationalist document, Gordon's attempt to begin the process of rescuing Canada from foreign control of the economy. The Finance minister levied a 30-per-cent takeover tax on sales of shares in Canadian companies to non-residents, and the 15-per-cent withholding tax on dividends paid to non-residents was reduced by 5 per cent for companies that were at least one quarter Canadian owned and increased by 5 per cent for firms with a lower proportion of domestic ownership. There were also changes to the depreciation allowance for companies with 25 per cent or greater Canadian ownership. Other noteworthy measures were special allowances for companies that hired older unemployed workers and the elimination of the 11-per-cent sales tax exemption on building materials and production machinery.

Gordon might have expected the criticism that fell upon him beginning June 14. The Governor of the Bank of Canada, Louis Rasminsky, had told the Prime Minister and Gordon that the withholding tax would cause trouble and might produce "massive attempts at liquidation" of foreign investment and precipitate another foreign exchange crisis.[3] He was right. The United States government was incensed at the takeover and withholding taxes,[4] and Canadian businessmen, hooked into the continental economy, quickly opened their own attacks on those same measures. The result of the protests at home and abroad forced Gordon on June 19 to withdraw the takeover tax. But the minister's troubles were not yet over, for his use of special assistants in preparing the budget came under assault, initially from Douglas Fisher, the NDP member for Port Arthur, Ontario. Were the "three bright boys" free of associations with their employers in the private sector? Could they have made personal gains because of their inside knowledge?[5] Those questions stung, and after Gordon unwisely stonewalled he had to reveal full details of the hiring of the assistants to the House.

By June 20, the battered Gordon had offered his resignation to Pearson. The Prime Minister refused to accept – he had enthusiastically approved the budget and could do little else – and the Cabinet that day agreed to give full support to Gordon in Parliament. Even so, the defence was tepid at best, and by July 8 Gordon had been forced to modify additional parts of his budget. The humiliation was completed in mid-July when the Kennedy administration proposed restrictive measures to be applied to foreign borrowings in the United States, and Gordon had to appeal to the U.S. Treasury secretary to exempt Canada from the restrictions that were sure to put further pressure on the Canadian dollar.[6]

Thus Gordon was crippled as Minister of Finance and the much-trumpeted Sixty Days of Decision sputtered to a halt in a first-class *brouhaha* that demonstrated the limitations of the new government. "Well!" Eugene Forsey wrote to a friend. "The government of all the talents, all the knowledge and all the virtues!"[7] In his semi-private correspondence, the Prime Minister supported his old friend: "I hope we have learned from our mistakes. I am sure Walter Gordon has." But in conversation he was much more critical. Arnold Heeney, who had worked closely with Pearson for twenty years, wrote in his diary that in two or three talks the Prime Minister "has been very frank concerning his political difficulties, notably re W.L.G. when his personal friendship and natural loyalty to the individual cuts right across the course of political wisdom. . . . LBP told me . . . that he hoped within a couple of months to have induced Walter to take another portfolio; he was afraid however that he would insist on resigning his seat."[8]

With astonishing swiftness, Gordon had fallen to the point where he had become a liability, even an impediment, to the proper functioning of Pearson's government. Although he retained his portfolio, there was nonetheless an element of personal tragedy in his fall; yet because of his superconfident mannerisms and his too obvious certainty that Liberals knew best, very few outside the Liberal party ranks could sympathize with him. For the government as a whole, the budget had serious consequences. When he met the executive of the National

Liberal Federation in Ottawa early in 1964, Pearson admitted that the budget had been "our major failure" but claimed that the country seemed to have forgotten that "we have accomplished a great deal. . . . The record has been a good one. . . . "[9] In many ways that was so. And yet the government was in terrible trouble, harassed in the House of Commons by the Tories, bedevilled by trouble-prone ministers, and beset by scandals.

The first scandal to become public concerned evidence that the Seafarers' International Union had contributed money to the campaigns of several Montreal Liberals. As Hal Banks, the SIU leader, was in the United States awaiting a decision on whether or not he was to be extradited to Canada to serve a jail term for contempt of court, there was understandable concern that the donations might have been made for a particular purpose. Then came charges that Lucien Rivard, a Montreal drug smuggler held in a Montreal jail pending extradition to the United States, had powerful friends in the government. Erik Nielsen, the Conservative M.P. for Yukon, and NDP Leader T.C. Douglas alleged that a lawyer for the American government had been offered a bribe to drop his opposition to bail for Rivard and that two of Justice minister Favreau's aides and Pearson's parliamentary secretary, Guy Rouleau, had added the government's weight to that request.[10] Favreau (who was also the Quebec leader since Lionel Chevrier had gone to London as High Commissioner at the end of 1963) had learned of the Rivard affair in late August 1964, and he had discussed it briefly with the Prime Minister on an aircraft on September 2. But nothing concrete had been done between that date and the Nielsen-Douglas revelations in Parliament on November 23, 1964.[11]

As a result, Favreau, an able and amiable man but not a shrewd parliamentary strategist, was led "like a lamb to the slaughter," or so Conservative House leader Gordon Churchill recalled.[12] Under questioning he denied the allegations. That same night Pearson saw the RCMP file on the case for the first time, and the next day he fired Rouleau. In the House, the Liberals agreed to an inquiry, and in response to an Opposition questioner Pearson said he had first heard of the Rivard case two days before when Favreau had told him the details at his home. The Prime Minister apparently had forgotten his earlier conversation with Favreau on the airplane. But within a day or two the House and the Press Gallery were awash with rumours that Pearson had known of the affair since September.

Despite appeals from colleagues and friends, Pearson remained silent. He was in the West on a political tour while Parliament worried over the details of the case, and when he returned to Ottawa the pressure to set the record straight began anew. One of those who made the attempt was Arnold Heeney, who had learned of the Rivard case from a deputy minister friend late in August. Heeney saw the Prime Minister on November 29, accompanied by Gordon Robertson, the Clerk of the Privy Council, and Tom Kent, policy secretary to Pearson. According to Heeney, all "shared the view that the P.M. would be in an exceedingly difficult, indeed false, position if the record were to stand as it was. Furthermore, I felt that the P.M. himself should make a strong effort to assert (resume?) the moral leadership which the demeanour of the Government so far had caused the public impression that Ministers were, to say the least, ignoring. . . ." When the meeting ended, Heeney expected Pearson to issue a statement making clear that Favreau had told him of the case in early September.

But nothing happened. Heeney learned that the question had been raised in Cabinet "and there had been opposition (notably from Walter Gordon) on the ground apparently that it would simply arouse further criticism and furor." Heeney was appalled: "I said that I thought it would be disastrous if the P.M. did not go ahead – even now – before the enquiry started December 15. Better to do it from a standing start than not at all. Otherwise the enquiry would almost certainly lead to a direct conflict over what was and was not reported to the P.M." Heeney then went to see Gordon but found the Finance minister "tired and depressed and without any idea as to what could be done . . . he said that no one but the P.M. could make the decision and he had not been asked for further advice."[13] In the end Pearson wrote on December 14 to Frédéric Dorion, Chief Justice of the Superior Court of Quebec and the inquiry commissioner, to explain his lapse in memory. "I did not want to appear unfair" to Favreau, Pearson later said, after having allowed the Justice minister to dangle for three weeks. The House of Commons was outraged, emotion already running high because of the flag debate, and Pearson was subjected to the worst barracking of his career, Tommy Douglas accusing him of misleading Parliament and concluded with a formal motion to refer the matter to the Committee on Elections and Privileges. In parliamentary terms, Pearson had been called a liar, and in the manoeuvring that followed the Liberals defeated the NDP motion 122 to 105. Pearson's honour had been upheld – barely.

The inquiry report appeared on June 29, 1965. Dorion concluded that Erik Nielsen was correct – bribes had been offered – and he blasted the men who had been involved. He was gentler with Favreau but did say that the minister "should have submitted the case to the legal advisers within his Department with instructions to complete the search for facts . . . and secured their views upon the possible perpetration of a criminal offence by one or several" of those involved.[14] Favreau's judgement had been called in question, and he offered his resignation to Pearson. Although Quebec ministers objected, Pearson accepted and, as he told the House, because Favreau "remains a man of unimpeachable integrity and unsullied honour, I have asked him to consider the acceptance of another post."[15] Ruined by the affair, Favreau became President of the Privy Council, a largely honorific portfolio.

While the Rivard case was at its peak, Pearson was also under pressure from Premier Jean Lesage to fire Yvon Dupuis, a Minister without Portfolio, who was suspected of taking a bribe in 1961 to accelerate the granting of a race track licence by the province. Lesage told Pearson that Montreal *La Presse* had the story and that the Union Nationale Opposition could be expected to raise it in the legislature. Forced to act, Pearson summoned Dupuis and told him he had two weeks to produce evidence why an RCMP investigation should not take place. By Christmas 1964, finally, the Prime Minister authorized the police to look into the case and, after seeing their report, on January 17, 1965, asked Dupuis for his resignation. The errant minister refused, and five days later, after the *Toronto Star* had some of the story, Pearson fired Dupuis.[16] (In the end, Dupuis was cleared in the courts.)

At the same time the Conservatives had begun to charge that another two ministers were involved in the bankruptcy of two Montreal furniture dealers. Maurice Lamontagne, the Secretary of State, it turned out, had taken delivery of $8,000 worth of furniture and had made no payments on the debt until the bankrupt company's creditor, the Bank of Montreal, had asked for the cash. René Tremblay, Minister of Citizenship and Immigration, had also bought furniture from the company and subsequently paid off the creditors. It was the tiniest of scandals, yet another uncovered by Erik Nielsen who had, he said, learned of the deals from a man he met on a train to Montreal, but it was sufficient to create innuendoes. What precisely was Lamontagne expected to do for the furniture dealers in return for their not asking for payment? The careers of both ministers were ruined, and the stench of scandal persisted.[17]

II

The scandals that ensnared it came to dominate the thinking of the Pearson government and preoccupy the press through 1964 and 1965. Every day seemingly brought new troubles for the Prime Minister and his shaky Cabinet, and over every acrimonious debate in Parliament hovered the shadow of minority government, obliging the Liberals to watch constantly lest some act of omission or commission push the opposition parties into coalition, produce a defeat in the House, and force an election at an inopportune time. The delicate balance in the Commons also gave the third parties more prominence than might otherwise have been the case, and Réal Caouette and Tommy Douglas won a genuine bargaining power as a result.

Yet the situation could not last indefinitely, and government strategists knew all too well that the next election had to be called at a time that best suited the Liberals. Here too were questions of strategy, the most important of which involved redistribution. Even if things went well, the Liberals estimated, the redistribution that was to take place on the census results of 1961 could not be put through Parliament before 1966. Once it was past the House, an eighteen-month delay was necessary to permit the reorganization of constituency associations by all the parties and a restructuring by the Chief Electoral Officer. In other words, if the Liberals did not go to the polls in 1965 they might well be stuck until late 1967 – and would Centennial year be the best of times for an election?

The arguments for an early election seemed compelling to those such as Walter Gordon who wanted to test the electorate quickly. In January 1965 – with polls showing the Liberals at 47 per cent and the Conservatives and NDP at 32 and 12 respectively – he told Pearson that the party's National Campaign Committee favoured a June election and estimated a gain of twenty-five seats.[18] A few months later Gordon was after Pearson again, still calling for a June or July election. The organization was ready, the economy was in good shape with unemployment at about 4 per cent, and Quebec "at the moment" was relatively calm. Moreover, the polls were still good (although the March Gallup poll showed both the Liberals and the Conservatives down in support), and if Diefenbaker decided to retire "a Conservative convention called for December or January" would tie "our hands . . . until the new leader was chosen." In political terms, the Finance minister said, "there will be no excuse for failing to take the initiative *when we can win*."[19]

But Pearson was reluctant. He hated campaigning, and the thought of another election against John Diefenbaker made him almost ill. The June date passed, and Gordon was soon urging an October election, prophesying 155 to 180 seats. "Diefenbaker is a real asset to us," he said, "and we should not risk waiting until someone takes his place." Moreover, the Dorion Report on the Rivard case was due. The campaign committee felt strongly "that firm and fast action is imperative following publication" and "any delay" in housecleaning where necessary "would be very damaging."[20] But again Pearson put off a decision, and by late summer 1965 the press had begun to argue against an election before redistribution. Tom Kent, Pearson's chief aide, however, still pressed for an early vote. The only people who objected were "those who don't like us but can't bear Diefenbaker . . . and good, sincere people who don't like elections and hope that if it is put off it will somehow be less 'dirty' and not do the harm to national unity that they fear from Diefenbaker." Kent added that "the rejection of Diefenbaker, if we achieve it, would be good for national unity."[21]

The crucial day was August 31. Gordon saw the Prime Minister that day to discuss new polls, which suggested the Liberals could win 150 to 155 seats. The issues were identified as the cost of living, unemployment, taxes, spending, and medicare; surprisingly, there was little concern about federal-provincial relations. "It would be a mistake to emphasize the Quebec problem," Gordon said, "not because we do not consider it the No. 1 domestic issue but because people in English-speaking Canada do not like being reminded of it. . . . Also every time we mention the 'two founding races', we offend unnecessarily the one-quarter of the population that belongs to neither. . . . " According to Gordon, the survey results argued that the issues should be "what we have done – prosperity . . . pensions, the flag, etc. An appeal for a strong Federal Government. . . . A request for a mandate to proceed with such programs as Medicare and improved educational and training facilities." And the proper strategy, Gordon added, was to leave Diefenbaker alone.[22]

Pearson fretted about the decision over the Labour Day weekend, but the decision to hold the election on November 8, 1965, was nonetheless made and announced on September 7. The Liberal strategy, as devised by the pollsters and Gordon and revised and expanded by Keith Davey, the National Campaign Director, was "Building the New Canada," which naturally demanded a Liberal majority government. With a majority, the party's secret strategy paper said, the Government and the Opposition both know where they are for the next four years. "We ask for a majority so that we can get on with the main job and be judged by how we do it."[23]

The Conservatives were no less eager than the Liberal strategists for an election. Waldo Monteith told Diefenbaker that he wanted the vote now and was confident the Chief could win. The people were "completely disenchanted" with Gordon and Pearson and the big issues were "One Canada," the erosion of central authority and the Liberals' catering to Quebec.[24] The party campaign committee set out the Conservative plan. In the first stage, the object was to hit at the government record and to stress bread-and-butter issues; in the last month, the candidates should stress national development. The Tories' objectives were to hold their rural vote and increase it, to target rural Quebec, Toronto, and Montreal (particularly working-class Montreal), as well as Vancouver and Newfoundland. It was a national campaign focused regionally.[25]

The NDP was in straitened circumstances, as usual. The Conservatives would raise more than $2 million and allocate $1.16 million to the constituencies; the NDP would budget $150,000 for their national campaign and be exultant when the Ontario party could raise and spend $250,000 during the election.[26] What worried the NDP planners was the appeal of majority government to an electorate tired of minority government and the wrangling between Diefenbaker and Pearson. Tommy Douglas had done his fair share of desk-pounding in Parliament too, but he had never attracted the odium that attached itself to the Prime Minister and the Leader of the Opposition. Thus for the NDP the issue was leadership – Tommy Douglas's transparent honesty against the mud-spattered Chief and the vacillating Mike.[27]

Social Credit and the Créditistes, divided in two since September 1963 when Réal Caouette had led most of the Quebec contingent in a breakaway, had demonstrated that a minor party when sundered was even less effective than when united. Caouette's forces were quick to appeal for support from "les petits gars," but their scarcely concealed efforts to save their own seats before all else did them little good. One Créditiste on the House Flag Committee had even offered his vote to the Conservatives in return for election expenses, a sure sign that collections were drying up in Quebec.[28] At the same time, as one of his followers told Robert Thompson, the Alberta M.P. and Social Credit leader, the Créditiste defection "dealt a very serious blow to the public image of Social Credit and its political effectiveness . . . [and] placed seriously in question before the public your status as leader. . . ."[29] The two parties were finished, and even Réal Caouette's fabled drawing power in the rural areas of Quebec had dwindled.

Diefenbaker's appeal had not diminished, however. The old Chief, turning seventy on September 18, toured the country by railway car, a striking contrast to the jet-setting Grits. "He cared enough to come," the Conservatives cheered, and the leader was glorying in a reunited party. George Hees and Davie Fulton had again pledged loyalty; Eddie Goodman was once more directing the campaign; and the party's opinion polls, showing the Liberals losing support during the campaign, looked better and better.[30] Diefenbaker played the Liberal scandals like a master – on warm nights he got an unfailing roar from the crowds when he said that "it was on a night like this" that Rivard, the dope peddler, had left his cell to water the prison ice rink – and escaped. It was great theatre, just as it was when Diefenbaker ran through a litany of the furniture scandals and bribes that had tormented the government. The names were French, and the Tory leader revelled in his mispronunciations and appeals for One Canada. In the code of the day, whatever Diefenbaker might have meant, he was unfailingly understood as wanting to put and keep Quebec in its place.

The Chief's supporters argued that he was not anti-Quebec. He used the scandals because those involved were Liberals, not because they were French speaking. He had no anti-French Canadian biases, they said; he simply did not understand Quebec. While he loved visiting country fairs in *La belle province* and even enjoyed his stumbling attempts to speak French, he simply equated Quebeckers with the Ukrainians he had grown up with in Saskatchewan – good people wanting to be accepted. Perhaps that was so, but even Diefenbaker's supporters had to rationalize what they were doing during the 1965 election. One slogan privately used around party headquarters in Ottawa was "Let's give the old bugger another chance," and three of the key planners jokingly agreed that if by chance the Chief won the election, one of them would go on the radio, accept the nation's plaudits, and then admit it was all a giant hoax. The three would then link hands and jump off the roof of the Chateau Laurier.[31]

There was even a chance that the election could be won. Pearson's self-doubts about the election were reflected in his lacklustre campaign. There was no oomph in the Liberal efforts, while Diefenbaker scored heavily with his attacks. Walter Gordon's assessment was that a majority was still possible, although in mid-October he expected losses in the Maritimes and on the Prairies but saw chances for large gains in Quebec. For Gordon, the issues remained the same, and he was convinced that a big push on the majority government issue could only do good.[32] The Liberals were bolstered by the return of Robert Winters, a minister in the St. Laurent government, running in York West, Ontario, and by the adhesion to the party of Gérard Pelletier, Jean Marchand, and Pierre Trudeau. Pelletier, a journalist, and Marchand, a labour leader, were much the best known; Trudeau, described by the *Round Table* in December 1965 as "an intellectual millionaire," was suspect to many Liberals for his scathing denunciations of Pearson on the nuclear issue in 1963.

The result, as the Montreal *Gazette* of November 10 described it, was that "Pearson wins but loses." The Liberals won only two seats more than they had in 1963, totalling 131 or two short of a majority. Diefenbaker also increased the Conservative ranks by two to 97, while the NDP went from 17 to 21 seats. The Créditistes and Social Credit were the main losers, dropping from 24 seats between them in 1963 to

9 and 5 in 1965. The Liberals had 40.2 per cent of the popular vote, the Conservatives 32.4, and the NDP 17.9. The election had turned on the Liberals' inability to sweep Quebec, where the Conservatives had held 8 seats and the Créditistes 9; the Liberals won only 56 of the 75 seats, at least 10 below expectations. On the Prairies, the Liberals had taken a lone seat against 42 for the Chief.

The post-mortems were many and various. Jack Pickersgill said the result had confirmed his hunch that Diefenbaker was a more formidable opponent than a new Tory leader would have been. "Undoubtedly by sickening the public with both 'old' parties Dief made a lot of extra votes for the NDP that they would never have got on their own merit." Pearson found the "total result . . . disappointing but the outlook is far from bleak." Yet he said to an old friend that his own preference was to get out: ". . . somebody might even give me a job at a university!"[33] And Walter Gordon, as the chief proponent of an election, felt obliged to give Pearson his resignation as Minister of Finance. In part that was a gesture that would allow the Prime Minister to replace a trouble-prone and sometimes troublesome minister; in part it was simply a recognition that after the Liberal failure Gordon's influence was severely weakened. Pearson did not protest much, later noting that as Gordon himself knew "he did not have the full confidence of the financial and business community which a Minister of Finance should enjoy."[34] Walter Gordon was gone from the Cabinet.

III

The election results, so closely duplicating those of 1963, unfortunately did not end the parade of scandals that had so tormented the last parliament. Pearson and Diefenbaker were still at the head of their parties, and so long as the two remained the bitterness that dominated the daily struggle in the House was certain to continue.

And continue it did. The next case to make the headlines concerned one George Victor Spencer, a postal worker in Vancouver, who had been recruited as a low-level spy by officials operating from the Soviet embassy in Ottawa. Spencer had no access to secrets of state, but he did provide his masters with details of the Post Office's security system and with data that could be used to create plausible backgrounds for deep-cover Soviet agents. The RCMP had apparently known of Spencer's activities for some time, but in May 1965 the police and the Department of External Affairs announced that two Soviet spies were to be expelled and the activities of Spencer, himself unnamed, were tossed into the press release for good measure. The

Prime Minister added that because the postal worker in question was about to die of cancer, no legal action would be taken against him.

The Spencer case, still unknown to the public as such, disappeared. But only for a time. Thanks to cobalt treatment, Spencer lived longer than anticipated, and a Vancouver reporter tracked him down. That stirred interest. Then "This Hour Has Seven Days," CBC-TV's flagship public affairs show that had won large audiences with an iconoclastic style and bold questioning of public figures, managed to have Justice minister Lucien Cardin confirm Spencer's existence on air.

Next it became known that Spencer had been fired by the Post Office and denied his pension, all without being prosecuted. That stirred up outrage in the Opposition and the press over the violation of Spencer's civil liberties. How could this man have been fired and deprived of his pension without being tried in open court for his alleged crimes? The Justice department told the Prime Minister quietly that although the facts were clear, "there are nevertheless such difficulties in the way of presenting this evidence to the Court as to raise a very serious doubt as to the success of a prosecution."[35]

The Cabinet spent some time considering the Spencer case over the Christmas recess, trying to decide whether or not to hold an inquiry. Pearson favoured an in camera hearing and was confident that, as "we had treated Spencer fairly," the government's course was completely defensible. But Cardin and a majority of the ministers disagreed sharply with Pearson's judgement. To appoint another inquiry inevitably would create the impression of government wrongdoing. Cardin had said as much in public, and, Pearson noted, his "repudiation" would have been interpreted as throwing another Quebec minister to the wolves. "He would have resigned."[36]

The Opposition continued its attacks on the government's position after the recess, and on March 4, 1966, David Lewis, the NDP M.P. for York South, Ontario, produced a telegram from Spencer asking for an inquiry. This blew away the argument that Spencer had never asked for an inquiry, one of the Liberals' pretexts for stonewalling on the issue. Spencer's telegram seemed to want to limit the inquiry's scope to the circumstances of his dismissal and his pension, and to Pearson that pointed a way out. We could "accept this kind of limited inquiry while rejecting the demand for a full one which would bring in security issues," he wrote. "We could save our face and give public opinion reassurance that the dismissal was just. . . ." The Prime Minister consulted some of his colleagues and won support; Cardin too "agreed that we should change front in the new circumstances. . . . There was not a word about resignation."

Thus Pearson announced the limited inquiry and associated Cardin with his statement "so that there would be no repudiation . . . either in fact or in appearance." But over the weekend, while the Opposition exulted in the Liberal surrender, and while the Liberals from Quebec fumed, Cardin decided to resign. The Quebec caucus furiously accused the Prime Minister "of having repudiated Cardin, tossed him aside, without even consulting him, etc., etc. Marchand felt that he should resign if Cardin did; so did [Léo] Cadieux [Associate Minister of National Defence] and [J.J.J.P.] Côté [Postmaster General]." As Pearson noted,"Things were really falling apart," and he applied all his formidable powers of persuasion to keeping Cardin in the government. But the Justice minister had come to detest Parliament, Ottawa, and his job, and he was adamant. Pearson soon discovered, however, that Cardin feared if he left, "his resignation would break up the government and lead to mine. He claimed that this would be a tragedy for Canada and especially for Quebec. . . . " Maurice Lamontagne and others persuaded Cardin that if he went they would *all* go, and the Justice minister relented. Cardin gave his decision to the caucus on Wednesday, March 9, 1966, and matters calmed down. Spencer was to have his inquiry and the government would stay together; Pearson had survived yet another crisis without the sacrifice of a Quebec colleague.[37]

But on March 4, Cardin had responded to a sharp attack from John Diefenbaker in the Commons by shouting out something about the "Monseigneur" case. Only a few insiders knew to what this referred until the Justice minister held a press conference on March 10. Cardin told the reporters, assembled to learn why he had decided to stay in the Cabinet, that although he had not seen the RCMP file, the case in question was worse than Britain's sex-and-security scandal involving John Profumo, a minister in the Macmillan government. Cardin added that one Gerda Munsinger had engaged in espionage before coming to Canada and that both Diefenbaker and Davie Fulton, his Minister of Justice, had known of the affair and had not referred it to the law officers of the Crown.

Cardin's accusations caused a sensation. The minister later confirmed that although he "had never seen the word 'Munsinger' spelled out . . . believe me, I knew what the facts were." In fact, Cardin had discussed the case with Pearson and Favreau earlier in an attempt to get the Prime Minister to use this weapon against Diefenbaker, but Pearson had refused, and Cardin had blurted out the slightly garbled pronunciation of Munsinger, he said, under the pressure of the House debate.[38] Favreau, it turned out, had also talked about the case with Fulton, warning him in a friendly way that it might be used against the Tories if the scandal campaign against the government continued. According to Fulton, that was proof that Cardin's interjection was far from accidental.[39]

The astonishment of the public increased when the *Toronto Star* discovered that Gerda Munsinger, far from being dead, was alive and well and living in Germany. Lurid stories soon appeared in the press, especially in Germany: "I will not be quiet about it," Munsinger breathlessly told the *Neue Illustrierte*. "I will tell you how it was. How it really was in my fast-living restless life . . . where I met the men of society who wanted to have my love." According to Munsinger, she had had an affair with Pierre Sévigny and also with George Hees, the Minister of Trade and Commerce in the Diefenbaker government.[40]

The result of the Cardin charges was the establishment of another royal commission under Supreme Court Justice Wishart Spence to investigate the Diefenbaker government's handling of the Munsinger case. The Spence Commission considered the evidence and heard testimony. The Conservatives, and especially Diefenbaker and Fulton, were fighting for their political lives, and some people were worried about the precedent that was being established. Joseph Sedgwick, a Toronto Conservative and one of the leading figures of the Ontario bar, told Fulton privately that the commission was "no better than a political witch hunt." The commissioner had been asked "to review decisions that were made in good faith, and which were purely political decisions. In my view," Sedgwick went on, "no Commissioner should be asked even to comment on the decisions of the leader of the Government, or his Ministers, whether to praise or condemn." The prime minister, he concluded, was answerable to the House and, in due course, to the country, not to anyone else.[41]

That was a good principle. And there were reasons to doubt Pearson's motives in the whole question. George Bain of the *Globe and Mail* wrote: "It is now apparent that for 16 months the Government had stood with the Munsinger case held like a pailful of slops over the heads of its chief political opponents . . . the inquiry that is now going on was brought into being by the desire for political revenge against the Government's tormenters . . . the protection of national security . . . had nothing to do with it."[42]

Bain was exactly right. In November 1964, at the height of the Opposition's scandalmongering, the Prime Minister had accepted a suggestion from J.W. Pickersgill, then Minister of Transport, that he should "counter the suspicions being created that members of Parliament are 'shady' characters" by instructing the RCMP, as Pearson wrote, "to let me know the details of any investigations made by them during the last 10 years in which a member was involved; let Diefenbaker know we are doing this."[43] Pearson duly spoke to the RCMP commissioner and on December 2, 1964, had received his report. This was the first time Pearson had learned of the Munsinger affair, the liaison between Sévigny, Associate Minister of National Defence in the Diefenbaker government, and Munsinger, a German-born prostitute in Montreal. It was a "particularly sordid affair," Pearson noted, but it would not have justified any intervention on his part except for the security aspect raised by Munsinger's involvement as a low-level Soviet agent in Germany. Diefenbaker had, again in Pearson's words, "merely reprimanded the Minister (who had certainly by now become a vulnerable person from a security point of view) and kept him in his most sensitive Ministerial post. It wasn't 'Go and sin no more'. It was 'Stay, and sin no more.' " As the Prime Minister added in a later diary note, "It can be imagined how great was the temptation to use this knowledge at a time when we were being subjected to every kind of slimy attack on grounds of corruption, integrity in Government, political morality, etc."[44]

As Pickersgill had proposed, Pearson wrote to Diefenbaker and met him on December 10, 1964. Pearson's account, written that day, noted that the Conservative leader "seemed tired and more than usually nervous." He had known of the Sévigny case, he said, "interviewed his minister, had satisfied himself that no security had been violated." Pearson added, "I shudder to think what he would have done to a Liberal P.M. who kept a Defence Minister on the job in these circumstances." It seems certain that Pearson hoped to persuade Diefenbaker to cool the scandal accusations against his government by letting the Conservative leader know that he was aware of the Munsinger case. Diefenbaker was equal to the challenge, however, and as Pearson wrote, "indulged in his own form of blackmail by telling me that when he took office, there was a very important security file – from Washington – in which I was involved. He was surprised, I think, when I identified it, said I knew all about it, would have no worry if it were ever made public and had, years ago, told the U.S. State Department just that! That ended the subject."[45] The file in question apparently contained accusations from a witness before a Congressional committee that Pearson had Communist connections.

This interview between the Prime Minister and the Leader of the Opposition had surely been extraordinary. Each man tried to blackmail the other with secrets from security files, and neither emerged with any credit whatsoever.

Nor was there much glory in the Spence inquiry. Diefenbaker and Fulton withdrew from the inquiry on May 18 in protest against Spence's conduct of it and the tactics of the commission counsel. That did not stop Spence, whose report, published on September 23, 1966, found that Pierre Sévigny had become a security risk because of the affair, even though there was no suspicion of disloyalty on his part. Diefenbaker was censured for failing to dismiss Sévigny and for not seeking the advice of his Cabinet, and Fulton, incredibly, was criticized for accepting the RCMP's word that there was no security breach without investigating further. George Hees was cited for a "regrettable" lack of discretion.[46] Parliament, the leaders of the parties, and the nation's political process were besmirched by this affair, from which no one emerged with either credit or reputation intact. Judy LaMarsh summed it up best: "Members scuttled from the House heads down, even though the drama lured them back to their seats as the lethal verbal slashing went on. They were sick, Parliament was sick, but the press had a field day."[47]

IV

The dreadful Munsinger affair and the less-than-satisfactory Spence inquiry reduced politics in Canada to an appalling state. In the House and throughout the country, the Liberals pointed the finger at John Diefenbaker and maintained that he alone was responsible for the debasement of Parliament; Conservatives, whether they supported the continuation of Diefenbaker at the head of their party or not, were almost unanimous in placing the blame on Pearson personally and on his government's apparently corruptible ministers; and the New Democrats, fortunately spared any direct involvement in the scandals, characteristically pointed at both parties and proclaimed their own innocence and pristine superiority. Everyone seemed to agree that renewal was needed if Parliament was to regain its position in the country and politics was again to be seen as an honourable profession. Renewal began first – but only with enormous travail – in the Progressive Conservative Party.

After the Cabinet revolt of February 1963 had been squelched, the unhappiness in certain quarters of the Tory party over the leadership of the Chief did not abate. Douglas Harkness, the Defence minister whose resignation had precipitated the crisis of confidence that destroyed the Conservative government, was one who remained adamant in his opposition. In June 1963, he wrote to a friend that the anti-Diefenbaker feeling had been responsible for the election of a Liberal in Calgary South in the election. "I was in considerable difficulty in Calgary North," he added, "because I was running as a regular Conservative candidate"; while many wanted to vote for Harkness, they "could not possibly cast a vote which would assist Diefenbaker in any way, and if I were elected it would mean one more seat to help keep him in power." There had to be a change of leaders, Harkness concluded. But as he wrote to the same friend in December, the caucus, while dissatisfied with the Chief, was not about to say so out loud: ". . . not more than two or three of the members at most are prepared to say publicly what the majority are saying privately." And it was the same across the country, "the same reluctance on the part of the Party members to come out and advocate a change in leadership."[48]

Part of the trouble arose from the minority situation in Parliament, which meant an election could come at any time. With the Liberal government so shaky, the Conservatives could not afford to be left leaderless by a party revolt at a critical time. That probably contributed to Diefenbaker's buoyant mood. In the fall of 1963 he wrote to the Lieutenant-Governor of Saskatchewan (one of his former M.P.s) that opinion polls showed the Progressive Conservatives up 3 per cent since the election and the Liberals up only two. The Pearson government was slipping, failing even to enjoy the traditional honeymoon. "The Pearson administration," he exulted, "started to die prematurely almost from the time of its birth."[49]

But opposition to Diefenbaker did show itself timidly at the party's annual meeting in Ottawa at the beginning of February 1964. Young Progressive Conservatives narrowly defeated a motion for a secret leadership ballot, and Student Conservatives on a secret ballot narrowly supported the leader 29 to 27. At the main meeting, the question of a secret ballot was fought for ninety minutes, and the Diefenbaker loyalists won by a 3-to-1 margin. A resolution of confidence in the leader, however, carried by a decidely larger margin with only about thirty delegates voting against. The frustrated Harkness wrote, "Over two hundred people to whom I spoke around the hotel . . . were anxious to see a change in leadership. . . . However, when the open vote on confidence came only between sixty and seventy stood up." Although the press had said that thirty opposed the Chief, he could name more than forty who rose and there were many others whose names he did not know. "It is very difficult to understand why so many people are afraid to publicly take a stand on a matter of this kind."[50]

But the next year at the P.C. Association National Executive meeting in Ottawa in February, the attacks against Diefenbaker were furious. The entire Quebec caucus had met in Montreal to lick collective wounds caused by Diefenbaker's anti-Quebec line and had issued a statement: "We have concluded, with real regret, that the direction that the party is now travelling can have no other result than to isolate Quebec Conservatives from the main body of the party." The problem was Diefenbaker: "On every issue touching the tap-roots of Confederation, the hopes and aspirations of French Canada have been distorted, misrepresented, and ignored . . . subjected to narrow, parochial, unreasoning criticism of the kind to which great issues should not be subjected." The conclusion was somber: ". . . the Conservative Party can no longer carry on under its present leadership and the policies which that leadership has engendered."[51] In the opinion of Quebec Tories, a leadership convention was necessary, and that became the focal point of the association meeting.

The key struggle was fought in the meeting of the National Executive. Léon Balcer, the Quebec leader in the federal house, was given the opportunity to read the Quebec statement. Then Diefenbaker spoke at length. The meeting was closed, but Davie Fulton's on-the-spot notes captured the flavour of the Chief's remarks:

> Those who opposed in 1956 and have continued to oppose ever since privately and publicly
>
> Those who have ambition will have opportunity in due course . . .
>
> . . . Gladstone won his last election at 84.
>
> You who have ambitions should not be other than hopeful
>
> Termites
>
> Balcer
>
> Press statements prepared by somebody else (attacks Pres. of U.S. – Kennedy
>
> – re attempted stoppage of shipments to Comm. China
>
> – in connection with crisis in foreign exchange – created by U.S. to help Liberals . . .
>
> Anti-Quebec? was I responsible in 1921-40? Was I the one who left caucus? and said I was anti-Quebec?
>
> . . . I am for one Canada – not separate.
>
> – I have no personal ambition – have had everything – don't care how you vote – but put yourself in my position. If you vote vs me you are voting for the [illegible] of Liberalism. I want to know if you want that . . .
>
> If you want a convention have it. Get rid of me. They offered me the Chief Justiceship of Canada – say more about that another time . . .
>
> Do what you will – I don't come to you as a supplicant.[52]

With its confused logic and rhetorical questions, that speech was vintage late Diefenbaker. The venom, the attacks on enemies within the party and on Liberals and Americans without were also classic.

But when the National Executive considered a vote on a secret questionnaire, Diefenbaker opposed the inclusion of a question involving a vote of confidence. The executive withdrew, considered the protest, and then decided to let the questions stand as drafted. The decision was challenged from the floor, and the motion to delete the confidence question carried 55 to 52, with the five-member executive abstaining. As the incredulous Harkness observed, had the executive voted "they would have supported their unanimous recommendation which would have given a majority against Diefenbaker." There was also a vote on whether or not a leadership convention should be called at once, the results of which, Harkness said, were "communicated only to Diefenbaker" while the National President, Dalton Camp, announced only that the recommendation was against a convention. Harkness was dubious: "I personally think it very probable that the ballot must have been in favour . . . because otherwise Diefenbaker would have been roaring from the rooftops that the meeting had voted against it."[53]

Diefenbaker was shaken by the narrow escape. On March 14 he summoned some of his supporters – Angus MacLean of P.E.I., Erik Nielsen of the Yukon, Waldo Monteith of Ontario, and Gordon Churchill of Manitoba – to Stornoway, his home, and told them that he was going to resign within two days. But on March 17, nothing having happened in the interim, Diefenbaker called his friends to his office. "Chief in high state of excitement," Monteith scribbled, " – 'this is it' and so on." Churchill urged the leader to remain, and on the next day Monteith noted that "Mike Starr wonders if he, Churchill and JWM[onteith] being used as pawns and Chief has no idea of resigning." The threat of resignation disappeared.[54]

However, some Quebec Conservatives were leaving. Remi Paul left the caucus in February and Balcer followed in April, charging that "the majority of members supporting Mr. Diefenbaker have nothing but contempt for French Canada and all that it represents." As a result, there was much speculation about the leadership, with men like George Hees and Davie Fulton campaigning almost openly.[55] But the Chief was equal to the threat, and with an election clearly on the way, he told the press on June 11 that the media should not spread idle gossip. He was the leader and would be for years to come.[56] Party unity in the face of the Grits and the election seemed restored, and in the 1965 campaign the hitherto rebellious Tories regrouped around the old man and fought with him a magnificent battle. The result was not victory, but it was closer than most pundits had thought possible in February 1965.

The election and its aftermath gave a pause to the leadership struggle. But it was only a pause. In early 1966, Diefenbaker named Dr.

James Johnston as the party's new National Director. "His first – and as some of his critics point out, his only – move in what he termed a thorough reorganization was to dispense with my services," Flora MacDonald wrote to her friends at Christmas 1966.[57] A long-serving senior headquarters staffer, popular with all factions in the party but not with Diefenbaker, Flora by being sacked rejuvenated the critics and increased their ranks. On May 19, 1966, Dalton Camp, the party's national president and hitherto a loyal supporter of the Chief, told a private gathering of Conservatives at Toronto's Albany Club that steps had to be taken to find fresh leadership before another election. A convention, he said, had to be held before the spring of 1967. Camp's strategy was based on the idea that there was little point in staging another direct challenge to Diefenbaker; instead he intended a crusade for the democratization of the party and for the principle that a leader, any leader, was responsible to his party and his performance had to be subject to review.[58] The test was to come at the National Progressive Conservative Association meeting at Ottawa in November 1966, and the issue was to be the selection of a national president, either Camp or a Diefenbaker candidate.

Dalton Camp was an advertising man, a shrewd assessor of winning slogans and strategies. He had worked at party headquarters in the 1950s, and he had played a major role in creating the Diefenbaker campaigns of 1957 and 1958 that swept the Conservatives into power. He was a Diefenbaker loyalist through 1963, but in the months that followed his attitude slowly had begun to change as Diefenbaker hung on to power and steadily diminished the party's base in urban middle-class Canada. Finally, by May 1966 he was ready to come out against the Chief – at least in a private address to party notables in Toronto – and his public "crusade," which began in September, led to the forced retirement of the old leader.

Within days of being launched, the Camp crusade began to win support. Riding associations and provincial party associations climbed aboard, and several prominent figures in caucus enlisted as well. The Chief's supporters were shaken by the extent of the support Camp drew. Gordon Churchill, for example, saw some of the leading figures in the Manitoba provincial party on October 2 and, to his surprise, found that they wanted him to urge Diefenbaker not to oppose the Camp review of the leadership. Winnipeg businessmen were against Diefenbaker, they argued, and their estimate was that at least sixty of the one hundred Manitoba delegates to the November meeting would support Camp. Churchill dutifully passed on the message to his leader, and Diefenbaker drew the appropriate message – Premier Roblin of Manitoba could no longer be counted upon for his support.[59]

But the caucus remained solid. Churchill surveyed the M.P.s and found that seventy were for the Chief, six were neutral, and only twenty were willing to say they opposed the leader. That heartened the Manitoba loyalist, and by October 20 he had found a candidate to oppose Camp for the party presidency: Arthur Maloney, a distinguished Toronto lawyer and an M.P. from 1957 to 1962.[60] The credibility of the old guard's candidate, to say nothing of the size of the loyalist caucus contingent, led some of the party chieftains to hold back their support for Camp. Davie Fulton, for example, wrote to his leadership campaign's shadow finance chairman to say, "We should not in any way attempt to interfere or frustrate" the Camp crusade "but should keep entirely aloof."[61] All aid short of help seemed to be the watchword.

Even so, Camp's troops were ready. They won control of the agenda for the association meeting and managed to have the vote for the presidency scheduled ahead of the resolutions on the leadership. They packed the convention floor and either sat on their hands during Diefenbaker's speech or hooted at him when, as Fulton wrote, "his speech grew progressively worse, more abusive and derogatory of all his predecessors, and all those who might have any hopes of succeeding him. As he grew more intolerant, so gradually the mood of his audience changed from one of cold respect to one of active hostility." Rattled by the boos, Diefenbaker blurted out, "Is this a Conservative meeting?" It was a sad denouement.[62]

The next day, November 15, Camp was re-elected over Maloney by 564 to 502 votes. Significantly, the three Conservative provincial premiers – Robarts of Ontario, Roblin of Manitoba, and Stanfield of Nova Scotia – supported Camp. Flora MacDonald was elected party secretary by a 4-to-1 majority, a sweeping vindication of a loyal worker and a repudiation of James Johnston as National Director. And on November 16, as the Diefenbaker supporters moved out of the hall to applaud the arrival of the Chief, the party delegates considered the leadership resolutions. Quickly the association accepted the necessity for a leadership convention and voted only a tepid motion of "support" for Diefenbaker. The Camp revolution was complete.

Characteristically, the caucus did not seem to realize the extent of the débâcle. As the leader argued that the caucus, not the party, determined leadership and as Camp's supporters were purged, the ever-faithful Churchill got a petition of support signed by seventy-one of the ninety-six members urging Diefenbaker to continue. His reasoning, Churchill wrote later, was based on his fear that as many as forty M.P.s might leave the party if Diefenbaker were forced out, and his petition, he believed, was necessary to keep the caucus together and block the formation of a new loyalist party.[63] It was a sad state of affairs, one that drove Conservatives to distraction. Joseph Sedgwick wrote to a caucus friend that no one wanted to see Diefenbaker "go out ignominiously. He had made his contribution and it was a great one, but he cannot, even in remote possibility, do a repeat." Now was the time for Diefenbaker's supporters to think of the party. "Might they not tell him, kindly but bluntly, that a return to power is beyond his grasp, and that he must go, soon, and gracefully. That is the favour they could do him, if they do not want to see him further humiliated." That was good advice, yet although some tried to follow it, the Chief and his supporters were in no mood to listen.[64]

Thus the planning for a leadership convention began in an atmosphere of bitterness and uncertainty. The bitterness was the fruit of past battles and present hostility between loyalists and Camp-ites. The uncertainty was the product of Diefenbaker's refusal to make clear his plans. Would he retire? The Chief's only utterance, a delphic one, came on TV on January 18, 1967, when he said that the delegates had to be selected on a democratic basis and the convention held as early as possible. "I know that some will interpret what I am saying as being a swan song. Let me say at once – this is no swan song. Those who will interpret it that way do not know me. I have never in the past, and I shall not now desert the course of a lifetime, of at all times upholding principle and standing for those things which in my opinion are good for Canada . . . ."[65]

By mid-February – with opinion polls showing the Conservatives at 25 per cent popular support, well behind the NDP (28 per cent) and Liberals (37 per cent) – the planning committee had picked Toronto as the site and fixed the first week in September 1967 as the date for the party's first leadership convention since 1956. Already the candidates were coming forward. Davie Fulton announced on January 19, bringing with him an organization he had been preparing since 1964 and that included able young Conservatives such as Joe Clark of Alberta and Brian Mulroney of Quebec.[66] George Hees was another early candidate, and in his train was John Bassett's Toronto *Telegram* (earlier promised to Fulton).[67] Michael Starr, Labour minister in Diefenbaker's cabinet and a loyalist, announced that he would run if the Chief did not; Senator Wallace McCutcheon decided to enter the race, arguing that his leadership could check socialism; and Alvin Hamilton, yet another loyalist, announced his candidacy in May. There were still more to come. Churchill had lined up more than fifty M.P.s who were prepared to support Diefenbaker, but he could not get the leader to commit himself. "God, I was mad at him," Churchill said. By mid-March, as a result, Churchill had begun to look elsewhere, and Donald

Fleming, the long-serving and long-suffering Finance minister through most of the Diefenbaker government, was his choice.[68]

Fleming was willing to listen to representations from Churchill, Waldo Monteith, and Ellen Fairclough, and he went across the country sounding out his chances, concluding that they were good. In part, Fleming was heartened by assurances that Stanfield and Roblin would not be candidates, and he had indications of sympathetic support from Union Nationale Premier Daniel Johnson of Quebec and Social Credit Premier Ernest Manning of Alberta, both influential quasi-conservatives. There was even a gesture in his direction from Premier W.A.C. Bennett of British Columbia. On June 7, therefore, Fleming tossed his hat into the ring.[69]

Dalton Camp was also thinking of his own prospects. He realized all too well that given his role in the ouster of the Chief he could not expect to unify the party. But the range of choice did not impress him, and he apparently believed that if he could not persuade Stanfield or Roblin to run, he himself must. Both premiers were under strong pressure from their supporters, but as the summer wore on, it seemed more and more likely that Camp had failed in his efforts to induce one of the new men to take the plunge. On July 19, finally, Stanfield decided to leave Nova Scotia, where he had been a long-lived and successful premier, to try for national prominence. He instantly garnered the support of Camp and his friends, an organization in being. But to the consternation of Camp and Stanfield – and to the utter horror of Fleming, who saw his support scatter – Duff Roblin also entered the contest on August 3. There were now Fleming and McCutcheon on the right, Hamilton and Starr on the left, and Fulton, Hees, Roblin, and Stanfield in the centre.

Soon there was a policy issue to concern the candidates and delegates. At a "thinkers' meeting" at Montmorency, Quebec, from August 6 to 10, 1967, the Conservatives argued bitterly over constitutional questions. Was Canada "two nations" or was it "one Canada"? The Montmorency delegates hit on the formula of "*deux nations*," which they translated as "two founding peoples,"[70] a neat piece of semantics. To many it seemed only a statement of the Canadian reality. But to John Diefenbaker, *deux nations* meant that his party was giving short shrift to those Canadians who were of neither French nor English origin and conceding an equality to French Canadians that he could not accept. The Chief kept his own counsel through the summer, and it was not until September 5, two days before the convention opened in Toronto, that he agreed to allow organization on his behalf to commence, even though no formal declaration of candidacy was made. What galvanized Diefenbaker into jumping in was the adoption of *deux nations* by the convention's policy subcommittee.[71] Even so, no one yet knew if the Chief would let his name go before the delegates.

When the convention opened amid the familiar hoopla of bands, balloons, and hospitality suites, there was no clear leader. Fleming had seen his guarantees of support dwindle after the premiers entered the leadership race, and Fulton had been hard hit by Stanfield's entry. When the Halifax Young PCs had balloted in June, they divided nine for Fleming, eight each for Fulton and Hees, and one for McCutcheon, but if Stanfield was a candidate, he would get all the votes but one.[72] That was symptomatic, although no one could yet judge definitively the extent of Stanfield's or Roblin's support. Neither man had served on the federal level, and although that was an advantage in that they had been relatively aloof from the prolonged blood-letting, it did mean that neither had any experience of Parliament.

The convention put all the candidates to the test. Still undeclared, Diefenbaker addressed the delegates in a sweltering Maple Leaf Gardens on September 7. His rambling speech was emotional in its attack on the two nations idea, and all the party stalwarts of past days were paraded in support of "One Canada." Diefenbaker urged the delegates to make the decision for him: "I cannot be interested in the leadership of this party under a policy that is borrowed from liberalism." Was that a declaration of candidacy? No one knew, and it was not until Friday morning's 10 A.M. deadline that Diefenbaker's papers were filed. Even that was largely an attempt to win time and not a firm decision to run. His tentative entry into the contest nonetheless swung support away from Fleming, Hamilton, and Starr, three candidates who had banked on the Chief's good will; their chances, never strong, were dealt the *coup de grâce*. But the two nations formula was resolved, in a strictly tactical sense, by the agreement of the convention co-chairmen to table the policy proposals. That was a gesture to Diefenbaker and, in a sense, a victory for his conception of one Canada.[73] But it was only tactical – the convention was not about policy, Montmorency notwithstanding, but about leadership.

The leadership balloting was long and wearying as the voting machines broke down. On the first ballot Stanfield led with 519 votes, trailed by Roblin with 347, Fulton with 343, Hees with 295, and Diefenbaker with 271. Well behind were McCutcheon, Hamilton, Fleming, and Starr, followed by two nuisance candidates. On the next ballot – and on two more – Stanfield increased his support, building his lead over Roblin. The fifth and final ballot saw Fulton throw his support to the Nova Scotian, and that was sufficient to elect Robert

Stanfield as leader, 1,150 to 969 for Roblin. It was a victory for Camp, something that Stanfield acknowledged by saying in his victory address that his first job was "to get along with that man Camp."[74]

As for Diefenbaker, his convention performance had been mismanaged from start to finish. He had decided to run only at the last moment, had foreclosed his opportunity to organize, and had gutted his friends' campaigns. He had forced the tabling of the two nations resolution, but his vehemence on the platform did the party little good in Quebec or with those who wanted to resolve the great Canadian issue. And yet, the Chief had gone down battling. As early as January 1967 he had told Churchill, "I will not resign – they will have to vote me out."[75] Vote him out they did, but Diefenbaker had lived up to his own conception of his role. As for his opponents, they were unanimously convinced that the Chief's poor convention showing had eliminated him as a political force. The defeat, Douglas Harkness said, "has put him in a position where he can do no further great damage."[76]

The new leader, Robert Stanfield, was vastly different from his predecessor. He was fifty-three, a well-off lawyer from the Stanfield underwear family who had gone into politics in his province, built up the Tory party through the dark days of the late 1940s and early 1950s, and then gone on to take power in 1956, keeping it for a decade. Awkward physically, stumbling in speech, Stanfield projected honesty, sincerity, and decency,[77] and people responded to him. The first Gallup poll after the convention showed the Conservatives up thirteen points to 43 per cent and the Liberals down seven points to 34. The Conservatives were back on the national scene in force, the Diefenbaker era was over, and the Stanfield age seemed set to begin.

CHAPTER 12

Conclusion

The mud-slinging in Parliament, the turmoil in Quebec, and the chill in Canada's relations with France did not markedly interfere with the great gala celebrations of the Centennial of Confederation. All across the country, and not least in Quebec, there were ceremonies and public events, speeches and parades to commemorate the survival of the country that the Fathers of Confederation had created a century before. Canada had survived; indeed, it had flourished and prospered despite depressions, two World Wars, a long Cold War, and the uncertainty and confusion engendered by continuous and often very bitter political and racial strife. Except for aberrations such as those of the Diefenbaker period, in the years since the Second World War the nation had made a good name for itself on the world stage, where Canada was genuinely honoured for its common sense and balanced views. At home the fertile land and the wealth of the country's resources, coupled with the native intelligence and talent of the citizenry, had provided a good life for the great majority of the twenty million Canadians. There were still problems of distribution, great inequities between rich and poor and between provinces and regions; there probably always would be. But the provinces and their people now accepted the idea of equalization as a goal, the idea that the basic minimum standard of living should be the same wherever Canadians resided. That was a concept that had been unknown in 1867; it was one that was new just ten years before the centennial, and while some still quibbled, equalization was by 1967 an accepted part of Canadian life.

But 1967 was intended to be a year for celebration. Planning for the centennial had begun as early as 1958. As with so many of the best ideas of the Diefenbaker period, the initial thrust came from Alvin Hamilton, the Minister of Northern Affairs and National Resources. A former high school teacher in Saskatchewan, Hamilton had asked for the views of his colleagues and officials on the best way to commemorate Canada's first century, and in December he wrote to the Prime Minister to urge that the primary focus of the celebration should be historical with organizations of every sort being encouraged to revise and rewrite their histories. The object, he said, was to make 1967 "a year of personal significance and of national importance."[1] This proposal was soon followed by letters to prominent academic historians. The minister told Donald Creighton of the University of Toronto, for example, "I believe that social history taught in our public and elementary schools for the last 25 years has certain limitations . . . social history, as one historical method has been exhausted for the time being at least." What was needed? To Hamilton, it was clear: ". . . a series of historical monographs on the Fathers of Confederation." And when he offered similar comments to the historian Hilda Neatby of the University of Saskatchewan, she replied that she was "in complete agreement . . . we need less exclusive attention to social history and more precise knowledge of the men and institutions that have formed and frame our national life."[2]

Despite Hamilton's proddings, the subsidization of a major series of biographies was not to be a feature of the centennial. What was to be done still remained unclear when the federal government in 1960 called a meeting of provincial representatives to get planning under way for 1967. John Archer, the Saskatchewan legislative librarian and provincial archivist, represented his province and reported to his premier that "there is simply no appreciation of the need for detailed planning, close executive control, and imaginative planning. . . . Questions on the provincial or community area of activity were met with such statements as – 'But this is a Canadian Centennial – we are all Canadians' while questions on the financial backing necessary for such projects as marking historic sites in provinces did not evoke a very ready answer. . . . I doubt many realize the conscious effort necessary to translate hopes into results." Saskatchewan in 1955 had staged a tremendously successful fiftieth anniversary celebration of its achievement of provincial status, and Archer knew what he was talking about.[3]

At that initial federal-provincial meeting, the Quebec representatives had raised the possibility of a world's fair in Montreal in 1967, and two years later Jean Drapeau, a mayor with a highly developed penchant for thinking big, won permission for his city to play host to a great exposition. Expo 67, as it came to be called, was a magnificent conception, but it was not without its problems in realization. In December 1963, for example, the project's construction manager reported that the city's share of the site preparation costs was escalating dramatically. The original estimates to prepare the islands in the St. Lawrence on which the fair was to be built had been $12 million. It was already evident that those costs would be at least $35 million; moreover, the city was building a grand subway ($30 million), contributing to the construction of an ice dam ($2 million) and to the costs of the World's Fair Corporation ($25 million), and building expressways, roads, and other facilities ($50 million) to handle the expected flood of visitors. It was obvious, the manager said, that Montreal's contribution was "out of all proportion when the benefits to be derived across Canada are considered."[4] Those benefits were expected to be substantial – the tax return on Expo 67 was estimated to be $230 million against a federal government cost of $148 million,[5] and the Bank of Montreal had estimated that the enormous stimulus that the fair would provide to the Canadian economy would exceed that of the construction of the St. Lawrence Seaway, the mega-project of the 1950s.[6]

There was much heart-burning among Drapeau's critics in Montreal, who called for bread (and sewage-treatment plants in a city that poured its untreated ordure into the St. Lawrence) before circuses, and in the rest of the country over the costs that Ottawa had to assume to ensure that Expo 67 was ready on time. Part of this was the age-old feeling that the Liberals were catering to Quebec for political purposes; part was a nascent concern that the federal government was contributing massive sums to build the infrastructure of a Quebec that might soon be going its own way towards independence. But the results ultimately seemed to justify the costs. Expo 67 was an unqualified triumph, a superbly designed, brilliantly planned world's fair that expressed the spirit of the new Quebec and Canada in a way that was completely winning. American reports positively gushed. *Time* greeted the fair's opening with the observation that "its very existence is a symbol of the vigor and enthusiasm of the Canadians who conceived an impossible idea and made it come true," while the *Washington Post* pontificated that "the Canadian, whose ego, individualism, and sense of personal worth, have long suffered in the shadow of the colossus to the south, will take a prideful look in the mirror and exclaim: 'We did it.' "[7] More important were the reactions of English-speaking Canadians to the Montreal many of them were seeing for the first time. "This city is the real, living end of it all," one Toronto visitor said. "You have to give them credit. It's not just Expo; they're really living in Montreal. I wish I could find a job here."[8]

It was true, too. Montreal's great office towers and lavish shopping districts were one aspect of life; another was the general *joie de vivre* so apparent on its streets. With unemployment low, wages generally good, and a new spirit of confidence abroad in Quebec, there seemed every reason for optimism. If only that spirit in Quebec had not seemed so threatening to English-speaking Canadians . . .

If those Canadians were warily congratulating Montreal on the success of Expo, they were more happily heaping praise on themselves in an extraordinary variety of publicly and privately financed celebrations. There was the Centennial Train, a brilliantly conceived travelling museum with a train whistle that played the first few bars of "O Canada." Where the train could not go, a caravan of tractor-trailers carried the same realistic recreation of a Great War trench, a Loyalist kitchen, and an eighteenth-century Quebec street.[9] There were also birthday parties in hundreds of cities and towns from Prince Edward Island to Vancouver Island and from Point Pelee to Yellowknife, there were Centennial arenas, pools, and parks constructed by the score (to the value of $90 million), and hundreds of books were published with the aid of the federal government's Centennial Committee, featuring its stylized maple leaf logo. There were, of course, the sombre assessments of editorial writers and the exuberant congratulatory appraisals of others.[10] Above all, the hundredth birthday celebrations combined with Expo to give Canadians a sense of national pride, which was natural enough in the circumstances and healthy too, and the feeling quickly spread that the good, grey outlook that had long been said to characterize Canadians was gone forever. In its place, if the press of 1967 can be believed, was a swinging, with-it nation. Suddenly Canada was fun. The new and happy patriotism was a good sign in a country where nationalism, as the Canadian Press put it, "was always regarded as a foreign disorder." So too was the simple fact that Bobby Gimby's tune "Ca-na-da," with its positively infectious melody, became almost inescapable: "Ca-na-da, we love you" seemed to say it all.

With the nation in this brief mood of exultation, political changes and problems should have seemed unimportant. They didn't. De Gaulle's "Vive le Québec libre" interjection had aroused passions, and the Prime Minister's virtual ordering of the French president out of the country seemed to many a suitable response. There had also been the Progressive Conservative party's leadership convention at Maple Leaf Gardens in Toronto in September, and that galvanized public attention. To some, it was tragic to see the old Chief go down to humiliating defeat, his vaunted sense of timing having finally deserted him. To others, it was almost exhilarating to see Robert Stanfield, the Premier of Nova Scotia, win the leadership of the Tories. Stanfield was no fire-breathing orator on the Diefenbaker model, but he was a transparently decent and honourable man.

Still, the Liberals remained in power, even though opinion polls showed that the Conservatives under their new leader were making rapid gains. Prime Minister Pearson was seventy, his health was becoming precarious, and the government he led, all too obviously mirroring the uncertainties of the 1960s, racked with divisions and plagued by leaks and scandals, often seemed to be rudderless.[11] Even so, when Pearson finally told a press conference on December 14, 1967, that he was going to retire, there was a sense of loss. The Prime Minister had been a fixture on the Ottawa scene since the end of the 1920s as a bureaucrat, a senior official, a Cabinet minister, Leader of the Opposition, and chief executive; there was no one in public life with his experience – or with his self-deprecating humour and potent, guileful charm.

There were contenders aplenty for the throne, however. Early in 1966 Pearson had told at least three of his ministers – Paul Martin, the Secretary of State for External Affairs, Mitchell Sharp, the Minister of Finance, and Paul Hellyer, the Minister of National Defence – that he did not intend to stay in office much longer. "If I was in your shoes," he told Hellyer, "I would begin talking to my friends."[12] Indeed, for a time Pearson seemed to be leaning toward the Defence minister as his favoured successor, telling Walter Gordon in March 1966 that "of the present Cabinet he thought Hellyer might be the best but obviously," Gordon added, "he has reservations." In fact, Pearson's comments on all his putative heirs were bleak: "He said Winters did not have the stuff," Gordon wrote after a talk in June 1966, "that Martin would be hopeless; that he was disappointed in Sharp and his vanity; that he just couldn't believe Hellyer was the man; and that while Allan MacEachen could be very good on occasion he could not be relied on."[13]

Pearson's views, while important, could not by themselves determine the leadership race. Once the candidates had been given the quiet nod to begin organizing, they leaped at the chance. Hellyer in particular was quick off the mark, setting up his shadow campaign team in 1966 and beginning to collect information on the sentiments of the party nabobs.[14] Later in the year fund raising began, and by early 1967 Hellyer's staff had prepared a budget for their *sub rosa* campaign before Pearson stepped down and a three-month post-resignation spending plan.[15] Nor was Hellyer alone. Mitchell Sharp's friends were also in the field, even beginning to talk informally with Hellyer's and Martin's people about convention deals.[16] The External Affairs minister's staff was equally busy,[17] bolstered by the support of 29 per cent of those questioned in a Gallup poll who thought their man likely to be Pearson's successor. Mitchell Sharp was next on the Gallup list, trailing badly at 13 per cent (even though Marshall McLuhan, the media theorist at the University of Toronto, pronounced his face perfect for television), Hellyer drew 11 per cent support, and John Turner, the young Registrar-General who would soon take the position of Minister of Consumer and Corporate Affairs, 4 per cent.[18]

It was striking that there were no Quebec ministers on either Pearson's list or the Gallup poll's, a reflection of the perceived weakness of the *rouge* ranks in Ottawa. Jean Marchand, the Minister of Manpower and Immigration, was popular with some – Walter Gordon, for example, was urging him to run – but Marchand was properly dubious about his fluency in English and his temperament. Maurice Sauvé, the Minister of Forestry and Rural Development, thought of himself as a possibility, but few others did. And a third, Pierre-Elliott Trudeau, the Minister of Justice, had been in Parliament only since the 1965 election and a minister only since April 1967; to many, he was simply too inexperienced to be given serious consideration for the top post. But to some Toronto professors and others, Trudeau was very much the right man for the times. Urged on by Marc Lalonde, one of Pearson's principal aides and a long-time Trudeau friend, the academics organized a petition that circulated through universities across the country at the end of 1967 and the beginning of the new year urging Trudeau to run for the leadership. Their reasoning, one participant later remembered, was that the Justice minister was "straight" on the constitution.[19]

There was also the Liberal "principle" of alternating French- and English-speaking leaders. If that principle (the very existence of which many denied) held, it was a francophone's turn, and Pearson for one told a friend a few days after his resignation statement that "he would favour a French Canadian (Marchand or Trudeau) at this time. . . ."[20] The Quebec wing of the Liberal party was thinking along those lines too, Marchand himself telling a friend that "the Quebecers [*sic*] seem to think some French Canadian should be a candidate and that Trudeau's (political) standing had improved & they might get behind him."[21]

By February, the Trudeau boom was in full cry, astonishing testimony to the public's desire for a fresh new face, no matter how untested its owner might be, and for relief from the acrimony that had characterized the political struggles between Pearson and Diefenbaker. The Justice minister's strong performance at the Quebec and Ontario Liberal party conclaves and at the federal-provincial constitutional conference at the end of January and the beginning of February had drawn him forcefully to popular attention, and the media eagerly spread his name along with potted summaries of his hard, clear constitutional views to every corner of the land. On February 16, Trudeau declared himself a candidate.

Three days later the Liberal government was defeated in the House of Commons on a single clause of an income tax bill. Pearson had been in the south on holiday, and Mitchell Sharp and others, against the cautionary advice of the government House leader, had urged that the vote be taken. The defeat had come on a question of substance, and although the government survived, thanks to Pearson's cajoling an inexperienced Stanfield, Sharp's hopes for the leadership did not. The Minister of Finance offered his resignation, but Pearson, supremely disenchanted by the shambles his colleagues had made of his last days in office, grimly refused it.

By the time of the leadership convention at the beginning of April, the leading candidates were Trudeau, Hellyer, Martin, and Robert Winters, Sharp having thrown his support, now much shrunken, to Trudeau before the convention opened. Martin, a vigorous sixty-four years old, seemed an ancient compared to Trudeau's forty-nine, and afterwards he lamented "the emergence of these young arrogant people. I did not know it existed. If I had known what I did three weeks before the Convention, I never would have gone into it – never in the world."[22] Winters, a self-proclaimed businessman-in-politics, had re-entered public life and the Cabinet in 1965 because he believed the government needed a strong voice from the private sector. "I soon found out that in a cabinet of 26 or 27 the hard cold realities of business were not popular," he said later.[23] They would not be popular with the majority at the convention, either. And Paul Hellyer, although four years younger than Trudeau, seemed to have come from an older and different political generation. The results, in retrospect, seemed predictable. Cheered on by an army of pretty mini-skirted workers, Trudeau led from the first, and on the fourth and final ballot he received 1,203 votes to 954 for Winters and 195 for John Turner, the one candidate who had refused to withdraw or to throw his support to anyone.

"The Liberal party couldn't have afforded to deny Trudeau the leadership in the face of the public adulation he aroused," a Cabinet minister told Peter Newman of the *Toronto Star*. "He was so patently what the public wanted. . . ." And Newman himself, swept up like so many of the media gurus in the extraordinary fervour that the charismatic Trudeau aroused, was among those who proclaimed that "the choice of Trudeau represents a unique opportunity for the revival of the Expo spirit that did so much for the Canadian psyche. . . . Trudeau," he wrote on April 8, the Monday after the convention, "could be the agent of a revival of Canadian political values, the end of the alienation that has removed most of the young generation from active involvement in our political process." For a time, that judgement seemed possible and even correct. More to the point, as a senior public servant wrote to a colleague overseas, the new prime minister and Liberal leader "at least knows what he stands for, and I really think it will be good for all concerned to have a first class French Canadian in charge again." Clearly Trudeau was not a man troubled by uncertainty; he knew precisely where he stood, particularly on constitutional questions, and that his intellect was first class no one could question. But his selection was a risk for the country and the Liberal party all the same, and one insider noted that no one knew what the new prime minister would do.[24] That was the truest judgement of all, but in April 1968, in the euphoria left by the Liberal convention, all the possibilities were open, and Canada seemed a changed country from what it had been only a few days before. A new era, the Trudeau era, had begun, destroying all prospects that Robert Stanfield might be the leader for the 1970s, and the doubts and hesitations that had dominated the nation since 1957 seemed to have been swept away in a splendid surge of optimism. In their place was a new decisiveness and leadership. Or so many Canadians believed.

SELECTED BIBLIOGRAPHY OF PRIMARY SOURCES

I. Manuscript Sources: Canada

Bank of Canada Archives, Ottawa
    Louis Rasminsky Papers*
    Bank of Canada Records*

Bishop's University Archives, Lennoxville, Quebec
    T.W.L. MacDermot Papers*

Canada Council, Ottawa
    Canada Council Records*

Department of External Affairs, Ottawa
    Department Records*
    John Starnes Papers*

Department of National Defence, Directorate of History, Ottawa
    Chairman, Chiefs of Staff Committee Records*
    Gen. Charles Foulkes Papers*
    A/ V/ M Max Hendricks Papers
    Office of Chief of the Defence Staff Records*
    Directorate of History Records*

John G. Diefenbaker Centre, Saskatoon
    John G. Diefenbaker Papers*

Fondation Lionel-Groulx, Institut d'histoire de l'Amérique français, Montréal
    Fonds André Laurendeau

Glenbow Archives, Calgary
    Progressive Conservative Party of Alberta Records
    Solon Low Papers

Massey College, University of Toronto, Toronto
    Vincent Massey Papers*

Privately held Papers
    Hon. Gordon Churchill Papers, Mill Bay, B.C.*

* Indicates closed or partly closed records.

Hon. Walter Gordon Papers, Toronto*
Hon. Paul Hellyer Papers, Toronto*
Robert I. Hendy Papers, Toronto*
Hon. J.W. Pickersgill Papers, Ottawa*
H.B. Robinson Papers, Ottawa*

Public Archives of Canada, Ottawa

A. *Government Records*
Committee on Election Expenses Records [R.G. 36]
Department of External Affairs Records
Department of Finance Records*
Royal Commission Records [R.G. 33]

B. *Private Papers*
René Beaudoin Papers
Laurent Beaudry Papers
Hon. R.A. Bell Papers*
R.B. Bryce Papers*
Réal Caouette Papers*
CCF/NDP Records*
Hon. Gordon Churchill Papers*
Hon. Brooke Claxton Papers
Hon. M.J. Coldwell Papers
Rt. Hon. J.G. Diefenbaker Papers*
Hon. T.C. Douglas Papers
Hon. George Drew Papers*
Hon. Donald Fleming Papers*
Eugene Forsey Papers
Hon. E.D. Fulton Papers*
Hon. Howard Green Papers*
Allister Grosart Papers
Hon. Alvin Hamilton Papers*
Hon. Douglas Harkness Papers*
A.D.P. Heeney Papers*
Hon. Paul Hellyer Papers*
H.W. Herridge Papers*
Howard Johnston Papers*
H.E. Kidd Papers
Rt. Hon. Jules Léger Papers*
Liberal Party of Canada Records*
Hon. Flora MacDonald Papers*
Hon. Paul Martin Papers*
Hon. J. Waldo Monteith Papers*
F.D. Mott Papers
Rt. Hon. L.B. Pearson Papers*
Hon. J.W. Pickersgill Papers*

* Indicates closed or partly closed records.

Progressive Conservative Party Records*
B.T. Richardson Papers
N.A. Robertson Papers*
Rt. Hon. L.S. St. Laurent Papers
Hon. Mitchell Sharp Papers*
Peter Stursberg Papers
Rt. Hon. Georges Vanier Papers*

Privy Council Office, Ottawa
Cabinet Conclusions [Minutes]*
Privy Council Office Records*

Queen's University Archives, Kingston, Ont.
Hon. T.A. Crerar Papers
J.J. Deutsch Papers*
Grant Dexter Papers
T.A. Kidd Papers
Norman Lambert Papers
Hon. J.M. Macdonnell Papers
W.A. Mackintosh Papers
J.R. Matheson Papers
Hon. J.J. McCann Papers
Hon. C.G. Power Papers
J.A. Stevenson Papers

Saskatchewan Archives, Regina
Hon. Allan Blakeney Papers*
W.G. Davies Papers*
Hon. T.C. Douglas Papers*
J.W. Erb Papers*
Hon. R.L. Hanbidge Papers
Woodrow Lloyd Papers*
E.A. Tollefson Tapes

Saskatchewan College of Physicians and Surgeons, Saskatoon
College Records*

University of British Columbia Archives, Vancouver
Leon Ladner Papers

University of Calgary Archives, Calgary
Bruce Hutchison Papers*

University of Victoria Archives, Victoria
Hon. G.R. Pearkes Papers*

York University Archives, Toronto
Oral History Programme Transcripts*
Robert Winters Papers

---

* Indicates closed or partly closed records.

II. Manuscript Sources: United States

Declassified Documents [Microfiche]

Dwight Eisenhower Library, Abilene, Kansas
  John Foster Dulles Papers*
  Oral History Transcripts
  Presidential Papers*
  White House Central Files*
  Ann Whitman Files

Lyndon B. Johnson Library, Austin, Texas
  Council of Economic Advisors Records
  M. Manatos Papers
  Oral History Transcripts
  Presidential Papers*
  White House Central Files*
  H.H. Wilson Papers

J.F. Kennedy Library, Boston, Mass.
  J.N. Behrman Papers
  Myer Feldman Papers
  Christian Herter Papers
  Oral History Transcripts
  Presidential Papers*
  White House Central Files*

U.S. Treasury Department, Washington, D.C.
  Treasury Records*

Yale University, New Haven, Conn.
  Walter Lippmann Papers

III. Interviews by Author
  G.C. Andrew
  J.R. Beattie
  R.B. Bryce
  Hon. Gordon Churchill
  Ramsay Cook
  James Coyne
  Hon. Paul Hellyer
  Rt. Hon. Jules Léger
  Al Johnson
  Geoffrey Pearson
  Hon. J.W. Pickersgill
  Louis Rasminsky
  Mrs. N.A. Robertson
  H.B. Robinson
  Malcolm Taylor

---

* Indicates closed or partly closed records.

NOTES TO CHAPTER ONE

1. F.H. Leacy, ed., *Historical Statistics of Canada* (Ottawa, 1983), A2-14.
2. Ibid., A67-69, A75-77.
3. Ibid., M55-56.
4. Ibid., M12-22.
5. *Canada Year Book, 1976-77* (Ottawa, 1977), p. 188.
6. Leacy, T147-62.
7. Quoted in Alan Green, *Immigration and the Postwar Canadian Economy* (Toronto, 1976), p. 21.
8. Ibid., pp. 31-32; Gerald Dirks, *Canada's Refugee Policy* (Montreal, 1977), pp. 190ff.
9. Green, p. 36; Freda Hawkins, *Canada and Immigration* (Montreal, 1972), pp. 125ff.
10. Green, p. 37.
11. Leacy, A385-416.
12. N. Levine, *Canada Made Me* (Ottawa, 1979), pp. 22-25.
13. Leacy, D205-22, D431-48.
14. N. Meltz and D. Stager, *The Occupational Structure of Earnings in Canada, 1931-75* (Ottawa, 1977), p. 165.
15. Leacy, B1-14.
16. Myrna Kostash, *Long Way from Home* (Toronto, 1980), p. 185.
17. Leacy, B75-81.
18. G. Grant, *Lament for a Nation: The Defeat of Canadian Nationalism* (Toronto, 1965), p. 40.
19. Leacy, G303-17.
20. Ibid., G329-40.
21. Ibid., G401-14.
22. Roy E. George, *A Leader and a Laggard* (Toronto, 1970), passim.
23. T.N. Brewis, *Regional Economic Policies in Canada* (Toronto, 1969), Chap. X; Philip Mathias, *Forced Growth* (Toronto, 1971).
24. On the Seaway's impact, see W.R. Willoughby, *The St. Lawrence Waterway* (Madison, Wis., 1961), pp. 218ff., 269ff.; Gerald Friesen, *The Canadian Prairies: A History* (Toronto, 1984), p. 429.
25. Leacy, Q131-36.
26. John Richards and Larry Pratt, *Prairie Capitalism: Power and Influence in the New West* (Toronto, 1979), p. 84.
27. Leacy, E175-77, E190-97.
28. J. Finkelman and S. Goldenberg, *Collective Bargaining in the Public Service* (Montreal, 1983), I, xxvii-xxviii, 4, 12.
29. Meltz and Stager, pp. 70, 170.
30. S. Ostry, *Unemployment in Canada* (Ottawa, 1968), p. 1.
31. Gérard Pelletier, *Years of Impatience, 1950-60* (Toronto, 1984), p. 30.
32. University of Calgary Archives,

Bruce Hutchison Papers, file 1.2.3., Hutchison to Grant Dexter, 17 Feb. 1955.

33. Queen's University Archives, Grant Dexter Papers, Dexter to Tom Kent, 4 Jan. 1956.

34. Public Archives of Canada [PAC], René Beaudoin Papers, vol. 5, Criticisms file, passim.

35. Quoted by Arthur Blakely in Montreal *Gazette*, 25 Oct. 1961.

36. PAC, Gordon Churchill Papers, vol. 2, Black Friday file, Churchill to Mona, "Sunday eve."

NOTES TO CHAPTER TWO

1. Saskatchewan Archives, Saskatchewan Homestead Records, #100470A – William Diefenbaker.

2. See Simma Holt, *The Other Mrs. Diefenbaker* (Toronto, 1982), passim; Bishop's University, T.W.L. MacDermot Papers, file /46, H.B. Robinson to MacDermot, 14 Oct. 1958.

3. See *Maclean's*, 29 Mar. 1958, 22-23.

4. University of Victoria Archives, George Pearkes Papers, vol. 7, interview transcript, 12 July 1967.

5. MacDermot Papers, file /46, H.B. Robinson letter, 14 Oct. 1958.

6. PAC, Gordon Churchill Papers, vol. 3, Manitoba file, Churchill to W. Dinsdale, 11 Oct. 1956.

7. Dalton Camp, *Gentlemen, Players and Politicians* (Toronto, 1970), p. 257.

8. Peter Stursberg, *Diefenbaker: Leadership Gained, 1956-62* (Toronto, 1975).

9. See John Meisel, *The Canadian General Election of 1957* (Toronto, 1962), pp. 18ff.

10. *Maclean's*, 24 Nov. 1956.

11. Churchill Papers, vol. 3, Alberta file, Churchill to W.J.C. Kirby, 24 Oct. 1956.

12. Ibid., Manitoba file, Churchill to Steen, 2 Nov. 1956; PAC, E. Davie Fulton Papers, vol. 7, Convention Organization file, E. Chambers to Fulton, 26 Oct. 1956.

13. Churchill Papers, vol. 2, Convention 1956 file, Churchill to Diefenbaker, 5 Oct. 1956.

14. Ibid., vol. 3, Manitoba file, 24 Oct. 1956.

15. Ibid., Churchill to C. Haig, 24 Oct. 1956.

16. Diefenbaker Centre, Saskatoon, John Diefenbaker Papers, Speeches, vol. 4, Press Conference, CBOT-TV, 8 Jan. 1957.

17. Fulton Papers, vol. 7, Convention 1956-General file, M.A. Macpherson to Fulton, 17 Dec. 1956; Churchill Papers, vol. 1, Personal file, Churchill to Roblin, 2 Jan. 1957; PAC, Peter Stursberg Papers, Balcer interview, n.d.; Pearkes Papers, vol. 5, Notebook 1956.

18. PAC, John Diefenbaker Papers, Sévigny to Diefenbaker, 19 Dec. 1956, ff.12825-6.

19. Glenbow Archives, Progressive Conservative Party of Alberta Records, file 9, "We Can Win With John".

20. See Camp, pp. 242ff., for a brilliant account of the convention, and Donald Fleming, *So Very Near* (Toronto, 1985), I, 322ff.

21. Saskatchewan Archives, T.C. Douglas Papers, Premier 130 file, Douglas to L.L. Lloyd, 3 Oct. 1956.

22. Queen's University Archives, C.G. Power Papers, vol. 13, 1957 Election file, NLF Memo to Liberal M.P.s and Senators, 6 Dec. 1956.
23. Churchill Papers, vol. 106, Election Organization file, "Forming the Government," Jan. 1954.
24. Stursberg Papers, Churchill interview, 25 May 1975; Gordon Churchill Papers (Mill Bay, B.C.), MS "Recollections of Political Life," Chap. X. But cf. Stursberg Papers, R.A. Bell interview, and Stursberg, *Leadership Gained*, pp. 43ff. In the 1957 election, total Conservative expenditures were $1,539,123 of which just over $1 million went to candidates. The party spent $337,683 on advertising, $10,000 on the ethnic vote, $42,788 on headquarters, and $45,559 on the leader's tour. Quebec ridings got $321,000, Ontario $407,600. PAC, Progressive Conservative Party Records, vol. 267, Provincial Liaison Meeting 1957 file, "Summary of 1957 Election Disbursements." For one candidate's expenses, see PAC, R.A. Bell Papers, vol. 7, Financial Committee file, Budget, n.d.
25. Churchill Papers, vol. 7, Election 1957 Organization file, Memo, 28 Feb. 1957, Notes, 4 and 7 March 1957; Churchill MS "Recollections," Chap. X; Patrick Nicholson, *Vision and Indecision* (Toronto, 1968), pp. 40ff.; and generally, PAC, Allister Grosart Papers.
26. Churchill Papers, vol. 7, Election 1957 Organization file, "Plans re Publicity," 31 Jan. 1957; vol. 1, Personal file, "Basis for Discussion," n.d.; Camp, pp. 253ff.
27. Ibid., pp. 259ff.; copy in Churchill Papers, vol. 1. Camp had many vicissitudes in his relations with Churchill and Grosart. See Camp, pp. 272-76.
28. PC Party Records, vol. 372, National Campaign Committee file, Minutes, 7 April 1957; PAC, Diefenbaker Papers, Diefenbaker to E. Goodman *et al.*, 29 March 1957, ff.02230ff.; Camp, pp. 280ff.
29. PAC, Diefenbaker Papers, Grosart memo, 24 April 1957, f.02305.
30. Diefenbaker Centre, Diefenbaker Papers, Speeches, vol. 4, "One Country, One Policy," n.d., vol. 5, Truro, May 1957.
31. Ibid., vol. 4, Press Conference, 8 Jan. 1957.
32. Stursberg Papers, Diefenbaker interview, 30 Oct. 1968.
33. PAC, Brooke Claxton Papers, vol. 77, Claxton to W.L. Gordon, 20 Mar. 1957.
34. York University Archives, Douglas How reminiscences, 28 June 1971; cf. Queen's University Archives, J.J. McCann Papers, vol. 3, Scrapbook, advt. in Arnprior *Chronicle*, 6 June 1957.
35. Power Papers, vol. 13, 1957 Election file, NLF Memo, 27 Feb. 1957; vol. 80, NLF file, Minutes of National Executive of NLF, 1 Feb. 1957.
36. 16 Apr. 1957. See also Winnipeg *Free Press*, 25-26 Apr., Calgary *Albertan*, 29 May 1957, *Toronto Star*, 17 Apr., 27 May 1957.
37. PAC, H.E. Kidd Papers, vol. 5, f.17, D.G. Mackenzie to D. MacTavish, 7 May 1957. See also R. Whitaker, *The Government Party* (Toronto, 1977), pp. 206ff., and Dale Thomson, *Louis St. Laurent, Canadian* (Toronto, 1967), pp. 504ff.
38. PAC, Paul Martin Papers, vol. 28, Election 1957 P.M. Visit file, Notes of Address, 5 June 1957.

39. Diefenbaker Centre, Diefenbaker Papers, Speeches, vol. 5, 14 and 29 May, 5 June 1957.
40. Stursberg Papers, Churchill interview, 25 May 1975.
41. PAC, Diefenbaker Papers, "Memo on Development," n.d. ff.00512ff. and Memos, 14 May 1957, ff.14550ff.; PAC, Alvin Hamilton Papers, vol. 137, Roy Faibish memo, Nov. 1956; Diefenbaker Centre, Diefenbaker Papers, Speeches, vol. 4, "Suggested Speech for Saskatoon," 1 Mar. 1957. On Hamilton in Saskatchewan, see Patrick Kyba, "Third Party Leadership in a Competitive Two-Party Province," *Saskatchewan History*, XXXVI (Winter, 1983), 1ff.
42. Power Papers, vol. 5, Crerar to Power, 21 May 1957; Robert Bothwell and William Kilbourn, *C.D. Howe* (Toronto, 1979), p. 325; Stursberg Papers, Walter Dinsdale interview, 15 Nov. 1973.
43. As in Kingston *Whig-Standard*, 27 May 1957. See the Liberal ad in the issue of June 7: "It's Agreed! The Liberals are Going Back! . . . The Tories Are Not Going In! Keep Kingston on the Government's Side!"
44. PAC, Diefenbaker Papers, Hogan to Grosart, 24 May 1957, ff.03258-60.
45. Queen's University Archives, T.A. Crerar Papers, vol. 132, Power to Crerar, 4 June 1957. Cf. Power Papers, vol. 6, Power to Hutchison, 28 May 1957.
46. PAC, Diefenbaker Papers, "Election Prediction," 10 June 1957, ff.03380ff.
47. Crerar Papers, vol. 105, Dexter to Crerar, 23 May 1957; Power Papers, vol. 6, Hutchison to Power, 4 June 1957. J.W. Pickersgill later noted, "It is curious that it is so easy with hindsight to see the signs of what happened . . . and how curious it is that practically no one saw them in advance." Pickersgill Papers (Ottawa), Hutchison file, Pickersgill to Hutchison, 15 June 1957.
48. See Meisel, pp. 235ff.; Douglas Papers, Premier 66D file, Douglas to Diefenbaker, 11 June 1957: "Black Friday has been avenged"; F.H. Underhill, "The Revival of Conservatism in North America," *Transactions of the Royal Society of Canada*, LII, Ser. III (1958), 14.
49. University of Calgary Archives, Bruce Hutchison Papers, file 2.1.6, Power to Hutchison, 17 June 1957; Power Papers, vol. 5, Power to Crerar, 14 June 1957. See also J.R. Mallory, "The Election and the Constitution," *Queen's Quarterly*, LXIV (Winter, 1958), 465ff.
50. Massey College, Vincent Massey Papers, Diary, 10-12 June 1957.
51. Privy Council Office, PCO Records, file C-20-3 1957, Cabinet Conclusion, 13 June 1957; Massey Diary, 14 June 1957; Pickersgill Papers, Harris file, Harris to Pickersgill, n.d.; Glenbow Archives, J.G. Gardiner interview, 3 and 5 Jan. 1962.
52. Massey Diary, 15 June 1957.
53. Ibid., 20 June 1957.
54. Ibid., 21 June 1957.
55. Based on Churchill MS "Recollections," Chap. XI; York University Archives, Oral History Programme, Angus MacLean interview, 24 Jan. 1969, Howard Green interview, 10 Apr. 1969, Fairclough interview, 3 Nov. 1968, Fulton interview, 9 Apr. 1969; Stursberg Papers, Diefenbaker interview, 26 Nov. 1973; Stursberg, *Leadership Gain-*

ed, pp. 62ff.; Fleming, I, 341ff.

56. John English, "The French Lieutenant in Federal Politics," unpublished CHA/CPSA paper 1983, p. 3. Overall, Diefenbaker's Cabinets had 18 per cent French-Canadian content compared to the 25 per cent in St. Laurent's and the 39 per cent in Pearson's. Paul Tennant, "French Canadian Representation in the Canadian Cabinet: An Overview," Ph.D. thesis, University of Chicago, 1970, p. 107.

57. Diefenbaker Centre, Diefenbaker Papers, Speeches, vol. 5, 22 June 1957. Diefenbaker did not speak French well, but he worked at it – as the carefully phoneticized speech texts indicate. See ibid., Speeches, vol. 12, Address in Quebec City, 3 July 1958.

58. For Monteith's account of his appointment, see PAC, Monteith Papers, vol. 1, Diefenbaker file, Monteith to Diefenbaker, 14 March 1974.

59. Massey Diary, 23 Mar. 1959. For another comment on the Quebec ministers, see Stursberg Papers, Bell interview, 26 July 1972.

60. PCO Records, file C-20-1, Memo, 20 June 1957 and att. Cabinet Document 54/57, 13 Mar. 1957.

61. H.B. Robinson interview, 16 May 1979; John Diefenbaker interview, 15 Feb. 1979; J.L. Granatstein, *The Ottawa Men: The Civil Service Mandarins, 1935-57* (Toronto, 1982), pp. 256ff. See also U.S. Treasury Department, Treasury Records, Acc. 68-A-5918, box 85, Can/0/20 (1957), biographical data on Joint U.S.-Canada Committee on Trade and Economic Affairs, 7-8 Oct. 1957.

62. J.W. Pickersgill interview, 20 Feb. 1979.

63. PAC, N.A. Robertson Papers, vol. 3A, Holmes to Robertson, 1 Aug. 1957.

64. Granatstein, pp. 266-67.

65. Pearkes Papers, vol. 14, unpublished comments on Lloyd, *Canada and World Affairs 1957-59*.

66. PAC, Howard Green Papers, vol. 9, Green to R.H. Winters, 6 July 1959.

67. Stursberg Papers, Roy Faibish interview, 27 Sept. 1973.

68. Churchill Papers, vol. 1, Personal file, Grosart to Churchill, 12 Nov. 1957.

69. Queen's University Archives, T.A. Kidd Papers, vol. 18, Patronage files.

70. PAC, R.B. Bryce Papers, Notebooks 1958; PCO Records, file C-20-1, Memo JRN to Bryce, 20 January 1959; Memo A.W. to Bryce, n.d.

71. Ibid., Halliday to Bryce, 6 January 1959.

72. Ibid., file C-20-2, Cabinet Agendas, e.g., 5 and 6 Dec. 1957; Pearkes Papers, vol. 7, interview, 23 Feb. 1967.

73. Massey Diary, 12 and 14 Oct., 4 Sept. 1957.

74. Stursberg Papers, Douglas interview, 4 Dec. 1972; J.G. Diefenbaker, *One Canada: The Memoirs of the Rt. Hon. John G. Diefenbaker* (Toronto, 1976), II, 64ff.

75. Hutchison Papers, file 1.2.3., Hutchison to Dexter, 8 Nov. 1957.

76. Thompson, pp. 523ff.

77. Martin Papers, vol. 351, Tape 5, Side 2, 100ff.

78. Claxton Papers, vol. 83, Political Comment file, Gordon to Claxton, 4 Dec. 1957.

79. Queen's University, Grant Dexter Papers, Memos, 9 and 23 Oct. 1957.

80. Hutchison Papers, file 1.2.4., Hutchison to Dexter, 12 Nov. 1957; Claxton Papers, vol. 83, Political Comment file, Kidd to Claxton, 5 Nov. 1957; Dexter Papers, Memo, 9 Oct. 1957; Power Papers, vol. 5, Crerar to Power, 18 Sept. 1957.

81. See Norman Ward, "The Liberals in Convention," *Queen's Quarterly*, LXV (Spring, 1958), 1ff.

82. L.B. Pearson, *Mike: The Memoirs of the Rt. Hon. Lester B. Pearson* (Toronto, 1975), III, 32.

83. Pickersgill Papers, Liberal Party in Opposition file, Pickersgill to J. Dickey, 23 Jan. 1958; Pickersgill interview, 5 Jan. 1983; MacDermot Papers, file /53, G.V. Ferguson to MacDermot, 8 Feb. 1958. The strategy was probably sound in intent. See, for example, Glenbow Archives, Solon Low Papers, f.130, Low to C. Schurter, 9 Oct. 1957.

84. Pearson, III, 33.

85. Stursberg Papers, Martin interview, 28 Nov. 1972. See also Dexter Papers, vol. 7, M. Sharp to Dexter, 5 Sept. 1958; Pickersgill Papers, Sharp file, Sharp to Pickersgill, 29 Aug. 1958; PAC, Donald Fleming Papers, vol. 60, file E2, K.W. Taylor to Fleming, 27 June 1958; PAC, B.T. Richardson Papers, vol. 4, f.9, J. Armstrong to Richardson, 4 Feb. 1958. The report is in PAC, Diefenbaker Papers, ff.00745ff. On how Diefenbaker learned of the report, see Nicholson, Chaps. IV-V; Diefenbaker, II, 64ff. See also Blair Fraser, *Maclean's*, 1 Mar. 1958, 2.

86. Massey Diary, 7 and 9 Nov. 1957.

87. PAC, M.J. Coldwell Papers, vol. 58, CCF #2 file, Coldwell to C. Fines, 2 Jan. 1958.

88. MacDermot Papers, file /53, Ferguson to MacDermot, 8 Feb. 1958.

89. Diefenbaker Centre, Diefenbaker Papers, Speeches, vol. 8, 12 Feb. 1958.

90. Stursberg Papers, Faibish interview, 27 Sept. 1973. The best account is Patrick Kyba, "The 'Vision' and the National Development Policy of the Diefenbaker Government," unpublished CPSA/CHA Paper, 1984.

91. Hutchison Papers, file 1.2.4., Hutchison to Dexter, 18 Feb. 1958. See also Claxton Papers, vol. 71, Claxton to D. Acheson, 24 Feb. 1958.

92. Power Papers, vol. 6, Power to Hutchison, 3 Mar. 1958.

93. C. Black, *Duplessis* (Toronto, 1977), pp. 406-8; Pierre Sévigny, *This Game of Politics* (Toronto, 1965), Chap. V.

94. Queen's University Archives, Norman Lambert Papers, vol. 2, Connolly to Lambert, 6 Mar. 1958; Whitaker, pp. 206ff.

95. Coldwell Papers, vol. 44, Saskatchewan Premier's Office file, Douglas to Coldwell, 5 Mar. 1958.

96. Diefenbaker Centre, Diefenbaker Papers, Speeches, vol. 9, 13 Mar. 1958.

97. PAC, Liberal Party of Canada Records, vol. 851, National Campaign Committee file, Connolly to Committee, 14 Mar. 1958.

98. Copy in Power Papers, vol. 13; H.E. Kidd Papers, vol. 6, f.9, Memo by D. MacTavish, 1 May 1958.

99. MacDermot Papers, file /53, Brooke Claxton, "The Reason Why," 16 Apr. 1958.

100. Pearson, III, 37.

101. Hutchison Papers, file 1.2.4., Hutchison to Dexter, Apr., May 1958.

102. Stursberg Papers, Baldwin interview, 7 Nov. 1973, Nielsen inter-

view, 5 Mar. 1973.

103. Gordon Churchill interview, 9-10 June 1983.

104. Stursberg Papers, Balcer interview, n.d.

105. Hamilton Papers, vol. 198, National Development file, Hamilton to Diefenbaker, 15 July 1959.

106. Diefenbaker Centre, Diefenbaker Papers, Speeches, 30 Nov.-9 Dec. 1960 file, extract from speech draft (in 9 Dec. 1960 file).

107. PC Party Records, vol. 352, Sévigny to Grosart, 28 Sept. 1960; see also vol. 335, Memo "re P.M.G.'s letter . . .," 18 Aug. 1961.

108. PCO Records, file R-20-N, Memoranda to Cabinet, 6 Aug. 1958 and 18 Feb. 1959; Joey Smallwood, *I Chose Canada* (Toronto, 1973), pp. 417ff.

109. Ibid., pp. 396ff.; Diefenbaker, II, 316ff.; H. Landon Ladd, "The Newfoundland Loggers' Strike of 1959," in W.J.C. Cherwinski and G.S. Kealey, eds., *Lectures in Canadian Labour and Working-Class History* (St. John's, 1985), pp. 149ff.

110. MacDermot Papers, file /53, Ferguson to MacDermot, 12 June 1958.

111. Diefenbaker, II, 256ff.

112. York University Archives, Fulton interview, 9 Apr. 1969.

113. Hamilton Papers, vol. 171, Faibish to R.G. Robertson, 7 Nov. 1958.

114. Fleming Papers, vol. 163, National Development Cabinet Committee file, Taylor to Fleming, 9 Dec. 1958.

115. Hamilton Papers, vol. 198, Northern Development file, Memo for Cabinet: Roads to Resources, 13 Nov. 1958; PCO Records, Cabinet Conclusions, 29-30 Jan., 3-4 Feb. 1958.

116. Douglas Papers, Premier 20 file, South Sask. River Dam Construction file, Notes . . ., 16 Mar. 1959.

117. Peter C. Newman, *Renegade in Power* (Toronto, 1963), p. 222.

118. Based on Hamilton Papers, vol. 130, Menzies file, Faibish to Menzies, 18 Feb. 1960; Queen's University Archives, J.A. Stevenson Papers, file 1, Martin to Stevenson, 10 Sept. 1957; Massey Diary, 26 July 1959; Gordon Churchill interview, 9-10 June 1983; Stursberg Papers, T.C. Douglas interview, 4 Dec. 1972; PAC, Jules Léger Papers, vol. 1, interview transcript, 22 Oct. 1980; H.B. Robinson interview, 18 Apr. 1983.

NOTES TO CHAPTER THREE

1. Saskatchewan Archives, T.C. Douglas Papers, file 115-(3-16), Spry to Douglas, 3 July 1957.

2. Trevor Lloyd, *Canada in World Affairs 1957-59* (Toronto, 1968), p. 66; J.G. Diefenbaker, *One Canada: The Memoirs of the Rt. Hon. John G. Diefenbaker* (Toronto, 1976), II, 197.

3. PAC, Gordon Churchill Papers, vol. 41, "Diversion of Canadian Imports . . ." 9 Aug. 1957.

4. PAC, Department of Finance Records, vol. 4192, file 8627/C212/U57, Plumptre to Fleming, 29 Dec. 1961; Queen's University Archives, Grant Dexter Papers, Memo, 9 Oct. 1957.

5. See Douglas Papers, file 115-(3-16), Spry to Douglas, 20 Sept. 1957.

6. Department of Finance Records,

vol. 4182, file 8522/U585-1 (1957), "Third Meeting of Joint Committee . . . 7-8 Oct. 1957." See also Donald Fleming, *So Very Near* (Toronto, 1985), I, 383ff.

7. Department of Finance Records, vol. 4192, file 8625-03/C2/2m, "Canadian Views . . ." att. to Schwartzmann to Plumptre, 22 May 1958.

8. Privy Council Office, PCO Records, file E-40-1, "Policy Issues Raised by European Regional Economic Developments," 28 Dec. 1959.

9. Department of External Affairs, External Affairs file 10364-40, Minutes, 28-29 June 1960.

10. Diefenbaker, II, 202.

11. External Affairs file 8490-B-40, vol. 4, Robertson to Minister, 27 Sept. 1960.

12. Department of External Affairs, H. Basil Robinson Papers, Note on Meeting, 10 Apr. 1961.

13. PAC, George Drew Papers, vol. 390, Robinson to USSEA, 26 Apr. 1961. See also Harold Macmillan, *At the End of the Day* (New York, 1973), pp, 10ff.

14. *Globe and Mail*, 17 Jan. and 12 Apr. 1961.

15. Ibid., 15 June 1961.

16. Drew Papers, vol. 390, Memos att. to Green to Drew, 17 July 1961. One academic study estimated that at most $55 million in trade would be lost by U.K. entry. S.F. Kaliski, "Canada, the U.K. and the Common Market," *International Journal*, XVII (Winter 1961-62), 17ff.

17. PAC, Howard Green Papers, vol. 7, "Meeting of Canadian Ministers with . . . Sandys," 13 July 1961. There are draft Canadian rejoinders attached.

18. PAC, B.T. Richardson Papers, vol. 5, file 4, Jane Armstrong to Richardson, 24 July 1961. The Canadian view is in PCO Records, Cabinet Conclusions, 15 July 1961.

19. *Globe and Mail*, 21 July 1961.

20. PAC, Donald Fleming Papers, vol. 156, file C13a, "Statement to CECC," 12 Sept. 1961; Fleming, II, 389ff.; Department of Finance Records, vol. 4326, file 8262-02/ 61, Minutes of CECC, 13 Sept. 1961; Peyton Lyon, *Canada in World Affairs 1961-63* (Toronto, 1968), pp. 448-49.

21. *Sunday Telegraph*, 24 Sept. 1961.

22. PCO Records, Cabinet Conclusions, 14 Sept. 1961.

23. Fleming Papers, vol. 148, file C13a-2, Bell to Fleming, 15 Sept. 1961. Gordon Churchill later said the Accra meeting was "the start of the ruin of relations with the United Kingdom." Interview, 9-10 June 1983.

24. House of Commons *Debates*, 28 Sept. 1961, pp. 9054ff.

25. *Globe and Mail*, 12 Sept. 1961; Fleming Papers, vol. 159, EEC Memos file, Firestone to Diefenbaker, 27 Sept. 1961; copy in PAC, Progressive Conservative Party files, vol. 341.

26. University of British Columbia Archives, Leon Ladner Papers, Diefenbaker file, Ladner to Diefenbaker, 14 Sept. 1961; see also *Globe and Mail*, 1 Aug. 1961.

27. Green Papers, vol. 7, "Report on Consultations . . . September 18 to 28, 1961."

28. Lyon, pp. 542-43.

29. Fleming Papers, vol. 158, file E1, Drew to Fleming, 8 Oct. 1961. For public opinion, see *Globe and Mail*, 18 Oct. and 7 Nov. 1961.

30. Dexter Papers, Memo of Simon Reisman conversation, 12 Oct.

1961. See also Green Papers, vol. 7, Robertson Memo for Minister, 10 Oct. 1961, and External Affairs file 12443-40, "Record of Meeting" between Diefenbaker and Macmillan, 30 Apr. 1962, where these themes are raised.

31. Fleming Papers, vol. 158, Notes on Conference, 18 Nov. 1961. Diefenbaker, II, 92, indicates that de Gaulle had told the Prime Minister the same thing in 1958.

32. Cited in Green Papers, vol. 7, Robertson Memo for Minister, 2 June 1962; Macmillan, *End of the Day*, p. 31.

33. Fleming Papers, vol. 158, file E1, O'Leary to Fleming, 22 Nov. 1961. Cf. *Globe and Mail*, 29 Nov. 1961.

34. Drew Papers, vol. 390, Commonwealth file, "Britain's Negotiations with the EEC," 7 Dec. 1961. See also Fleming Papers, vol. 156, file E1, Drew to Fleming, 21 Dec. 1961.

35. Dexter Papers, Memo, 12 Oct. 1961; H. Basil Robinson interview, 21 Apr. 1983; J.L. Granatstein, *A Man of Influence: Norman A. Robertson and Canadian Statecraft, 1929-68* (Ottawa, 1981), p. 335.

36. Green Papers, vol. 7, 2 Jan. 1962.

37. *Round Table* (March 1962), 204; Macmillan, *End of the Day*, pp. 115-16.

38. External Affairs file 12447-40, vol. 50, Memo for Minister, 5 Apr. 1962 and att. See also ibid., Minutes of meetings, 26-27 Mar. 1962 and ibid., file 6731-40, Drew to Prime Minister, 6 Apr. 1962.

39. Ibid., file 12447-40, Drew to Prime Minister, 9 Apr. 1962.

40. Ibid., Record of Meeting, 30 Apr. 1962.

41. Robinson Papers, Macmillan to Diefenbaker, 13 Aug. 1962.

42. Green Papers, vol. 7, Memo for Ministers, 13 Aug. 1962; Lyon, p. 460.

43. PCO, Cabinet Conclusions, 30-31 Aug. and 3 Sept. 1962. See also Green Papers, vol. 7, Cabinet Committee on Commonwealth and Common Market minutes, and memos in Churchill Papers, vol. 70 and vol. 73, Prime Minister file, Churchill to Diefenbaker, 4 Sept. 1962.

44. *Sunday Observer*, 16 Sept. 1962.

45. Green Papers, vol. 7, Minutes of Meeting of Commonwealth Prime Ministers 1962, 11 Sept. 1962.

46. 12 Sept., 16 Sept. 1962.

47. Ibid., 18 Sept. 1962; Macmillan, *End of the Day*, pp. 130ff.

48. Green Papers, vol. 7, "Possible Breakdown of Brussels Negotiations," 17 Jan. 1963.

49. Ibid., "Canada's Attitude to British Entry," 31 Aug. 1962.

50. On the background to Canadian policy, see Frank Hayes, "South Africa's Departure from the Commonwealth, 1960-1," *International History Review*, II (July, 1980), 453ff.; Brian Tennyson, *Canadian Relations with South Africa* (Washington, 1982).

51. External Affairs file 11827-40, Memo, Robinson to Commonwealth Div., 20 Feb. 1959.

52. Ibid., Memo, Robinson to USSEA, 28 Jan. 1960.

53. PAC, R.B. Bryce Papers, Telephone notes, 7 Apr. 1960.

54. Diefenbaker, II, 210-11; Department of External Affairs, State Papers 1-1961/1, "South Africa's Application to remain a member of the Commonwealth," 4 Feb. 1961.

55. Ibid.; Diefenbaker, II, 211-12; Ramsay Cook, "The South African Referendum," *Canadian Forum*

(Dec. 1960), 196-97.

56. Drew Papers, vol. 390, Commonwealth file, Bryce to Prime Minister, 20 July 1960. Bryce remembered that the British were the secretaries of the study group – "like Communists, they were always willing to be secretary." Bryce interview, 13 Feb. 1979. Membership of the study group is given in PAC, E. Davie Fulton Papers, vol. 67, Commonwealth Prime Ministers #4 file, "Constitutional Development of Commonwealth," 23 July 1960.

57. External Affairs file 11827-40, "Future Relationship Between South Africa and the Commonwealth," 30 Aug. 1960.

58. Ibid., various drafts of "South Africa and the Commonwealth," Oct.-Dec. 1960.

59. Ibid., file 50085-J-40, Bryce to Glazebrook, 20 Jan. 1961.

60. PCO Records, file F-2-1(b)-4, Robinson to USSEA, 3 Nov. 1960.

61. External Affairs file 11827-40, telegram, 15 Nov. 1960; Harold Macmillan, *Pointing the Way, 1959-61* (London, 1972), p. 293.

62. Ibid., pp. 294-96.

63. External Affairs file 50085-J-40, Memo, Robinson to USSEA, 9 Jan. 1961; Diefenbaker, II, 216-17.

64. External Affairs file 50085-J-40, Robinson to USSEA, 11 Feb. 1961; PCO Records, Cabinet Conclusions, 11 Feb. and 25 Feb. 1961.

65. Ibid., file F-2-1(b)-4, Bryce pen notes, 9 Mar. 1961.

66. Ibid. and Bryce to Prime Minister, 9 Mar. 1961. See also Diefenbaker, II, 218-19.

67. Hayes, 471-73.

68. State Papers, 1-1961/3A, Minutes of Meeting of Commonwealth Prime Ministers, 13 Mar. 1961; Diefenbaker, II, 219.

69. Confidential source. See also Fulton Papers, vol. 67, Notebook, Commonwealth Prime Ministers' Meeting 1961, and PCO Records, file F-2-1(b)-4, Bryce pen notes, 14 Mar. 1961.

70. Tennyson, pp. 167-68; Hayes, 476-77; J.A. Stevenson, "Mr. Diefenbaker and South Africa," *Commentator*, V (Apr. 1961), 15.

NOTES TO CHAPTER FOUR

1. Bank of Canada *Annual Report 1957*, p. 15.

2. PAC, Donald Fleming Papers, vol. 165, Fiscal and Monetary Policy file, "Chartered Banks – Prime Interest Rates," n.d.

3. Privy Council Office, PCO Records, file C-20-3 1957, Cabinet Conclusions, 7 Nov. 1957.

4. PAC, Department of Finance Records, vol. 4123, file C20, Fleming to C. Allison, 11 Feb. 1958; ibid., vol. 4122, file C20, Diefenbaker to Premier W.A.C. Bennett, 20 May 1958, says the same.

5. PAC, L.B. Pearson Papers, vol. 7, "Bank of Canada Report," n.d., quoting Earl Rowe, George Hees, and Davie Fulton.

6. Ibid., statements of 14 and 16 Mar. 1957 in Halifax *Chronicle-Herald* and Vancouver *Province*.

7. See Department of Finance Records, vol. 4123, file C20, J.M. Macdonnell to Fleming, 10 Apr. 1958, for one minister's attempt to cool the situation.

8. Fleming Papers, vol. 167, Mone-

tary Chronology 1954-57, n.d.

9. James Coyne interview, 16 Nov. 1982.

10. PAC, Peter Stursberg Papers, Fleming interview; Donald Fleming, *So Very Near* (Toronto, 1985), 2 vols.

11. House of Commons *Debates*, 10 Aug. 1956, p. 7351, 1 Feb. 1960, p. 599.

12. R.M. Campbell, "The Diefenbaker Years Revisited: The Demise of the Keynesian Strategy in Canada," *Journal of Canadian Studies*, XVIII (Summer 1983), 109.

13. PCO Records, file G-89-U, "Possible Federal Government Measures to Stimulate Employment," 7 Nov. 1957, by J.F. Parkinson.

14. Ibid., "Check List of Programmes . . .," 22 Jan. 1958. The Cabinet actions are detailed in ibid., Cabinet Conclusions, 3 Feb. 1958.

15. Queen's University, J.M. Macdonnell Papers, vol. 8, O.J. Firestone to Macdonnell, 19 Aug. 1958, encl. "Economic Conditions Turn Upwards," 18 Aug. 1958.

16. A.F.W. Plumptre, *Three Decades of Decision: Canada and the World Monetary System, 1944-75* (Toronto, 1977), p. 159. See also J.G. Diefenbaker, *One Canada: The Memoirs of the Rt. Hon. John G. Diefenbaker* (Toronto, 1976), II, 267ff.

17. Bank of Canada *Annual Report 1958*, p. 28.

18. Macdonnell Papers, vol. 8, Fleming to Macdonnell, 12 Dec. 1958.

19. R.B. Bryce interview, 3 Nov. 1982; Coyne interview, 16 Nov. 1982. Complaints continued into 1959. See, e.g., Fleming Papers, vol. 42, file B7, Eric Stefanson, M.P., to Diefenbaker, 26 Sept. 1959.

20. See the comments in *The Report of the Royal Commission on Banking and Finance* (Ottawa, 1964), pp. 454-55.

21. Department of Finance Records vol. 4100, file B30, Taylor to Fleming, 6 Nov. 1958. A later memo on 19 Dec. 1958 set the real deficit for 1958-59 at $900 million and projected those for 1959-60 at $800 million and 1960-61 at $500 million. Ibid., "Some Preliminary Notes on the Budgetary Outlook and Budget Policy," 19 Dec. 1958.

22. Ibid., vol. 4104, file B30 1959, 17 Mar. 1959.

23. PCO Records, file B-10, Memo for Prime Minister, 20 Mar. 1959.

24. PAC, R.A. Bell Papers, vol. 19, Bank of Canada file, 15 Aug. 1959.

25. Fleming Papers, vol. 42, file B7, 4 Sept. 1959. See also H.S. Gordon, *The Economists vs. the Bank of Canada* (Toronto, 1961), p. 30; Fleming, II, 69-71.

26. See J.W. Pickersgill Papers (Ottawa), Sharp file, Mitchell Sharp to Pickersgill, 30 Sept. 1959; Fleming Papers, vol. 42, file B7, Dr. J.A. Sullivan to Fleming, 7 Oct. 1959: Coyne had ruined the Liberals and will ruin us.

27. Queen's University, Grant Dexter Papers, Memo, 4 Nov. 1959; see also University of British Columbia Archives, Leon Ladner Papers, Diefenbaker file, Ladner to Diefenbaker, 18 Nov. and reply, 23 Nov. 1959, one instance where Diefenbaker did not blame the bank.

28. Hamilton interview, 19 Apr. 1983; Churchill interview, 9-10 June 1983; Coyne letter to author, 25 Jan. 1984; Churchill Papers (Mill Bay, B.C.), Memo, "Election Comments 1962," 1 Oct. 1962. Churchill launched his own attack on Coyne in parliament. See House of Commons *Debates*, 21 Mar. 1960,

p. 2262, and Winnipeg *Free Press*, 24-25 Mar., 4 and 11 Apr. 1960 for comment.

29. Senate Standing Committee on Banking and Finance, *Minutes*, 10 July 1961, p. 62.

30. Ibid., pp. 65-66; Coyne interview.

31. Bank of Canada Archives, Bank of Canada Records, address, 16 Nov. 1959.

32. Ibid., address, 18 Jan. 1960. See also House of Commons *Debates*, 18 Jan. 1961, pp. 50ff.

33. Fleming Papers, vol. 42, file B7, Fleming to Ladner, 5 Feb. 1960.

34. Bank of Canada Records, address, 5 Oct. 1960.

35. PAC, Alvin Hamilton Papers, vol. 198, National Development Fund file, note, n.d., from Roy Faibish.

36. Pearson Papers, N2, vol. 92, Coyne file, 6 Oct. 1960.

37. Department of Finance Records, vol. 4099, file B30 1961, 14 Oct. 1960.

38. Senate Standing Committee on Banking and Finance, *Minutes*, 10 July 1961, p. 67.

39. In J.T. Saywell, ed., *The Canadian Annual Review [CAR], 1960* (Toronto, 1961), p. 180.

40. House of Commons *Debates*, 21 Feb. 1961, pp. 2265ff. See Pearson in ibid., 20 Feb. 1961, pp. 2200ff., and Fleming, II, 309ff.

41. Fleming Papers, vol. 143, file E2, pen note, n.a., n.d. *CAR 1961*, pp. 198-99, indicates the areas of agreement between Fleming and Coyne early in 1961. See Peter Stursberg, *Diefenbaker: Leadership Gained, 1956-62* (Toronto, 1975), p. 232.

42. Pearson Papers, N2, vol. 94, 17 Feb. 1961. See D.C. Smith and David Slater, "The Economic Policy Proposals of the Governor of the Bank of Canada," *Queen's Quarterly*, LXVIII (Spring, 1961), 196ff., an example of a sharply critical and influential academic assault.

43. Coyne interview; Bryce interview, 2 Nov. 1982; Dexter Papers, letter, J.T. Bryden to Fleming, 7 Apr. 1961; Bell Papers, Bryden to Fleming, 28 June 1961. Fleming denied knowing of the pension raise until March 1961 (*Globe and Mail*, 27 June 1961).

44. Fleming, II, 313-14; Dexter Papers, Bryden to Fleming, 7 Apr. 1961. The Dexter Papers contain mimeo. copies of the letters Coyne released during the fight with the Cabinet.

45. Fleming, II, 314; PCO Records, Cabinet Conclusions, 23 Mar. 1961.

46. Ibid., 30 Mar. 1961.

47. Ibid., 1 May 1961; Fleming, II, 319.

48. PCO Records, Cabinet Conclusions, 2 May 1961.

49. Ibid., 26 and 27 May 1961; Stursberg Papers, Fleming interview. See also Fleming Papers, vol. 167, pen notes re meeting with chartered bankers, 15 May 1961, and Plumptre memo, "Budget Meeting at 4 p.m. tomorrow."

50. PCO Records, Cabinet Conclusions, 8 June 1961; Fleming, II, 320-21.

51. Stursberg Papers, Fleming interview; Coyne interview.

52. Dexter Papers, Coyne to Fleming (two letters), 9 June 1961.

53. Ibid., Coyne's press release, 13 June 1961; Coyne interview.

54. House of Commons *Debates*, 7 July 1961, p. 7694.

55. PCO Records, Cabinet Conclusions, 8 June 1961; Stursberg Papers, R.A. Bell interview.

56. Coyne interview; Bryce interview.
57. PCO Records, Cabinet Conclusions, 8 June 1961; Fleming, II, 321.
58. Peter C. Newman, *Renegade in Power* (Toronto, 1963), p. 309.
59. Dexter Papers, press release, 13 June 1961.
60. Ibid., Coyne to Fleming, 13 June 1961.
61. PAC, Paul Martin Papers, vol. 352, Tape 11, Side 1, p. 7. See also Denis Smith, *Gentle Patriot: A Political Biography of Walter Gordon* (Edmonton, 1973), p. 95; L.B. Pearson, *Mike: The Memoirs of the Rt. Hon. Lester B. Pearson* (Toronto, 1975), III, 49.
62. House of Commons *Debates*, 14 June 1961, pp. 6314ff.
63. Stursberg Papers, Diefenbaker interview.
64. Coyne interview; Stursberg Papers, Diefenbaker interview; J.W. Pickersgill interview, 10 Nov. 1982; Stursberg Papers, Fleming interview; Senate Standing Committee on Banking and Finance, *Minutes*, 10-13 July 1961, passim; *Globe and Mail*, 14 June 1961; Bell Papers, vol. 19, Bank of Canada file, Bell to C.A. Bounsell, 28 June 1961. Cf. Pickersgill Papers, Harris file, Harris to Pickersgill, 25 July 1961.
65. Dexter Papers, Memo, 15 Feb. 1961, att. to press release, 19 June 1961. Coyne's memo drew no official or ministerial response in February. After the memo became public, C.M. Isbister of Finance drafted a refutation for Fleming's use. Copy in Bell Papers, vol. 24, file Finance-Coyne, 20-21 June 1961.
66. 21 June 1961.
67. *Globe and Mail*, 22 June 1961.
68. Ibid., 23 June 1961.
69. PCO Records, Cabinet Conclusions, 20 June 1961.
70. Stursberg Papers, Diefenbaker interview; Fleming, II, 343-44.
71. Stursberg Papers, Bell interview.
72. Dexter Papers, Coyne to Fleming, 26 June 1961.
73. Ibid.; *Globe and Mail*, 8 July 1961. Coyne said his purpose in making that charge was "to smoke Diefenbaker out" and make him respond. Interview.
74. *Globe and Mail*, 8 July 1961.
75. Queen's University Archives, T.A. Crerar Papers, vol. 90, Crerar to Agnes, 20 July 1961.
76. Walter Gordon, *A Political Memoir* (Toronto, 1977), p. 78.
77. Senate Standing Committee on Banking and Finance, *Minutes*, passim; Dexter Papers, Coyne statement, 11 July 1961; *Globe and Mail*, 11-14 July 1961.
78. Senate Standing Committee on Banking and Finance, *Minutes*, 12 July 1961, pp. 205-6.
79. PAC, H.W. Herridge Papers, vol. 17, Bank of Canada Coyne file, Herridge to C.B. Garland, 16 July 1961.
80. Dexter Papers, Coyne statement, 13 July 1961.
81. PCO Records, Cabinet Conclusions, 8 June 1961.
82. Fleming Papers, vol. 42, Rasminsky file, 1 Aug. 1961.
83. PCO Records, Cabinet Conclusions, 8 June 1961.
84. Fleming Papers, vol. 42, Rasminsky file, Taylor to Fleming, 14 July 1961; PCO Records, Cabinet Conclusions, 8 June 1961.
85. Bank of Canada Archives, Louis Rasminsky Papers, file LR76-552-1, 21 July 1961. The letter is not discussed in Fleming's lengthy memoir.
86. 18 Nov. 1961; Bryce interview.
87. Rasminsky interview, 8 Nov.

1982.

88. Ottawa *Journal*, 10 Aug. 1961.

89. House of Commons *Debates*, 18 Nov. 1963, p. 4856. The legal opinions are in Rasminsky Papers, file LR76-575-4.

90. *CAR, 1961*, pp. 95-96.

91. Rasminsky Papers, file LR76-607-2(a), Memo, 2 Jan. 1962 att. to Rasminsky to Fleming, 2 Jan. 1962.

92. 9 Mar. 1962.

93. Rasminsky Papers, file LR76-291, "Canada 1961 – Article VII Consultations"; ibid., D. Hudon to Rasminsky, 14 and 21 Feb. 1962.

94. *CAR, 1962*, pp. 178-79.

95. PCO Records, file F-1-5, Report to Mr. Rasminsky, 2 May 1962.

96. Ibid., Cabinet Conclusions, 2 May 1962; ibid., file F-1-5, "Notes Left with PM," 29 Apr. 1962; PAC, R.B. Bryce Papers, telephone notes, 1 May 1962.

97. PCO Records, file F-1-5, Report to Mr. Rasminsky, 2 May 1962. Smith, *Gentle Patriot*, p. 107, suggests that the IMF persuaded the government to peg the dollar. There is no evidence of this. Gordon Churchill noted that the decision to devalue was made by only five ministers and considered this "inexcusable." Churchill Papers (Mill Bay, B.C.), MS "Recollections," Chap. XV.

98. Stursberg Papers, Diefenbaker interview; Diefenbaker, III, 119-20; Fleming, II, 494-97.

99. Hamilton interview, 19 Apr. 1983; Stursberg Papers, Walter Dinsdale interview and Fleming interview.

100. PCO Records, file F-1-5, pen note, 21 June 1962; ibid., Cabinet Conclusions, 2 May 1962.

101. Rasminsky Papers, file LR76-523-24, Memo, 31 May 1962. Cf. Diefenbaker, III, 121-23.

102. Canadian Press dispatch, 8 June 1962; Diefenbaker, III, 131; Stursberg Papers, Fleming interview.

103. Rasminsky Papers, file LR76-522-182, Plumptre to Bryce, 10 June 1962.

104. Stursberg Papers, Fleming interview.

105. Quoted in Newman, p. 330. On the election use of the devaluation, see Diefenbaker, III, 123; Pearson, III, 59.

106. PAC, Progressive Conservative Party Records, vol. 387, Campaign Strategy 1962 file, Private and Confidential Memo, n.d., and vol. 384, Election 1962, National Campaign Committee file, "Meeting of the National Campaign Committee . . . 15-16 Apr. 1962."

107. See Hamilton Papers, vol. 130, Brian Mulroney file, Mulroney to Faibish, 5 Jan. 1962: "We have no organizers, no public relations men, no press liaison people – in short nothing."

108. "The June 1962 Election: Break-up of Our Party System?" *Queen's Quarterly*, LXVIII (Autumn, 1962), 337.

109. PAC, CCF Records, vol. 440, Correspondence Candidates 1962 file, Carl Hamilton to B. Mather *et al.*, 6 Apr. 1962; see also Joseph Wearing, *The L-Shaped Party* (Toronto, 1981), pp. 30ff., and Christina McCall-Newman, *Grits* (Toronto, 1982), Part I.

110. PAC, Liberal Party of Canada Records, vol. 692, Pre-Campaign Strategy 1961-62 file, "Pre-Campaign Strategy," n.d.; Election 1962 file, "1962 Election Advertising," n.d. The Liberals' Rule One was ". . . don't attack Diefenbaker. . . . Never – repeat never – refer to him. Always attack the Tories without

names." Wearing, p. 35.

111. PAC, Flora MacDonald Papers, vol. 30, Progressive Conservative Election Material File, "A Study of Voter Attitudes toward National Party Leaders and Probable Election Issues," Apr. 1962; *CAR, 1962*, p. 12.

112. Desmond Morton, *Social Democracy in Canada* (Toronto, 1977), p. 20. See also Gad Horowitz, *Canadian Labour in Politics* (Toronto, 1968) and Desmond Morton with Terry Copp, *Working People* (Ottawa, 1980).

113. CCF Records, vol. 374, file NCNP IIf, "Summary of a Discussion upon a Campaign to gain Support of 'Other Liberal-Minded Persons,' " n.d.

114. Herridge Papers, vol. 8, file 4, Herridge to Rev. F. Job, 29 July 1962.

115. Ibid., vol. 51, file 6, Argue to Fisher, 10 Jan. 1962.

116. CCF Records, vol. 449, Douglas Correspondence, Hamilton to Douglas, 26 Feb. 1962.

117. Michael Stein, *The Dynamics of Right-Wing Protest in Quebec* (Toronto, 1973), Chaps. II-III.

118. PAC, Réal Caouette Papers, vol. 4, programme electorale file 1963-4, Lettre aux députés . . ., n.d.; vol. 4, finance 1962 file, "Rémarques du trésorier provincial . . .," n.d.

119. Ibid., vol. 2, Association des Femmes Créditistes files, correspondence 1961-65, M. Lajeunesse to M. Smith, 10 May 1962. See also M. Pinard, *The Rise of a Third Party* (Toronto, 1971).

120. Stursberg Papers, John Fisher interview.

121. Glenbow Archives, Progressive Conservative Party of Alberta Papers, file 20, Campaign Memo No. 28, 25 May 1962.

122. Ladner Papers, Diefenbaker file, Ladner to Diefenbaker, 22 June 1962; Diefenbaker, III, 129: "The turning point," Diefenbaker called it.

123. *CAR, 1962*, p. 21.

124. PAC, Paul Hellyer Papers, vol. 245, NLF Election 1962 file, Tels., 21 May, 15 June 1962.

125. Queen's University Archives, C.G. Power Papers, vol. 5, Connolly file, Memos, 30 Apr., 22 May, 7 June 1962.

126. Ibid., vol. 6, Power to Hutchison, 29 May 1962; *CAR, 1962*, p. 19; D.V. Smiley, "Canada's Poujadists," *Canadian Forum* (Sept. 1962), 121-23; H. Pilotte, "Réal Caouette: Fuhrer ou Don Quixote?" *Le magazine Maclean* (septembre, 1962), 18ff.

127. Bell Papers, vol. 9, Election Results National file, "Analysis of 1962 General Election," n.d.; PAC, Douglas Harkness Papers, vol. 89, Election 1962 envelope, David Brown to Harkness, 22 June 1962.

128. Martin Papers, vol. 197, "Implications of the Popular Vote, 18 June 1962," 20 Aug. 1962.

129. Churchill Papers (Mill Bay), "Election Comments 1962," 1 Oct. 1962, MS "Recollections," Chap. XV.

130. PAC, Georges Vanier Papers, vol. 21, Diefenbaker and Pearson file, Memo, n.d.

131. Power Papers, vol. 13, 1963 Election file, Pearson to Power, 23 July 1962.

132. Patrick Nicholson, *Vision and Indecision* (Toronto, 1968), p. 111.

133. Churchill Papers, vol. 105, Hogan to Churchill, 5 Oct. 1962.

134. Rasminsky Papers, file LR76-

523-41, "Possible Plan of Action," 12 June 1962.

135. PCO Records, file F-1-16(d), "Memorandum on Emergency Financial Measures," 17 June 1962.

136. Press Release of 22 June 1962, copy in Rasminsky Papers, file LR76-523.

137. PCO Records, file F-1-16(d), "Points to Include . . ." 22 June 1962 and "Programme Given Us by Mr. Fleming," 22 June 1962.

138. Rasminsky Papers, file LR76-523-44, Rasminsky to Diefenbaker, 23 June 1962; ibid., file LR76-523, Rasminsky to Diefenbaker, 23 June 1962. See also ibid., Taylor to Fleming, 23 June 1962, making the same points, and Fleming, II, 516ff.

139. Bank of Canada Records, file PR/BR/-12, 24 June 1962. It is worth noting that the U.S. gave aid without stint. See J.F. Kennedy Library, Boston, Mass., J.F. Kennedy Papers, POF, vol. 90, Treasury 2/63, Fowler to Bundy, 22 Feb. 1963; W.L. Gordon Papers (Toronto), file U-10, Rasminsky to Gordon, 9 May 1963.

140. E.g., Harkness Papers, file 46-99(2), Fleming to Harkness, 27 June 1962. For opposition, see PCO Records, Cabinet Conclusions, 4 July 1962.

141. See Rasminsky Papers, file LR76-543, Ad Hoc Committee on Balance of Payments (Longer Term Measures), 28 June 1962, and Fleming Papers, vol. 162, Cabinet Committee on Balance of Payments, Minutes, 2 Aug. 1962 and passim.

142. Rasminsky Papers, LR76-523, Rasminsky to Cromer, 3 July 1962.

143. Bank of Canada Records, PR/EF-17, press release 13 Nov. 1962.

144. *CAR, 1962*, pp. 190-91.

NOTES TO CHAPTER FIVE

1. Department of External Affairs, External Affairs file 26-EBR-40, Heeney to Pearson, 10 May 1956.

2. Dwight Eisenhower Library, Abilene, Kans., Eisenhower Papers, file PPF1-F-107(4), Merchant to Eisenhower, 14 July 1958.

3. United States Treasury Dept., Treasury Records, Acc. 68-A-5918, Box 87, file Can/9/30, Scope and Objectives Paper for Canada-U.S. Ministerial Committee on Joint Defense, 4 Nov. 1959.

4. The best account is in J.T. Jockel's unpublished MS, "No Boundaries Upstairs: Canada, the United States and North American Air Defence, 1945-58," Chaps. III-V.

5. Department of National Defence, Directorate of History, Office of Chief of Defence Staff Papers, Combined Defence-NORAD file, Memo, CAS to CGS, 17 July 1958, att. as Annex A to "NORAD", 14 June 1967; J.G. Diefenbaker, *One Canada: The Memoirs of the Rt. Hon. John G. Diefenbaker* (Toronto, 1977), III, 18.

6. [U.S.] Declassified Documents [microfiche], (78) 238C, Report by Chief of Staff, U.S. Air Force to the JCS . . ., 5 Dec. 1955.

7. Ibid., Partridge to Chief of Staff, 9 Sept. 1955.

8. This became a political issue later. See Trevor Lloyd, *Canada in World Affairs 1957-59* (Toronto, 1968), pp. 31-32.

9. Directorate of History, Records, file 79/24, G/C Weiser to AOC, 21

Dec. 1956 and att. report, "Integration of Operational Control . . ., " 22 Oct. 1956.

10. Ibid., Gen. Charles Foulkes Papers, NORAD Consultation file, "Steps in Development of Integration," 4 Dec. 1957.

11. Directorate of History, Records, file 73/778, Aide Memoire, 12 June 1957; Foulkes Papers, NORAD Consultation file, "Steps in Development . . ."

12. York University Archives, Oral History Programme, Pearkes interview, 7 Apr. 1969; University of Victoria Archives, Pearkes Papers, Gen. H.D. Graham interview, 24 Sept. 1970, and Air Chief Marshal F.R. Miller interview, 20 June 1967.

13. Office of Chief of Defence Staff Papers, Answer to Questions file, Extract, 5 Aug. 1957. "There it is, approved," Pearkes told Foulkes. Cited in R.H. Roy, *For Most Conspicuous Bravery* (Vancouver, 1977), p. 289.

14. Pearkes Papers, vol. 19, Pearkes to Diefenbaker, 8 June 1965; Privy Council Office, PCO Records, Cabinet Conclusions, 31 July 1957. Cf. PAC, Jules Léger Papers, vol. 1, interview transcript, 22 Oct. 1980.

15. House of Commons, Special Committee on Defence, *Minutes*, 31 May 1963, p. 510; Pearkes Papers, vol. 19, Pearkes to Diefenbaker, 8 June 1965; Diefenbaker, III, 17.

16. PCO Records, file D-28-3(f), Holmes to Bryce, 31 July 1957.

17. Docs. in ibid., and in Department of External Affairs, External Affairs file 50309-40; Diefenbaker, III, 22-23; J.L. Granatstein, *A Man of Influence: Norman A. Robertson and Canadian Statecraft, 1929-68* (Ottawa, 1981); Jon McLin, *Canada's Changing Defense Policy, 1957-1963* (Baltimore, 1967), pp. 44ff.; Directorate of History, Records, file 73/778, Smith to Pearkes, 18 Oct. 1957; Lloyd, pp. 33-34.

18. External Affairs file 50309-40, Robertson to External, 6 Nov. 1957.

19. Extract, 16 Dec. 1957, in PCO Records, file D-28-3(f).

20. Office of Chief of Defence Staff Papers, Answer to Questions file, Léger to Minister, 2 Dec. 1957; Foulkes's view is in PCO Records, file D-28-3(f), Foulkes to USSEA, 26 Nov. 1957 and reply, 11 Dec. 1957 and 3 Jan. 1958. See also docs. in External Affairs file 50309-40; and PAC, Howard Green Papers, vol. 8, Memo, 12 June 1957.

21. Lloyd, p. 29.

22. James Dow, *The Arrow* (Toronto, 1979), pp. 85ff.; Robert Bothwell and William Kilbourn, *C.D. Howe* (Toronto, 1979), pp. 266-67.

23. Dow, pp. 92-95.

24. This account is based on Foulkes Papers, "The Story of the CF-105 Avro Arrow, 1952-62," a paper by Foulkes, and on Directorate of History, Records, file 181.003 (D5427), "The CF 105 (Arrow) Programme," n.d.

25. PCO Records, file D-28-3(f), Foulkes to Bryce, 21 July 1958; Directorate of History, Chairman, Chiefs of Staff Committee Records, Minutes of Special Meetings, Memo of Discussions, 18 July 1958; ibid., file 181.003 (D5427), "CF-105 Programme." On the Bomarc, see R.H. Clark, "Canadian Weapons Acquisition: The Case of the Bomarc Missile," M.A. thesis, Royal Military College, 1983; PCO Records, file D-28-3(f), Memo to Cabinet Defence Committee, 8 Aug. 1958, and "Progress Report on Implementation of Decisions . . . 21 Sept. 1958."

26. Docs. in External Affairs files, Washington 3-2-2-9 and 4-12-6;

Granatstein, *Man of Influence*, pp. 318-20; Diefenbaker, III, 36. Pearkes's biographer (Roy, p. 314) notes that the USAF had no aircraft on drawing boards with the CF-105's capabilities. True, but the Arrow had been designed to fly in the North, and the USAF (and the RAF) had little need for that.

27. PCO Records, file D-28-3(f), Memo to Cabinet Defence Committee, No. 9/58.

28. Ibid., file C-20-9(a)-M, Cabinet Defence Committee Minutes, 21 Aug. 1958; PAC, Douglas Harkness Papers, vol. 84, file 1, Memo to Cabinet, 22 Aug. 1958.

29. Ibid., vol. 14, file 2, "The Nuclear Arms Question and the Political Crisis Which Arose from It in January and February, 1963."

30. PCO Records, file C-20-9(a)-D, "Continental Air Defence – Foreign Policy Implications," 14 Aug. 1958.

31. Ibid., file D-28-3(f), Bryce pen notes, 26 Aug. 1958; York University Archives, Pearkes interview.

32. PCO Records, Cabinet Conclusions, 28 Aug., 7 and 21 Sept. 1958. Diefenbaker, III, 36, gets the date of the Cabinet decision wrong.

33. PCO Records, file D-28-15, Halliday to O'Hurley, 9 Dec. 1958. Cf. file D-28-3(f), "Progress Report," 24 Dec. 1958, which indicates that Avro had made proposals for concluding the Arrow development.

34. Chiefs of Staff Committee Records, Minutes of Special Meetings, 5 Feb. 1959.

35. PAC, Gordon Churchill Papers, vol. 23, Memo to Cabinet, 6 Feb. 1959. See PCO Records, file C-20-9(a)-M, Cabinet Defence Committee Minutes, 5 Feb. 1959; ibid., Cabinet Conclusions, 17 Feb. 1959; PAC, Paul Hellyer Papers, vol. 167, CF-105 file, contains a paper dated 5 Feb. 1959 that sets out the Chiefs' agreement in full.

36. PCO Records, Cabinet Conclusions, 17 Feb. 1959.

37. PAC, A.D.P. Heeney Papers, vol. 2, Memoirs 1959 file, Diary, 29 Mar. 1959.

38. External Affairs file, Washington 3-2-2-7, Washington to External, 1 Sept. 1959. See also Foulkes Papers, "The Story."

39. External Affairs file 50309-40, Holmes to SSEA, 25 Aug. 1959.

40. Ibid., Washington 3-2-2-7, External to Washington, 27 Aug. 1959.

41. Ibid., two tels., Washington to External, 28 Aug. 1959, and file 50309-D-40, Memo, Robinson to USSEA, 31 Aug. 1959.

42. Ibid., Washington 3-2-2, "Lessons from Skyhawk," 11 Sept. 1959, att.

43. Ibid., file 50309-D-40, Memo, Robinson to USSEA, 31 Aug. 1959.

44. Ibid., Washington 3-2-2, Memo, 4 Sept. 1959.

45. Ibid., "Lessons," 11 Sept. 1959, and file 50309-D-40, Memo, SSEA to Prime Minister, 10 Sept. 1959.

46. Eisenhower Papers, Ann Whitman files, Eisenhower Diary, vol. 49, Telecons, Apr. 1960, Call, 8 Apr. 1960. See Lawrence Martin, *The Presidents and the Prime Ministers* (Toronto, 1982), p. 179.

47. Heeney Papers, vol. 1, Ambassador to US file, Memo of Conversations, 30-31 Aug. 1960; PCO Records, Cabinet Conclusions, 17 Feb. 1961.

48. Heeney Papers, vol. 15, US Ambassador file, Heeney to Diefenbaker, 20 Feb. 1961; J.F. Kennedy Library, Boston, Mass., J.F. Kennedy Papers, POF Canada Security

1961, vol. 113, Merchant to Secretary of State, 11 Apr. 1961.

49. Ibid., Memorandum for the President, 17 Feb. 1961; Martin, pp. 185ff.

50. Kennedy Papers, POF Canada Security 1961, vol. 113, Trip to Ottawa (D) file, "Trends in Canadian Foreign Policy," 2 May 1961, and Canada Security (C) file, Biographical material, May 1961.

51. Heeney Papers, vol. 2, Diary, 18 Mar. 1962.

52. H.B. Robinson interview.

53. The Americans, Charles Ritchie, the new ambassador in Washington, said, "are beginning to give us the cold shoulder and their reaction to any Canadian official visitor is a snub." Moreover, the word that Canada was in disfavour "swiftly percolated down into every department of the United States Administration." *Diplomatic Passport* (Toronto, 1981), p. 186; *Storm Signals* (Toronto, 1983), p. 2.

54. PCO Records, file F-2-8(a), Wigglesworth to Diefenbaker, 11 July 1960.

55. Department of External Affairs, John Starnes Papers, Memo, "The Cuban Situation," 13 July 1960, and Bryce memo for Robertson, 15 July 1960.

56. External Affairs file 2444-40, Robertson to SSEA, 25 Oct. 1960. Diefenbaker later denied any such suggestion. Robert Reford, *Canada and Three Crises* (Toronto, 1968), p. 164.

57. Heeney Papers, vol. 2, Memoirs 1961 file, Diary, 12 Mar. 1961.

58. External Affairs file 2444-40, Moscow to External, 19 Oct. 1962.

59. PAC, R.B. Bryce Papers, notebook, 22 Oct. 1962, and blue notebook, 21-22 Oct. 1962; External Affairs file 244-40, Memo for Prime Minister, 22 Oct. 1962; PCO Records, file F-2-8(a), Memo for Prime Minister, 22 Oct. 1962.

60. Kennedy Papers, NSF files, vol. 20, Tel., American Embassy, Ottawa, 22 Oct. 1962.

61. Harkness Papers, vol. 14, file 2, "Nuclear Arms Question." Parts of this were printed in the Ottawa *Citizen*, 22 Oct. 1977.

62. Foulkes Papers, NORAD Consultation file, Slemon to Foulkes, 3 Mar. 1965.

63. Harkness Papers, "Nuclear Arms Question." This differs from the account in Jocelyn Ghent, "Canada, the United States and the Cuban Missile Crisis," *Pacific Historical Review*, XVIII (May 1979), 169.

64. Harkness Papers, "Nuclear Arms Question"; PCO Records, Cabinet Conclusions, 23 Oct. 1962.

65. Ibid., file F-2-8(a), Bryce Memo for Prime Minister, 23 Oct. 1962; Harkness Papers, "Nuclear Arms Question"; Ghent, 169-70.

66. Diefenbaker later said the alert was immediate. PAC, Peter Stursberg Papers, Diefenbaker interview.

67. Granatstein, *Man of Influence*, p. 352; Diefenbaker, III, 80ff.; External Affairs file 2444-40, Washington to External, 23 Oct. 1962; House of Commons *Debates*, 22 Oct. 1962.

68. PCO Records, Cabinet Conclusions, 24 Oct. 1962.

69. Harkness Papers, "Nuclear Arms Question."

70. PCO Records, file F-2-8(a), Memo for Bryce, 20 Nov. 1962. See J.T. Saywell, ed., *Canadian Annual Review, 1962* (Toronto, 1963), p. 128.

71. Harkness Papers, "Nuclear Arms Question"; Peyton Lyon, *Canada*

in World Affairs 1961-63 (Toronto, 1968), pp. 52-54; *CAR, 1962*, pp. 133ff.; Pierre Sévigny, *This Game of Politics* (Toronto, 1965), pp. 253, 257.

72. House of Commons *Debates*, 25 Jan. 1963, p. 3127.

73. Ibid., 20 Feb. 1959, p. 1223.

74. Office of Chief of Defence Staff Records, Nuclear Stockpiling file, Tel., Washington to External, 12 Dec. 1957; Memo to Cabinet Defence Committee, 3 Jan. 1958; PCO Records, file C-20-2, Bryce to Prime Minister, 9 Jan. 1958.

75. Office of Chief of Defence Staff Records, Nuclear Stockpiling file, Foulkes to CGS *et al.*, 13 Jan. 1958, Foulkes to Sparling, 21 Jan. 1958, Pearkes to Smith, 21 Jan. 1958.

76. PCO Records, file C-20-3 1958, Cabinet Conclusions, 9 Dec. 1958, and file C-20-9(a)-D, Memo for Cabinet, 3 Nov. 1959; Harkness Papers, vol. 89, "Aide Memoire on Undertakings to Acquire Nuclear Weapons . . .", n.d. [early 1961]. See also Declassified Documents, (81) 174A, National Security Council Memo, "Canadian Access to Nuclear Weapons in Peacetime," 12 Dec. 1958.

77. Churchill Papers, vol. 82, Memo to Minister, n.d. [Feb. 1963]; York University Archives, Pearkes interview; Diefenbaker, III, 63ff., treats this but fails to mention Norstad's appearance at the Cabinet.

78. Hellyer Papers, vol. 167, "Sequence of Events Leading to the Procurement of the F-104 . . .", 11 Apr. 1967; PCO Records, file C-20-9(a)-M, Cabinet Defence Committee Minutes, 27 June 1959.

79. Eisenhower Papers, Whitman files, Staff Notes, "Memo of Conference with President, 10 June 1959"; PCO Records, file D-1-5(b), A.E. Ritchie to USSEA, 24 Mar. 1960, and Record of Cabinet Decision, 3 May 1960; ibid., Memo, D.B.D. to Bryce, 30 May 1960.

80. York University Archives, Oral History Programme, Green interview, 10 Apr. 1969.

81. Granatstein, *Man of Influence*, pp. 338ff.; External Affairs file 50309-40, "Visit to NORAD and SAC Headquarters . . ." 16 Mar. 1959; ibid., file 50309-A-40, Robertson to Minister, 23 Oct. 1959.

82. York University Archives, Pearkes interview; University of Victoria, Pearkes Papers, Pearkes interview, 13 Apr. 1967.

83. Heeney Papers, vol. 1, Ambassador to US file, Memo of Conversations with Prime Minister, 30-31 Aug. 1960. This was the period when J.M. Minifie's *Peacemaker or Powder-Monkey* (Toronto, 1960) was very popular.

84. PAC, Donald Fleming Papers, vol. 162, Black Binder, "Cabinet Defence Committee Report" presented to Cabinet, 6 Nov. 1959; Heeney Papers, vol. 2, Chap. 15 file, Diary, 17 Nov. 1960.

85. PCO Records, Cabinet Conclusions, 6 Dec. 1960 and file N-4, "NATO Long Term Planning," 6 Dec. 1960. This External Affairs paper specifically referred to Canadian decisions to equip Canada's NATO forces with nuclear weapons. See also Churchill Papers, vol. 81, F.R. Miller to Minister, 11 Feb. 1963.

86. Diefenbaker, III, 71; External Affairs file 50219-AL-2-40, Robertson to SSEA, 5 Dec. 1960. The Cabinet decision was the product of an agreement negotiated by Bryce, Robertson, and F.R. Miller. See ibid., file 50219-AM-40, Bryce to

Robertson and Miller, 30 Nov. 1960. But cf. Green Papers, vol. 3, Robertson to Minister, 5 Dec. 1960.

87. Ibid., Robertson to SSEA, 14 Feb. 1961; PCO, Cabinet Conclusions, 14 Feb. 1961, att. Cab. Doc. 67/61, "Disarmament-Canadian Policy, 1961," 13 Feb. 1961.

88. Harkness Papers, vol. 84, envelope 1, Bryce to Harkness, 2 Mar. 1961; H.B. Robinson Papers (Ottawa), Robinson to Robertson, 21 Feb. 1961; PCO Records, Cabinet Conclusions, 14 Feb. 1961.

89. Ibid.; External Affairs file 50219-AM-40, Ignatieff to USSEA, 4 May 1961; Harkness Papers, vol. 84, envelope 1, Harkness to Green, 4 May 1961, and reply, 5 May 1961.

90. Green Papers, vol. 8, NATO and Nuclear Weapons file, External to Geneva, 18 May 1961.

91. PAC, L.B. Pearson Papers, N2, vol. 49, LePan to Pearson, 21 Feb. 1962.

92. Kennedy Papers, NSF Canada, vol. 20, Diefenbaker correspondence, Merchant to Secretary of State, 26 Feb. 1961, 4 and 5 Aug., 20 Sept. 1961.

93. Ibid., POF, vol. 113, Briefing Memorandum, 11 May 1962; Granatstein, *Man of Influence*, pp. 349-50; Ottawa *Citizen*, 14 July 1965.

94. *CAR, 1962*, p. 32; Diefenbaker, III, 141ff.

95. Gordon Churchill Papers (Mill Bay, B.C.), MS "Recollections," Chap. XV.

96. PCO Records, Cabinet Conclusions, Oct. 30, 1962; see J.M. Ghent, "Did He Fall or Was He Pushed? The Kennedy Administration and the Fall of the Diefenbaker Government," *International History Review*, I (Apr. 1979), 246ff.

97. Harkness Papers, "Nuclear Arms Question"; Office of Chief of Defence Staff Records, Defence Policy – Canada-US Relations file, CJS(W) to CCOS, 14 Feb. 1963, re talk with Nitze.

98. Harkness Papers, vol. 89, CAS to Minister, 21 Jan. 1963. Eighteen months were required to get the Voodoos to readiness. Ibid., "Nuclear Arms Question." See John Hilliker, "The Politicians and the 'Pearsonalities'," CHA Paper 1984, 22ff.

99. See, e.g., University of Calgary Archives, Bruce Hutchison Papers, file 1.2.5, V. Sifton to Pearson, 9 Dec. 1959, and reply, 30 Dec. 1959; PAC, J.W. Pickersgill Papers, vol. 256, NLF file, Hellyer memo, 14 Feb. 1962; *Globe and Mail*, 22 and 30 Mar. 1962.

100. Pearson Papers, N2, vol. 49, Memo, 27 Feb. 1962.

101. Ibid., W.A. Curtis to Pearson, 29 Mar. 1962.

102. Ibid., reply, 5 Apr. 1962.

103. Stursberg Papers, LaMarsh interview, 28 May 1975.

104. Pearson Papers, N2, vol. 22, Pearson to B. Hutchison, 18 Dec. 1962.

105. J.W. Pickersgill Papers (Ottawa), Pearson file, Pickersgill to Pearson, 3 Jan. 1963.

106. Lyon, pp. 130-36.

107. J.T. Saywell, ed., *Canadian Annual Review, 1963* (Toronto, 1964), p. 287. Diefenbaker, III, 8 offers the Chief's opinions on the switch. The most famous critique of the Liberal position is P.-E. Trudeau, "Pearson ou l'abdication de l'esprit," *Cité Libre* (avril, 1963), 7ff.

108. Lyon, pp. 138, 540; L.B. Pearson, *Mike: The Memoirs of the Rt.*

Hon. Lester B. Pearson (Toronto, 1975), III, 71.

109. Pearson Papers, N3, vol. 31, file 100.8 White Paper, Hellyer to Pearson, 24 Aug. 1964. See also ibid., vol. 32, file 109.11 Policy Confidential, Paul Martin to Pearson, 19 Feb. 1964.

110. York University Archives, Oral History Programme, Goodman interview, 5 Feb. 1970; Harkness Papers, "Nuclear Arms Question"; *CAR, 1963*, pp. 288-89; Diefenbaker, III, 153-55.

111. House of Commons *Debates*, 21 Jan. 1963, p. 2897.

112. Donald Fleming, *So Very Near* (Toronto, 1985), II, 581ff.; Churchill Papers, vol. 81, Memo, n.d., and Churchill MS "Recollections," Chap. XVI; Green Papers, vol. 8, Aide memoire, 11 Jan. 1963, att. to Memo for Minister, 4 Feb. 1963, and ibid., 15 Jan. 1963; PCO Records, Cabinet Conclusions, 8 Feb. 1963.

113. House of Commons *Debates*, 25 Jan. 1963, pp. 3125-28; Harkness Papers, "Nuclear Arms Question."

114. PAC, J.W. Monteith Papers, Diary, 25 Jan. 1963.

115. Lyon, p. 153.

116. Harkness Papers, "Nuclear Arms Question."

117. Ibid.; Lyon, pp. 157-58.

118. Green Papers, vol. 9, docs. att. to Memo for Minister, 1 Feb. 1963 and Robertson to Prime Minister, 30 Jan. 1963.

119. Kennedy Library, Sorensen Oral History Transcript, 26 Mar. 1964.

120. Confidential source.

121. Declassified Documents, (78) 301E, Col. Burris to Vice-President Johnson, 6 Feb. 1963. Butterworth later said the press release had gone from the embassy to State where it was seen by George McGhee, George Ball, and Rusk, and then to the White House where it won Bundy's OK. Ghent, "Did He Fall," 262.

122. PAC, Georges Vanier Papers, vol. 29, Dissolution file, Memo, 31 Jan. 1963; vol. 21, Diefenbaker and Pearson file, pencil notes, n.d.

123. Harkness Papers, "Nuclear Arms Question."

124. Ibid.; Monteith Diary, 3 Feb. 1963.

125. Ibid., 3 Feb. 1963; Diefenbaker, III, 160ff.; Patrick Nicholson, *Vision and Indecision* (Toronto, 1968), pp. 230ff.

126. According to the diary of T.W.L. MacDermot, then a gossipy External Affairs officer, McCutcheon raised $200,000 for Diefenbaker and gave it to him in February on the understanding he would step down. (Bishop's University, MacDermot Papers, Diary, 12 Apr. 1963). There is no confirmation of this.

127. Sévigny, p. 278; Diefenbaker, III, 163; Peter C. Newman, *Renegade in Power* (Toronto, 1963), pp. 370ff.

128. Stursberg Papers, T.C. Douglas interview, 4 Dec. 1972.

129. Ibid., Marcoux interview, 20 June 1975; Caouette interview, 10 Sept. 1975; Sévigny, p. 269; Diefenbaker, III, 165-66. Cf. *Montreal Star*, 30 Jan. 1963; Thompson's letter in *Globe and Mail*, 2 Mar. 1968.

130. Stursberg Papers, Lewis interview, 29 Aug. 1975.

131. Monteith Diary, 6 Feb. 1963. See also Jack Horner, *My Own Brand* (Edmonton, 1980), pp. 55-56; Nicholson, pp. 260ff.; Sévigny, pp. 281-82; Diefenbaker, III, 172; Harkness Papers, "Nuclear Arms

Question"; R.A. Bell letter in *Globe and Mail*, 20 Jan. 1983.

132. Monteith Diary, 9 Feb. 1963; Sévigny, pp. 284-85.

133. Monteith Diary, 13 Feb. 1963; Stursberg Papers, Bell interview, 26 July 1972.

134. Pickersgill Papers (Ottawa), Weir file, Pickersgill to Weir, 8 Feb. 1963.

135. Stursberg Papers, Bell interview.

136. PAC, Alvin Hamilton Papers, vol. 129, Churchill file, Faibish to Churchill, 30 Jan. 1963.

137. PAC, Liberal Party Records, vol. 688, Correspondence and Memos, Jan.-Feb. 1963 file, "Memo on Conclusions to be Drawn from the January Survey," 16 Jan. 1963.

138. Ibid., vol. 689, National Office General Correspondence file, "Strategy for Victory," 12 Feb. 1963.

139. Stursberg Papers, Camp interview, 13 June 1975; LaMarsh interview, 28 May 1975; Judy LaMarsh, *Memoirs of a Bird in a Gilded Cage* (Toronto, 1969), pp. 36ff.; Liberal Party Records, docs. in vols. 705 and 696.

140. Glenbow Archives, Progressive Conservative Party of Alberta Records, file f-2, Camp to Constituency Presidents, 13 Feb. 1963.

141. Stursberg Papers, Camp interview. The Liberals were using Lou Harris, Kennedy's pollster, but the other parties did not know this. See Montreal *Gazette*, 9 September 1971. For additional offers of Kennedy aid, see Pearson, III, 80-81; Bruce Hutchison, *The Far Side of the Street* (Toronto, 1976), pp. 260-62. For the impact of U.S. intervention in Pearson's view, see A.E. Ritchie's letter in *Globe and Mail*, 13 Dec. 1983.

142. J.M. Beck, "The Election of 1963 and National Unity," *Dalhousie Review*, XLIII (Summer 1963), 146.

143. Monteith Papers, vol. 1, Election file, Speech, 23 Feb. 1963; ibid., Diefenbaker correspondence, Monteith to Diefenbaker, 24 Feb. 1963, and reply, 28 Feb. 1963; Monteith Diary, 26-27 Feb. and 4 Mar. 1963.

144. Lyon, p. 541.

145. PAC, R.A. Bell Papers, vol. 13, Speeches 1963 file, "Issues of 1963 Campaign."

146. Churchill MS "Recollections," Chap. XVI. Churchill and Green agreed on a campaign press release that affirmed the Fleming Committee report. PAC, Churchill Papers, vol. 82, Draft Statement file, 6 Mar. 1963.

147. *CAR, 1963*, p. 22.

148. Kennedy Papers, POF, vol. 113, Canada Security 1963, W.H. Brubeck to Bundy, 5 Apr. 1963.

149. Stursberg Papers, Bell interview.

150. Kennedy Papers, POF, vol. 90, Treasury 2/63, Dillon to Kennedy, 25 Feb. 1963.

151. See Churchill MS "Recollections," Chap. XVIII; Winnipeg *Tribune*, 25 July 1963; House of Commons *Debates*, 27 May 1963, pp. 319-22, 6 and 8 Apr. 1965, pp. 31-32, 131ff. The letter is in PAC, Churchill Papers, vol. 105, Election 1963-Butterworth file; see also Bryce Papers, telecon notes, 5 Apr. 1963.

152. See Kennedy Papers, White House Central Files, vol. 43, C043, Salinger memo, 6 Apr. 1963.

153. Ibid., POF, vol. 113, Canada Security 1963, Memo for Rusk, 29

Mar. 1963. The remarks are in Lyon, pp. 203-4.

154. The Tory attack infuriated the military. See Foulkes Papers, Air Defence file, "The Truth About the Bomarc," n.d.; Directorate of History Records, file 74/425, Dunlap to ADC COS Conference, 28 May 1963.

155. Liberal Party Records, vol. 698, Reports to Pearson file, Davey to Pearson, 15 Mar. 1963, and vol. 694, Election 1963 Correspondence and Reports file, Gordon to Pearson, 20 Mar. 1963; Pearson, III, 78-79.

156. Liberal Party Records, vol. 698, Reports to Pearson file, Davey to Pearson, 8 Mar. 1963.

157. See, e.g., *Globe and Mail*, 2 Apr. 1963. Only the Ottawa *Journal*, Winnipeg *Tribune*, Vancouver *Province* and Fredericton *Gleaner* stayed Tory. PAC, CCF Records, vol. 442, Douglas Correspondence, W.E. McLaughlin letter, n.d. The Conservatives spent $1,797,512. PAC, Flora MacDonald Papers, vol. 46, "General Election Campaign," n.d. The Liberals spent $917,574 on advertising alone. W.L. Gordon Papers (Toronto), Election Expenses file, Statement of Campaign Operations to May 31, 1963.

158. *CAR, 1963*, pp. 34ff.; Bell Papers, vol. 1, Election 1963 file, "Analysis of 1963 General Election"; J.L. Granatstein, "The Armed Forces' Vote in Canadian General Elections, 1940-68," *Journal of Canadian Studies*, IV (Feb. 1969), 6ff.

159. See, e.g., Granatstein, *Man of Influence*, pp. 355-56; Ritchie, *Storm Signals*, p. 46.

160. Yale University Archives, Walter Lippmann Papers, Sec. III, vol. 59, file 351, Butterworth to Lippmann, 20 May 1963.

NOTES TO CHAPTER SIX

1. Pickersgill remarks, "Canada Council 25th Anniversary Dinner," 14 June 1982, mimeo., as amended in letter to author, 25 March 1984. See also Pickersgill's account in his *My Years with Louis St. Laurent* (Toronto, 1975), pp. 318-19.

2. Lamontagne remarks, "Canada Council 25th Anniversary Dinner," pp. 28-29.

3. *Report of the Royal Commission on National Development in the Arts, Letters and Sciences* (Ottawa, 1951), pp. 370ff. See also Claude Bissell's paper, "The Massey Commission and Canadian Culture," presented at Carleton University in 1983.

4. Vincent Massey, *What's Past Is Prologue* (Toronto, 1963), p. 453.

5. Massey College, Vincent Massey Papers, Diary, 4 Jan. 1955.

6. Ibid., 6 Jan. 1956.

7. Ibid., 22 Sept., 15 Oct. 1956.

8. Claude Bissell, *Halfway up Parnassus* (Toronto, 1974), p. 46.

9. Canada Council Records, Ottawa, Pre-Council Material file, "Cultural Progress in Canada," 13 Nov. 1956.

10. Bissell, p. 47; Carl Berger, *The Writing of Canadian History* (Toronto, 1976), p. 179.

11. Part of St. Laurent's speech in the House, like most of the draft bill, was prepared in the Privy Council Office, largely by Peter Dwyer, who

eventually joined the Canada Council. See Privy Council Office, PCO Records, file C-34 (1957).

12. Glenbow Archives, Solon Low Papers, f. 131, Low to I. Watts, 23 Apr. 1957.

13. Queen's University Archives, T.A. Crerar Papers, vol. 99, Crerar to A.K. Cameron, 8 Feb. 1957.

14. PAC, Brooke Claxton Papers, vol. 72, Canada Council file, note, n.d.

15. See Frank Milligan, "The Ambiguities of the Canada Council," in David Helwig, ed., *Love and Money: The Politics of Culture* (Toronto, 1980).

16. A.W. Trueman, *A Second View of Things* (Toronto, 1982), p. 137.

17. Canada Council Records, Claxton file, memos, passim.

18. PCO Records, file C-34-2, Bryce to Hill *et al.*, 16 Apr. 1957.

19. Massey Diary, 16 June 1957.

20. Claxton Papers, vol. 77, Claxton to Walter Gordon, 20 Mar. 1957.

21. Hugo McPherson, "Gilding the Muses: The Canada Council," in A. Rotstein, ed., *The Prospect of Change* (Toronto, 1965), p. 332; Frank Milligan, "The Canada Council As a Public Body," *Canadian Public Administration*, XXII (Summer 1979), 285; Canada Council Records, Trueman file 1957-61, Bissell to Trueman, 12 Sept. 1961.

22. PCO Records, file C-3-1, Fullerton to Chairman, Canada Council, 21 Jan. 1963; Canada Council Records, Minutes, 30 Apr., 1 May 1957.

23. Ibid., 5-6 May 1958, 18-19 July 1958; Agenda book, 6-7 Oct. 1959; Minutes, 2-3 Feb. 1959. Trueman remained director until 1965, when he was replaced by Jean Boucher. Bussière left at the same point and was succeeded by Peter Dwyer.

24. Ibid., Minutes, 30 Apr., 1 May 1957; Claxton Papers, vol. 72, Trueman memo, "Notes on Conversations with People in New York," Feb. 1958.

25. Canada Council Records, MacKenzie file, MacKenzie to Trueman, 10 Oct. 1957.

26. Bissell cited in McPherson, p. 331; Milligan, "Ambiguities," pp. 69-70.

27. Canada Council Records, Bissell file, Trueman to Bissell, 26 July 1960. In early 1962, Diefenbaker named Col. D.B. Weldon, a London businessman, chairman; in 1964 Montreal lawyer Jean Martineau succeeded to the post.

28. Trueman, p. 152.

29. University of British Columbia Archives, Leon Ladner Papers, Ladner to Diefenbaker, 11 Apr. 1960, and Ladner to H.C. Green, 11 Apr. 1960.

30. Canada Council Records, [Peter] Desbarats interview file, "Submission concerning need of increase . . ." 7 Nov. 1960.

31. PCO Records, file C-3-1, Bryce to Prime Minister, 5 Dec. 1960.

32. Ibid., Bissell to Diefenbaker, 8 Dec. 1960.

33. *Canada Council Annual Report 1963-4*, p. 1ff.

34. Cited in ibid., *1964-5*, pp. 1-2.

35. Canada Council Records, Director's file 1962-5, 19 Mar. 1965.

36. Ibid., unfiled Memo to Secretary of State, Dec. 1964.

37. Trueman, p. 157. In 1967-68, the government gave the council $17 million, raising its level of support that year to $21.5 million.

38. "Canada Council Support to the Arts 1957-8 to 1981-2," 31 Aug. 1982. Data provided by the Canada Council. If 1981 equals $1.00, the

purchasing power of a dollar in 1959, for example, was $3.23 and in 1967 $2.74.

39. Ibid.

40. Canada Council Records, Minutes, 30 Apr.-1 May 1957.

41. Ibid., Minutes, Executive Committee, 18 June 1957.

42. Ibid., Minutes, 19-20 Aug. 1957. At its meeting on 7-8 Oct. 1957, the Grands Ballets was given $10,000. Ibid., Minutes. And on 2-3 Feb. 1958, the council declared itself satisfied that the National had met the conditions demanded and authorized the second $50,000 grant. Ibid., Minutes.

43. *Report*, p. 202.

44. See, e.g., the careful account in Ken Johnstone, "Ballet," in M. Ross, ed., *The Arts in Canada* (Toronto, 1958), pp. 54-56; also Max Wyman, *The Royal Winnipeg Ballet* (Toronto, 1978), pp. 101-2.

45. Claxton Papers, vol. 72, "Notes on Conversations with People in New York," Feb. 1958.

46. By 1968-69, 40 per cent of the country's dancers earned less than $4,000 and none more than $15,000. Laurent Mailhot et Benôit Melançon, *Le Conseil des Arts du Canada* (Montréal, 1982), pp. 221-22.

47. The *Canada Council Annual Report to March 31, 1959*, pp. 32-33, noted that ballet, opera, and symphony had to be subsidized in all countries; in the U.K., in fact, the Arts Council devoted half its budget to the support of four major companies. Carter's report is in Canada Council Records, Carter Survey Ballet 1959 file.

48. Canada Council Records, Minutes, 19-20 May 1959, 17-19 Aug. 1959.

49. In a 1963 speech, Dwyer said frankly that regional and linguistic concerns virtually obliged the council to support three companies, even though this stretched council resources. Address to University of Michigan, Mar. 1963, copy in Canada Council Records.

50. Claxton Papers, vol. 81, Mackintosh to Claxton, 28 Aug. 1959, and reply, 14 Sept. 1959.

51. Canada Council Records, memo 30 May 1960, att. to Minutes, 30-31 May 1960.

52. Ibid., "Standards of the National Ballet," 20 Feb. 1961, att. to Minutes, 20-21 Feb. 1961. The 1961 tour was "the most disastrous single season in the ballet's history." Herbert Whittaker, *Canada's National Ballet* (Toronto, 1967), p. 95.

53. Canada Council Records, Ballet Survey 1961 file, Bissell to Dwyer, 16 May 1961.

54. Ibid., Minutes, 23-24 May 1961. A memo, "The National Ballet Guild of Canada," 4 Sept. 1961, att. to Minutes, 4-5 Sept. 1961, indicates the National's acceptance.

55. Ibid., Minutes, 20-21 Nov. 1961; Ballet Survey file, Dwyer-Kirstein correspondence, 14, 16 Aug., 1 Sept. 1961.

56. Wyman describes the fiasco of the Royal Winnipeg's attempt to live up to its name during a Royal visit in 1959. Wyman, pp. 109-10.

57. Canada Council Records, Kirstein file, Report, n.d.; ibid., Ballet Survey file, Buckle Report 1962; ibid., Dwyer to Bissell, 18 May 1961. Glover's report has not been found. In the council's *Annual Report 1963-4*, p. 16, Dwyer wrote that the council had chosen to follow the policy of *laissez danser*.

58. Dwyer later said that council's

goal was to build "support services for the arts," such as the National Ballet School. "We think it important . . . to develop our own actors rather than to receive from training elsewhere a pint-sized Gielgud dripping mannerisms, or a brand-new Brando dripping methods." Address to Associated Councils of the Arts 1969 Seminar, Ste Adèle, copy in Canada Council Records. On Dwyer's earlier career in intelligence, see John Sawatsky, *Men in the Shadows* (Toronto, 1980), pp. 119ff.; Robert Fulford, "The Canada Council at Twenty-five," *Saturday Night* (Mar. 1982), 36-37.

59. Canada Council Records, Minutes, 26 Mar. 1962.

60. Ibid., 14-15 May 1962.

61. Ibid., Memo att. to Minutes, 30 June 1963.

62. Ibid., Memo, "Re Ballet," 3 June 1963.

63. By 1967, the National's budget was over $1 million with box office receipts covering only 45 per cent. Grants from the council, the province, and Toronto added more than $250,000, and donations covered most of the rest. Whittaker, p. 94.

64. Ibid., p. 217.

65. Ibid., p. 121.

66. Dwyer's address to the Canadian Conference of the Arts, 1967, copy in Canada Council Records; ibid., address to Canadian Music Council, 1 Apr. 1966; but cf. James Beveridge, "Culture and Media in Canada," *American Review of Canadian Studies*, III (Spring 1973), 135ff., Robert Fulford, "General Perspectives on Canadian Culture," ibid., 115ff., and Bill Glassco in *Globe and Mail*, 1 June 1985, p. CS5, all of which make the point that American influences were still dominant.

67. F.H. Leacy, ed., *Historical Statistics of Canada* (Ottawa, 1983), W340-438; Canada Council Records, Desbarats interview file, Canada Council Submission to Prime Minister, 7 Nov. 1960.

68. *Canada Council Bulletin* (No. 6), *Canada's Universities*, Summer 1960. This bulletin was cancelled and not sent in this form.

69. Senate Standing Committee on Finance, *Minutes*, 9 June 1960, p. 9.

70. Douglas Fullerton, *The Dangerous Delusion* (Toronto, 1978), p. 38.

71. Senate Standing Committee on Finance, *Minutes*, 15 Apr. 1959, p. 9. Universities not founded when the Canada Council was established were deemed ineligible.

72. G.E. Beament to Claxton, 10 Apr. 1958, att. to Canada Council Records, Minutes, 5-6 May 1958.

73. Trueman, pp. 155-56.

74. Canada Council Records, Minutes, 7-8 Oct. 1957.

75. Ibid., 23-24 May 1961; *Canada Council Bulletin*, No. 6; Fullerton, pp. 37-38; list of Quebec grants in *Canada Council Annual Report 1961-2*, p. 55.

76. Leacy, W340-438, W466-74, W519-32; S141-47: University capital expenditures rose from $38 million in 1957 to $259.3 million in 1967. Total operating and capital costs rose from $100,265,000 in 1955 to $1,616,190,000 in 1970. Provincial expenditures on universities increased from $140 million in 1961-62 to $350 million five years later.

77. See, e.g., John McLeish, *A Canadian for All Seasons* (Toronto, 1978), p. 223.

78. *Canada Council Bulletin*, No. 3 (Summer 1959).
79. Canada Council Records, Address by Trueman to Montreal Canadian Public Relations Society, 9 January 1963. See also S.D. Clark, "The Support of Social Science Research in Canada," *Canadian Journal of Economics and Political Science*, XXIV (May, 1958), 141ff.
80. Canada Council Records, Minutes, 30 Apr.-1 May 1957.
81. Ibid., 19-20 Aug. 1957.
82. Ibid., 28 Mar. 1958; ibid., Scholarship Policy file 1958-9, Memo, 27 Mar. 1958.
83. *Canada Council Annual Report to March 31, 1959*, p. 12.
84. The outside agencies, however, were destined for the chop. In June 1963 the Canada Council abruptly informed the Humanities Research Council and the Social Science Research Council that it now would do its own adjudications. The academic councils were shaken by the swift brutality of the move, but there was nothing they could do about it. See McLeish, pp. 183-85; docs. in Canada Council Records, Scholarship Policy 1962-3 file. The Canada Council soon set up discipline panels and a final review panel to determine awards. See Canada Council Records, Scholarship Policy 1964 file; Doc. 467, 31 Mar. 1964.
85. Non-resident scholarships were also dropped. See Ruth Lor Malloy, "The Canada Council and Its International Aspects," *Exchange* (Fall, 1970), 16.
86. Canada Council Records, Scholarship Policy 1959-61 file, "The Scholarship and Fellowship Programme: Report and Recommendations," 29 January 1960. Leacy, W475-85, indicate 7,760 full-time university teachers in 1960 and 24,733 in 1970. In 1960, 43 per cent had doctorates; in 1970, 51.2 per cent.
87. *Canada Council News*, II (Jan. 1965).
88. Robert Parise, *Georges-Henri Lévesque* (Montréal, 1976).
89. Canada Council Records, Lévesque file, letter 1 Apr. 1960.
90. Memo in ibid., 23 Mar. 1960. Trueman, pp. 140-41, said that Quebec members of the council were strongly pressured by applicants who regarded them almost as M.P.s with a duty to lobby.
91. Canada Council Records, MacKenzie file, Memo, 21 Apr. 1960.
92. Ibid., Minutes, 21-22 Nov. 1960, Appendix 11.
93. It is worth noting that the council, like all of Ottawa, essentially functioned only in English in this period. Application forms were in both languages, of course. In addition, there was a sexist cast to the council's forms and regulations – spouses were invariably female, for example, and the council did not pay travel expenses for the husbands of winners as they were deemed to hold jobs; wives of winners were given travel expenses. The council was not different from other agencies in this era.
94. Canada Council Records, Desbarats interview file, Submission, 7 Nov. 1960.
95. Ibid., Minutes, 14-15 May 1962.
96. Ibid., 3-4 June 1963, 31 May-1 June 1965, 20-21 Feb. 1967. See also F.E.L. Priestley, *The Humanities in Canada* (Toronto, 1964), pp. 46-47.
97. *Canada Council Annual Report 1963-4*, p. 1ff.

98. Canada Council Records, Minutes, 10-11 Feb. 1964, "General Observations on the Development of Graduate Studies in Canada," 10 Feb. 1964.

99. Ibid., Minutes, 4-5 Apr. 1966, "Pre-Doctoral Fellowships," 11 Mar. 1966. By 1967, more than half of Canadian doctoral candidates abroad were supported by the council. Ibid., Ford Foundation file, J. Boucher to E.A. Ritchie, 20 Apr. 1967.

100. Ibid., Minutes, 20-21 Feb. 1967, "Report on the 1965 Survey of Pre-Doctoral Award Holders," 20 Feb. 1967. Ph.D.s awarded in Canada in 1955 were 266; by 1970, there were 1,625. Leacy, W504-12. M.A.s in the same period increased from 1,459 to 9,638, B.A.s from 13,757 to 67,100. By 1968 controversy had begun over the numbers of non-Canadians teaching in Canadian universities. Robin Mathews and James Steele of Carleton University argued that between 1961 and 1968 the proportion of non-Canadians rose from 25 to 51 per cent, that 58 per cent of new appointments between 1963 and 1965 went to non-Canadians, and that from 1965 to 1967 the figure rose to 72 per cent. Their data were attacked. See Mathews and Steele, *The Struggle for Canadian Universities* (Toronto, 1969), pp. 85ff. The figures of Ph.D. production in Canada suggest the difficulties involved in getting sufficient university faculty without having recourse to foreigners.

101. *Canada Council News*, I (July, 1964).

102. Canada Council Records, Desbarats interview file, Statistical page; *Canada Council Annual Report 1964-5*, p. 49.

103. Canada Council Records, Minutes, 28 Mar. 1958, 5-6 May 1958.

104. Ibid., 20-21 Aug. 1962.

105. Social Science Research Council, *Annual Report 1970-71*. p. 20, forecast the completion of the series in 1974-75. The experience with the Centenary Series stands in contrast to the general mood of the time. See H. Blair Neatby, "The Gospel of Research: The Transformation of English-Canadian Universities," *Transactions of the Royal Society of Canada*, XX Ser. IV (1982), 275ff.; and Philip Cercone, "The Aid to Scholarly Publications Programme, 1940-83," *Social Sciences in Canada*, XI (Sept. 1983), 9. See also R.H. Hubbard, ed., *Scholarship in Canada, 1967* (Toronto, 1968) for an authoritative survey.

NOTES TO CHAPTER SEVEN

1. *Saskatchewan Medical Quarterly*, XXIV (Sept. 1960), 148.

2. *Interim Report of Advisory Committee on Medical Care to the Government of Saskatchewan 1961* (Regina, 1961), p. 58; Saskatchewan Archives, T.C. Douglas Papers, Cabinet Secretary 13(2), Cabinet Conference on Planning and Budgeting, Nov. 1958, vol. 2, Forward Planning Proposals. [All references to Douglas Papers are to those in Regina unless otherwise noted.]

3. Malcolm Taylor, *Health Insurance and Canadian Public Policy* (Montreal, 1978), Chap. II; Ken MacTaggart, *The First Decade* (Toronto, 1973), p. 15. A 1948 revision of this resolution is quoted in A.W. Johnson, "Biography of a Govern-

ment: Policy Formulation in Saskatchewan," Ph.D. thesis, Harvard Univ., 1963, p. 619. On the early attitudes of the Canadian Medical Association, see R. Bothwell and J. English, "Pragmatic Physicians: Canadian Medicine and Health Care Insurance 1910-45," in S. Shortt, ed., *Medicine in Canadian Society* (Montreal, 1981), pp. 479ff.

4. Taylor, Chap. IV; Queen's University Archives, J.M. Macdonnell Papers, vol. 17, file 16, "Hospital Insurance and Diagnostic Services," 15 Nov. 1957.

5. Douglas Papers, file 19 (1-19-1), Douglas to Diefenbaker, 8 Aug. 1957; PAC, Department of Finance Records, vol. 4133, file F20(1957), Notes, 26 Nov. 1957.

6. Douglas Papers, file 570a(14-24), "Conference . . . on Health Insurance Planning," 5 Jan. 1951. Ibid., file 562, Douglas to J. Waterfield, 30 Mar. 1954.

7. MacTaggart, p. 17; docs. on Douglas Papers, file 570(14-24) and file 137(14-28a).

8. See Taylor, pp. 266ff., which offers reasons for the CCF decision to go for medicare; also Douglas Papers, file 574(14-28-1), A.J.M. Davies to doctors, 12 Apr. 1960, encl. copy of transcript of TV debate, 20 Mar. 1960.

9. Ibid., Cabinet Secretary 13(2) file Cabinet Conference . . . Nov. 1958.

10. Saskatoon *Star-Phoenix*, 27 Apr. 1959.

11. Saskatchewan College of Physicians and Surgeons, Saskatoon, College Records, Council Minutes, 28 Sept. 1959.

12. Ibid., 18-19 Oct. 1959.

13. Ibid., 21 Oct. 1959. Cf. "Why Do Doctors Fear Government Entry into the Medical Care Field?" *CMA Journal*, 9 June 1962, 1072.

14. SCPS Records, file 3C, Peacock to doctors, 16 Nov. 1959, and file P-7-2-1, Peacock to doctors, 29 Oct. 1959.

15. Douglas Papers, Cabinet Secretary 13-2 file, Minutes of Cabinet Conference on Planning and Budgeting, 23-27 Nov. 1959.

16. Ibid., file 575a(14-28-2), Douglas to Thompson, 1 Dec. 1959; Saskatchewan Archives, Woodrow Lloyd Papers, file 14d(1411), Dr. Roth to Dr. Acker, 26 Nov. 1959.

17. Text in SCPS Records, "Correspondence re Medical Care Insurance Plan" binder. Basic books on the medicare issue are Taylor; R.F. Badgely and S. Wolfe, *Doctors' Strike* (Toronto, 1967); E.A. Tollefson, *Bitter Medicine* (Saskatoon, 1964 [?]).

18. Saskatchewan Archives, J.W. Erb Papers, file 181C4, Deputy Minister of Public Health to Douglas, 22 Jan. 1960.

19. Ibid., Statement by Dr. Davies, n.d.; SCPS Council minutes, 7-8 Feb. 1960, 1 Mar. 1960; ibid., 1 Mar. 1960, 1-2 May 1960, 16 Oct. 1961; Kurt Hall, unpublished MS on health policy in Saskatchewan, Chap. VIII, p. 22.

20. SCPS Records, Council minutes, 1 Mar. 1960.

21. Ibid., file 2-18-6, Dr. Leishman to Davies, 11 Apr. 1960.

22. Douglas Papers, file 574(14-28-1), encl. with Dr. Davies to doctors, 12 Apr. 1960.

23. Lloyd Papers, Medical Care Programme file, Panel Discussion CKBI-TV, 18 May 1960; SCPS Records, file 2-18-6, Dr. Taylor to Madam, 26 May 1960; Regina *Leader-Post*, 25 May 1960; SCPS Records, file 2-18-6, Dr. Anderson to F.B. Strong, 10 May

1960; J.T. Saywell, ed., *Canadian Annual Review, 1960* (Toronto, 1961), pp. 24-27.

24. Weyburn *Review*, 2 June 1960; Saskatoon *Star-Phoenix*, 25, 27 May 1960.

25. Douglas Papers, file 575b, Press Release, 9 June 1960.

26. Quoted in E.A. Tollefson, "The Saskatchewan Medicare Controversy," *Saskatchewan Bar Review*, XXVII (1962), 32, and in W.P. Thompson, *Medical Care: Programs and Issues* (Toronto, 1964), p. 63.

27. SCPS Records, Dalgleish file, CMA statement.

28. Ibid., file 2-18-6, Special Medical Assessment Fund, Balance Sheet, 12 June 1960; Council minutes, 9-10 July 1960.

29. Ibid., Steering Committee file, Minutes, 30 July 1960.

30. Ibid., Council minutes, 16-17 Oct. 1960.

31. Regina *Leader-Post*, 22 Oct. 1960.

32. PAC, T.C. Douglas Papers, vol. 1, file 18-45, Douglas to D. Swailes, 21 Mar. 1960; and vol. 2, corr. on file 18-45-3.

33. E.g., see Saskatchewan Archives, Froher Tapes, esp. interviews with M. Shumiatcher, 9 Dec. 1978, and Dr. C.J. Houston, 18 Oct. 1979.

34. Erb Papers, file 181C1, Memo, 28 Aug. 1961.

35. Interim Report. See also Saskatchewan Archives, Allan Blakeney Papers, Medical Care Plan 1962 file, Dr. Ann Rivkin brief, Feb. 1962.

36. Douglas Papers, file Premier 817, NDP Caucus Minutes, 28 Sept. 1961; Johnson, p. 638.

37. SCPS Records, Newsletter, 12 Oct. 1961.

38. *Saskatchewan Medical Quarterly*, XXV (Dec. 1961), 263ff. See the careful analysis of the act and the CMA principles in Tollefson, *Saskatchewan Bar Review*, XXVII, 36ff.

39. Lloyd Papers, file 325b(13-1-15), Memo for file, 29 Nov. 1961.

40. SCPS Records, Council minutes, 16-17 Dec. 1961.

41. Regina *Leader-Post*, 13 Jan. 1962. Also ibid., 1 Mar., 19 Apr. 1962, and Moose Jaw *Times-Herald*, 19 Apr. 1962; SCPS Records, Council minutes, 9-10 June 1962.

42. Ibid., Correspondence re Medical Care Insurance Plan binder, Davies to Dalgleish, 2, 22 Mar. 1962 and reply, 15 Mar. 1962.

43. Ibid., Minutes of Meeting, 28 Mar. 1962; Saskatchewan Archives, W.G. Davies Papers, file 1-13-2, pen notes, n.d. On the flaws in the college plan, see A.E. Blakeney, "The Saskatchewan Experience," *American Medicine: The Forensic Quarterly*, XXXVII (Nov. 1963), 464.

44. SCPS Records, Minutes of Meeting, 1 Apr. 1962.

45. Blakeney Papers, file Addenda II.4, pen notes of meeting, 31 Mar. 1962 [*sic*: 1 Apr. 1962]. See also Johnson, p. 650.

46. Blakeney Papers, Minister of Public Health, II.4 file, "Analysis of the Proposal . . .", 13 Apr. 1962; SCPS Records, Minutes of Meeting, 11 Apr. 1962; see Saskatchewan Archives, E.A. Tollefson Tapes, Blakeney interview, 25 May 1966. But cf. ibid., Erb interview, which suggested the government was on the verge of accepting the SCPS position.

47. Davies Papers, file 1-13-2, pen notes, "College Proposals," n.d.

48. SCPS Records, Newsletter, 18 Apr. 1962.

49. Tollefson Tapes, Erb interview, suggests pure coincidence. Lloyd's address is in Lloyd Papers, file 216(13-1-K). *Saskatchewan Medical Quarterly*, XXVI (Sept. 1962), 105.
50. Ibid., p. 107.
51. *Maclean's*, 16 June 1962, 67. SCPS Records, Newsletter, 11 May 1962.
52. Lloyd Papers, file 413, Caucus minutes, 6 May 1962; ibid., Cabinet Secretary, file 1-3-23b, Cabinet Memo, 7 May 1962, 14 May 1962, and file 230c(13-1-2), Memos, 4, 6 June 1962; SCPS Records, Steering Committee folder, Minutes, 6 June 1962; Lloyd Papers, file Premier 231, Lloyd to MLAS and Candidates, 23 May 1962.
53. A survey of Saskatchewan editorials collected in the Davies Papers, vol. 14, file 181D, found 41 against medicare and none in favour, news stories opposed to medicare 125, in favour 86, and neutral 70. See also A.E. Blakeney, "Press Coverage of Medicare," *Queen's Quarterly*, LXX (Autumn, 1963). I am indebted to Pat Brennan for help here.
54. 23 May 1962; 26 May 1962. See also Taylor, pp. 307ff.
55. Docs. on SCPS Records, file 2-18-11; ibid., Minutes of General Committee for Emergency Services, 3 June 1962, and Council minutes, 10 June 1962; *Globe and Mail*, 23 June 1962.
56. Lloyd Papers, file 27-8, Spry to D. Tansley, 7 June 1962.
57. *Globe and Mail*, 20 June 1962. See also A.P. Darcil, "Saskatchewan Imbroglio," *Canadian Doctor* (July 1962), 23ff.; Taylor, pp. 300-301.
58. SCPS Records, Council minutes, 19-20 June 1962; ibid., SCPS Newsletter, 27 June 1962; Lloyd Papers, file 216(13-1-K), Statement, 22 June 1962; Taylor, pp. 304ff. See also PAC, F.D. Mott Papers, vol. 33.
59. SCPS Records, file P7-0-1, Lloyd to Dear Physician, 26 June 1962; Lloyd Papers, file Premier 214, Radio address, 26 June 1962.
60. Blakeney Papers, Addenda II.15 file, Memo, 12 July 1962; SCPS Records, Council minutes, 29-30 June 1962.
61. Cf. W.W. Wigle, president-elect of the CMA: "No one died for lack of medical care. Some people were a little inconvenienced . . . ." "Saskatchewan – Before, During and After," *CMA Journal*, 8 Sept. 1962, 574.
62. *Globe and Mail*, 3 July 1962.
63. *New York Times*, 7 July 1962; Lloyd Papers, file 235f (13-1-5), Brockelbank to Dalgleish, 6 July 1962.
64. *Globe and Mail*, 7, 11 July 1962. See also *Financial Post*, 14 July 1962, and SCPS Records, file 4-5-14, CMA Public Relations Committee minutes, 15 July 1962.
65. *Globe and Mail*, 10 July 1962; Lloyd Papers, file Premier 214, radio address, 9 July 1962. On July 12 the NDP caucus was told that sixty-two doctors were working under the act. Ibid., file 413, Caucus minutes, 12 July 1962.
66. *New York Times*, 11, 12 July 1962; *Globe and Mail*, 12 July 1962; Hall MS, Chap. VIII, pp. 82-83.
67. Blakeney Papers, file II.5, Strategy Committee Notes, 9 July 1962.
68. Lloyd Papers, Premier 230 file, Memo of Conversation Lee-Goldenberg, 5 July 1962; Blakeney Papers, file II.12, R. Clarke to Blakeney, 7 July 1962 and atts.
69. Blakeney Papers, file II.5, Strategy Committee notes, 9 July 1962.

70. Lloyd Papers, file Premier 230, "Notes on Discussions of the Cabinet Strategy Committee," n.d.
71. Lord Taylor, "Personal View," *British Medical Journal*, XXVII (Jan. 1968), 246. I am grateful to Peter Neary for drawing this to my attention.
72. Lloyd Papers, file 235g(13-1-5), Dalgleish to Lloyd, 9 July, and reply 13 July 1962.
73. Ibid., Dalgleish to Lloyd, 14 July, and reply, 17 July 1962; SCPS Records, Dalgleish file, Dalgleish to A. Hill, 10 July 1962.
74. *Globe and Mail*, 13,14, 17 July 1962; Jeanine Locke, "Our Town Will Never Be the Same," *Star Weekly*, 4 Aug. 1962, 2ff.
75. SCPS Records, Speech by Dr. Dalgleish, 18 July 1962; *New York Times*, 19 July 1962.
76. Lloyd Papers, file 27-9 Cabinet Secretary, Lord Taylor transcript, n.d. A CMA account is in SCPS Records, file 4-0-2, A.D. Kelly to Members of Executive Committee. See also Kelly's "Saskatchewan Solomon," *CMA Journal*, 25 Aug. 1962. The Saskatoon agreement is in Lloyd Papers, file 230c(13-1-2).
77. Blakeney Papers, Addenda II.13 file, Blakeney to D. Lewis, 24 July 1962.
78. SCPS Records, Newsletter, 23 July 1962.
79. *Globe and Mail*, 24 July 1962.
80. Lloyd Papers, file Premier 210, Lloyd to D. Lewis, 21 Aug. 1962; ibid., file Premier 232, T. Lee to G. Cadbury, 10 Aug. 1962.
81. Ibid., file 14a(1413), "Community Health Associations," 20 Aug. 1962; cited in ibid., file 43e-5, Lloyd to Dalgleish, 10 Sept. 1962. See Tollefson tapes, Dr. Wolfe interview, 1 June 1966.
82. R. Spasoff and S. Wolfe, "Trends in the Supply and Distribution of Physicians in Saskatchewan," *CMA Journal*, 6 Mar. 1965, 523-28; MacTaggart, pp. 130-31; but cf. SCPS Records, Dalgleish's "The Saskatchewan Experience," address in Montreal, 4 Mar. 1963.
83. Lloyd Papers, file Premier 240a, "Physicians Requesting Payment by MCIC."
84. Ibid., file Premier 232, Taylor to Lloyd, 15 Mar. 1963. See also Joan Hollobon, *Bungle, Truce and Trouble* (Toronto, 1963); Hall MS, Chap. VIII, p. 91.
85. Blakeney Papers, file 43e-2, Memo, Molnar to Clarkson and Tansley, 22 Oct. 1963; Lloyd Papers, file 460, Lloyd to Coldwell, 27 Apr. 1964; PAC, M.J. Coldwell Papers, vol. 27, Lloyd file, Lloyd to Coldwell, 9 Apr. 1964.
86. Tollefson tapes, Thatcher interview, 26 May 1966. See also E.A. Tollefson, "The Aftermath of the Medicare Dispute in Saskatchewan," *Queen's Quarterly*, LXXII (Autumn, 1965), 453ff.
87. PAC, J. Waldo Monteith Papers, vol. 2, "Memorandum on the National Health Program," 20 Oct. 1960, esp. pp. 48ff.
88. See, e.g., docs. on PAC, R.G. 33/78, vol. 37, file 4-0, vol. 39, file 7-2 and 6-2.
89. PAC, Stursberg Papers, Hall interview, 30 Apr. 1974.
90. R.G. 33/78, vol. 39, file 7-2, 3 July 1964; J.T. Saywell, ed., *Canadian Annual Review, 1964* (Toronto, 1965), p. 394.
91. R.B. Bryce interview, 3 Nov. 1982; R.G. 33/78, vol. 45, "Discussion with Province of Ontario . . ." 8-9 Apr. 1965, etc.; vol. 37, file 4-0, Manning to Pearson, 3 July 1969.

92. Johnson interview, 21 Mar. 1983.
93. Taylor, pp. 364-66; Department of Finance Records, vol. 4719, file 5515-04(65/1)-1, Johnson memo for file, 8 July 1965 and vol. 4854, file 5508-2, Johnson to Bryce, 16 July 1965.
94. Stursberg Papers, LaMarsh interview, 28 May 1975.
95. PAC, Fulton Papers, vol. 128, Medicare file, Manning to Fulton, 11 Aug. 1966.
96. Taylor, pp. 370-72; Walter Gordon, *A Political Memoir* (Toronto, 1977), pp. 247-48; Judy LaMarsh, *Memoirs of a Bird in a Gilded Cage* (Toronto, 1968), pp. 323-25.
97. Queen's University Archives, John Matheson Papers, MacEachen to M.P.s, 25 Aug. 1967.
98. Fulton Papers, vol. 128, Medicare file, Fulton to R.D. Pilling, 6 Nov. 1967.
99. W.L. Gordon Papers (Toronto), Pearson file, Gordon to Pearson, 1 Nov. 1967; Gordon, pp. 294-95, 306.
100. Denis Smith, *Gentle Patriot: A Political Biography of Walter Gordon* (Edmonton, 1973), pp. 333-36; Gordon Papers, Pearson file, "Medicare," pen memo for Cabinet, 20 Nov. 1967.
101. Ibid., Gordon to Pearson, 19 Jan. 1968 (not sent); Gordon, pp. 306-7.
102. Taylor, pp. 376ff.

NOTES TO CHAPTER EIGHT

1. G. Ignatieff, MS "Pearson's Postwar Decade."
2. W.L. Gordon Papers (Toronto), Pearson file, "re Mike Pearson," 5 Dec. 1972. This sentence is omitted from Gordon's *A Political Memoir* (Toronto, 1977), p. 331.
3. Hellyer interview, 29 Mar. 1983.
4. Based on interviews with Geoffrey Pearson, 10 Jan. 1979, Rt. Hon. Jules Léger, 17 Nov. 1978, Mrs. N.A. Robertson, 23 Oct. 1978, G.C. Andrew, 29 Apr. 1978; Thomas Barman, *Diplomatic Correspondent* (New York, 1969), pp. 252-54; and C.S.A. Ritchie, "One of the Great Negotiatiors . . .", *International Perspectives*, March/April, 1973, 54.
5. University of Victoria, George Pearkes Papers, vol. 3, Report of Resolutions Committee, General Meeting, P.C. Association of Canada, 30 Nov.-2 Dec. 1959.
6. See esp. PAC, L.B. Pearson Papers, N3, vol. 62, file 306 Conf., Kent to Prime Minister, 7 Apr. 1964.
7. Ibid., N7, vol. 3, Canadian Flag file, pencil memo, n.d. [17 May 1964].
8. Queen's University Archives, T.A. Crerar Papers, vol. 91, Creighton *et al.* to Pearson, 27 May 1964. The Canadian Institute of Public Opinion in June 1964 found 2-to-1 support for Pearson's design.
9. 21 May 1964 in J.T. Saywell, ed., *Canadian Annual Review, 1964* (Toronto, 1965), p. 23.
10. Ibid., p. 25; J.G. Diefenbaker, *One Canada: The Memoirs of the Rt. Hon. John G. Diefenbaker* (Toronto, 1977), III, 221ff.
11. PAC, Paul Hellyer Papers, vol. 57, Flag file, Hellyer to A. Davidge, 16 Sept. 1964.
12. PAC, Gordon Churchill Papers, vol. 91, Flag Debate file, Pickersgill note, n.d.

13. Ibid., vol. 105, Diefenbaker file, Memo, 24 July 1964.
14. Gordon Papers, Pearson file, Memo to Prime Minister, 31 Aug. 1964.
15. Pearson Papers, N3, vol. 291, file 912.1 Policy, Pearson to R. Marcotte, 30 Sept. 1964; *CAR, 1964*, p. 29.
16. PAC, J.W. Monteith Papers, vol. 13, Flag Committee Minutes, 21 Sept.-28 Oct. 1964. Cf. Diefenbaker III, 225.
17. Gordon Churchill Papers (Mill Bay, B.C.), MS "Recollections," Chap. XIX.
18. Paul Hellyer Papers (Toronto), Diary, 15 Feb. 1965.
19. The best account is J.F. Keeley, "Cast in Concrete for All Time? The Negotiation of the Auto Pact," *Canadian Journal of Political Science*, XVI (June 1983), 281ff.
20. Bank of Canada Archives, Louis Rasminsky Papers, LR76-560-1, Memo from Commissioner, 8 Nov. 1960; ibid., LR76-560-2, Report of the Royal Commission . . . Tariff Proposals, 27 Apr. 1961; PAC, Donald Fleming Papers, vol. 162, Cabinet Committee on Balance of Payments, 2 Aug. 1962; J.F. Kennedy Library, Christian Herter Papers, vol. 7, Tel. Rusk to Embassy Ottawa, 24 Oct. 1963 and Hudec memo, 30 Oct. 1963.
21. Herter Papers, vol. 7, "Legal Aspects . . .," 9 Dec. 1963; Kennedy Library, J.N. Behrman Papers, vol. 8, McNeill to Undersecretary of Commerce, 23 Apr. 1964.
22. PAC, Department of Finance Records, vol. 3496, file 8705-01, Record of Cabinet Decision, 11 June 1964; Behrman Papers, vol. 8, "Report on the Canadian Auto Tariff Remission Scheme," n.d.
23. Herter Papers, vol. 14, Trezise and McNeill to Hodges and Ball, 29 Sept. 1964; Department of Finance Records, docs. in vol. 3946, file 8705-01.
24. Lyndon B. Johnson Library, H.H. Wilson Papers, vol. 1, Canada file, Wilson to Moyers, 25 Nov. 1964 (2 memos).
25. Gordon, p. 169. Gordon told the Liberal caucus that to get the Auto Pact Canada had to exempt *Time* and *Reader's Digest* from legislation to control foreign influence in the magazine industry. "I said I did not like the *Time* exemption any more than they did, but this was the price we had to pay. . . ." Denis Smith, *Gentle Patriot: A Political Biography of Walter Gordon* (Edmonton, 1973), p. 231. Pearson flatly denied any trade-off: *Mike: The Memoirs of the Rt. Hon. Lester B. Pearson* (Toronto, 1975), III, 134.
26. Johnson Library, L.B. Johnson Papers, NSF Records, vol. 8, Memos to President, Bundy to President, 18 Jan. 1965.
27. Ibid., Council of Economic Advisers Records, mf. 44, Joint U.S.-Canadian Committee on Trade and Economic Affairs 1967 file, Position Paper, n.d.
28. Lawrence Martin, *The Presidents and the Prime Ministers* (Toronto, 1982), p. 219; PAC, Paul Martin Papers, vol. 352, tape 11, side 2, pp. 28ff. See figures in *Globe and Mail*, 29 Mar. 1980, 27 Feb. 1982.
29. John Holmes, "Canada and the Vietnam War," in J.L. Granatstein and R.D. Cuff, eds., *War and Society in North America* (Toronto, 1971), pp. 186ff.
30. Charles Taylor, *Snow Job* (Toronto, 1974), pp. 5ff.; Ramesh Thakur, "Peacekeeping and Foreign

Policy: Canada, India and the International Commission in Viet Nam 1954-65," *British Journal of International Studies*, VI (1980), 125ff. The best account is Douglas Ross, *In the Interests of Peace: Canada and Viet Nam 1954-1973* (Toronto, 1984).

31. Johnson Papers, National Security Files, Aides Files, Memos to President, box 1, vol. 3, Bundy to President, 21 Apr. 1964; "Canada and the Pentagon Papers," *Canadian Forum* (Sept. 1973), 9.

32. Ibid., 9-10. See also Taylor, pp. 47ff.; Martin, p. 223.

33. "Canada and the Pentagon Papers," passim; Johnson Papers, National Security Files, Aides Files, Memos to President, box 2, vol. 7, Bundy to President, 23 Dec. 1964; Johnson Library, Oral History Transcripts, Chester Cooper interview, 9 July 1969.

34. Pearson, III, 138-39; Taylor, p. 39; Martin, p. 225.

35. Ibid., p. 226; Pearson, III, 139ff.; Charles Ritchie, *Storm Signals* (Toronto, 1983), pp. 81ff.

36. York University Archives, Robert Winters Papers, Correspondence 1940-69, unmarked file, Winters to daughter, 16 Dec. 1966 and att. See also Martin, p. 227; Taylor, pp. 38-39; Holmes, pp. 184ff.

37. See Cyril Levitt, *Children of Privilege: Student Revolt in the Sixties* (Toronto, 1984).

38. Claude Bissell, *Halfway Up Parnassus* (Toronto, 1974), Chap. VIII.

39. See Ian Hamilton, *The Children's Crusade* (Toronto, 1970).

40. See Gary Moffatt, *History of the Canadian Peace Movement* (St. Catharines, Ont., n.d.), pp. 81ff.

41. House of Commons *Debates*, 10 May 1967, p. 57. See, on Paul Martin's role, his *A Very Public Life* (Toronto, 1985), II, 423ff.

42. Gordon, pp. 281-82; Smith, p. 323.

43. Martin Papers, vol. 252, Memos to Minister, M. Jeffries to Martin, 15 May 1967.

44. Gordon Papers, Pearson file, pen note, 17 May 1967, 23 May 1967, and Gordon to Pearson, 19 May 1967, unsent.

45. Ibid., NATO meeting file, pen note, n.d.; Queen's University Archives, John Matheson Papers, vol. 15, file 68a, "Memo re Special Caucus Conference, 23-4 September 1967," p. 26.

46. Martin Papers, vol. 357, External Affairs 1967 file, "A private discussion . . ." 25 May 1967.

47. Gordon Papers, file E-50, Gordon to G. Awde, 5 Oct. 1967; Matheson Papers, vol. 15, file 68a, Caucus Conference.

48. W.L. Gordon, *Troubled Canada* (Toronto, 1961), p. 127; see Gordon Papers, docs. in file F2-C4.

49. Rasminsky Papers, file LR76-593-1, Rasminsky to J. Fayerweather, 1 Apr. 1971; and file LR76-575-14, Extracts from Bank of Canada Record, 30 Jan. 1967; Kennedy Papers, NSF Records, vol. 19, Tel. Butterworth to Secretary of State, 29 July 1963.

50. Gordon Papers, Pearson file, Memo to Prime Minister, 5 Nov. 1963; Gordon, *A Political Memoir*, p. 351; Rasminsky Papers, file LR76-576-1-9, Note of Telephone Call, 30 July 1963; Kennedy Papers, NSF Records, vol. 19, Tel., 29 July 1963.

51. Gordon, *A Political Memoir*, p. 214.

52. Rasminsky Papers, file LR76-576-4-11, Ritchie to External, 9 Aug.

1966, and file LR76-576-4-13, 11 Nov. 1966.

53. Joseph Wearing, *The L-Shaped Party* (Toronto, 1981), pp. 73ff.

54. Gordon Papers, Pearson file, pen memo, 22 Dec. 1966 and 29 Dec. 1966; Notes of Matters to discuss with Mike on 29 Dec. 1966 and Memo, Gordon to Pearson, 29 Dec. 1966.

55. Ibid., Memo, 4 Jan. 1967.

56. Ibid., 18 Jan. 1967. See Gordon, *A Political Memoir*, App. 7, which omits the derogatory reference to Pearson.

57. Ibid., Conversation with LBP, 9 Feb. 1967, and pen memo, 23 Feb. 1967; Memo by Hon. E.J. Benson, 24 Feb. 1967; "Notes of my remarks to Cabinet yesterday . . ." 24 Feb. 1967; Memo of Discussion in the PM's Office, 24 Feb. 1967.

58. Ibid., "The Commitments Made to Me," 7 Mar. 1967. A book-length account is John Fayerweather, *The Mercantile Bank Affair* (New York, 1974).

59. Matheson Papers, vol. 15, file 68a, Memo re Special Caucus Conference, 23-24 Sept. 1967.

NOTES TO CHAPTER NINE

1. R.L. Raymont, "The Evolution of the Structure of the Department of National Defence 1945-1968," a report to the Task Force on Review of Unification of the Canadian Armed Forces, 30 Nov. 1979, copy in Department of National Defence, Directorate of History. See also University of Victoria Archives, George Pearkes Papers, [R.H. Roy] Interview with General C. Foulkes, 5 June 1967, transcript.

2. Raymont report.

3. Directorate of History, Records, file 101.009 (D53), Memo, Foulkes to F.R. Miller, 23 May 1957; ibid., Foulkes Papers, Integration file, "Study on a Reorganization of Canadian Armed Forces," Nov. 1957; Pearkes Papers, Foulkes interview.

4. Ibid. See also *Royal Commission on Government Organization, Report 20: Department of National Defence* (Ottawa, 1962) for a critical look at defence organization. Cf. Directorate of History, Records, file 78/165, Gen. R.M. Withers, "Integration/Unification Paper," 27 Jan. 1978, p. 7.

5. PAC, Paul Hellyer Papers, vol. 314, Memo, Nov. 1962. For Hellyer's earlier views, see J.W. Pickersgill Papers (Ottawa), vol. 256, NLF file, Memo, 14 Feb. 1962. See also Judy LaMarsh, *Memoirs of a Bird in a Gilded Cage* (Toronto, 1969), pp. 18ff.; David Burke, "The Unification of the Canadian Armed Forces: The Politics of Defense in the Pearson Administration," Ph.D. thesis, Harvard Univ., 1975, 92ff.

6. Hellyer interview, 29 Mar. 1983; PAC, Paul Martin Papers, vol. 352, Tape 11.1, p. 20.

7. Paul Hellyer Papers (Toronto), Hellyer to Pearson, 31 Dec. 1962.

8. PAC, Hellyer Papers, vol. 422, "Proposals for a Liberal Defence Policy," n.d. [21 Dec. 1962]. See also Gellner's "Background to Canadian Unification," in *Brassey's Annual 1967*, pp. 98ff.

9. R.I. Hendy Papers (Toronto), Hellyer to Irene Downham, 30 Sept. 1966; PAC, Hellyer Papers, vol. 60, "Defence Expenditures in Relation to Total Federal Government Expenditures," 6 Sept. 1966; Hellyer

interview; House of Commons Special Committee on Defence, 17-18 Dec. 1963, Third Report to House, p. 805.

10. Hellyer interview.

11. PAC, Hellyer Papers, vol. 52, "Report of the Ad Hoc Committee on Defence Policy," 30 Sept. 1963.

12. Ibid., vol. 422, Hellyer to Pearson, 25 Sept. 1963.

13. Directorate of History, Records, file 73/1223, Ser. IV, Defence Policy Review 1963, Sutherland to Minister, 30 Sept. 1963.

14. Department of External Affairs, External Affairs files, file 3-2-2, Washington Embassy, Memo for Ambassador, 10 Oct. 1963; Foulkes Papers, Tackaberry files, R.J. Gray to R.B. Tackaberry, 1 May 1969.

15. Directorate of History, Chairman, Chiefs of Staff Committee Records, Canadian Defence Policy, vol. 2, N.A. Robertson to F.R. Miller, 19 Aug. 1963, and Hellyer to Paul Martin, 31 Oct. 1963.

16. Hellyer interview; PAC, Hellyer Papers, vol. 60, "Background to the White Paper on Defence," n.d., by G/ C William Lee.

17. Ibid., vol. 7, White Paper file, letters and memos, 20 Dec. 1963.

18. Ibid., vol. 52, Martin to Hellyer, 21 Dec. 1963.

19. Ibid., vol. 167, Hellyer to Pearson, 27 Dec. 1963. See T. Robertson, "The Real Reason for Putting Them All Together," *The Canadian*, 15 Oct. 1966, which suggests this; Pearson, however, said this was not his reason. PAC, L.B. Pearson Papers, N4, vol. 37, file 100.82 Policy, R.O'H[agan] to Prime Minister, 29 Aug. 1966.

20. Chairman, Chiefs of Staff Committee Records, White Paper file, Hellyer to Miller, 30 Dec. 1963.

21. Hellyer Papers (Toronto), Diary, 7 and 8 Feb. 1964. The issue of civilian control is dealt with in R.B. Byers, "Canadian Civil-Military Relations and Reorganization of the Armed Forces: Whither Civil Control?" in H. Massey, ed., *The Canadian Military* (Toronto, 1972), pp. 197ff.

22. Hellyer Papers (Toronto), Diary, 10, 12, and 22 Feb. 1964. Rayner's later account is in Hendy Papers, "Comments on Page 2," att. to Hellyer to Downham, 30 Sept. 1966.

23. PAC, Hellyer Papers, vol. 315, Minutes of Cabinet Committee on External Affairs and Defence, 24 Mar. 1964. Cf. Walter Gordon, *A Political Memoir* (Toronto, 1977), p. 279.

24. PAC, Hellyer Papers, vol. 430, Comments on Burke thesis.

25. *White Paper on Defence* (Ottawa, 1964), pp. 17ff.

26. Directorate of History, Records, file 80/225, folder 72, Commander B.C. Thillaye, "Thoughts on the Profession of Arms in Postwar Canada."

27. Ibid., folder 9, Address to Canadian Club, Toronto, 3 Oct. 1966. See also J.L. Granatstein, "All Things to All Men: Triservice Unification," in S. Clarkson, ed., *An Independent Foreign Policy for Canada?* (Toronto, 1968), pp. 141ff. PAC, Hellyer Papers, vol. 60, "TRIO" and "Charge No. 2" refer to this.

28. Hellyer Papers (Toronto), Diary, 26 Mar. 1964; House of Commons *Debates*, 26 Mar. 1964, pp. 1485-86; PAC, Hellyer Papers, vol. 60, "Background to the White Paper," prints the Chiefs' messages; Directorate of History, Records, file 73/230, CNS "Remarks on the White Paper,"

May 1964.

29. Gellner in *Commentator*, May, September 1964; J.T. Saywell, ed., *The Canadian Annual Review 1964* (Toronto, 1965), pp. 215-16.

30. L. Beaton, "The Canadian White Paper on Defence," *International Journal*, XIX (Summer 1964), 364ff.; C. Girard, *Canada in World Affairs 1963-65* (Toronto, 1980), pp. 272-74; V.J. Kronenberg, *All Together Now* (Toronto, 1973), pp. 9ff. Less favourable was NDP defence critic Andrew Brewin in *Stand on Guard* (Toronto, 1965), pp. 95ff.

31. Copy in PAC, Hellyer Papers, vol. 7, "Report to Chiefs of Staff Committee, An Organization for Canadian Forces Headquarters," 16 Apr. 1964; copy in Directorate of History, Records, file 101.009 (D102), folder 1.

32. Hellyer Papers (Toronto), Diary, 31 July 1964.

33. Ibid., 1 Aug. 1964.

34. Ibid., 19 Nov. 1964.

35. Directorate of History, Records, file 73/220, Minutes of Chief of Defence Staff Conference, 19-20 Nov. 1964; *Globe and Mail*, 6 Oct. 1966; J.T. Saywell, ed., *The Canadian Annual Review 1966* (Toronto, 1967), p. 237. Material in Directorate of History, Records, file 112.11.003(D3) indicates morale difficulties from 1963 on.

36. Hendy Papers, Hendy to Hellyer, 6 Jan. 1965.

37. PAC, Hellyer Papers, vol. 430, transcript of interview by W.A.B. Douglas, 1 Nov. 1978. See also Kronenberg, passim, and Burke "Unification." pp. 221-22.

38. PAC, Hellyer Papers, vol. 60, "Background to the White Paper"; Hendy Papers, Hellyer to Downham, 30 Sept. 1966.

39. Hellyer Papers (Toronto), Diary, 29 Mar. 1965.

40. Ibid., 7-8 June 1965. See also Directorate of History, Records, file 73/1213, for minutes and papers of the Central Integration Coordination Group.

41. Ibid., Defence Council Minutes, 19 Oct. 1964 and att. memo, 13 Oct. 1964; ibid., file 112.11. 003(D3), Integrated Defence Program-1967-Book 1, Part A, foreword, 12 July 1966; Burke, "Unification," pp. 364ff.

42. W.L. Gordon Papers (Toronto), Pearson file, Memo to Prime Minister, 21 Nov. 1964.

43. Hellyer Papers (Toronto), Diary, 28 Sept. 1964.

44. Ibid., 27 Oct. 1964.

45. Raymont report, pp. 15ff. Hellyer's version was that the RCAF wanted a new American-made fighter-bomber, the F-4, but there was insufficient money to pay for this aircraft. Thus the department was looking for something to keep the aviation industry alive, to let airmen relearn the tactical support role, and to convert to an advanced trainer when a tactical fighter reached the top of the priority list. "The airmen," Hellyer said, "could never accept the fact that their requirements shouldn't come first. They wanted the F-4 and they wanted it then." When the paper rating the A-7 and the A-4 was produced, the RCAF knew that Hellyer would not accept them and their ranking was designed to force him to buy the F-4 "at a time when there was no way that purchase could be justified on the basis of an 'integrated' force." PAC, Hellyer Papers, vol. 430, Comments on Burke thesis.

46. Hellyer Papers (Toronto), Diary, 21 Dec. 1965.
47. PAC, Hellyer Papers, vol. 7, "Summary Record of the Discussion at Defence Council on 21 Dec. 1965 . . ."
48. Hellyer interview.
49. Ibid.; Burke, "Unification," p. 232; PAC, Hellyer Papers, vol. 235, Personal file, M. Goldfarb to A. Scott, 25 Aug. 1966.
50. Hellyer Papers (Toronto), Hellyer to Pearson, 27 Jan. 1966, and reply, 4 Feb. 1966. The same letter in Pearson Papers, N4, vol. 276, file 100.8, is dated 7 Feb. 1966. Hellyer's memo to Cabinet setting out the changes to the National Defence Act was dated 3 Aug. 1966 and called for a 164-clause bill. Cabinet Document 470/66, copy in PAC, Hellyer Papers, vol. 422. See generally, T. Axworthy, "Soldiers Without Enemies: A Political Analysis of Canadian Defence Policy, 1945-75," Ph.D. thesis, Queen's Univ., 1979, and R.B. Byers, "Reorganization of the Canadian Armed Forces: Parliamentary, Military and Interest Group Perceptions," Ph.D. thesis, Carleton Univ., 1970.
51. Burke, "Unification," pp. 253ff.
52. PAC, Hellyer Papers, vol. 430, Comments on Burke thesis; Hendy Papers, Miller to Hendy, 27 Mar. 1967.
53. Hellyer Papers (Toronto), Memo, Lee to Hellyer, 7 June 1966; PAC, Hellyer Papers, vol. 430, Douglas interview transcript. On Allard's views, see his *Mémoires du Général Jean V. Allard* (Boucherville, Qué., 1985), passim and pp. 369ff.
54. The best printed account is David Burke, "Hellyer and Landymore: The Unification of the Canadian Armed Forces and an Admiral's Revolt," *American Review of Canadian Studies*, VIII (Autumn 1978), 3ff.
55. House of Commons Standing Committee on National Defence, *Minutes*, 23 June 1966, pp. 336-37.
56. The list of senior officers retired between 1 Jan. 1965 and 30 Aug. 1966 comprised seventy-nine names. See Parliamentary Return 3003, 5 Oct. 1966, copy in PAC, Hellyer Papers, vol. 60. By Aug. 1966, only two of the thirteen most senior officers had held their posts longer than one month. A.K. Cameron, "The Royal Canadian Navy and the Unification Crisis," in J.A. Boutilier, ed., *RCN in Retrospect 1910-68* (Vancouver, 1982), p. 341.
57. Quoted in Burke, "Unification," p. 266.
58. Ibid.; *Globe and Mail*, 16 July 1966; Allard, pp. 382-83.
59. Pearson Papers, N4, vol. 37, file 100.82, Pearson to Hellyer, 16 July 1966 and 17 Aug. 1966; Hellyer to Pearson, 11 Aug. 1966.
60. Hendy Papers, tel. Hendy to Groos, 29 June 1966.
61. Ibid., Hilborn to J.G.K. Strathy *et al.*, 25 July 1966, and Hilborn to Landymore, 10 Aug. 1966.
62. This account is based on the Hendy Papers and on D.T. Simcoff, "The Opposition of the Progressive Conservative Party, the Tri-Service Identities Organization, and Senior Officers to Bill C-243 . . ." M.A. thesis, Univ. of Manitoba, 1974, pp. 37ff.; PAC, Hellyer Papers, vol. 49, material on TRIO file; W.A. Morrison, *The Voice of Defence: The History of the Conference of Defence Associations* (Ottawa, 1982), pp. 194ff.
63. Hellyer Papers (Toronto), Diary, 18 and 19 July 1966. Cf. Cameron, p. 341; J. Brock, *With Many Voices*

(Toronto, 1983), II, 217-18.
64. Hellyer Papers (Toronto), Diary, 2 Aug. 1966.
65. Ibid., 9 Aug. 1966.
66. Hendy Papers, Hellyer to Downham, 30 Sept. 1966.
67. House of Commons *Debates*, 4 Nov. 1966, pp. 9574-78.
68. Hellyer Papers (Toronto), Diary, 9, 10, and 14 Nov. 1966. Cf. Brock, II, 245.
69. Hellyer Papers (Toronto), Diary, 7 Dec. 1966.
70. *Toronto Star*, 15 Feb. 1967; Brock, II, 254ff.; Hendy Papers, Harkness to Hendy, 24 Jan. 1967, indicates TRIO also passed along questions.
71. House of Commons Standing Committee on National Defence, *Minutes*, 14 Feb. 1967, pp. 950ff.
72. Ibid., 15 Feb. 1967, p. 1060.
73. Hellyer Papers (Toronto), Diary, 16 Feb. 1967.
74. Ibid., 23 Feb. 1967.
75. Ibid., 24 Feb. 1967; *Globe and Mail*, 24 Feb. 1967; Brock, II, 293ff.
76. Hellyer Papers (Toronto), Diary, 28 Feb. 1967; *Globe and Mail*, 28 Feb., 1 Mar. 1967.
77. PAC, Hellyer Papers, vol. 430, Comments on Burke thesis.
78. Hellyer Papers (Toronto), Diary, 1, 2 Mar. 1967.
79. Hellyer interview. But cf. *Globe and Mail*, 1 Apr. 1967.
80. Foulkes Papers, Defence Committee 1967 file, Winch to Foulkes, 24 Feb. 1967. The guillotine was a new procedure sanctioned by the 1965 Standing Orders. See *Globe and Mail*, 19 Apr. 1967.
81. Ibid., 21 Nov. 1966; Kildare Dobbs, "Hellyer and the Admirals," *Saturday Night* (Sept. 1966), 21ff.

NOTES TO CHAPTER TEN

1. Fondation Lionel-Groulx, Institut d'histoire de l'Amérique français, Fonds André Laurendeau, vol. 7, f.59, Ballantyne-Laurendeau Correspondence, 12 Sept. 1956 ff.
2. See Ramsay Cook, "The Canadian Dilemma," *International Journal*, XX (Winter 1964-65), 3.
3. Fonds Laurendeau, vol. 8, f.63, Léger to Laurendeau, 30 Sept. 1960. On Léger to 1960, see Micheline Lachance, *Le Prince de l'Eglise* (Montréal, 1982). See also Michael Behiels, *Prelude to Quebec's Quiet Revolution* (Montreal, 1985).
4. Fonds Laurendeau, vol. 8, f.63, Laurendeau to Léger, 18 Oct. 1960.
5. Ibid., f.64, Laurendeau-Frère Pierre-Jérôme [J.-P. Desbiens] Correspondence.
6. *Census of Canada 1961*, series 1.2-9, Population: Official Language and Mother Tongue.
7. Fonds Laurendeau, vol. 8, f.67, Forsey to Laurendeau, 7 Nov. 1961. See also Forsey's "Canada: Two Nations or One?" *Canadian Journal of Economics and Political Science*, XXVIII (Nov. 1962), 485ff.; Ramsav Cook, "A Time to Break Silence," *Canadian Forum* (July 1963).
8. *Le Devoir*, 20 janvier 1962. See also Marc LaTerreur, *Les Tribulations des Conservateurs au Québec: de Bennett à Diefenbaker* (Québec, 1973), Chap. VIII.
9. Fonds Laurendeau, Royal Commission files, Committee on French-English Relations file, Resumé of Discussion, 21 Feb. 1962.

10. Quoted in Cook, "Dilemma," 9.
11. Fonds Laurendeau, vol. 9, f.69, Groulx to Laurendeau, n.d.
12. House of Commons *Debates*, 17 Dec. 1962, pp. 2722-26; L.B. Pearson, *Mike: The Memoirs of the Rt. Hon, Lester B. Pearson* (Toronto, 1975), III, 67-69. See also Fonds Laurendeau, Journal des rencontres avec les premiers provinciaux, 189; Peter Stursberg, *Lester Pearson and the Dream of Unity* (Toronto, 1978), pp. 7ff.
13. PC 1963-1106, 19 July 1963; Pearson, III, 240-41.
14. Fonds Laurendeau, Royal Commission files, Notes et Réflexions file, note, n.d.
15. Ibid., vol. 9, f. 73, J.-P. Desbiens [Frère Pierre-Jérôme] to Laurendeau, 22 Aug. 1963.
16. PAC, R.G. 33/80, vol. 220, Minutes of 4th Meeting, 6 Nov. 1963.
17. Ibid., Minutes of 6th, 7th, 8th Meetings; H.B. Neatby interview, 11 Dec. 1982.
18. Fonds Laurendeau, Royal Commission files, "Bulletin de la Recherche," n.d.
19. Ibid., Oliver file, Oliver to Laurendeau and Dunton, 16 Sept. 1964.
20. Neatby interview.
21. R.G. 33/80, vol. 220, Minutes of 1st Meeting, 4 Sept. 1964.
22. Ibid., docs. 102E, 5 Dec. 1963, 157F, 3 février 1964, 529E, 10 Dec. 1964, 720E, 29 Sept. 1965, 378E and 380F, 13 July 1964.
23. Fonds Laurendeau, Journal, 24ff.; R.G. 33/80, doc. 340F, 2 juillet 1964.
24. PAC, Liberal Party of Canada Records, vol. 1024, poll of 25 Jan. 1964.
25. Fonds Laurendeau, Royal Commission files, annexe II to 17e réunion, 15 juin 1964.
26. R.G. 33/80, vol. 220, 17th Meeting, 15 June 1964; 18th Meeting, 2 July 1964, annex II.
27. Fonds Laurendeau, Journal, 25, 30, 40.
28. Ibid., pp. 275ff.; Neatby interview.
29. R.G. 33/80, vol. 220, 19th Meeting, 2-3 Sept. 1964. On the origins of the preliminary report, see Fonds Laurendeau, Journal, 82, 90ff., 129ff.
30. *Preliminary Report of the Royal Commission on Bilingualism and Biculturalism* (Ottawa, 1965), p. 13.
31. Fonds Laurendeau, Royal Commission files, Colombie-Britannique correspondance file, F. Walden to Dr. G. Moreau, 15 Nov. 1965. See Pearson, III, p. 241 for Pearson's response to the preliminary report. The sharpest Quebec assault on the report came in *Cité Libre* (décembre 1965) where the theology, analysis, and sentiments of the commission were denounced. See also Denis Monière, *André Laurendeau* (Montréal, 1983), pp. 324-26.
32. J.T. Saywell, ed., *Canadian Annual Review* [*CAR*] *1965* (Toronto, 1966), p. 44.
33. R.G. 33/80, vol. 122, Tim Creery, "Notes on Premier Lesage's Western Tour," 14 Nov. 1965, doc. 751E; ibid., vol. 220, 38th Meeting, 15-17 Nov. 1965.
34. Fonds Laurendeau, Royal Commission files, Morrison file, Neil Morrison to G.F. Davidson, 25 Feb. 1966; ibid., budget file, P. Findlay to Co-Chairmen, 8 Nov. 1967.
35. *Report of the Royal Commission on Bilingualism and Biculturalism* (Ottawa, 1967), Book I.

36. Fonds Laurendeau, Royal Commission files, La réaction de la presse file, "Press Reactions to Vol. 1, March 1968."
37. Liberal Party of Canada Records, vol. 1024, poll, 23 Dec. 1967.
38. PAC, R.G. 33/46 vol. 571, Bilingualism file, Study Gp. No. 13 on Education, 11 Oct. 1961, "Notes on Problem of Bilingualism."
39. Privy Council Office, PCO Records, doc. on file A-35 (1959).
40. *Report of the Royal Commission on Organization of Government* (Ottawa, 1963), IV, 107.
41. Gary Caldwell, "The Participation of French Canadians in the Department of External Affairs," M.A. thesis, Université Laval, 1965, pp. 10-11; J.L. Granatstein, *A Man of Influence: Norman A. Robertson and Canadian Statecraft 1929-68* (Ottawa, 1981), pp. 359-61.
42. Fonds Laurendeau, Royal Commission files, "The Meaning of the Present Day System," Jan. 1962.
43. PAC, L.B. Pearson Papers, N3, vol. 24, file 043, Martin to Pearson, 12 June 1963; Department of External Affairs, External Affairs file 3-2-1, Robertson to Minister, 27 May 1963.
44. Ibid., Robertson to Minister, 27 July 1963.
45. E.g., see ibid., Robertson to Minister, 4 Sept. 1963.
46. Fonds Laurendeau, Royal Commission files, Anderson file, A.G. Instruction 63/8, 11 Dec. 1963.
47. W.L. Gordon Papers (Toronto), Pearson file, Memo to Prime Minister, 2 Jan. 1964.
48. Fonds Laurendeau, Royal Commission files, Entrevue No. 7 file, Interview, 18 Mar. 1965.
49. Pearson Papers, N3, vol. 24, file 043 Conf., Robertson to Pearson, 26 July 1965. See also Stursberg, pp. 314-15.
50. Liberal Party of Canada Records, vol. 716, Bi-Bi file, L. Francis to Pearson, 8 Jan. 1964.
51. R.G. 33/80, doc. 982E, 15 June 1966.
52. Ottawa *Journal*, 3 Mar. 1966; Pearson Papers. N4, vol. 32, file 043.3 Pers. and Conf., Pearson to Pepin, 8 Mar. 1966.
53. 8 Apr., 9 avr. 1966.
54. 26 Apr. 1966.
55. Pearson Papers, N4, vol. 32, file 043.6, Pers. and Conf., Cadieux to Prime Minister, 27 Nov. 1967; Lalonde to Prime Minister, 5 Dec. 1967 and Pitfield to Prime Minister, 1 Mar. 1968. See also J.V. Allard, *Mémoires du Général Jean V. Allard*(Boucherville, 1985), Chap. VIII.
56. PAC, Gordon Churchill Papers, vol. 28, Dominion-Provincial Conference (Oct. 1960), file, pencil note, n.d.
57. See Jean-Luc Pepin, "Cooperative Federalism," *Canadian Forum* (Dec. 1964), 206ff.; Ramsay Cook, *Canada and the French-Canadian Question* (Toronto, 1966), pp. 22, 67-68, 163-64.
58. On the elections of 1960 and 1962, see V. Lemieux, ed., *Quatre Elections provinciales du Québec* (Québec, 1969) and P.E. Trudeau, "l'Election du 22 juin 1960," *Cité Libre* (sept. 1960), 3ff. On Lesage's first two years, see Dale Thomson, *Jean Lesage and the Quiet Revolution* (Toronto, 1984), Part II.
59. On the strike see Gérard Pelletier, *Years of Impatience, 1950-1960* (Toronto, 1984), Chap. VIII.
60. Pearson Papers, N2, vol. 64, Pearson to T.A. Stone, 26 Mar. 1962. See also Richard Daignault, *Lesage* (Montréal, 1981), pp. 115ff., and Dale Posgate and Ken

McRoberts, *Quebec: Social Change and Political Crisis* (Toronto, 1976), Chap. VI.

61. PCO Records, file H-2-7(a), Bryce to Prime Minister, 17 Nov. 1961. See other docs. this file for detail on the P.C. plan.

62. See docs. in ibid. (1963), and Paul Hellyer's assault on the proposal in PAC, Hellyer Papers, vol. 167, "Canada Pension Plan: A Critique of Cab. Doc. 77/63 and Alternative Plan," 17 June 1963.

63. The Pearson government, most notably LaMarsh and Tom Kent, tried to use the pension plan against Premier Robarts in the election of 25 Sept. 1963, but this effort failed dismally. See docs. in PCO Records, file H-2-7(a), and Gordon Papers, Pearson file, Note for Mr. Pearson, 8 Aug. 1963.

64. Claude Morin, *Quebec Versus Ottawa* (Toronto, 1975), p. 7; Stursberg, p. 186.

65. Quebec's budgets were increasing at a staggering rate: in 1959, the budget proposed $419 million in operating expenses and $97 million in capital expenditures; in 1966 the figures were $1.74 billion and $318.7 million respectively. Daignault, p. 133. See also Thomson, pp. 186ff.

66. Pearson Papers, N3, vol. 62, Robertson to Pearson, 6 Apr. 1964.

67. Ibid., Kent to Prime Minister, 7 Apr. 1964.

68. Judy LaMarsh, *Memoirs of a Bird in a Gilded Cage* (Toronto, 1969), p. 127. The resulting CPP provided $104 a month (plus the $75 old age pension) to contributors who had paid 3 per cent of income (with their employers paying half).

69. Pearson Papers, N3, vol. 62, file 306 Pers., Pearson to Lesage, 22 Apr. 1964.

70. J.W. Pickersgill Papers (Ottawa), Lesage file, Pickersgill to Lesage, 22 Apr. 1964.

71. Fonds Laurendeau, Journal, 125-26.

72. Ibid., 142.

73. Jean Provencher, *René Lévesque: Portrait of a Québécois* (Toronto, 1975), p. 199.

74. See Cook, Chap. V, for a good discussion of associate state status; see also Cook in *Globe and Mail*, 3 Aug. 1967, on special status. On the strength of separatist sentiment in late 1963, see Peter Gzowski, "This Is the True Strength of Separatism," *Maclean's*, 2 Nov. 1963.

75. Also printed in *Canadian Forum* (May, 1964), pp. 29ff. On *Cité Libre*'s origins, see Pelletier, Chap. V, and Behiels, pp. 61ff.

76. See Hellyer Papers, vol. 52, Report to Minister file, Gen. Walsh to Minister of National Defence, Feb. 1964; Fonds Laurendeau, Journal, 209. On the Front pour la libération du Québec, see Louis Fournier, *F.L.Q.: The Anatomy of an Underground Movement* (Toronto, 1984), Part I.

77. P.E. Trudeau, *Federalism and the French Canadians* (Toronto, 1968), p. 212. For the contrasting views of *Le Devoir* in this period, see F. Dumont *et al.*, eds., *Idéologies au Canada français, 1940-76* (Québec, 1981), I, 101ff.

78. Fonds Laurendeau, Journal, 209.

79. PAC, Forsey Papers, vol. 5, Spry file, Forsey to G. Spry, 2 July 1964; vol. 3, Fulton file, Forsey to D. Fulton, 1 May 1964 and 2 July 1964.

80. Gordon Papers, Constitutional Amendment file, Cabinet Doc. 385/64, "Constitutional Amendment in Canada," 25 Aug. 1964. For

the Saskatchewan opinion, see Saskatchewan Archives, T.C. Douglas Papers, file 771 (23-35-4).

81. Gordon Papers, Constitutional Amendment file, Cab. Doc. 385/64.

82. Ibid., Bryce to Minister, 25 Sept. 1964.

83. *CAR 1964*, pp. 79-80. Eugene Forsey wrote to Diefenbaker to urge that he not "appear to be simply saying 'No' to anything and everything Quebec demands. . . ." Forsey Papers, vol. 3, Forsey to Diefenbaker, 17 Mar. 1965.

84. Guy Favreau, *The Amendment of the Constitution of Canada* (Ottawa, 1965).

85. Pearson, III, 252-53.

86. Cf. ibid., 220. See Pelletier and Trudeau's explanation of their decision to go to Ottawa in *Cité Libre* (oct. 1965), 3-5.

87. Published in Montréal, 1965. See also the UN programme in J.-L. Roy, *Les Programmes électoraux de Québec* (Montréal, 1971), II, 405ff.

88. Lesage urged his friends in Ottawa to delay any showdown with Johnson to make it "more difficult . . . for him to dissolve the legislature and use a fight with Ottawa as an electoral issue." Pickersgill Papers, Lesage file, Lesage to Pickersgill, 8 July 1966.

89. *CAR 1966*, p. 51. See PAC, Department of Finance Records, vol. 4854, file 5508-2, "Shared Cost Programs," 17 Dec. 1965 and other docs. on file.

90. 2 April 1966 in *CAR 1966*, p. 52. See Thomson, pp. 403-5.

91. Peter C. Newman, *The Distemper of Our Times* (Toronto, 1968), p. 326. See also P. Godin, *Daniel Johnson* (Montréal, 1980), II, 302-4.

92. See P.E. Trudeau, *A Canadian Charter of Human Rights* (Ottawa, 1968) and *Federalism for the Future* (Ottawa, 1968). For a Quebec critique, see Morin, Chap. XI. See also Trudeau's "A Constitutional Declaration of Rights" in Trudeau, *Federalism and the French Canadians*, pp. 52ff., and his proposals for constitutional reform in ibid., pp. 3ff.

93. This section has benefited greatly from my reading of draft chapters of John English's book on "Canada and World Affairs 1965-67," for which courtesy I am most grateful.

94. Pearson, III, 260-61; PAC, Paul Martin Papers, vol. 357, External Affairs 1967 file, Memo for Prime Minister, 24 Jan. 1967.

95. Ibid., vol. 225, Memo, Martin to Pearson, 24 Feb. 1967.

96. PAC, Jules Léger Papers, vol. 1, Cadieux file #2, Cadieux to Léger, 23 nov. 1964.

97. Ibid., Léger to Cadieux, 25 nov. 1964 and Cadieux to Léger, 19 nov. 1964.

98. *Round Table* (July 1967), 343.

99. Pearson Papers, N3, vol. 63, file 305, R.G. Robertson to Pearson, 29 Apr. 1965; Canada Council Records, Ottawa, Programme of Cultural Relations with Countries of French Expression, Dec. 1963; External Affairs file 3-2-1, N.A. Robertson to Minister, 27 July 1963.

100. Léger Papers, vol. 1, Cadieux file #2, Cadieux to Léger, 23 nov. and 3 dec. 1964.

101. Pearson Papers, N3, vol. 62, Martin to Pearson, 26 Apr. 1965. See Thomson, pp. 427ff.

102. Pearson Papers, N3, vol. 62, Martin to Pearson, 26 Apr. 1965.

103. Ibid., vol. 63, file 306, R.G. Robertson to Pearson, 27 Apr. 1965.

104. See ibid., vol. 62, Robertson to Pearson, 14 May 1965; see also Queen's University Archives, J.M. Macdonnell Papers, vol. 59, Paul Gérin-Lajoie to Macdonnell, 20 May 1965.

105. Léger Papers, vol. 1, Cadieux file #2, Léger to Cadieux, 25 nov. 1964.

106. Ibid., vol. 4, Martin file, Léger to Martin, 3 Feb. 1965.

107. Ibid., vol. 1, Cadieux file #2, Memo for USSEA, Jan. 1967 by J.H.

108. Martin Papers, vol. 357, External Affairs 1967 file, Memo for Prime Minister, 24 Jan. 1967.

109. Ibid., vol. 381, tape 8, side 1, pp. 22ff.; ibid., vol. 225, Pearson to Premier Johnson, 29 June 1967; Pearson Papers, vol. 258, docs. on file 846/F815 Conf.; and esp. Martin Papers, vol. 357, External Affairs 1967 file, Report from Department of External Affairs on the de Gaulle visit, 14 Aug. 1967.

110. Ibid., vol. 381, tape 8. See also Martin's *A Very Public Life* (Toronto, 1985), II, 594ff. Cf. Godin, *Johnson*, II, 214.

111. Martin Papers, vol. 357, External Affairs 1967 de Gaulle Visit file, SSEA to Pearson, 24 July 1967.

112. Léger Papers, Cadieux file #1, Cadieux Memo for Prime Minister, 10 Jan. 1968. For Johnson, see Godin, II, 232ff.; for Lesage's response, see Daignault, p. 249.

113. Jean Chapdelaine interview, 23 May 1983.

114. Martin Papers, vol. 357, Memo of telecon, SSEA and Ambassador, 25 July 1967.

115. Pearson, III, 267. See also T. Hewat, ed., *De Gaulle File* (London [?], n.d.), pp. 49ff., and R. Lescop, *Le Pari québécois du Général de Gaulle* (Montréal, 1981).

116. Martin Papers, vol. 357, de Gaulle visit file, Report from Department of External Affairs, 14 Aug. 1967; ibid., vol. 381, tape 8.

117. Ibid., vol. 357, External Affairs, Jul-Sep 1967 file, talk Martin-Couve, n.d.; ibid., vol. 381, tape 8.

118. Ibid., vol. 227, De Gaulle speeches file, Press Conference, 27 Nov. 1967.

119. Address given at Canadian Culture: International Dimensions Conference, University of Waterloo, 24 May 1983.

120. Daignault, pp. 249-50.

121. Provencher, pp. 233, 239ff.; Peter Desbarats, *René* (Toronto, 1976), p. 135; and esp. Graham Fraser, *P.Q.: René Lévesque and the Parti Québécois in Power* (Toronto, 1984), Chap. III. W.D. Coleman's *The Independence Movement in Quebec, 1945-80* (Toronto, 1984), is a very good account.

NOTES TO CHAPTER ELEVEN

1. W.L. Gordon Papers (Toronto), Post-Election Problems file, 1963, D. Stanley to Gordon, 16 Apr. 1963, J.W. Holmes to Gordon, 18 Apr. 1963, etc.

2. Privy Council Office, PCO Records, file F-1-8, Records of Cabinet Decision, 11 and 13 June 1964; L.B. Pearson, *Mike: The Memoirs of the Rt. Hon. Lester B. Pearson* (Toronto, 1975), III, 103-4; Denis Smith, *Gentle Patriot: A Political Biography of Walter Gordon* (Edmonton, 1973), pp. 146-49.

3. Bank of Canada Archives, Louis Rasminsky Papers, LR76-549, "Some

Comments on the Budget," 31 May 1963.

4. See Charles Ritchie, *Storm Signals* (Toronto, 1983), p. 52.

5. Peter Stursberg, *Lester Pearson and the Dream of Unity* (Toronto, 1978), pp. 126ff.; David Smith, *The Regional Decline of a National Party* (Toronto, 1981), pp. 155ff.; Judy LaMarsh, *Memoirs of a Bird in a Gilded Cage* (Toronto, 1968), p. 64.

6. Smith, pp. 172ff.

7. PAC, Forsey Papers, vol. 3, Knowles file, Forsey to S. Knowles, 25 July 1963.

8. PAC, Pearson Papers, N3, file 251-63 Personal and Conf., Pearson to C. Curtis, 15 July 1963; Queen's University Archives, T.A. Crerar Papers, vol. 131, Pearson to Crerar, 9 July 1963; PAC, A.D.P. Heeney Papers, vol. 2, Memoirs n.d. file, Diary, 23 Aug. 1963.

9. PAC, Election Expenses Committee Records, vol. 4, National Exec. Committee meeting, National Liberal Federation, 7 Mar. 1964.

10. The best account is Richard Gwyn, *The Shape of Scandal* (Toronto, 1965). See also Peter C. Newman, *The Distemper of Our Times* (Toronto, 1968), pp. 264ff.; PAC, Stursberg Papers, Nielsen interview transcript, 5 Mar. 1973; and John Diefenbaker, *One Canada: The Memoirs of the Rt. Hon. John G. Diefenbaker* (Toronto, 1977), III, 227ff. On Banks, see esp. W.E. Kaplan, "Communism, Corruption and Reform: A History of Maritime Unions in Canada, 1935-1967," unpublished M.A. thesis, Univ. of Toronto, 1985.

11. See "The Pearson Papers" in *Toronto Star*, 15 Mar. 1969; Pearson, III, 151ff.

12. Churchill Papers (Mill Bay, B.C.), MS "Recollections," Chap. XX.

13. Heeney Papers, vol. 2, Memoirs Chap. 18 file, diary, 5 Dec. 1964 and Dorion Inquiry file, typed diary entry and atts. Cf. LaMarsh, p. 148.

14. *Report of the Commissioner the Honourable Frédéric Dorion* (Ottawa, 1965), p. 135.

15. Newman, p. 276.

16. Ibid., pp. 281-83; Pearson, III, 164-65.

17. Stursberg Papers, Nielsen interview; Pearson, III, 161-62.

18. Gordon Papers, Pearson file, Gordon to Pearson, 5 Jan. 1965.

19. Ibid., 31 Mar. 1965; Pearson, III, 198.

20. Gordon Papers, Pearson file, Gordon to Pearson, 25 June 1965.

21. Pearson Papers, N3, vol. 60, file 304-1965.3, Kent to Pearson, 10 Aug. 1965; Pearson, III, 201-3.

22. Ibid., 203-4; Gordon Papers, Pearson file, Gordon to Prime Minister, 31 Aug. 1965.

23. Ibid., NLF, Davey to candidates, 23 Sept. 1965, and atts.

24. PAC, J.W. Monteith Papers, vol. 1, Diefenbaker file, Monteith to Diefenbaker, 31 Aug. 1965; Diefenbaker, III, Chap. X.

25. PAC, Alvin Hamilton Papers, vol. 207, Campaign Committee Meeting 1965 file, "Election Strategy," n.d., and R.A.F. [?] memo to Diefenbaker, 31 Aug. 1965.

26. PAC, CCF/NDP Records, vol. 366, Federal Executive Minutes, 12-13 Mar. 1965; PAC, Flora MacDonald Papers, vol. 46, PC Financial File, "Recapitulation, 1 September 1965-31 January 1966"; Election Expenses Committee Records, vol. 6, Notes file, J. Bury to H. Noble, 28 Jan. 1966.

27. CCF Records, vol. 366, Federal

Executive Minutes, 11 Sept. 1965.

28. Monteith Papers, vol. 13, Notes re Special Flag Committee, n.d.

29. PAC, Réal Caouette Papers, vol. 19, Memo, J.M.R. to R.N.T., 1 Oct. 1963.

30. See Diefenbaker, III, 261-62; Stursberg, *Dream of Unity*, pp. 128-30.

31. Confidential source.

32. Gordon Papers, Pearson file, Gordon to Pearson, 18 Oct. 1965.

33. J.W. Pickersgill Papers (Ottawa), Harris file, Pickersgill to Walter Harris, 16 Nov. 1965; Pearson Papers, N4, vol. 59, file 304-1965.5 Personal, Pearson to T.W.L. MacDermot, 24 Nov. 1965.

34. See Gordon Papers, Pearson file, Memos, 5 Dec. 1965 and 15 Jan. 1966; LaMarsh, pp. 74-75; Pearson, III, 209.

35. Pearson Papers, N4, vol. 276, file 100.6, Cardin to Pearson, 15 Nov. 1965 and att. memo, 28 Sept. 1965.

36. Ibid., "The Spencer and Munsinger Crises."

37. Ibid.; see also "The Pearson Papers," *Toronto Star*, 17 Mar. 1969.

38. Stursberg Papers, Cardin interview, 15 May 1975.

39. Stursberg Papers, Fulton interview, 5 Oct. 1972; ibid., Nielsen interview; Gordon Churchill in Winnipeg *Free Press*, 2 Apr. 1969; House of Commons *Debates*, 14 Mar. 1966, p. 2615.

40. PAC, R.G. 33/96, vol. 3, translations, 27 Mar., 3 Apr. 1966. See also Hees's interview with Pearson in Pearson Papers, N4, vol. 276, file 100.6, "Spencer and Munsinger Crises," postscript, 22 Mar. 1966.

41. PAC, Fulton Papers, vol. 123, Munsinger file, letter, 7 July 1966.

42. *Globe and Mail*, 29 Apr. 1966. See also Bain in ibid., 18-20 Mar. 1969.

43. "The Pearson Papers."

44. Pearson Papers, N4, vol. 35, file 100.2 "The Munsinger Case," 4 May 1966; ibid., vol. 276, file 100.6 "The Spencer and Munsinger Crises," 21 Mar. 1966.

45. Pearson Papers, N4, vol. 35, file 100.2, Munsinger, Diary, 10 Dec. 1964; Diefenbaker, III, 269-70; Churchill MS "Recollections," Chap. XXIII. See also R.W. Bowen, "No Refuge but Suicide," *Canadian Forum*, May 1984, 13-15.

46. See on the Spence Report, Diefenbaker, III, 272-73.

47. LaMarsh, p. 163.

48. PAC, Douglas Harkness Papers, vol. 91, Harkness to J.W. Murphy, 20 June, 3 Dec. 1963.

49. Saskatchewan Archives, R.L. Hanbidge Papers, box 1, file 1f, Diefenbaker to Hanbidge, 18 Oct. 1963.

50. Harkness Papers, vol. 91, Harkness to H.R. Milner, 13 Feb. 1964; Peter Stursberg, *Diefenbaker: Leadership Lost* (Toronto, 1976), p. 105.

51. Copy in Queen's University Archives, J.M. Macdonnell Papers, vol. 59; Diefenbaker, III, 221.

52. Fulton Papers, vol. 102, 1965 National Exec. Meeting file, pencil notes, 6 Feb. 1965.

53. Harkness Papers, vol. 91, Harkness to Milner, 1 Mar. 1965; Stursberg, *Leadership Lost*, pp. 115ff.

54. Monteith Papers, vol. 1, Mar. 1965 file, Notes, 14-18 Mar. 1965; Churchill, MS "Recollections," Chap. XXI; cf. Diefenbaker, III, 239-41.

55. E.g., see Fulton Papers, vols. 90-92, "Sussex" files.

56. CIPO data showed 48 per cent of

Conservatives and 64 per cent of all Canadians wanted Diefenbaker to retire (30 June 1965).

57. MacDonald Papers, vol. 42, Xmas memo 1966; Stursberg, *Leadership Lost*, pp. 164-65.

58. See R. McKeown, "The Man Who Caged the Lion," *Weekend*, 12 Aug. 1967, p. 2.

59. Ibid., and Churchill MS "Recollections," Chap. XXIV.

60. PAC, Churchill Papers, vol. 107, "re Camp revolt," 18 Nov. 1966; R. Coates, *The Night of the Knives* (Fredericton, 1969), passim; Diefenbaker, III, 273ff.; Jack Horner, *My Own Brand* (Edmonton, 1980), pp. 75ff.

61. Fulton Papers, vol. 92, Mitchell file, Fulton to Mitchell, 11 Oct. 1966.

62. Ibid., vol. 102, Criticism: Diefenbaker and Annual Meeting file, Fulton to G. Lodwick, 9 Dec. 1966; Stursberg, *Leadership Lost*, pp. 170ff.; Newman, pp. 142-45.

63. Churchill MS "Recollections," Chap. XXIV; Churchill Papers, vol. 107, "re Camp Revolt" and att. list of signers and non-signers; Douglas Fisher and Harry Crowe, Toronto *Telegram*, 16 Nov. 1966.

64. Macdonnell Papers, vol. 59, Sedgwick to R.A. Bell, 2 Dec. 1966 and Bell to Sedgwick, 12 Dec. 1966; Monteith Papers, vol. 1, Diefenbaker file, draft letter Monteith to Diefenbaker, 17 Jan. 1967.

65. J.T. Saywell, ed., *The Canadian Annual Review 1967* (Toronto, 1968), pp. 24-25.

66. Fulton Papers, vol. 90, Clark file.

67. Ibid., vol. 92, Bassett-Fulton correspondence.

68. Churchill MS "Recollections," Chap. XXV. On Diefenbaker's views, see PAC, B.T. Richardson Papers, vol. 16, file 161, Diefenbaker to Richardson, 20 June 1967.

69. Ibid., Memo on P.C. Convention, 10 Sept. 1967; Churchill interview, 9-10 June 1983; Donald Fleming, *So Very Near* (Toronto, 1985), II, 662ff.

70. See Dalton Camp, "Reflections on the Montmorency Conference," *Queen's Quarterly*, LXXVI (Summer, 1969), 185ff.

71. Gordon Churchill, "Deux Nations or One Canada: John Diefenbaker at the 1967 Conservative Convention," *Canadian Historical Review*, LXIV (Dec. 1983), 597ff.

72. Fulton Papers, vol. 110, Nova Scotia file, J. Miller to L. Murray, 26 June 1967. Cf. Monteith Papers, vol. 1, Fleming file, Monteith to Fleming, 26 Sept. 1967.

73. Churchill, "Deux Nations"; Diefenbaker, III, 282-83; Forsey Papers, vol. 3, Diefenbaker to Forsey, 20 Sept. 1967.

74. D. Peacock, *Journey to Power* (Toronto, 1968), Chap. III.

75. Churchill, "Deux Nations."

76. Harkness Papers, vol. 91, Convention 1967 file, Harkness to L. Haw, 12 Sept. 1967.

77. Peter Aucoin, "The Stanfield Era," *Dalhousie Review*, XLVII (Autumn, 1967), 400ff.; P. Grescoe, "The Key to Understanding Bob Stanfield," *The Canadian* (11 Nov. 1967).

NOTES TO CHAPTER TWELVE

1. PAC, R.A. Bell Papers, vol. 104, file A-7-8, Hamilton to Prime Minister, Dec. 1958.

2. Ibid., Hamilton to Fairclough, 20

Oct. 1958 and Neatby to Hamilton, 26 Mar. 1959.

3. Saskatchewan Archives, T.C. Douglas Papers, file 791(23-54), Memo on Inaugural Meeting, n.d.

4. W.L. Gordon Papers (Toronto), World's Fair file, R. Shaw to P. Dupuy, 5 Dec. 1963.

5. Ibid., Memo to Dupuy, Dec. 1963.

6. Ibid., "Economic Implications of Montreal's World's Fair," 19 Dec. 1963.

7. Vancouver *Sun*, 1 May 1967.

8. Harry Boyle, "Something Magical Has Happened," *Weekend Magazine*, 1 July 1967.

9. Vancouver *Sun*, 1 May 1967.

10. See, e.g., Winnipeg *Free Press* and *Globe and Mail*, 1 July 1967.

11. Senior Liberals agreed. See, e.g., York University Archives, Robert Winters Papers, box 1, Government file, C. Neiman to Winters, 23 Mar. 1966.

12. Paul Hellyer interview, 29 Mar. 1983. Pearson's account was different. Gordon Papers, Pearson file, Memo of Conversation with Pearson, 15 Jan. 1966.

13. Ibid., pen memo, 15 Mar. 1966, and memo, 14 June 1966.

14. PAC, Hellyer Papers, vol. 279, POL Notes file, G.C. Van Roggen to Hellyer, 26 Jan. 1967.

15. Ibid., Politics file, "Proposed Ontario Budget," n.d. and vol. 147, docs. on Federal Politics file.

16. Ibid., vol. 279, Politics file, "Private Report on lunch with Mike McCabe," n.d.

17. PAC, Paul Martin Papers, vol. 272, Agenda envelope, "Aims to be Discussed," 30 Oct. 1967.

18. PAC, Liberal Party of Canada Records, vol. 1024, poll, 20 Dec. 1967.

19. Ramsay Cook interview, 16 Aug. 1984; Toronto *Star*, 13 Jan. and 8 Apr. 1968. Perhaps surprisingly, John Diefenbaker wholeheartedly agreed. He did not know who would win the leadership, he wrote, but "if it is Trudeau (who stands for One Nation, not two, and no 'Special Status' for Quebec) I would be concerned for P.C. party hopes in the next General election in spite of his Leftist background." PAC, Diefenbaker Papers, Family Series, Diefenbaker to Elmer Diefenbaker, 9 Feb. 1968, f.5972. See also Martin Sullivan, *Mandate '68* (Toronto, 1968), Chap. XIII.

20. Gordon Papers, Pearson file, pen memo, 19 Dec. 1967.

21. Ibid., memo, 28 or 29 Dec. 1967.

22. Martin Papers, vol. 351, tape 1, side 2, pp. 74-75. See also Martin's *A Very Public Life* (Toronto, 1985), II, 606ff.

23. Winters Papers, box 1, Government federal file, Winters to B. Danson, 25 Feb. 1969.

24. PAC, Jules Léger Papers, vol. 2, general correspondence, R.G. Robertson to Léger, 3 Apr. 1968, and J.J. Connolly to Léger, 10 Apr. 1968.

Index

THE CANADIAN CENTENARY SERIES

A History of Canada in Nineteen Volumes

The Canadian Centenary Series is a comprehensive history of the peoples and lands which form the Dominion of Canada.

Although the series is designed as a unified whole so that no part of the story is left untold, each volume is complete in itself. Written for the general reader as well as for the scholar, each of the nineteen volumes of *The Canadian Centenary Series* is the work of a leading Canadian historian who is an authority on the period covered in his volume. Their combined efforts have made a new and significant contribution to the understanding of the history of Canada and of Canada today.

W.L. Morton (d. 1980), Vanier Professor of History, Trent University, was the Executive Editor of *The Canadian Centenary Series*. A graduate of the Universities of Manitoba and Oxford, he was the author of *The Kingdom of Canada; Manitoba: A History; The Progressive Party in Canada; The Critical Years: The Union of British North America, 1857-1873;* and other writings. He also edited *The Journal of Alexander Begg and Other Documents Relevant to the Red River Resistance*. Holder of the honorary degrees of LL.D. and D.LITT., he was awarded the Tyrrell Medal of the Royal Society of Canada and the Governor General's Award for Non-Fiction.

D.G. Creighton (d. 1979), former Chairman of the Department of History, University of Toronto, was the Advisory Editor of *The Canadian Centenary Series*. A graduate of the Universities of Toronto and Oxford, he was the author of *John A. Macdonald: The Young Politician; John A. Macdonald: The Old Chieftain; Dominion of the North; The Empire of the St. Lawrence* and many other works. Holder of numerous honorary degrees, LL.D. and D.LITT., he twice won the Governor General's Award for Non-Fiction. He had also been awarded the Tyrrell Medal of the Royal Society of Canada, the University of Alberta National Award in Letters, the University of British Columbia Medal for Popular Biography, and the Molson Prize of the Canada Council.

Ramsay Cook, Professor of History, York University, co-author with R.C. Brown of *Canada 1896-1921*, volume 14 of the series, is the Executive Editor of *The Canadian Centenary Series*, 1983.